HOMELANDS AND DIASPORAS

I0038741

HOMELANDS AND DIASPORAS

Holy Lands and Other Places

———————

Edited by

ANDRÉ LEVY AND ALEX WEINGROD

STANFORD UNIVERSITY PRESS

Stanford, California 2005

Stanford University Press
Stanford, California

© 2005 by the Board of Trustees of the Leland Stanford Junior University. All rights
reserved.

No part of this book may be reproduced or transmitted in any form or by any means,
electronic or mechanical, including photocopying and recording, or in any information
storage or retrieval system without the prior written permission of Stanford University
Press.

Printed on acid-free, archival-quality paper

Library of Congress Cataloging-in-Publication Data
Homelands and diasporas : holy lands and other places / edited by André Levy
and Alex Weingrod.
    p. cm.
    Includes bibliographical references and index.
    ISBN 0-8047-4771-7 (cloth : alk. paper)—ISBN 0-8047-5079-3 (pbk. : alk. paper)
    1. Jewish diaspora.   2. Israel and the diaspora.   3. Jews—Identity.   4. Palestinian
Arabs—Ethnic identity.   5. Social integration.   6. Memory—Social aspects.
7. Ethnicity—Political aspects.   8. Ethnicity—Social aspects.   I. Levy, André.
II. Weingrod, Alex.
DS134.H65 2004
956.9405—dc22

                                                                2004011640

Typeset by G & S Typesetters, Inc. in 10/13 Aldus

Original Printing 2005

Last figure below indicates year of this printing:
14   13   12   11   10   09   08   07   06   05

CONTENTS

Lisa Anteby-Yemini received her B.A. in Anthropology from Brandeis
University and her Ph.D. from the Sorbonne in Paris. Since 1997 she
has been a CNRS researcher working at the French Research Center
in Jerusalem, and also teaching at Ben-Gurion University of the
Negev. Her research focuses on Ethiopian Jews in Israel as well as
wider issues of migration, diaspora, and transnationalism.

Avner Ben-Amos is a historian of education, and Head, Department of
Educational Policy and Management, School of Education, Tel Aviv
University. He is the author of *Funerals, Politics and Memory in
Modern France 1789–1996*, as well as articles on political rituals,
civic education, and collective memory.

Efrat Ben-Ze'ev completed her doctorate at the Institute of Social and Cultural Anthropology, University of Oxford, writing on the memories
of Palestinian refugees. She currently holds a position at the Ruppin
Academic Center, and is affiliated with the Truman Institute at the
Hebrew University of Jerusalem. She has published on Palestinian
politics of taste and smell, on the intersection of Palestinian oral history and Israeli army documents, and on conflicts surrounding a museum exhibition in Jerusalem.

Ilana Bet-El is a political analyst specializing in conflict resolution. Currently based in Brussels, she worked for the United Nations in Bosnia
during and after the war (1995–97), and subsequently became Senior
Adviser on the Balkans. She holds a Ph.D. in history from the University of London, and has lectured in history at Tel Aviv University.
Her book *Conscripts: Lost Legions of the Great War* was published
in 1999.

Jonathan Friedman is Directeur d'Etudes at the Ecole des Hautes en Sciences Sociales, Paris, and Professor of Social Anthropology at the
University of Lund, Sweden. He is the author of *Cultural Identity
and Global Process; Globalization, The State and Violence*, and nu-

merous articles on anthropological theory, globalization, and culture and the practices of identity.

Sari Hanafi has a Ph.D. degree in sociology from Ecole des Hautes en Sciences Sociales, Paris (1994). He is Director of Palestinian Refugee and Diaspora Centre, Shaml. His work has focused on economic sociology and network analysis among Palestinian refugees, relationships between diaspora and center, returnees, and the sociology of international relations.

Hanna Herzog is Professor in the Department of Sociology and Anthropology at Tel Aviv University, and Head of the Society and Politics Program at the Academic College of Tel Aviv-Yaffo. Her books include *Political Ethnicity — The Image and the Reality* (Hebrew); *Realistic Women — Women in Israeli Local Politics* (Hebrew); *Gendering Politics — Women in Israel*; and *Sex, Gender, Politics — Women in Israel* (with other authors) (Hebrew).

André Levy teaches anthropology in the Department of Behavioral Sciences, Ben-Gurion University of the Negev. His Ph.D. dissertation from the Hebrew University (1996) was titled "Jews Among Muslims: Perceptions and Reactions to the End of Casablancan Jewish History." He is the author of various book chapters and articles that deal with topics such as diasporas, identities, minority-majority relations, and pilgrimages.

Edna Lomsky-Feder is a senior Lecturer in the School of Education, Hebrew University of Jerusalem. She has conducted research on the war and military in Israel, and her publications include *As If There Was No War: Life Stories of Israeli Soldiers*, as well as many articles. She recently collaborated with Tamar Rapoport on a research project studying Russian-Jewish immigration in Israel.

Fran Markowitz teaches anthropology in the Department of Behavioral Sciences at Ben-Gurion University of the Negev. She is the author of *A Community in Spite of Itself* and *Coming of Age in Post-Soviet Russia*, and is co-editor of *Sex, Sexuality and the Anthropologist*.

Susan Pattie is a Senior Research Fellow at University College, London. She received her Ph.D. in Cultural Anthropology from the University of Michigan, and does research on Armenians and other diaspora peoples. Her book *Faith in History: Armenians Rebuilding Community* is based on fieldwork in Cyprus and London with Cypriot Armenians.

Tamar Rapoport is Associate Professor at the School of Education, Hebrew University of Jerusalem. She has conducted research on religiosity, gender and education, gender and social movements, and gender and knowledge. Her latest research project, conducted together with Edna Lomsky-Feder, concerns Russian-Jewish immigrants in Israel.

Efrat Rosen-Lapidot is a Doctoral Candidate in the Department of Sociology and Anthropology, Hebrew University of Jerusalem. Her current research deals with social and cultural characteristics of a Jewish-Tunisian community under the French Protectorate, and the dynamics of community revival after its dispersion.

Ida Simon-Barouh is a Social Anthropologist at the Centre National de la Recherche Scientifique (France)—Laboratoire Asie du Sud-Est et Monde Austronesien (LASEMA-CNRS), Paris, and the Centre d'Etude et de Recherche sur les Relations Inter-Ethniques et les Minorités (CERIEM), Université de Haute Bretagne, Rennes. She is the author of *Le Cambodge des Khmers Rouges. Chronique de la vie quotidienne*, as well as articles on ethnicity and minorities in France and Cambodians at home and overseas, and is the editor of *Migrations internationales et relations inter-ethniques*.

Alex Weingrod is Emeritus Professor of Anthropology in the Department of Behavioral Sciences, Ben-Gurion University of the Negev. Among his publications are *The Saint of Beersheba* and (with M. Romann) *Living Together Separately: Arabs and Jews in Contemporary Jerusalem*.

Pnina Werbner is Professor of Social Anthropology at Keele University and is Research Administrator of the International Centre for Contemporary Cultural Research (ICCCR) at the Universities of Manchester and Keele. She is the author of "The Manchester Migration Trilogy," which includes *The Migration Process: Capital, Gifts and Offerings Among British Pakistanis; Imagined Diasporas Among Manchester Muslims;* and *Pilgrims of Love: The Anthropology of a Global Sufi Cult*.

As often is the case, the idea for this book originated in a casual discussion between the editors. We were intrigued by the almost instant changes and daily paradoxes of life around us, and, more to the point, by the revival of the notion of "diaspora" as a means to define and perhaps explain some of the more striking features of this brave new world. As a first step towards educating ourselves, we organized a year-long university seminar in which, together with our students, we began to explore the meanings of "diaspora" and how the concept might be used. The next step—organizing a conference on the topic—was, in retrospect, almost inevitable. In June 1999, we invited about twenty participants to take part in a three-day conference in Beersheba where we began to unravel the topic. Many of the presentations were excellent, the discussions were focused and sometimes heated, the food, drink, and friendship satisfying: and hence, with some urging from the editors and patient enthusiasm from the contributors, this book was on its way.

The conference was held under the auspices of the Chilewich Family Chair in Studies of Social Integration at the Ben-Gurion University of the Negev, and we thank the Chilewich family for their continuing generous support. This was the second such event sponsored by the Chilewich Family Chair. The first conference was held in 1980, and it too resulted in a book (*Studies in Israeli Ethnicity: After the Ingathering,* 1985) that was based mainly upon conference presentations. The differences between the two books is instructive. The first book was focused entirely upon Israel, and it sought to sum up, from the perspective of the 1980s, the various ways in which "ethnicity" had become a major force in shaping Israeli social, cultural, and political life. The main topics were social stratification and assimilation, political mobilization, and "constructing identities"—in other words, the articles ranged over many of the key issues that continue to be raised in contemporary studies of ethnicity.

In certain respects this book can be seen as a logical continuation of the "ethnicity" theme. "Homelands and diasporas" take off where ethnicity ends. Like "ethnic groups," the term "diasporas" refers to minorities set within larger societies. But then the resemblance fades, and important differences, both historical and conceptual, are emphasized. Since diaspora communities are also linked to their "homelands" and continue to be engaged with their fates and futures, they persist for long stretches of time. Jews and Armenians may have been the "classic diasporas"—but the term is also appropriate (and enlightening) when applied to many others. The present plethora of diasporas is an outgrowth of new global trends—world migrations that spread millions of persons into new places, modern modes of communication and transportation that permit persons to be both "here and there" at practically the same moment, deep changes in some nation-states in which more federative allegiances and multiple identities are developed, and a great deal more. Conceptually, "diaspora" stresses multiplicity and critiques the uniformities so often demanded by the nation-state: "diasporics" are not "citizens of the world," but they prosper in the new cultural fusions that may emerge along the borders. These are concepts appropriate to the end of the twentieth century and the beginning of the twenty-first—movement and migration are at their core, and these are among the hallmark features of the current age. What is more, they have a truly global reach: many of the chapters in this book analyze how Israelis, both Jews and Arabs, continually wrestle with the many ironies of their "homeland and diaspora," while, moving in a comparative direction, other chapters consider Armenians, Pakistanis, African-Americans, and Cambodians who are similarly engaged in defining "who they are" as they build their lives "at home and away."

We gratefully acknowledge the following journals and publishers for permission to use previously published material: "Commemoration and National Identity: Memorial Ceremonies in Israeli Schools," in *Between "I" and "We": The Construction of Identities and Israeli Identity*, ed. Azmi Beshara, pp. 129–51 (Tel Aviv: Van Leer Institute and Hakibbutz Hameuchad Publishing House, 1999) (in Hebrew); "Rethinking the Palestinians Abroad as Diaspora: The Relationships Between the Diaspora and the Palestinian Territories," *Hagar, International Social Science Review* (Spring 2003) 4(1); "A Community That Is Both a Center and a Diaspora: Jews in Late Twentieth Century Morocco," *City and Society* (2001) 13(2):247–72; "Visit, Separation, and Deconstructing Nostalgia: Russian Students Travel to Their Old Home," *Journal of Contemporary Ethnography* (2000) 29(1):32–57; and "The Place Which Is Diaspora: Citizenship, Religion and Gender in the Making of Chaordic Transnationalism," *Journal of Ethnic and Migration Studies* (2002) 28(1):119–34.

HOMELANDS AND DIASPORAS

Introduction

On Homelands and Diasporas:
An Introduction

ALEX WEINGROD AND ANDRÉ LEVY

There is a certain anachronistic, old-new ring to the title of this book. The twinned terms "homeland" and "diaspora" have been in common use for many years, indeed, for centuries. They are likely to conjure up images of nineteenth-century European romanticism, taking us back to earlier days of heroic-sounding nationalism and movements of national regeneration and return. For some, "homeland" may strike a negative tone, especially when it is said to be a "fatherland" or, for that matter, even a "motherland." "Diaspora" too seems overly laden with dark tones of grief and gloom. What is more, in this new millennium the world is often described as a "global village" without boundaries, a totally new configuration in which world-wide markets and instant information technologies have made nationalism redundant and individuals more cosmopolitan. Why, then, place these old-sounding terms at the center of this book?

The reasons are that, following an interlude of a half-century or more, some of today's new social realities are once again being conceptualized in terms of "homeland" and "diaspora." The primary reason for this rediscovery is the massive present-day movement of millions of persons from place to place, from continent to continent, and from one nation-state to another. There can be little doubt that modern large-scale migrations have a revolutionary, global significance whose impacts are, at the least, political, social, economic, and cultural. Depending upon their point of orientation and theoretical interests, social scientists have conceptualized these movements in different ways. To cite some of the competing terms, they may be labeled as "international migrations," "transnational movements," creating "trans-ethnic solidarities," and, alternatively, as establishing new relationships between "homeland and diaspora." Each of these conceptualizations (and there are others) frames the issues differently, and then proceeds to set its own specific agenda of questions, processes, and consequences.

3

To be more specific, researchers in a variety of academic disciplines—notably political science, sociology, anthropology, history, and cultural studies—have increasingly become engaged with the issues posed by a world in which the millions of persons "on the move" no longer reside in a common place (their homeland, perhaps), but instead have moved to far-distant places (diasporas, perhaps), and yet continue to be or feel connected with one another in various significant ways. These continuing relationships, both real and imagined, between "home" and "away," "here" and "there," "homeland" and "diaspora," form the major topic of this book.

The classic "old" diasporas were the Jews, the Greeks, and the Armenians, peoples who lost or were driven from their ancient homelands and then resided in different lands as dispersed minorities (*diaspora* is a Greek word, meaning, appropriately, "scattered seeds"), and yet continued to both dream and plan to someday "return home." These classic diasporas have an ancient vintage—the Jewish diaspora has continued for more than two thousand years, and Armenians too have lived in their diaspora for centuries. This list should also include the Gypsies, wanderers in their diaspora for many hundreds of years, and the black populations who, beginning in the fifteenth and sixteenth centuries, were brutally wrenched out of Africa and dispersed as slaves to different parts of the Americas.

Today's "new" diasporas are considerably different. Depending upon the particular definition and usage, there are likely to be many more of them, and they are scattered about as a result of the global trends that shape the contemporary world. As we know, these new diasporas have emerged from the world-wide movement of millions of persons, which in turn has been caused by global inequalities, modern information and production technologies, powerful multi-national corporations that frequently shift production across the world, as well as the more familiar "old-fashioned" reasons of famine and war. At another level, diasporas can also be seen to thrive in a world made up of nation-states: inasmuch as they practice exclusivity, nation-states relegate "others" to long-term minority status at best, brutal elimination at worse. Being "new," the more recent diasporas have been in place for only one or several generations, and they too retain a variety of ties to as well as memories of their homeland. In his recent book *Global Diasporas*, Robin Cohen lists such diverse groups as Lebanese traders, English colonists in India and Australia, Palestinian refugees, Japanese managers and technicians living abroad, and a great many others, as instances of different types of diasporas (Cohen 1997).

The basic terms of reference have also been revised and given different meanings. In the older vocabulary, "homeland" was commonly depicted as a sacred place filled with memories of past glory and bathed in visions of nobility and renaissance. Paradoxically, in the new discourse "homelands" sometimes fade out of view entirely, or, as noted above, they become nation-states that by definition repress minorities and place limits upon their cultural and other freedoms. The tone and meaning of "diaspora" are also transformed. According to the old usage "diasporas" were commonly depicted as melancholy places of exile and oppression that restricted social and cultural fruition; in the words of the Armenian poet Sylva Gaboudikian, quoted by Susan Pattie in Chapter 2, diaspora is a place where the homeland (symbolized by the walnut tree) spills its blessed fruit "to nourish foreign soils." In sharp contrast, in the current view "diasporas" are enthusiastically embraced as arenas for the creative melding of cultures and the formation of new "hybridic," mixed identities. To be part of a diaspora is, presumably, to be "on the cutting edge" of new cultural and other formations. The terms of presentation have, in other words, shifted from a kind of theology to politics, psychology, and sociology.

Is this old-new shift just a clever sleight-of-hand, another bit of post-modernist fluff, or does it instead focus upon important issues and uncover new realities? Is it merely confusing, or might the "confusion" in fact be productive and enlightening?

This sudden multiplicity of what are being called "diasporas" might be confusing. Definitions obviously are required, since without them practically any migration to every place can be seen to have produced its "diaspora." (The "Californian diaspora" in Seattle, the "English diaspora" on the Costa del Sol, or Westerners attached to Indian ashrams, as well as the many other contemporary instances of travelers, sojourners, or expatriates, seem to clearly be outside of our range [Tölölyan 1996 : 10].) Yet perhaps this is exactly the point. James Clifford, one of the more cogent analysts of diaspora, has argued that "in the late twentieth century, all or most communities have diasporic dimensions. . . . Some are more diasporic then others" (1997:254). Now whether there are different "types" of relations both within and between migrating communities, including those that by no stretch of the imagination are diasporas (such as Californians in Seattle or Englishmen on the Spanish coast), or, instead, an indefinite gradation depending upon the particular mix of "dimensions," the value of resurrecting "diaspora" and "homeland" is that this perspective invites a fresh look at some clearly important issues. There are many examples. Are all contemporary minorities "ethnic groups," or might some be better understood as "diasporas" that are as much influenced by links to their "homeland" as they are to the "hosts" among whom they reside? Do "homelands" always influence "diasporas," or are their relationships sometimes reversed, and why? Under what circumstances can or might a "diaspora" become a "homeland," and what are the dynamics of these changing relationships? What are the consequences of (as it were) living in two places at the same time, and what conditions or circumstances make doing so possible?

These are by no means idle questions. As some of the chapters in this book show, for Moroccan Jews, or for Armenians and Cambodians living "abroad," new centers may challenge the traditional homelands, and there are continuous, changing patterns of transnational influence that affect persons wherever they reside. There are, moreover, what might be called "spaces in-between" in which some persons commonly move back and forth across borders and consequently compose enduring cross-diaspora frameworks. To sum up, by placing homeland and diaspora at the center of our analysis, we reopen some old problems for fresh analysis, and also pose and develop an agenda of new topics.

These themes are considered in this book in two closely connected ways. First, viewed theoretically, as the chapters unfold it becomes clear that "homeland" and "diaspora" are not absolute givens, isomorphic and precise, but are instead considerably more complex and contingent. For example, "land" and "homeland" are not always overlapping terms. A particular geographic area—a "land"—may be considered to be a "homeland" by more then a single community of persons, and their "diasporas" will also be located in quite different places. Similarly, there may be circumstances in which a "diaspora" begins to take on some of the qualities of a "homeland," and vice versa. In this regard the "homeland"-"diaspora" pair is opened to question and problematized. Second, these issues as well as others are examined with specific reference to both "old" and "new" diasporas. Practically a third of the book (five chapters) focuses upon what is undoubtedly the classic historical case of homeland and diaspora: the Jews, including Jews living in the homeland, Israel, as well as those living in a number of different diasporas. Several other chapters deal with Palestinians in Israel as well as those living abroad in the Palestinian diaspora. This broad focus upon Israel, Jews, and Palestinians offers a vivid example of contesting visions of "land" and "homeland": both groups view the same "land" as their exclusive "homeland," and their different "diasporas" are also mobilized and have become engaged in this long-lasting dispute. In addition to these, other chapters consider such dispersed and transnational populations as Armenians, Cambodians, Pakistanis, and African-Americans. This broadly comparative range has many advantages. We can apply the discourse and terms of reference developed regarding the "new diasporas" to the analysis of an old classic case, and comparisons with other historically different situations also allow us to better understand what is unique and general in the current debates on transnational communities.

Types and Dimensions

If, as is rightly claimed, we live in a "world on the move," then which among the millions of migrants are those who can properly be said to be living "in diaspora," and which are those who are just plain "migrants," "transnationals," or "ethnics"? Or, in other words, what are the defining features of the terms "diaspora" and "homeland"? These questions require clarification in order to understand how the chapters in this book are related to the rapidly growing literature in what has already been called "diaspora studies."

Taken as a whole, this literature can be seen to move in one of two quite different directions. Some analysts, notably Safran (1991), Cohen (1997), Tölölyan (1991), and others, first define "diasporas" and thereby distinguish them from other categories of persons "on the move" (migrants, exiles, expatriates, refugees, tourists, sojourners, ethnics, transnationals, to list other prominent types). Then, with their definition in hand, they proceed to analyze a range of issues that take place in the concrete historical or contemporary communities that fit their definition. Taking a somewhat different position, Shuval emphasizes the inherent ambiguities and proposes a complex typology consisting of variables that would identify "different types of diasporas and the dynamics that differentiate among them" (2000:41). In contrast, Clifford (1997), Appadurai (1996), Bhabha (1990, 1994), Hall (1990), and many others tend to use the term in a looser, more metaphoric sense and consequently they may discover "diasporic features" among a wider range of migrating groups. For these scholars certain historical moments, social contexts, and political-cultural processes are more important than whether a specific community neatly fits the type. Perhaps not surprisingly, many of those in the category of "typologists" are political scientists and sociologists, whereas "diaspora as metaphor" is more prominent in the work of scholars associated with cultural studies and anthropology.

However, the differences between them are deeper and much more interesting than mere differences between competing academic disciplines. Indeed, it is fair to say that each camp has a fundamentally different agenda. As befits sociologists and political scientists, the "typologists" are primarily interested in better understanding why and how different kinds of diasporas have emerged, and they also have a considerable interest in the on-going dynamics of diaspora-homeland relationships. The "diasporists," on the other hand, are more concerned with showing how the phenomenon of "diaspora" may contradict and ultimately subvert the internal exclusivity of modern nation-states. For these researchers, transnational communities are a postcolonial development that challenges national borders and the sovereignty of the nation-state, and their interest is mainly focused on diaspora as places where multi-culturalism, hybrid identities, and mixed cultural formats become possible. To be sure, these contrasts are probably overdrawn, and yet "diaspora studies" as a field certainly includes within it these and other different agendas and contrasting perspectives.

Safran's 1991 article in the first issue of the journal *Diaspora* is a good example of the first approach. Safran presents six defining features of diasporas, both classic and modern: (1) they are "expatriate minority communities" that were dispersed from an original center and subsequently became established in two or more foreign places; (2) they continue to maintain mythical or other attachments to their homeland; (3) as a foreign minority they are not fully accepted by, or in fact are alienated from, the host societies within which they live; (4) they continue to dream of in the future returning to their original and true home; (5) those living in diaspora are also concerned or actively engaged in the maintenance and restoration of their homeland; and (6) their group consciousness is to a considerable degree maintained by these homeland-connected aspirations and activities. Safran slips in a qualification when he writes that sharing "several of the . . . characteristics" is adequate to be defined as diaspora (Which characteristics? How many are "several"?), and yet his intent in framing a set of criteria that distinguish diasporas from other types is clear. Even though others who follow the "typological" approach (such as Cohen in his *Global Diasporas*) have been critical of this phrasing and its application to specific cases, they follow a similar path in analyzing the historical emergence and continuity of both old and new diasporas.

What items or issues compose the agenda of diaspora studies as seen from this perspective? Some of the issues are straightforwardly historical. For example, Safran (1991), Cohen (1997), Band (1996), Stratton (1997), and the Boyarins (1993), as well as others, have returned to examine the case of Jews as the classic "original" diaspora. In much the same vein, Chaliand and Vernon (1983) have considered the Armenians, Chadney (1984) writes about Sikhs in Vancouver, Wang (1991) discusses overseas Chinese, Hourani (1992) examines the Lebanese spread over several continents, and other researchers have traced the historical development and dynamics of still other dispersed communities and places. There is, in other words, a rich and growing literature that both documents and analyzes the establishment and continuity of a number of modern diasporas. Beyond history, some fascinating cases of homeland-diaspora relations have also been studied. For example, how the "Rushdie affair" became a *cause célèbre* among Pakistanis living in England, and how it influenced relationships both within the Pakistani minority and between it and the English majority, is a recent case in point (Werbner 1996). Moreover, as political scientists such as Sheffer, Weiner, and Safran have pointed out, diaspora communities can also have significant influence upon events "in the homeland." "Living permanently in two places," with multiple interests and perhaps allegiances as well, may also pose dilemmas of "dual loyalties" (Jews between Israel and the United States or Europe and Chinese in their links to both the United States and China are two examples). Finally, Tölölyan (1996) and Anthias (1998) have also sought to unravel the meanings of "diaspora" as it contrasts with "ethnic group," and thereby to underline both the problems inherent in both terms and the different realities that they seek to uncover.

How are these issues and themes considered in this book? In Chapter 1, Pnina Werbner offers a fresh, multi-layered model of homeland-diaspora ties in the contemporary world. There are, she claims, powerful currents that sweep back and forth between homeland and diaspora, as well as between the various diaspora communities. These are not merely memories of a once-upon-a-time past, but are due, more profoundly, to the fact that "many diasporas are deeply implicated both ideologically and materially in the nationalist project of their homeland." Diaspora communities are increasingly characterized by their striving to obtain multiple citizenship both for themselves and for their fellow diasporics located in other places: in fact, this is a hallmark feature that "typifies contemporary diasporas." Werbner then builds her analysis around the concept of "chaorder," which depicts the links between homeland and diaspora as chaotic and uncontrolled, nonpredictable and spontaneous—yet operating within an orderly framework. Here she draws a parallel (her "little fable") with Visa credit cards—there, too, a huge number of transactions are made without there being any overarching control mechanism. What lends "order" to these typically contradictory, competitive relations is the moral sense of "co-responsibility" that orients the ongoing, intimate links between them. The dimensions and dynamics of "co-responsibility" are then considered in the specific case of Pakistanis living in England. Werbner argues that cultural performances make the bonds real, and her analysis of proliferating Sufi cults in Manchester and Bradford traces out how "chaorder" works on the ground. Political organizations thrive, including those in which women are prominent, and in the process the "Pakistani diaspora" at times becomes a "Muslim diaspora" that is alert to the struggles and concerns of Muslim communities across the globe. Indeed, in the current world political-cultural crisis, Muslim diaspora communities in Europe, the United States, and Asia suffer from what she calls "Islamophobia," a "fear of Muslims": "September 11 highlighted the vulnerability of Muslim diasporas in the West, caught up in international conflicts not of their own making." Co-responsibility has its obvious perils in a world of nation-states, and yet these far-flung diaspora communities continue to organize and to claim their rights in multiple settings.

What social and cultural processes unfold as diaspora communities reconsider their ties to their all-too-real "homeland"? This question is posed in several chapters, and perhaps most directly in Chapter 2, Susan Pattie's consideration of the Armenians, one of the old, "classic" diasporas. Like Werbner, she too sees "chaorder," what is phrased as a "tangled mass of approaches" to the problematics of defining and maintaining "Armenian-ness" in Armenian diaspora communities. What complicates matters is that Armenia, the ancient homeland that is now an independent state, is politically fractured and economically underdeveloped, and longings for return among diaspora communities must be balanced with the fact that a million Armenians have lately left the "homeland," many for a safer haven in California! The older Armenian diaspora communities—those in Cyprus, London, Beirut, or Jerusalem—are therefore engaged in re-negotiating their relationships with one another, and, most important, re-designing the contents of their own Armenian identity. Pattie skillfully cites the work of contemporary Armenian poets, politicians, and artists to illustrate the apparently endless, contentious search for the meaning of "being Armenian" in the diaspora: the ingredients include, among others, conflicting images of the homeland (which includes both the modern nation of Armenia and Hayastan, the much larger, historic "land of the Armenians"), speaking the language, maintaining the Armenian Church, putting an emphasis upon family ties and relationships, and a great deal more. She correctly draws parallels between the Armenians and the Jews—and also between Armenia and Israel. Whether "there is a positive side to diaspora" is a question that both Armenian and Jewish nationalists find to be "extremely provocative, even blasphemous." On the reverse side, nationalism and the state—both Armenia and Israel—are sometimes subjected to searching criticism by diasporics themselves. This dialogue is, in short, often harsh and contentious, as partisans on all sides debate the passionate issues that structure their lives both "here and there."

While Pattie mainly focuses on the changing dynamics of homeland-diaspora ties, Levy's analysis in Chapter 3 of Morocco as a "symbolic home-land" for Morocco's dispersed Jews essentially problematizes this conceptualization itself. Indeed, his chapter suggests a radical reformulation of the usual ways of thinking about "homeland"-"diaspora" relationships.

Levy disputes what he calls the "solar system model"—that is, the commonly accepted belief that the "homeland" is like a "sun" which maintains the attention and interest of the various diaspora communities that circle around it like satellites. The issues are not so simple and one-directional, he argues, and in making his case Levy explores the changing patterns of daily practice that have lately emerged between Moroccan Jews, Morocco, and Israel.

Only about five thousand Jews remain in Morocco—the rest, more then a quarter of a million persons, immigrated to Israel, France, Canada, and the United States. Like Jews everywhere, in Morocco too Jews had through time seen themselves to be in exile and longed to return to the mythic homeland. While many have returned to the "real homeland," Israel, they also have begun to see Morocco as their "symbolic homeland." Levy tells the story from the perspective of the numerically small but still lively Jewish remnant. Interspersing ethnographic vignettes with broader analysis, he relates why some Jews in Morocco choose to bury their dead in the local Casablanca cemetery rather then transporting them for burial in Israel. The debate over how Hebrew should be taught to Jewish youngsters living in Morocco is shown to have equally substantial symbolic significance: is Hebrew the language of holy texts, or the language that Israelis speak in Tel Aviv? Moreover, not only have those remaining carved out a small place for themselves, in recent years the much larger number of Moroccan Jews living in France, Israel, and Quebec have also developed a kind of nostalgia for and symbolic identification with Morocco. This is expressed in such matters as trips—practically pilgrimages—back "home" to Morocco, and a growing literature of films and books that presents the past in glowing colors. In short, Morocco has become both a diaspora and a center, and, as Levy demonstrates, "the relationships between diaspora and homeland, or better, these very classifications, may be fluid, historically conditioned, and even multidirectional."

This re-formulation has broad theoretical consequences for "diaspora studies." What is "diaspora" and what constitutes "homeland" are not necessarily obvious and clear in the complex contemporary world of movement and migration. Indeed, the anthropological analysis of Israel and the Diaspora shows that the paradigm itself requires reconsideration. Relationships between "homeland" and "diaspora" are anything but static, and, in fact, immigration often sets off processes which are unexpected and richly paradoxical. This point is elaborated upon in several other chapters. For example, in Chapter 9, Anteby-Yemini's analysis of the movement of thousands of Ethiopian Jews to Israel shows how by immigrating to the "homeland" they also became part of the "Ethiopian diaspora," and, even more broadly, the "Black diaspora." Similarly, as Rapoport and Lomsky-Feder indicate in their study of Russian Jewish students in Israel, in Chapter 12, by immigrating to Israel they too became part of the "greater Russian diaspora." In brief, "homeland" and "diaspora" are not fixed categories, and the complex links between dispersed populations that share common memories and culture needs to be carefully sorted out and evaluated.

Two chapters in this section are devoted to a consideration of the Palestinian diaspora. In Chapter 4, Sari Hanafi presents a broad-scaled analysis of how this particular constellation is presently emerging, and in Chapter 5, Efrat Ben-Ze'ev focuses on how the past is constructed by the different generations of Palestinians living in the diaspora. Hanafi argues that, in the post-Oslo period, the concept of diaspora is both applicable and useful for understanding the Palestinians who reside outside of the Palestinian territories. These populations include, for example, Palestinians living as refugees in Syria, Lebanon, and Jordan, others living and working in the Gulf States and Egypt, and still others who have mainly settled in Europe, the United States, and Latin America. Conceptualizing them as "diasporas," is preferable to "refugees," "assimilated people," a "population in transit," or "transnationals," since this paradigm emphasizes the "importance of the multi-polar connectivity between the different peripheral communities and between them and the Palestinian territories." There are varieties of relationships both within and between the diasporized communities—"familial networks sometimes with a family council, village clubs . . . national and nationalistic-religious networks usually based on the different popular organizations connected with the Palestinian Liberation Organization (PLO) or pro-Hamas." On the other hand, the "center" in the Palestinian territories is still emerging and continues to be engaged in often violent conflict with Israel. A "Palestinian national identity" is also in the process of becoming constructed. Hanafi concludes that the Palestinians may be considered to be a "diaspora with a weak center of gravity," and that in this instance the forms of relationship between "homeland" and "diasporas" are relatively new, uncertain, and still being negotiated.

This wide-ranging presentation is complemented by Ben-Ze'ev's detailed study of how the different Palestinian generations construct and reconstruct their past. Ben-Ze'ev focuses upon what were, until 1948, three Palestinian villages located south of Haifa; some of the villagers and their children still live in Israel, while the others are dispersed in Jordan, the West Bank, the United States, and in other countries. Their former village, where none of them now live, is "their homeland," and therefore they are said to be living in "the Palestinian diaspora." Ben-Ze'ev's major theme is a classic topic in diaspora studies: she asks how the first and second generation, no longer living in "the homeland," picture and represent their past (that is, the village). The older generation, men and women who had actually experienced the village, and are now exiled from it, retain memories of specific place, events, smells, and colors. These memories are frequently expressed in the telling of long, convoluted, and not altogether coherent stories about the once-upon-a-time village and its people. In contrast, the younger adult generation—men and women who are literate, including persons with advanced professional and academic degrees—are uneasy with these tales of the past, and they therefore have found other ways to commemorate the village, and, by implication, to reconstruct the past. Some have traveled back to the village; together with their parents and children, they return to see and experience what continues to be their place, "their village." Others are engaged in making their own detailed records of the past. These include personal and family archives of old photographs, maps, historical accounts— whatever can be located that presents an "objective" documentation. In addition, in recent years richly detailed "memorial books" that depict and celebrate the village have also been assembled. In brief, the adult second generation of Palestinians has not lost its interest or fierce passion regarding the past, but instead is constructing a different form of narrative.

While they may question or even problematize certain features of the paradigm, all of the chapters in this section are framed in terms of "homeland" and "diaspora." In contrast, Jonathan Friedman's essay (Chapter 6) offers a critique of some key elements in this formulation. Friedman casts a skeptical eye on the brave new world of "globalism" and "diaspora." A world on the move? Hardly, he argues, since barely 3 percent of the world's population is involved in global migrations. The outpouring of books and articles on this theme is an "elite discourse"—the world as seen from the jet plane and conference circuit—and it often mistakes "movement" for "culture." Taking issue with those who celebrate diaspora since it presumably produces "hybridity," he reminds us that, to the contrary, "diaspora formation is based in a process of identification, and with the material and symbolic practices that are bound up with such identification." What is needed, he implies, is a wider framework for analysis as well as a deeper comparative historical perspective. Friedman argues that the growing number of "diasporas" should be interpreted not so much as an attack upon the nation-state as a symptom of the changing world-wide system. "Ethnic groups" can become "diasporas" when the effective power of state hegemony wanes and the state itself becomes "an instrument for global capital accumulation." This is a powerful critique: it is not, as we have been urged to see, that the state is necessarily weakened or transformed by transnationalism and diaspora, but rather that nation-states themselves are able to adapt to the "new world order" of global capitalism.

In addition to these analyses of homeland-diaspora ties, this book also takes a closer look at political and cultural changes that are taking place within homelands themselves. This is an important and somewhat neglected theme. As was previously pointed out, the growing literature on homelands and diasporas has primarily been focused on the latter: the field is called "diaspora studies," and the journals have the title "Diaspora" rather then, say, "Homeland and Diaspora." The literature is replete with statements to the effect that there is a continuous interaction between them—changes taking place in the "homeland" will affect the outlooks and ideologies of those in the "diaspora"—and yet little attention has actually been given to this topic (Safran; Tölölyan). Several chapters deal directly with this subject. More particularly, they consider Israeli Jews and Israeli Palestinians as "homeland communities," and reflect upon how changes taking place in the "homeland" may influence their diasporas.

The chapters written by Ben-Amos and Bet-El, Herzog, and Anteby-Yemini directly address some major core issues in the Israeli homeland. Ben-Amos and Bet-El's presentation of "memorial ceremonies" in Israeli schools provides an insightful analysis of several pivotal themes—namely, how agencies of the state actively seek to inculcate a "national identity" among school-age youngsters, and, correlatively, how the elements that compose that identity become re-fashioned over time. Israeli national holidays (including several that were deliberately invented for the purpose) are meant to create common symbols and understandings among Israel's diverse, heterogeneous population, and, ultimately, to forge an "Israeli collective identity." The state-sponsored schools have been charged with promoting these common beliefs, understandings, and emotional identifications, and several commemorations that are celebrated each year form the topic of Ben-Amos and Bet-El's analysis. The three secular holidays that they select for study— Holocaust and Heroism Day, Memorial Day, and Jerusalem Day—follow one another in a regular spring pattern of personal sadness and presumed collective commitment, and the "deep impression that they make on adolescents" is meant to embed some of the essential features of "Israeliness." The authors first trace the history of these as well as other "invented traditions," and they then proceed to analyze common or significant features in the ceremonies' structure. Although the teachers and students could select from different texts recommended by the Ministry of Education, the yearly commemorations have by now become "traditional," or better, codified. Ben-Amos and Bet-El then go on to provide an interpretation of the meanings of the texts and events. What is being conveyed, they argue, is an interpretation of history as well as markers of identity that are founded upon a set of binary oppositions that strike at the core of Israeli life and culture: "Jews/non-Jews, Zionist-Jews/diaspora Jews, Israelis/Arabs, Ashkenazi/Sephardi, men/women." Individual and collective "Israeli identity" is built out of these repeated commemorations, and in their analysis of some of the texts (poems, songs, letters from fallen heroic soldiers or the ghetto dead) the authors point to the growing emphasis upon nationalism and the continued "national struggle" against enemies. Interestingly, they also note that while the canonical texts that are employed are repeated and deemed sacred, in recent years a few schools have selected other texts and more critical interpretations (what the authors term "subversive commemoration"), and that this resistance has provoked intense public debate.

How does the Palestinian minority living in Israel relate to the changing definitions of "being Israeli"? Herzog considers the problems and paradoxes that are presently faced by a growing number of Israeli Palestinians. Her presentation focuses on a particular group of Israeli Palestinian women—they are mainly younger women, often well educated, and their principal defining feature is that they have become activists in Israeli peace organizations. This is an especially interesting group, since they are regularly in contact with other peace activists, including both Israeli Jews and Palestinians living in the West Bank. Her presentation focuses upon the dilemmas that emerge from their marginality: as in the society at large, in peace organizations, too, the Israeli Palestinian women are often patronized and dominated by Israeli Jews, and they are also made to feel inferior by the "real Palestinians," those living on the West Bank and Gaza. Adopting an ideology of "feminism" also does not offer a path to true equality and attaining the women's aspirations. Herzog concludes, however, that in negotiating their own identity these women have also begun to find their own particular voice and political position. By implication, at least, their outlooks also have an impact upon "what it means to be an Israeli."

Anteby-Yemini's study of Ethiopian Jewish immigrants in Israel considers "the homeland" (and "diasporas" too) from the perspectives of those who only recently returned "home." More then fifty thousand Jews immigrated from Ethiopia to Israel during the 1980s and 1990s. Their situation is anything but simple. As the title of her chapter suggests ("From Ethiopian Villager to Global Villager"), their new life-situation as a small Ethiopian Jewish minority has set off a number of different, perhaps contradictory, processes. Now citizens of Israel, they actively enter into various local and national contexts: they wish to "become Israelis," albeit on their own terms, and like others they attend state-sponsored schools, serve in the army, vote in elections, and the like. They also suffer from racial prejudice, and Anteby-Yemini reports how Ethiopian Jews have staged large demonstrations to protest against discrimination. At the same time, some have also begun to travel back to Ethiopia as tourists and entrepreneurs, and they return home with Ethiopian spices, clothes, videos, and tales of their adventures. In this sense they are for the first time becoming part of a transnational Ethiopian community that includes Jews and non-Jews, and their identity as "Ethiopians" takes on entirely new meanings. What is more, Anteby-Yemini goes on to show how, for some, alienation from the dominant majority Israeli society, as well as involvement with contemporary "global processes," have lead to the development of a new Black "diasporic consciousness." Based on TV imagery, music, and dress, some youngsters "dress more and more like urban black youth on the model of American inner cities and rastafarian patterns." Ironically, having returned to Israel, the homeland, a growing number of Ethiopian Jews are also constructing new identities as participants in a global "Black diaspora." This is a critical point, and she argues that it should bring us to adopt a new perspective in studies of Israel (and, by implication, of other homelands): henceforward, events need to be understood in "the interplay between the local Israeli context, the former society of origin and the global dimension of 'world culture.'" This is surely a complex and challenging task—and yet this "local-national-global" paradigm seems realistic, and it is also likely to lead to new and different understandings.

Diaspora and Diasporism

We turn next to examine the theoretical interests that are expressed in the second broad meaning given to "diaspora"—that is, what was previously termed "diaspora as metaphor." The studies that fall under this heading derive from a different set of issues, and they consequently move in rather different directions.

The impetus behind this body of work can be found in new scholarly interests and orientations, as well as in the real-world changes that have taken place in the last several decades. With regard to theory, this line of inquiry derives from a critique of nationalism and the nation-state, and the work of Benedict Anderson in his *Imagined Communities* (1983) figures prominently in the outlook and analysis. Anderson described the modern nation-state as a kind of fiction held together not just by geography and "interests," but also by constructed mythologies of origin and blood that were popularized by the media, and particularly by "print-capitalism." Among the many devious features of nationalist ideology was the emphasis upon the exclusive "who we are"—what in more recent literature has been translated to mean cultural and racial "essentialism." This exclusivity in origin and, presumably, in culture too, defined and restricted who were the *"real* French" or the *"true* Egyptians," and thereby also ruled out other groups, and minorities in particular, from being "authentic" or "full" members of the nation-state.

How is this related to the new "diasporism"? Hall, Gilroy, Bhabha, Appadurai, Clifford, and others who write in this genre have adopted the phrasing of "diaspora" as a way to emphasize the powerful cultural and other relationships between minorities living in several different countries (for example, between Blacks in England and African-Americans in the United States), as well as their ties of myth, dream and memory to their historical "homeland." Diaspora in this sense means rejecting the path of assimilation into the dominant majority. The reasons for doing so are often complex: in some instances they are racially different—"persons of color" who have been marginalized and excluded—or belong to religious and other minorities that are discriminated against by the majority, and in other cases they are minority groups who for various reasons desire to separate themselves from the dominant society and culture. Based upon lengthy experience with their hosts, members of these groups are intimately acquainted with the codes of conduct of the majority, and yet they also wish to maintain their own collective identity, ways-of-living, and real or imagined connections to their "homeland." As Susan Pattie puts it in her analysis of the Armenian dispersion, diaspora communities wish to continue living "on their own terms" without becoming fully a part of or entirely assimilated within their host society. Diasporas therefore challenge and may transform the exclusivity of the nation-state: their insistent voice may ultimately move the society towards a greater acceptance and recognition of difference.

What is mainly at stake is the position and role of minorities in the contemporary world, and, in particular, the space allotted to them within the frameworks of the nation-state. In addition to this political and cultural critique, a number of major changes have also weakened the exclusive bonds and commitments demanded by nations and states. A series of factors are usually cited in explaining this radical shift. First, global migrations have poured new populations into numerous states across the world. Many nations that previously perceived themselves to be "homogeneous" in cultural and racial terms (such as Sweden and Austria) suddenly find themselves with more mixed populations, just as in the more heterogeneous states (like the United States, Nigeria, and Australia) the growing size and number of "minority groups" continues to pose major national issues. Second, the power and success of global capitalism challenge state boundaries. Crucial sectors of the world economy are now dominated by "multinationals," and as a result many key, far-reaching decisions are made without regard to borders or national allegiance. Third, a variety of new federative frameworks have also been created—the European Community is probably the best example—and consequently the unilateral power of many states has declined. Dual citizenship has also become more common, so that a growing number of persons enjoy citizenship rights in more then a single state. We should also take note of the "anti-colonial" or "post-colonial" thrust to this argument. Many of the millions on the move are the former "colonial peoples" who have migrated to the previously dominant colonizing societies (Pakistanis, West Indians, and Indians to England, North Africans and others to France), and this ironic twist also finds expression in the new "diasporic dialogue." Finally, it should not be imagined that these changes have taken place smoothly or without opposition and resistance. On the contrary, globalization and the multinationals have their fierce opponents on the political left; immigration, multi-culturalism, and the new federative frameworks are equally opposed by the right; and in certain situations members of these otherwise opposed political camps may also forge ad hoc coalitions (sometimes under nationalist banners) in order to resist change.

Diaspora-as-metaphor appears prominently in many recent studies of migrating groups. According to this perspective "diasporas" are a sub-species of transnational minorities (in Tölölyan's positive phrasing they are "the exemplary communities of the transnational movement"), and research has focused on understanding how they construct their own distinctive cultural identity that melds ties with the "homeland" together with the contexts and everyday experiences in their new land. Not surprisingly, since marginal minorities have frequently been studied by anthropologists (these are, after all, "anthropology's people") they have been especially involved in much of the on-the-ground ethnographic research. On the other hand, some of the key theoretical formulations (for example, the notion of "hybridity," as well as the emphasis placed upon "identity," both individual and collective) originated or were emphasized in cultural studies, as researchers in these and other disciplines have focused attention on the "diasporic features" that characterize some minority cultures.

What topics frame the agenda of these studies? First, emphasis is typically placed upon "diaspora" populations—including links and exchanges between those living in several locales—and considerably less attention is given to the "homeland." In some instances the "homeland" may have a kind of mythic meaning, but how on-going social or political developments in the "homeland" influence the "diaspora" is not a primary issue. Second, many studies have focused upon ways in which minorities design their own distinctive cultural styles—in music, dance, dress, film, and other creative designs—and how these quickly changing patterns challenge or otherwise interact with those of the "majority culture." Gilroy's research on minority Black cultural styles in England during the 1960s and 1970s has been especially influential in this regard (Gilroy 1991). Third, even though the daily experience of minority-group members may be harsh and frustrating, in many of these studies diaspora life is depicted as being vibrant and internally creative. A good example of this "glorification of diaspora" is the positive imagery given to an old classic diaspora, the Jews. This is most pronounced in the work of the Boyarins (Boyarin and Boyarin 1993), and it has also been favorably picked up by Clifford and others. (Goiten's encyclopedic research on Jews in the Mediterranean Arab world [1967] is frequently cited as an instance of "positive diaspora.") The moral of these studies is that minorities sometimes live harmoniously for long periods together with majorities, while, in contrast, modern nationalism not only represses minorities but also fails to be culturally enriching and creative. Fourth, although homelands are not central to these studies, the "to-and-fro" movement of persons between homeland and diaspora is underscored. Diasporas prosper in an age of charter flights, Internet and e-mails, cell phones and videos, and the immediacy that these provide. Fifth, since "diaspora-as-metaphor" turns attention away from the issues of how minorities become assimilated to the alternative perception that they may persist and prosper, research has focused on how new "hybrid identities" and "mestizo cultures" are constructed. To be sure, this paradigm contains an unresolved dilemma. Minority communities are said to maintain inner vitality and resist the pressures of assimilation into their "host society"; what is more, "hybrids" are valued since they presumably have mastered their host's cultural codes and are thus able to move easily from one cultural platform to another. Yet the nagging doubts remain: are these "hybrids" an expression of the creative relations between minorities and majority, or are they merely marginal cosmopolitans living in a dream and with no place to go?

Many of the themes of "diaspora as metaphor" are considered in this book. Markowitz's rich analysis of the Black Hebrews is an excellent example. The Black Hebrews (their official name is the African Hebrew Israelite Community) are a small African-American community, some of whose members have immigrated to Israel, where they mainly settled in the "dusty desert town of Dimona." Markowitz locates the origins of their journey in the huge problematic of being Black in White America: "the binary of race overpowered the ... multiplicity of hybridity," and they therefore set out in search for the Homeland that would enable a more fulfilled life. Consequently, when they (as she puts it) "looked for origins in Africa, they found their way to Israel." As evangelical Christians the Black Hebrews took inspiration from the Old Testament tales of flight and return, and ultimately they came to see themselves as the "true Children of Israel." They are a widely dispersed community: some remain in their diaspora residences in Chicago, Detroit, and Washington, they also maintain a small outpost in Ghana, and several thousand of the Black Hebrews presently live in the "homeland," Israel. This is, to say the least, a remarkable and complex tale, and Markowitz traces the development of their ideology of "Israel is Africa, Africa is Israel," showing how "claiming the pain" may bridge the gaps between past and present. By locating the analysis in the swiftly changing frames of past and present events, her detailed presentation emphasizes the ways in which their "culture" is constantly being refashioned. Indeed, she concludes that "the African Hebrew Israelite Community . . . is a transnational diasporic and returning society-in-the-making, always struggling to make its claims for hybridity visible." Even though their saga is undoubtedly unique, the Black Hebrew vision of "diaspora and return" also echoes trends that resound within other post-colonial Black communities.

Ida Simon-Barouh's analysis of Cambodians living overseas (mainly in France) is also concerned with "diaspora as metaphor." As always, the circumstances are complicated. To begin with, Cambodia itself is practically a metaphor, since the "Cambodian nation" is new, a composite made up mainly of Khmer together with smaller numbers of "others," primarily Chinese and Vietnamese, all of whom also blend together in a variety of complex ways. What is more, those persons who in Europe and North America are labeled "Cambodian" are primarily refugees who fled from Pol Pot's evil butchery that killed millions during the mid-1970s. Could "Cambodia" be their homeland? Perhaps, although this relationship has not as yet crystallized. Simon-Barouh notes that even though the second generation in particular has become more engaged with the larger society, important features of "Cambodian culture" also appear to be retained over time. This is best illustrated in Cambodian Buddhism, and most vividly in the pagodas that have been built in Paris and other cities where Cambodians have settled. In addition, many have begun to visit "back home," and they also join together to raise funds that are sent back to Cambodia in order to rebuild village pagodas that were destroyed during the devastation of the Pol Pot regime. What the author calls "Cambodianity," meaning the changing definition of being Cambodian "in the dispersion," thereby takes on new meanings, and these relationships may develop further into those of a "diaspora-homeland."

Before continuing, it is important to again point out that while the twin poles that have guided us thus far—"diaspora as typology," and "diaspora as metaphor"—provide a useful heuristic device for critically analyzing the recent research regarding diasporas, the differences between them should not be over-emphasized. Although each approach has its own agenda and proceeds in different directions, there also is considerable common ground and overlap between them. For example, studies that problematize the "homeland-diaspora" relationship (such as Levy's analysis of Morocco's Jews) are also deeply concerned with how the nation-state structures "minority relations," just as research on the neglected theme of "homelands" is vital to both agendas. These and other areas of common interest should be kept in mind as we now turn to explore how travel and movement are intimately bound up with the study of homelands and diasporas.

The Spaces in Between

In this final section we return to some of the questions that were raised earlier, and also proceed to critically consider some features of the "homeland-diaspora" paradigm. Do the terms "diaspora" and "homeland" exhaust all of the possibilities in the relationship, or are there also other relevant and important dimensions? Must a particular place and community of persons be *either* a "diaspora" or a "homeland," or may a diaspora also become a homeland, and why?

Our first topic has to do with travel and movement. Whether real or mythical, the twinned pair "homeland" and "diaspora" refers to landscapes, sites, and groups of persons who are situated apart and at a distance from each other. For some, these places and persons are barely known and mainly imaginary, while for others they are well acquainted and highly tangible.

Now since there are on-going relationships between those living or situated in far-off, different places, there also is an area or a "space" between them. Depending upon the particular situation, these spaces vary in distance, in their relative difficulty and form of passage, and in their internal construction and organization. For example, the "spaces" may be composed of dispersed family members living in different places who periodically gather together for family events, or networks of merchants or intellectuals who from time to time interact in various different locales. These spaces and interactions are a regular feature of "homeland-diaspora" relations, and they therefore need to be given proper attention. In other words, an expanded model might include "homeland," "diaspora," and the "spaces in between."

This is more a matter of empirical observation then formal logic. These "spaces in between" are filled with travelers and movement; as was previously emphasized, one of the features that marks "homeland and their diasporas" is that persons often travel back and forth between them. This is an ancient tradition—the Greeks, Armenians, and Jews journeyed between their diaspora communities, and from diaspora to homeland and vice versa, as merchants, pilgrims, religious specialists, and plain voyagers. As Clifford and other analysts of diasporas have emphasized, in this present era of charter flights and instant communication technologies the frequency and importance of travel has hugely expanded (Clifford 1997; Appadurai 1996). These are persons who, for a variety of reasons, are intermittently but also regularly both "here" and "there," at "home" and "away." "Spaces in between" mark off the routes and travels of groups and individuals journeying from place to place, from "diaspora" to "homeland" and back again.

What features characterize the "spaces in between"? Depending upon the particular historical and other circumstances, there clearly is a wide spectrum and range of difference. For our purposes we focus briefly on two quite different formats or types. Adopting Marc Augé's terminology, one type can be called "non-places." These are artificial, impersonal places such as international airports and high-speed roadways through which solitary travelers pass in almost silent motion from one locale to another. A second type can be called "places en route." These are, in contrast, spaces between homelands and diasporas, such as a charter flight made up of pilgrims, or the voyage of persons who are connected in various ways and are traveling with some common purpose that, however loosely, links them together.

Augé's "non-places" are produced by what he calls "supermodernity"— that is, the great changes in scale and the "overabundance of events" that characterize the present-day world. "Non-places" designate two different yet complementary realities: spaces formed in relation to certain ends (transport, transit, commerce, leisure), and the relations that individuals have with these spaces" (Augé 1995:94). With regard to the first, "non-places" typically are creations of the state (airports and border crossings), or they are licensed and overseen by state agencies (hotel chains and refugee camps), and they therefore are expressions of the state's power to define and control its citizens and others. How do "supermoderns" relate to these places? How do they design their lives in a world of non-places? Aihwa Ong's depiction of a Chinese investor "based" in San Francisco records a classic reply: "I can live anywhere in the world, but it must be near an airport" (Clifford 1997:257). This is, presumably, a "cool" world without deep social connections, with the exception perhaps (or at least Clifford surmises) of close family and kinsmen. "Homeland and diaspora" are barely relevant in these instances: "nonplaces" (such as airports and border crossings) must of necessity be passed through, but the non-place world of "solitary individuality" where "the fleeting, the temporary and ephemeral" are dominant motifs are hardly features of homelands and their diasporas (Augé 1995:78).

In contrast, "places en route" represent a radically different configuration, the other edge of the spectrum. Neither sanitized nor solitary (as are "non-places"), these spaces are composed of persons who are "in circuit" between diaspora and homeland, or between several diaspora communities. Many are regular or veteran voyagers—merchants, religious and commercial entrepreneurs, poets, and teachers—while others are "first-timers," on their initial trip to "the homeland." During the journey they are both "here and there," periodically "back and forth," even "betwixt and between": being "en route" means that this space is infused with the practical and symbolic features of both "home and "away." As they travel by plane, ship, or bus, their conversations may be carried on in different or "mixed" languages; some persons identify themselves with songs or key phrases that carry intimate symbolic meanings; and arguments may break out regarding how to correctly interpret past or present events. In brief, "spaces en route" are typically animated and "hot," filled with a babble of mixed tongues and usually high expectations. Including both "home and away" may produce confusions and uncertainties: and yet these spaces are a kind of preparatory platform where persons may "try out" how they wish to appear. Being in motion, the issue is not "who you are" but "where you are," and the constraints and opportunities of the "where" suggest or impose the identities that may be fashioned.

Some features of "spaces en route" appear as key themes in a number of chapters. Jews who immigrated from Ethiopia and the former Soviet Union are among the most recent arrivals in Israel, and it is therefore not surprising that many among them have also returned to visit the places where they formerly lived. Anteby-Yemini's analysis indicates how, among Ethiopian Jews, their travels back to Ethiopia are intimately related to constructing their new identities as "Ethiopian Israelis." Lomsky-Feder and Rapoport's chapter on the return visits to Russia of Russian Israeli university students provides additional dimensions. These visits are termed "the little journey," in contrast with the "big journey," the students' immigration to Israel during the 1990s. Inevitably, they contrasted and compared their previous lives in Moscow, St. Petersburg, or Kiev with their present situation in Israel. In the authors' apt phrasing, they were "transient homecomers," anxious about what they would find "back home" and how they would react, while, at the same time, seeking to "try out" their new Israeli identities. Of course, their reactions were mixed: some felt wonderfully at home ("Moscow is mine!"), even though they deplored the "Russian character" and crass materialism; others discovered a new sense of connection with Jews remaining in Russia; and still others found that they had returned "as Israelis," displaying their new Israeli identity. Clearly, they were in a complex, puzzling situation. By immigrating to Israel they had chosen the Jewish homeland over the diaspora—but in the process, they also left their "cultural homeland" and in this sense became part of the "Russian diaspora." In the end, they were able to "deconstruct nostalgia" for Russia itself, while at the same time their "revered Russian culture" continued to be prized and in many respects represented *the* meaningful cultural center in their lives.

Rosen-Lapidot's analysis of the processes involved in building "new configurations of identity" among a relatively small community of Jews who formerly lived in Bizerte, a port town situated along the Tunisian coast, also focuses upon movement and identity. The entire Jewish population of Bizerte left their homes during the immigration waves of the 1950s and 1960s; many families immigrated to Israel, although a substantial number also moved to France and mainly settled in Paris. Until the last decade or so they seem to have been primarily engaged in establishing themselves in their new lands. More recently, however, they banded together to form an organization of former Bizerte Jews, and Rosen-Lapidot depicts some of the ways in which they have been "anchoring, placing, centralizing and preserving past entities." Bizerte Jews in Israel and Paris "found one another" and began to undertake some joint organizational activities. Principal among these were various activities involved in reconstructing and preserving the old Jewish cemetery in Bizerte itself. French, their native language in Tunisia, also creeps back into their Israeli lives, as their "new identities" begin to include acceptable francophone as well as Hebrew elements. Their past, in other words, is being refashioned anew, and in this process Tunisia-Paris-Israel becomes a reconstituted, energized axis of activity.

Finally, in bringing this introduction to a close, we return full circle to where we began: homeland and diaspora. In the opening paragraphs these terms were taken more or less uncritically, as if it were clear and obvious which place was which—either "homeland" or "diaspora." Now, at the end of this review, there are many more doubts, and it is not at all certain what label is appropriate to what situation. There are many examples. Russian Jews return to "the homeland," and in the process they also become part of the "Russian diaspora." Markowitz's Black Hebrews are an especially intriguing instance. Israel is for them a kind of "homeland within a homeland," in most respects the United States is their cultural center, and they can also be seen as being part of the Black Diaspora. How should this be conceptualized? Obviously, this is a case so complex that it defies attempts at neat classification. And, if this were not enough, Levy's analysis of Moroccan Jews details how, after many returned from the diaspora to the homeland, Morocco itself has become a new center for the dispersed communities of Moroccan Jews. There are, in short, ironic, paradoxical processes at play within the complex links between homeland and diaspora. If nothing else, we conclude that labels and types are not enough to comprehend the changing interactions between these transnational communities, and that research needs to more carefully examine how their relative attractive power and position continuously takes new twists and directions.

REFERENCES

Anderson, Benedict. 1983. *Imagined Communities: Reflections on the Origin and Spread of Nationalism*. London: Verso.
Anthias, Floya. 1998. "Evaluating 'Diaspora': Beyond Ethnicity?" *Sociology* 32(3):557–80.
Appadurai, Arjun. 1996. *Modernity at Large: Cultural Dimensions of Globalization*. Minneapolis: University of Minnesota Press.
Augé, Marc. 1995. *Non-Places: Introduction to an Anthropology of Supermodernity*. London and New York: Verso.
Band, Arnold. 1996. "The New Diasporism and the Old Diaspora." *Israel Studies* 1:323–32.
Bhabha, Homi K. 1990. *Nation and Narration*. London and New York: Routledge.
———. 1994. *The Location of Culture*. London and New York: Routledge.

Boyarin, Daniel, and Jonathan Boyarin. 1993. "Diaspora: Generation and Ground of Jewish Identity." *Critical Inquiry* 19(3–4):693–725.

Chadney, James G. 1984. *The Sikhs of Vancouver*. New York: AMS Press.

Chaliand, Gérard, and Yves Vernon. 1983. *The Armenians: From Genocide to Resistance*. London: Zed Books.

Clifford, James. 1997. "Diasporas." In *Routes: Travel and Translation in the Late Twentieth Century*, ed. J. Clifford, pp. 244–77. Cambridge, Mass., and London: Harvard University Press.

Cohen, Robin. 1997. *Global Diasporas: An Introduction*. Seattle: University of Washington Press.

Gilroy, Paul. 1991. *"There Ain't No Black in the Union Jack": The Cultural Politics of Race and Nation*. Chicago: The University of Chicago Press.

Goiten, Shlomo D. 1967. *A Mediterranean Society*. 6 vols. Berkeley and Los Angeles: University of California Press.

Hall, Stuart. 1990. "Cultural Identity and Diaspora." In *Identity: Community, Culture, Difference*, ed. J. Rutherford, pp. 222–37. London: Lawrence & Wishard.

Hourani, Albert, and Nadim Shehadi, eds. 1992. *The Lebanese in The World: A Century of Emigration*. London: Centre for Lebanese Studies.

Safran, William. 1991. "Diasporas in Modern Societies: Myths of Homeland and Return." *Diaspora* 1(1):83–99.

Shuval, T. Judith. 2000. "Diaspora Migration: Definitional Ambiguities and a Theoretical Paradigm." *International Migration* 35(5):41–57.

Stratton, Jon. 1997. "(Dis)placing the Jews: Historicizing the Idea of Diaspora." *Diaspora* 6(3):301–29.

Tölölyan, Khachig. 1996. "Rethinking Diaspora(s): Stateless Power in the Transnational Moment." *Diaspora* 5(1):3–36.

Wang, Gungwu. 1991. *China and the Chinese Overseas*. Singapore: Times Academic Press.

Werbner, Pnina. 1996. "Allegories of Sacred Imperfection: Magic, Hermeneutics, and Passion in the Satanic Verses." *Current Anthropology* 37:55–86.

PART ONE

Changing Diasporas

CHAPTER 1

The Place Which Is Diaspora: Citizenship, Religion, and Gender in the Making of Chaordic Transnationalism

PNINA WERBNER

Introduction: The Place of Diaspora

Some time ago I listened to a BBC Radio 4 program on Jewish religious music. The speaker, a sophisticated musicologist, compared different styles of *hazanut*, Jewish cantorial devotional singing, in different Jewish traditions, performed historically by different Jewish communities in different parts of the world. His repeated phrase in drawing these comparisons was to the way "the Jews in the Diaspora" made music; not the Jews *of* the diaspora, not diasporic Jews, but the Jews living *in* the diaspora. He was referring, I realized, to a place—the diaspora—but that place was the whole world, with the exception, perhaps, of a small but focal center, a point of origin. Yet although he seemed to be referring to a non-place ("not-Zion/Palestine/Israel"),[1] a kind of limbo, the place of diaspora he was reflecting upon was, in his description, an incredibly intricate network of places marked by great cultural variability and historical depth; a place of many different heterogeneous "traditions." This paradox, of the one in the many, of the place of a non-place, of a global parochialism, is what makes diasporas a typical transnational formation. In this chapter I shall argue that like many such formations, diasporas are *chaorders*, chaotic orders, which are inscribed both materially and imaginatively in space, time, and objectifying practices.

The problematics of space and territory have been a key focus of the renewed debates on diaspora. Against the prototypical historical example of the dispersed Jewish diaspora, imaginatively oriented toward return to a lost homeland, the stress in the new discourse of diaspora has been on the positive dimensions of transnational existence and cosmopolitan consciousness (Hall 1990:235; Boyarin and Boyarin 1993; Gilroy 1993; Clifford 1994). The powerful attraction of diaspora for postcolonial theorists has been that,

29

as transnational social formations, diasporas challenge the hegemony and boundedness of the nation-state and, indeed, of any pure imaginaries of nationhood. The creative work of diasporic intellectuals on the margins is celebrated for transgressing hegemonic constructions of national homogeneity.

The more recent scholarly riposte to this view has highlighted the continued imbrication of diasporas in nationalist rhetoric, and critiqued the celebration of rootlessness as an aestheticizing move which is both ahistorical and apolitical (Fabricant 1998; see also Werbner in Leonard and Werbner 2000). So, too, the new postmodern interpretation challenged simplistic paradigms of diasporas as scattered communities yearning for a lost national homeland, whether real or imaginary. The growing consensus is, by contrast, that such imagined attachments to a place of origin and/or to a collective historical trauma are still powerfully implicated in the late modern organization of diasporas. Diasporas, it seems, are both ethnic-parochial *and* cosmopolitan. The challenge remains, however, to disclose how the tension between these two tendencies is played out in actual situations.

The currently emergent consensus in the literature is that many diasporas are deeply implicated both ideologically and materially in the nationalist projects of their homelands. Very often, these may be emancipatory and democratic. Thus Basch et al. (1993) report on the critical democratic politics of Grenadans, Haitians, and Filipinos based in New York in lobbying for the removal of authoritarian regimes in their respective countries, and Tölölyan (1996) describes the emancipatory socialist diasporic project of the Armenian community, a feature shared with other anti-colonial diasporic movements. The early Zionist project was universalist, secular, democratic, and socialist (Shanin 1988). African-Americans mobilized against the apartheid regime in South Africa, Chinese-Americans protest against human rights violations in China, and Cuban-Americans against the communist regime of Castro. Jewish peace groups in the United States and Canada have rejected expansionary anti-Palestinian moves by right-wing Israeli governments (Sheffer 1996, 1999).

But by the same token, diasporics often feel free to endorse and actively support ethnicist, nationalistic, and exclusionary movements. They engage in "long distance nationalism" without accountability (Anderson 1992, 1994): they support the IRA, Hindu nationalist movements (Gopinath 1995: 315–16), Greek Cypriot separatism (Anthias 1998), or religious zealotry in Israel. With regard to this, the ability of diasporas to actively participate and intervene in the politics of the homeland has been greatly enhanced and facilitated by the spectacular development of global media and communication technologies. Although transnationalism is by no means a new phenomenon, today sending societies often encourage such participation while receiving societies range from those which refuse to assimilate newcomers to those, such as Britain and the United States, which tolerate cultural pluralism, dual citizenship, and transnational activism as never before (Foner 1997).

A key question raised in this chapter is the historical processes which have generated the move from "incipient" diaspora to "mobilised" diaspora (Sheffer 1995). Taking Pakistani migrant-settlers in Britain as an example, I argue that the social formation of a diaspora is a predictable process which replicates itself transnationally. Yet it is not the product of any central organizing force able to control the multiple goals pursued by local diaspora communities. Diasporic organizations retain their autonomy along with a capacity to switch agendas and shift orientations in response to local predicaments or world historical events.

Dispersed Communities of Co-Responsibility

By definition, a diaspora is a transnational network of dispersed political subjects. One key feature of certain kinds of diasporas (Jews, Muslims, Armenians) is that they are connected by ties of *co-responsibility* across the boundaries of empires, political communities, or (in a world of nation-states) nations. I use the notion of co-responsibility in preference to usual evocations of "solidarity" or "loyalty" to indicate:

(a) that the planetary flow of cultural goods, philanthropic giving, or political support between diaspora communities and their homeland possesses a vector and a force, ranking diaspora communities globally by wealth, political clout, and cultural authenticity or production;

(b) that diasporas do not necessary have singular centers. On the contrary, they may recognize and foster multiple concerns and more than one sacred center of high value (Goldschmidt 2000);

(c) that diasporas are not simply aesthetic communities; nor are they merely reflections of the displaced or hybrid consciousness of individual diasporic subjects. On the contrary, diasporas are usually highly politicized social formations.

This means that the *place* of diaspora is also a historical location, not merely an abstract, metaphorical *space*. Diasporas need to be grasped as deterritorialized imagined communities which conceive of themselves, despite their dispersal, as sharing a collective past and common destiny, and hence also a simultaneity in time.[2] In existing beyond the nation-state with its fixed boundaries and clearly defined categories of inclusion and exclusion, of participatory rights and duties, citizenship and loyalty, diasporas as scattered, uncontained and uncontainable minorities have historically been the target of racialized and xenophobic nationalist imaginings. Thus Jews in the diaspora were conceived in the racist imagination as the nefarious leaders of both communist and capitalist international conspiracies—a hidden, malignant presence in the body politic of the pure nation. More recently, such imaginaries have been transposed by the extreme right onto the new Muslim diasporic presence in Europe. Writing about Scandinavia, Tore Bjorgo reports that in their racist discourses, migrants and asylum seekers are represented by the Scandinavian right as "pioneers" in a Muslim army of conquest. According to this theory, the "so-called refugees" have come to establish "bridgeheads" for Islam in Norway. This is part of an evil Muslim conspiracy to establish global Islamic rule (Bjorgo 1997:60).

For Scandinavian neo-Nazis, the plot is even thicker: immigration is presented as a strategic weapon in the hand of "the Jews" in their ongoing race war against "the Aryans" (ibid.:62).

The neo-Nazi assumption is thus of an alliance between Jews and Muslims, in which the latter have become the instruments of a Jewish will to global domination.

Although such conspiracy theories are openly expressed only by a small minority in Europe and the West today, there are other, apparently more acceptable, discourses which nevertheless presume an irreconcilable and unbridgeable cultural, "civilizational," if not racial, gulf between "Islam" and "the West." Fear of Muslims, Islamophobia, takes more quotidian forms as well, embedded in stereotypical assumptions and pronouncements regarding the status of women in Islam, arranged marriages, or the inherently fanatical, violent, and irrational tendencies of Muslim leaders and their followers (on Islamophobia, see the Runnymede Trust 1997). The further point of such discourses is that these alien qualities and attributes have come to be implanted in the Western body itself, no longer simply confined to its "bloody boundaries," as Huntington has described Islam's relations with the rest of the world (1993:35), but extending within and across them. A substantial Muslim diasporic presence has emerged in Europe and the West, and even some Western liberals who pride themselves on their enlightened tolerance appear concerned about the capacity of this culturally "alien" presence, as they see it, to "integrate." Such doubts have surfaced especially since the Rushdie affair and the Gulf war, and most recently, after September 11, all of which seemed to expose the chasm between so-called Western "values" and Islamic ones. (In the Gulf war Muslims in Britain expressed open support for Saddam Hussein. They remain vociferous in their objections to war with Iraq, but have joined forces with a wider anti-war coalition.)

September 11 highlighted the vulnerability of Muslim diasporas in the West, caught up in international conflicts not of their own making. Almost universally, they objected to the war in Afghanistan and refused to believe that any Muslim could have perpetrated the attack on the World Trade Center. Although they condemned the attack on the twin towers, many at the same time declared their support for the Taliban, while a few young British Muslims were even found fighting in Afghanistan on their side.

All this points to the fact that, in being nomadic and transnational, able to transverse political boundaries and settled cultures, diasporas such as Jews and Muslims which have a global reach appear in the eyes of others to be sites of mysterious power, sometimes disguised, sometimes open and public. But how is the illusionary and sometimes very real power of such diasporas created? How is a diaspora produced and reproduced in time through its scattered, discrete "communities"? My question does not refer to the political-economic or historical reasons for such dispersions, although this is a question to which I will return below. Instead, I want to address a somewhat neglected dimension of diasporic formation: the material, moral, and organizational features that underpin the creation of new diasporas and the predatory expansion of old ones into new territories.

My question can be put differently: what makes a diaspora community settled in a particular country "diasporic" rather than simply "ethnic"?[3] What turns a country (for example, Britain) from a permanent place of settlement, an adopted home, into a place of diaspora? The model of diasporic reproduction I propose to put forward here draws on the contemporary world of global finance with its radically new forms of decentralized expansion in order to advance a theory of transnational diasporic formation.

The New Global Chaorder

Credit cards such as Visa now have a turnover of trillions of pounds annually.[4] From being a mere bank card of the California-based Bank of America, Visa has become a global guarantor of money transactions. At the present time, it is rapidly penetrating at an increasingly accelerated rate beyond the northern hemisphere into the rest of the world. Yet no one owns Visa. It has, it seems, no value and no shareholders. It is not quoted on the stock market. It is not managed through an elaborate command structure. It is not, in other words, a normal multinational firm. Its headquarters are a relatively small, insignificant building in San Francisco, and it has other similarly modest regional headquarters. The big banks do not have a monopoly over it. Visa is not a commodity. Despite their gigantic stake in it, banks can put no value on it—and it cannot be bought or sold. Moreover, any firm can buy into Visa: Pet Plan (an English pet insurance scheme), Keele University, Barclays Bank. All a firm has to do in order to become a cardholder is to comply with the rules of the game and honor the multi-lateral agreements these imply. In all other respects cardholders act as competitors: they compete with one another for customers; they offer bonuses and incentives in their attempts to lure customers away from rival Visa card holders; they compete, individually, with other credit cards such as American Express or MasterCard.

According to its inventor, Visa works through a system of "chaorder," rather like the way biological growth and replication occur in nature: leaves multiply by following DNA rules without a central command structure. At the same time, organic interdependency is an essential feature of plant life. So, too, Visa companies sprout independently but depend on the mutual honoring of credit by all the firms contracted into the system, if they are to continue to exist and grow.

Chaordic Diasporas

Diasporas resemble, I suggest, my little fable about the Visa credit card because they too reproduce and extend themselves without any centralized command structures. Governments may try to manage their diasporas, but ultimately such attempts must fail. Neither the Pakistani or Israeli governments nor the keepers of the Kaaba in Mecca, control the Pakistani, Jewish, or Muslim diasporas. The locations of diaspora are relatively autonomous of any center, while paradoxically they continue to recognize the center and to acknowledge at least some obligations and responsibilities to it and to the larger whole. Moreover, in any particular location, chaorder is the principle of organization: diasporic groups are characterized by multiple discourses, internal dissent, and competition for members between numerous sectarian, gendered, or political groups, all identifying themselves with the same diaspora. The question of who owns a diaspora and its foundational myths—the holocaust, Zionism, the Partition of India, Pakistani Independence, the rise of the Prophet of Islam—is a highly contested one. What is subsumed under a single identity are a multiplicity of opinions, "traditions," subcultures, lifestyles, or modalities of existence, to use Avtar Brah's apt terminology (1996).

Sufi Cults as Chaordic Organizations

An example of the chaordic expansion of diasporas is the transnational spread of Islamic mystical Sufi cults to the West. To begin, it should be said that there is nothing new about Sufism as a global religious movement. Sufis began their itinerant existence in the tenth century A.D., and have carried the Message of Islam from the Near East to South Asia, Indonesia, and West Africa.[5] Officially, Sufis claim to belong to named *tariqa* or orders, but none of these orders have centers or real command structures. What they share, notionally, are ways or paths toward Allah; *wazifas*, secret formulas and sequences of prayers for disciples to follow. These lead them through the different "stations" on the mystical journey toward experiential revelation. In reality, Sufi cults focus on living or dead saints as regional cults, organized very much along the same lines as other regional cults (see Richard Werbner 1976 and 1989), with a center and branches of it. These branches extend across national boundaries wherever disciples happen to settle. The foundation of a branch follows a predictable pattern, as it develops its materiality (in the form of a mosque, for example) and ritual practice is enhanced. It may start with little more than a group which meets regularly to perform *zikr*, the rhythmical chanting in unison of the name of Allah. It may progress to holding monthly *gyarvi sharif* ritual meetings in which sacralized food is cooked and distributed in commemoration of the birth/death of Abdul Qadr Jilani, one of the founding saints of South Asian Sufism. It may gain its own *khalifa*, vicegerent or deputy, recognized by the Center (or miraculously, by God). It may even distribute *langar* (sacralized food, freely offered) on a daily, weekly, monthly, or annual basis.[6]

Sufi regional cults are not particularly exclusive, although this varies somewhat. Disciples may follow more than one saint, attend more than one annual *'urs* festival in commemoration of a departed saint, and—in the absence of the disciples' "own" saint to whom they have sworn allegiance—happily attend the festivals of another saint, even from a different Sufi order. At the same time, however, Sufi regional cults are locked into thinly disguised competition with each other for disciples; having many disciples, an enormous gathering at saintly festivals, certainly proves that a saint is a great saint, a *wali*, friend of God. Like other regional cults, Sufi cults wax and wane, with the sacred center of the cult rising to great prominence or sinking into oblivion (see Werbner 1996c; also 2003). Within South Asia, there are the recognized cults of the great Sufi saints who brought Islam to the subcontinent, and their places of burial draw millions annually. But there is no obligation to perform pilgrimage to these places. A minor saint in the back streets of a dilapidated part of a slum in a large city may draw devotion from a circle of local disciples (see Frembgen 1998). Sufism is thus extremely chaordic, having the capacity to expand across boundaries while remaining local and even parochial, recognizing its extensions while practicing locally.

Transnational Sufi cults outside Pakistan or India form one materially embodied way of being diasporic. Saints, disciples, and followers move in predictable pathways between major and minor sacred centers, especially on festive occasions. Sufi regional cults are located "in" the diaspora, rather than being simply "diasporic." The discourses and practices they perpetuate are a way of living and seeing things, and their movements in space, their material exchanges across space, constitute one dimension (modality, perspective) of the Pakistani global diaspora today, and, even more broadly, of the Muslim global diaspora. In Britain, there are by now a large number of cults centered on local *khalifa* or saints (*pirs*), and they commonly recognize sacred genealogical links to saints located in different parts of Pakistan. Each cult forms a network of saintly brothers and sisters (*pir-bhai/bhen*) with centers or branches in a dozen British cities: Bradford, Manchester, Birmingham, Luton, London, and so forth.

In my recent research on such orders, I interviewed members of six very different orders, all located in Manchester, each with a local leader and an extensive national and international network. Disciples and saints regularly visit each other's centers in other cities on a weekly or monthly basis, and keep in regular contact with the cult center in Pakistan. Reciprocally, saintly leaders of the cults from Pakistan visit their followers in Britain, often staying for several weeks or months.

There are other chaordic manifestations of diaspora. Some Pakistanis belong to Pakistani political parties. I once interviewed a man who spent three hours trying to explain to me the intricacies of factional alignments and conflicts in the Pakistan People's Party. This was a time when the party had just split, before Benazir Bhutto first became president. President Zia was in power, and many leaders of the party were exiled in Britain. As a local leader, this man was quite clearly living entirely "in" the diaspora. It filled his thoughts and life. England was an incidental accident of political geography which he happened to be located in, to be disregarded as almost unreal. More recently, Benazir Bhutto—facing corruption charges in Pakistan—made Britain her permanent abode. Although her role in Pakistan as party leader has been undermined, she has nevertheless reinvigorated the diasporic politics of the Pakistan People's Party in Britain.

Elsewhere, as in my monograph *The Migration Process* (Werbner 1990), I have written about processes of Pakistani migration and community formation, culminating in the building of the Central Manchester *Jamia* mosque. What makes the Pakistani communities which have emerged throughout Britain diasporic, rather than simply ethnic or religious, is an orientation in time and space—toward a different past or pasts and another place or places. What makes these diasporas into communities is categorically *not* their unity. Like Sufi cults, people "buy into" "their" diaspora in quite different, materially embodied ways. Some people set up Urdu poetry reading circles. They meet every month to recite poetry in each other's company. Others set up religious discussion groups. They meet in mosques, homes, or restaurants to talk about Islam. Such groups host visiting poets or religious experts from Lahore, London, or Delhi (see Leonard 2000).

Second, diasporas are embodiments of cultural, political, and philanthropic sentimental *performances.* Beyond the imaginary, they exist through *material* flows of goods and money, through gestures of "giving" or *khidmat*, public service. Often these three dimensions of materiality—culture, politics, and philanthropy—are intertwined. Members of the diaspora mobilize politically to defend or protest against injustices and human rights abuses suffered by co-diasporics elsewhere. They raise money, and donate ambulances, medicines, blankets, and toys for them. They visit them to celebrate Eid together (see Werbner 1996a).

The diaspora is in one sense not a multiplicity at all, but a single place, which is the world. When people suffer elsewhere, it hurts. The pain demands action. In this respect diasporas are fraternities or sororities. When Muslim women in Bosnia or Kosovo or Kashmir are raped or their husbands tortured, it hurts Pakistani women in England. When Palestinian women are evicted from their homes, the pain is felt in other places as well. African-Americans mobilized politically in favor of sanctions against apartheid South Africa. Irish Americans mobilized to support the IRA. The main Jewish lobby supports the Israeli government in the name of existential claims to survival.

But when the homeland's politics disappoint or become too controversial, diasporans can turn their attention elsewhere. If Israel no longer lives up to its utopian Zionist vision, the silent majority of diaspora Jews turn their back on it and preoccupy themselves with the Holocaust or the plight of Russian

Jewry, just as Pakistanis in Britain, disillusioned with the endemic corruption of their country's politicians and civil servants, turn their back on Pakistan and preoccupy themselves with other, transnational Muslim causes where Muslims are the victims of atrocities and human rights abuses.

Ultimately, there is no guiding hand, no command structure, organizing the politics, the protests, the philanthropic drives, the commemoration ceremonies, the poetry, and the devotional singing styles of diasporas. No single representation by a diasporic novelist or film maker, even in a single country, can capture this diversity or define its politics. What people buy into is an orientation and sense of co-responsibility. The rest is up to their imaginative ability to create and invest in identity spaces, mobilize support, or manage transnational relations across boundaries. Chaorder defines this complex combination of shared rules and focused competitiveness.

Diasporic Citizenship

The diasporas of the Old World—the Phoenicians, the Greeks, the Jews, the Armenians—were protected traders and sojourners. In the Ottoman empire, they constituted set-apart religious communities, *dhimmis*, physically and economically protected but without the right to political representation. In pre-Enlightenment Europe, the Jews formed an occupational group of money lenders, petty traders, and menial workers, confined to urban ghettos and at the mercy of autocratic and anti-Semitic regimes. Even today, Turkish and Maghrebian settlers in Germany, and Palestinians in the Gulf, have no citizenship rights.[7] In general, however, in a post-Liberal world of nation-states, there has been a radical change in the civic and political status of many, though as we have seen, not all, diasporics. No longer defined as permanent strangers, they expect as a right to be granted full citizenship in their country of settlement. They have become, in a sense, also "ethnics."

Although citizenship is still grasped by some as an exclusionary identity denoting singular loyalty to a particular national collectivity, in reality, people bear multiple collective loyalties and quite often multiple formal citizenships. The claims, duties, and rights attached to these memberships and loyalties are played out in the public domain in various complex ways. There is thus a growing interest in what citizenship might mean, first, in the context of a postnational world in which rights and duties are no longer defined exclusively within the boundaries of nation-states (Soysal 1994), in which human rights movements are both transnational and often anti-national, and in which the cultural sphere of identity politics has challenged the private/public divide (Zaretsky 1995: 252 passim).

The possibility of combining transnational loyalty and local national citizenship *as a right* has increased the influence of diasporics on world politics as never before. Hence Benjamin Netanyahu, the right-wing Israeli prime minister, could appeal over the head of the president of the United States to the Republican right and the Moral Majority, along with the so-called "Jewish lobby," against the American government's attempts to advance the Oslo peace accords. Irish American senators play a part in the Northern Ireland settlement (or are asked to "stay away" for fear of jeopardizing it). Sanctions against Apartheid South Africa were strongly supported by the African American community.

Diasporic political influence on Western international policy depends, however, on the existence of organized diasporic political lobbies. Political lobbies test the skills of diaspora activists to the limit. They require clear agendas, sophisticated diplomacy, large sums of money, access to the media, and an ability to influence public opinion through ethnic mobilization in a united front. Incipient diasporas often acquire such skills only through trial and error, over lengthy periods. Although in Britain ethnic leaders have ready access to politicians and MPs (Werbner 1996a), this in itself does not translate into effective political clout without the other ingredients. New, experimental transnationally oriented diasporic organizations often disintegrate in the face of internal divisions or local opposition by rival communal groups. Even the very successful British parliamentary Kashmir caucus (see Ellis and Khan 1998) appears to have collapsed when confronted with Indian intransigence. Building up such organizations at the national level is not easy, and most organizations fail to reproduce themselves over time. The following example illustrates this process of mobilization and collapse. It is interesting also because it concerns an activist women's transnational organization.

Gender and Diaspora

Arguments about gender and diaspora have so far tended to stress the patriarchal dominance of male diasporic leaders, the exploitation of diasporic women, or their cultural invocation as objects of the male gaze (Anthias 1998; Gopinath 1995). It is therefore worth noting that in some diasporas women have built up powerful transnational diasporic organizations in the past century. This is certainly the case for the Jewish diaspora, which has witnessed the founding of very large national and transnational women's philanthropic organizations comprised of millions of members, oriented toward raising funds for welfare, education, and health in the homeland or elsewhere in the diaspora. These organizations sustain major hospitals, a network of nursery schools, and special secondary and higher educational facilities. However, when these organizations are still small, women often find themselves blocked by male activists if they attempt to claim an autonomous space for women's transnational activities.

My own research on a Pakistani women's organization in Manchester revealed clearly how the local micropolitics of the diasporic public sphere come to be intertwined with transnational diasporic political activism. Al Masoom, an organization which rose to prominence during the 1990s, began as a philanthropic association officially aiming in the long term to build a cancer hospital for children in Pakistan. Meanwhile, the organization raised funds to treat visiting Pakistani children suffering from rare diseases. It also collected clothing, jewelry, and appliances for the dowries of young women from impoverished backgrounds in Pakistan.

In transcending the construction of their local identity as "victims"—as a doubly oppressed racialized minority women's group—the Pakistani women activists redefined their social positioning not only in Britain, but also globally and transnationally. They literally rewrote the moral terms of their citizenship—from passive to active, from disadvantaged underclass to tireless workers for the public good, from racialized minority to an elite cadre of global citizens responsible for the plight of the needy of the Islamic *ummah* and of their national homeland. Theirs was a battle to capture the moral high ground and, in the process, to define themselves as active citizens, rightfully and legitimately able to claim a place and voice in the *Pakistani, British* public sphere. To achieve this, the women organized themselves to work for transnational causes (see also P. Werbner 1996c, 1998a, 1999).

As the women encountered male resistance to their philanthropic work, their efforts became increasing spectacular. They organized a series of public marches, inviting other women's organizations in the city to join them to protest against human rights violations and atrocities in Bosnia and Kashmir. Manchester was the only city to send women's groups to London for a pro-Kashmir march from Hyde Park past the House of Commons to Downing Street, in a national march organized by the Pakistan People's Party. Representatives of al Masoom twice traveled over land to the border of Bosnia, driving through Europe in the middle of winter in order to bring medical aid, food, clothing, and two ambulances to the refugee camps on the outskirts of Zagreb. In their activism the women were supported by British MPs and the press. At its height the organization could mobilize hundreds of families in Manchester for its fund-raising events. It received donations from British hospitals and support from other English and Muslim transnational organizations.

For a while this group came to be recognized as an equal actor in the local diasporic public sphere. Leaders were invited to all major public events in Manchester, and met with the Lord Mayor, MPs, visiting politicians from Pakistan, the High Commissioner, and other dignitaries. But the organization lacked a fully developed feminist consciousness, a national support network, and the educational resources and experienced personnel needed to sustain its momentum. The leader, a charismatic woman, began to pursue her own personal interests at the expense of the group. In the end, the organization collapsed amidst accusations of corruption. Male elders' hegemony in the diasporic public sphere was triumphantly reinstated.

Conclusion

To prove their identification with their homeland and other diasporic causes, members of diaspora communities must constantly confront their local invisibility through public acts of mobilization and hospitality and through demonstrations of generosity which reach out beyond their present communities. They must be seen to contribute real material or cultural goods *across* national boundaries through their political lobbying, fund-raising, or works of poetry, art, and music. Pakistani diasporans create havens of generosity for visitors from Pakistan (especially distinguished ones), as well as for refugees and tourists. In return, these itinerants bear witness that the idolatrous wasteland of Britain has been appropriated and civilized.

This stress on active identification in the making of diaspora echoes our recent call to analyze the materiality of diaspora (Leonard and Werbner 2000), the embeddedness of diasporic subjectivities, the sites of "double and multiple consciousness," in "structures of diasporic polity and collective being" (Tölölyan 1996: 28). These can only be achieved through "doing" (ibid.: 16) or, more broadly, through *performance*. The invisible organic intellectuals of diasporic communities engage in constant practical ideological work— of marking boundaries, creating transnational networks, articulating dissenting voices, lobbying for local citizenship rights or international human rights—at the same time that they re-inscribe collective memories and utopian visions in their public ceremonials or cultural works.

The imagination of diaspora, according to Stuart Hall (1990), is hybrid, mediated by the creative products of diasporic artists in their places of settlement. Global diasporas thus exist through the prism of the local. There is no cultural essence defining a diaspora. Identities are always positioned and in flux (Gilroy 1993; Bhadha 1994; Brah 1996). But the politics of diaspora are, in this view, the politics of artistic representation. This *aestheticizing* of diaspora as high cultural or popular text denies the extraordinary promiscuity of cultural representations and performances that constitute diaspora as a political imaginary, the institutional, material, embodied nature of much diasporic activism. By contrast, in this chapter I argue for a need to grasp the organizational and moral, as well as aesthetic, dimensions of diaspora in order to understand its political and mobilizing power. Such a view questions whether diasporas are always enlightened, progressive, or anti-nationalist. We need just as much to come to terms with diaspora's local parochialisms and heterogeneity, its internal arguments of identity.

An adequate response to the aestheticization of the diaspora concept entails, as I have argued, a radical conceptual rethinking, that is, a recognition that the imagination of diaspora is constituted by a compelling sense of *moral co-responsibility* embodied in material performance which is extended through and across space. For half a century Pakistani settler-citizens in Britain have worked to build a British Pakistani diasporic community oriented toward its homeland, Pakistan. They raise money for this homeland, commemorate its founding moments, and criticize its defects; they contribute vast sums to it at times of disaster and war. They host visiting dignitaries and dream of return, just as they support their national cricket team with wild displays of enthusiasm. In this respect they form a conventional diaspora focused on a national homeland.

However, at the same time Pakistanis have also redefined themselves as a *Muslim* diaspora. To invent a Muslim diaspora has entailed a refocusing on the Islamic peripheries—on minority Muslim communities, often persecuted and displaced, beyond the Islamic heartland. Pakistanis in Britain have rediscovered their connection to Palestine, Bosnia, Chechnya, Kashmir. In their fund-raising efforts they work with major Muslim transnational non-governmental organizations such as Islamic Relief or the Red Crescent. Indeed, on reflection it seems evident that the Muslims of India have always harbored a diasporic consciousness. For example, in the 1920s the pan-Indian *khilafat* movement, which arose with the aim of saving the Ottoman caliph, expressed this diasporic political consciousness even though it was founded on a gross misreading of the real geopolitics of the time (Alavi 1997). Pakistan, like Israel, is the nationalist fulfillment of a diasporic vision. As religious Muslims, Pakistanis embrace a religious aesthetic which they are willing to defend at a very high material and personal cost, as the Rushdie affair demonstrated.

Being a *Muslim* diasporan does not entail an imperative of physical return to a lost homeland. It enables Pakistanis to foster and yet defer indefinitely the fulfillment of the myth of their return home, while asserting their present responsibility for fellow diasporan Muslims—their membership in a transnational moral community. A key development in this postcolonial sense of moral co-responsibility, evident also among Muslims, has been the struggle of diasporas resident in the democratic West to secure citizenship and human rights for co-diasporans living as minorities beyond the West. In addition, the Muslim diaspora also opens up a diasporic space of critical dissent against corrupt Muslim and Western leaders everywhere—in the Islamic heartland, Pakistan, and also in the West. Through performative pronouncements of dissent, Pakistani settlers re-center Britain as a significant locus of diasporic action.

"Buying in" to diaspora today in the West thus includes the struggle for local citizenship and fighting for the citizenship rights of co-diasporics elsewhere (or assisting them to escape discrimination "there" by shifting them to a new haven "here," in the place where citizenship rights are guaranteed). This process of playing on multiple citizenships is what typifies contemporary diasporas and makes the chaorder they represent quite different from that of earlier, pre-national diasporas.

But being a Muslim diasporan is not the final ontological truth for Pakistanis. It remains in tension with an equally compelling diasporic orientation toward a South Asian popular and high cultural aesthetic (see also Bhachu 1995). It is an aesthetic embodied in a flow of mass cultural products from the subcontinent and a nostalgic reinscription in ritual and ceremonial of the pungent tastes and fragrant smells, the vivid colors and moving musical lyrics of a lost land. These, more than any diasporic novel written in English, stamp South Asia indelibly on subjects' diasporic bodies. The puritanical intellectual sobriety of Islam is for the majority of Pakistani settlers in Britain countered by the sheer pleasure of South Asian food and dress, films and poetry, music and dance. Yet the transnational diaspora these performances embody is a *depoliticized* one that demands from its members nothing except enjoyment and consumption. There is no sense here of a moral or politically grounded transnational subjectivity, of responsibility for another, even of a return. As a transgressive aesthetic, however, South Asia has nevertheless become for marginalized groups—women and youth—a source of powerful counter-narratives in their struggle with Muslim male elders to define the agendas and diasporic consciousness of British Muslim South Asians (Werbner 1996a, 1996b, 1999).

Can this traveling aesthetic of desire emanating from South Asia (itself an invented and imposed category) be said to constitute a "diaspora"? Amitav Ghosh argues that South Asians form a diaspora of the "imagination" (1989:76), embodying an "epic" relationship between center and peripheries. In extending this definition, what needs to be recognized is the power of mass cultural production and trade to underwrite transnational communities in the postcolonial world (see Ong and Nonini 1997). Exported from South Asia (more rarely, from the West), this packaged culture constitutes South Asian transnational communities otherwise divided politically and morally into national diasporas (Indian, Pakistani, Bangladeshi, Sri Lankan) and religious ones (Muslim, Hindu, Sikh, Jain, Buddhist, Christian). In the case of Pakistanis—who are mostly devout Muslims—South Asia can perhaps best be seen as the original locus of a powerful *counter-diaspora*, transgressively interrupting pure narratives of origin and faith or over-policed boundaries.[8]

At the outset of this chapter I proposed that diaspora is a place which is both a non-place and a multiplicity of places, a place marked by difference. I suggested that this place emerges chaordically, without centralized command structures, but in a highly predictable fashion. In incipient diasporas, organizations are often tentative and short lived, highly vulnerable to local intra-communal struggles and conflicts or to personal shortcomings. Some organizations, such as national political lobbies, require resources of knowledge, skill, and finance which only established diasporas can mobilize. At the same time, the expansion of Sufi orders and Pakistani national political parties into the West reveals that Pakistani diasporic formation is highly predictable. This has been reflected in the proliferation of Pakistani diasporic organizations mirroring the full conflictual sectarian, cultural, and regional diversity of the subcontinent. New diasporic communities form through the usual patterns of growth and expansion and recreate ties to a place of origin and a shared history, and hence also to a sense of common destiny, without homogenizing themselves globally. As Leonard (2000) shows in a comparison between Canadian and American South Asians, each diasporic "community" is unique, historically contingent, and different. Nevertheless, they all share certain common parameters which this chapter has attempted to sketch out: above all, in the case of the most powerful diasporas, a sense of co-responsibility extending across and beyond national boundaries.

REFERENCES

Alavi, Hamza. 1997. "Ironies of History: Contradictions of the Khilafat Movement." In *Muslim Identities in Plural Societies*, ed. Mushirul Hasan. New Delhi: Manohar. Also published in *Comparative Studies of South Asia, Africa and the Middle East* 17(1):1–17.

Anderson, Benedict. 1983. *Imagined Communities*. London: Verso.

———. 1992. *Long Distance Nationalism: World Capitalism and the Rise of Identity Politics*. Werthem Lecture. University of Amsterdam: Centre for South Asian Studies.

———. 1994. "Exodus." *Critical Inquiry* 20:314–27.

Anthias, Floya. 1998. "Evaluating 'Diaspora': Beyond Ethnicity?" *Sociology* 3(32):557–80.

Basch, Linda, Nina Glick Schiller, and Cristina Szanton Blanc. 1993. *Nations Unbound: Transnational Projects, Postcolonial Predicaments and Deterritorialized Nation-States*. Reading: Gordon & Breach.

Bhachu, Parminder. 1995. "New Cultural Forms and Transnational South Asian Women: Culture, Class and Consumption among British Asian Women in the Diaspora." In *Nation and Migration: The Politics of Space in the South Asian Diaspora*, ed. Peter van der Veer, pp. 222–44. Philadelphia: University of Pennsylvania Press.

Bhabha, Homi. 1994. *The Location of Culture*. London: Routledge.

Bjorgo, Tore. 1997. "'The Invaders,' 'the Traitors,' and 'the Resistance Movement': The Extreme Right's Conceptualisation of Opponents and Self in Scandinavia." In *The Politics of Multiculturalism in the New Europe: Racism, Identity and Community*, ed. Tariq Modood and Pnina Werbner, pp. 54–72. London: Zed Books.

Boyarin, Daniel, and Jonathan Boyarin. 1993. "Diaspora: Generation and the Ground of Jewish Identity." *Critical Inquiry* 19:693–725.

Brah, Avtar. 1996. *Cartographies of Diaspora: Contesting Identities*. London: Routledge.

Cheyette, Bryan. 1996. "'Ineffable and Usable': Towards a Diasporic British-Jewish Writing." *Textual Practice* 10(2):295–313.

Clifford, James. 1994. "Diasporas." *Cultural Anthropology* 9(3):302–38.

Eaton, Richard. 1987. *Sufis of Bijapur, 1300–1700: Social Roles of Sufis in Medieval India*. Princeton, N.J.: Princeton University Press.

———. 1993. *The Rise of Islam and the Bengal Frontier, 1204–1760*. Berkeley: University of California Press.

Ellis, Patricia, and Zafar Khan. 1998. "Diasporic Mobilization and the Kashmir Issue in British Politics." *Journal of Ethnic and Migration Studies* 24(3): 471–88.

Fabricant, Carole. 1998. "Riding the Waves of (Post)Colonial Migrancy: Are We Really in the Same Boat?" *Diaspora* 7(1):25–51.

Foner, Nancy. 1997. "What's New About Transnationalism? New York Immigrants Today and at the Turn of the Century." *Diaspora* 6(3):355–75.

Frembgen, Jörgen W. 1998. "The Majzub Mama Ji Sarkar: 'A Friend of God Moves from One House to Another.'" In *Embodying Charisma: Modernity, Locality and the Performance of Emotion in Sufi Cults*, ed. Pnina Werbner and Helene Basu. London: Routledge.

Ghosh, Amitav. 1989. "The Diaspora in Indian Culture." *Public Culture* 2(1): 73–78.

Gilroy, Paul. 1993. *The Black Atlantic: Modernity and Double Consciousness*. London: Verso.

Goldschmidt, Henry. 2000. "'Crown Heights Is the Centre of the World': Reterritorializing a Jewish Diaspora." Special issue on "The Materiality of Diaspora: Between Aesthetics and 'Real' Politics," ed. Karen Leonard and Pnina Werbner. *Diaspora* 9(1).

Gopinath, Gayatri. 1995. "'Bombay, U.K., Yuba City': Bhangra Music and the Engendering of Diaspora." *Diaspora* 4(3):303–22.

Hall, Stuart. 1990. "Cultural Identity and Diaspora." In *Identity: Community, Culture, Difference*, ed. J. Rutherford. London: Lawrence & Wishart.

Hock, Dee W. 1999. *The Birth of the Chaordic Age*. San Francisco: Berrett-Koehler Pub.

Huntington, Samuel P. 1993. "The Clash of Civilizations?" *Foreign Affairs* (Summer).

Leonard, Karen. 2000. "State, Culture, and Religion: Political Action and Representation among South Asians in North America." Special issue on "The Materiality of Diaspora: Between Aesthetics and 'Real' Politics," ed. Karen Leonard and Pnina Werbner. *Diaspora* 9(1).

Leonard, Karen, and Pnina Werbner, editors. 2000. Special issue on "The Materiality of Diaspora: Between Aesthetics and 'Real' Politics" *Diaspora* 9(1).

Ong, Aihwa, and Donald Nonini. 1997. *Underground Empires: the Cultural Politics of Modern Chinese Transnationalism*. New York: Routledge.

Safran, William. 1991. "Diasporas in Modern Societies: Myths of Homeland and Return." *Diaspora* 1(1): 83–99.

Shanin, Teodor. 1988. "The Zionisms of Israel." In *State and Ideology in the Middle East and Pakistan*, ed. Fred Halliday and Hamza Alavi, pp. 222–56. London: Macmillan Education.

Sheffer, Gabriel. 1995. "The Emergence of New Ethno-National Diasporas." *Migration* 28:5–28.

———. 1996. "Israeli-Diaspora Relations in Comparative Perspective." In *Israel in Comparative Perspective*, ed. Michael J. Barnett, pp. 53–83. New York: SUNY Press.

———. 1999. "From Israel Hegemony to Diaspora Full Autonomy: The Current State of Ethno-National Diasporas and the Alternatives Facing World Jewry." In *Jewish Centers and Peripheries: Europe Between America and Israel Fifty Years After World War II*, ed. S. Ilan Troen, pp. 41–64. Somerset, N.J.: Transactions Publishers.

Soysal, Yasmeen N. 1994. *Limits of Citizenship: Migrants and Postnational Membership in Europe*. Chicago: University of Chicago Press.

Tölölyan, Khachig. 1996. "Rethinking Diaspora(s): Stateless Power in the Transnational Moment." *Diaspora* 5(1): 3–36.

Werbner, Pnina. 1990. *The Migration Process: Capital, Gifts and Offerings among British Pakistanis*. Oxford: Berg.

———. 1996a. "Public Spaces, Political Voices: Gender, Feminism and Aspects of British Muslim Participation in the Public Sphere." In *Religion and Politics in Europe* (provisional title), ed. P. S. van Koningsveld and W.A.R. Shadid. Leiden.

———. 1996b. "Fun Spaces: On Identity and Social Empowerment among British Pakistanis." *Theory, Culture and Society* 13 (4).

———. 1996c. "Stamping the Earth with the Name of Allah: Zikr and the Sacralising of Space among British Muslims." *Cultural Anthropology* 11(3).

———. 1998a. "Diasporic Political Imaginaries: A Sphere of Freedom or a Sphere of Illusions." *Communal/Plural: Journal of Transnational and Crosscultural Studies* (May).

———. 1998b. "*Langar*: Pilgrimage, Sacred Exchange and Perpetual Sacrifice in a Sufi Saint's Lodge." In *Embodying Charisma: Modernity, Locality and the Performance of Emotion in Sufi Cults*, ed. Pnina Werbner and Helene Basu. London: Routledge.

———. 1999. "Political Motherhood and the Feminisation of Citizenship: Women's Activism and the Transformation of the Public Sphere." In *Women, Citizenship and Difference*, ed. Nira Yuval-Davis and Pnina Werbner, pp. 221–45. London: Zed Books.

———. 2000. "Introduction: The Materiality of Diaspora—Between Aesthetics and 'Real' Politics." Special issue on "The Materiality of Diaspora: Between Aesthetics and 'Real' Politics," ed. Karen Leonard and Pnina Werbner. *Diaspora* 9(1).

———. 2001. *Imagined Diasporas among Manchester Muslims: The Public Performance of Pakistani Transnational Identity Politics*. Oxford: John Curry.

———. 2003. *Pilgrims of Love: The Anthropology of a Global Sufi Cult*. Bloomington, In.: Indiana University Press.

Werbner, Richard. 1976. *Regional Cults*. London and New York: Academic Press.

———. 1989. *Ritual Passage, Sacred Journey: The Process and Organisation of Religious Movement*. Washington, D.C.: Smithsonian Institution Press.

Westerlund, David, and Eva Evers Rosander, eds. 1997. *African Islam and Islam in Africa: Encounters between Sufis and Islamists*. London: Hurst Co.

Yuval-Davis, Nira. 1997. "Ethnicity, Gender Relations and Multiculturalism." In *Debating Cultural Hybridity*, ed. Pnina Werbner and Tariq Modood. London: Zed Books.

Zaretsky, Eli. 1995. "The Birth of Identity Politics in the 1960s: Psychoanalysis and the Public/Private Division." In *Global Modernities*, ed. Mike Featherstone, Scott Lash, and Roland Robertson, pp. 244–59. London: Sage.

NOTES

Previously published in *Journal of Ethnic and Migration Studies* (2002) 28(1): 119–34. www.tandf.co.uk. Reprinted with permission.

1. Cheyette (1996:296) cites Lyotard's view that "the jews have been the object of *non-lieu*," non-place or no place, which follows Heidegger's writings on this subject.

2. On the simultaneity in time of imagined communities see Anderson 1983. On some key features of diasporas see Tölölyan 1996.

3. This question is discussed importantly by Tölölyan 1996.

4. The term "chaorder" was coined by Dee W. Hock, inventor of the Visa credit card (see his new book, Hock 1999). I base my account here on an interview with Hock aired on Radio 4 in 1998.

5. For recent discussions see Eaton 1987, 1993; Westerlund and Rosander 1997.

6. For a more elaborate discussion of *langar*, see Werbner 1998b.

7. Very recently, Germany for the first time passed a law allowing for dual citizenship.

8. On such transgressions, see Bhabha 1994.

CHAPTER 2

New Homeland for an Old Diaspora

SUSAN PATTIE

The most widely viewed treatment of Armenian diaspora/homeland relations in recent years must be Atom Egoyan's film *Calendar*, a portrayal of a
triangulated love relationship involving people and places. The Western and
Middle Eastern diasporas and the Republic of Armenia are each represented,
as Egoyan himself plays a non-Armenian-speaking diasporan photographer
on assignment in Armenia to capture images of the country for a calendar.
His wife, a Middle-Eastern born Armenian, acts as interpreter, and soon begins an affair with their chauffeur and self-appointed guide-teacher, a native
of Armenia. The experience of something potentially emotionally powerful,
both the disintegration of his marriage and the encounter with Armenian
space, a typical Egoyan device, is mediated at all times. The photographer
seems to live through the lens of his cameras, content to learn only what is
absolutely necessary to the completion of his project as he conceived it while
still away from the land itself. The chauffeur does not accept the assigned
role of passive helper, and attempts to present a different version of Armenia and Armenian history. The interpreter, as one might expect, is caught
in between, but gradually drifts toward the chauffeur-guide as symbol of
homeland. She is, finally, more at home with what she is discovering, with a
flawed but lively "reality," and less comfortable with the purposeful detachment of her husband, Mr. Western Diaspora.

The movie continues to unfold, but this brief depiction provides a focus
on a vital aspect of homeland/diaspora relations in the Armenian world.
There has been and continues to be variety within the diaspora, including in
the ways in which homeland is conceived and individuals and communities
act on those ideas. Since 1991, with the independence of the Republic of Armenia, there is increasing convergence on the idea of that state as homeland
for all Armenians, though, as discussed below, this is a new development for
many in diaspora. As in the film, images of homeland as constructed in di-

aspora often are idealized, content-less, beautiful, and unproblematic (other than, crucially, their unavailability). One can project anything onto the landscape. On the other hand, the inhabitants, their different-ness, their surprising "other-ness," are a shock. Unlike in the film, a diaspora Armenian does not have to travel to Armenia to discover this. Over one million Armenians have emigrated from the Republic since independence, and many are moving to Los Angeles.

In this chapter, we will look at constructions of identity in diaspora intertwined with changing visions and evolving relations with a homeland. This includes varied conceptions and symbolizations of a homeland (and of diaspora) over time, from life under the rule of empires through genocide, dispersal, and a focus on survival, to the recent independence of the Republic of Armenia. Over the last ten years, discussion of diaspora within the social sciences has proliferated and questions raised include the implications that diasporas have for their homelands and for the multi-cultural states in which they live. William Safran asks if it is possible that diaspora communities pose a more serious challenge to their host societies than do other minorities, since they test the limits of pluralism (Safran 1991:96–97). In a more positive vein, others such as James Clifford (1997) and Paul Gilroy (1987/1991) suggest that diaspora is not really about longing for another space, but rather about an effort to be part of the host country on one's own terms. This leads to a question that nationalists find extremely provocative, even blasphemous: Is there a positive side to diaspora? These are some of the issues explored in this chapter.

Like identity itself, the concepts of Return, Homeland, and Diaspora are all continually in the process of construction. They interact with each other and other factors, within both the Armenian world and the varied contexts within which Armenians live. The dominance or popularity of a particular attitude toward these ideas provides a backdrop against which many other opinions may be formulated, whether in simple rejection or more complex elaboration. These others may underline or undermine, and some will themselves gain in importance and popularity as social and political contexts change. These minor voices are not difficult to find, and they form a significant part of the variation in identity around the Armenian world.

The New Homeland?

An attempt to rein in the perceived centrifugal forces at work in the Armenian world was behind the first Armenia/Diaspora Conference, held in

Yerevan, Armenia, in September 1999. Some 6,000 delegates attended from around the world. Their selection was rather haphazard, and the conference was finally organized only after determined, last-minute heroic efforts, but the effect was important. The symbol of one concrete homeland, Armenia, was further solidified, and the diaspora was drawn, at least partially, into the realities of nation-state politics.[1]

A popular slogan leading up to the conference was "One Nation, One Homeland." Vartan Oskanian, the Secretary for Foreign Affairs (himself from the diaspora) suggested a change: "One Nation, One State." The Committee on Communication, made up of diaspora Armenians, went further, beginning its report by stating that the Diaspora is, and is not, a single entity, suggesting relations between Armenia and "Armenians abroad" take this diversity into account. In addition to the government and various countries' representatives, two poets were invited to give an official address at the conference. Their speeches extended the oppositions outlined in this discussion and in the film above.[2] The first poet, Sylva Gaboudikian, born in the Soviet period in Armenia, lamented the ways in which "Western culture" has encroached on the "national culture," and hoped that new structures in Armenia would be able to help not only internal rebuilding, but communities in diaspora "remain Armenian." The second, diaspora writer Vahe Oshagan, took a much looser approach to what and who is Armenian, emphasizing that one does not have to speak Armenian to be counted. "One nation, yes; one fatherland, yes; but one culture? This is a question."

Until recently there has been no center-periphery to Armenian life. The state of Armenia, under Soviet rule until 1991, was not acknowledged by all as "the" or even "a" homeland. Particularly after independence, an increasing number of vertical links have been established with Armenia—yet lateral links between diaspora individuals and communities remain crucial. These are connected to each other through family, economic, and ethnic political ties, and are still marked by diverse cross-cutting affiliations between families and their villages, towns, and countries of origin. Iranian-Armenians in London may establish a circle of friends and colleagues within that country, remain close to others still in Iran, while helping with charitable work in Armenia or visiting the country as tourists. Cypriot-Armenians share the political concerns of their Greek and Turkish neighbors, look to Beirut as the closest major Armenian center, go to London for visits with relatives, and visit Armenia to gauge potential investment opportunities or appropriate aid. All share an interest in the burgeoning Los Angeles community, where it seems every Armenian today has family and makes at least one trip to attend a wedding. Below the surface of these activities is the symbolic level of homeland and diaspora relations, and the shifting from a long-ing for places of lived experiences to a refining of an idealized homeland. In-herent in this shift is the continuing redefinition of what it means to be Ar-menian and how one can live productively, as an Armenian, in diaspora.

Poetry in Motion

Like other peoples around the Middle East and Caucasus, Armenians have long used poetry as a public expression and discussion of ideals, and most community events include recitations of poetry. The following is "The Wal-nut Tree," a well-known poem by Sylva Gaboudikian (1985).

> There is a walnut tree
> Growing in the vineyard
> At the very edge of the world.
>
> My people, you are like
> That huge ancient tree—
> With branches blessed by the graces
>
> But sprawling
> Over the small corner of land
> Roots and arms spread out
> And spilling your fruit
> To nourish foreign soils.

This poem, written during the Soviet period in Armenia, does not men-tion the word "homeland," but it is understood and presented as a problem, being small, somehow isolated at the edge of the world, and connected with an inevitable sense of loss. Among other themes familiar to Armenian audi-ences is the walnut tree itself, symbolizing longevity and productivity, a long history and connections. The dispersion of fruit is rendered slightly more positively than is usual in such poetry, although it is still clearly far from ideal. By including both negative and positive elements, the poem is es-pecially effective in conjuring up the range of feelings of Armenians for their diaspora.

The Armenian Diaspora

There is great deal of discussion among Armenians about the concept of diaspora, in terms of the definition of the word and the ways in which diaspora is experienced and whether, of course, there is an "ideal" diaspora. John Armstrong (1982) has suggested that the Armenian diaspora most closely resembles the "archetypal" or, in Safran's word, "ideal" diaspora of the Jews (Safran 1991), In attempting to define diaspora, Safran includes a belief in an eventual Return to the true homeland and, in the meantime, a commitment to supporting the homeland. Robin Cohen, in his *Global Diasporas*, takes issue with the emphasis that Safran places on homeland, and notes that the concept of homeland itself is problematic, that some people are diasporic though their concept of homeland was created after dispersion, and that there may be "positive virtues" in living in diaspora. He writes, "The tension between an ethnic, a national and a transnational identity is often a creative, enriching one" (Cohen 1997:24).

For Armenians, this tangled mass of approaches to the question of ethnic identity and diaspora/homeland relations is highly appropriate. Doing fieldwork in the diaspora, first in Cyprus and London and lately in the United States, I find examples to fit nearly any position offered, and one has to conclude that the vitality of the diaspora itself must be due in great part to its complexity and flexibility. However, among these positions is a particularly vociferous one—found most often among political activists—that the Armenian diaspora is entirely negative in its very nature—that is, both in its reason for being and in its dispersion from some version of the homeland. Cohen, too, describes the Armenians as an example of a "victim diaspora" (along with Jews, Palestinians, Irish, and Africans), people who have survived and been displaced by catastrophe, the memories of which continue to bind them together on some level (1997:31).

For many centuries, the Armenian world has been based on interconnected communities without an umbrella government of their own. The vast majority of people remained on the territory of their ancestors in what is now eastern Turkey and the Caucasus. From Byzantine times onward, however, the forced transfer of Armenian populations and voluntary migration have continued to create new diaspora centers, including Iran, Istanbul (Constantinople), and parts of Africa, India, Europe, and Russia. In his "The Historical Evolution of the Armenian Diasporas," Rouben Adalian notes that from early times each progressive relocation "opened a new chapter in the history of the Armenian diaspora" (1989:81). The clash and conflict of empires in and over the region brought new influences to be absorbed, and following the end of Byzantine rule, Armenians found themselves in the midst of Islamic peoples, Arabs, Turks, Persians (after their own conversion). In the empires under which they lived, a sizable number of Armenians became thoroughly integrated, to the point of taking on positions of power (for example, in the Byzantine empire), rising to be commanders of military units and marry into royalty.[3] In addition to forced dispersion, the old Armenian diaspora was also formed by trade networks, by economic migration going on at least since the tenth century. Adalian believes that it is at this point that people living in communities in diaspora began to speak of themselves as "living in exile."

Characteristics of the Contemporary Armenian Diaspora

Although this diaspora is indeed an old one, in this century it has been transformed entirely, in terms of numbers and geography, and in its very nature. The genocide and deportations at the end of the Ottoman Empire resulted in the deaths of well over one million Armenians and the near emptying of the old lands. The great dispersion of survivors that followed increased the size of some of the old diaspora centers as well as establishing new ones. Today, there are roughly seven million Armenians in the world, and more than half live in diaspora, including in the former Soviet Union, outside the Republic of Armenia.[4] As was noted earlier, the Los Angeles area has become the largest diaspora population center.

As in the past, the cement of diaspora communities, within and between them, is family. Networks of people related through descent or marriage remain of great importance, though the specific ways in which this is true have changed. The national church and the political parties and cultural organizations that have grown up over the last hundred years provide an infrastructure and public face linking communities on a more formal level. The Armenian Apostolic Church has provided a primary identity alongside kin and locale; indeed, during the Ottoman years, through the *Millet* system, the church gained explicit political authority. The church remains a central symbol in diaspora as well as in the republic, where it plays a powerful role in the new politics of nation-building and diaspora networking.

Though the Armenian diaspora is more widely spread than ever at the end of this century, modern innovations have made connections quicker, easier, and fundamentally different than in earlier times. Telephones, jets, fax machines, the Internet, international banking and finance, and the various media all serve to pass information immediately, but they also reinforce the role of kin as a resource, wherever and however far away they may reside. The concept of "home" for many is mobile and nomadic, more synonymous with family than with a particular place. The experience of place, whether present or known through memory, is always about people and their relationships, as well as about the physical surroundings. Diaspora is "place" on a large scale, encompassing a wider range of relationships, a grander network of known and possibly knowable people.

Visions of Homeland(s)

As it is for other peoples, homeland for Armenians is and has been a contested and evolving notion. It is shaped by the personal memories and experiences, ambitions and hopes of people at particular times, and by the desires and plans (and varying degrees of success of these plans) of intellectuals, teachers, priests, and political leaders. The question of return is equally ambiguous, as people have been haunted by the memories of the smells and sights of their old village or town while gradually becoming more at home in their new space, in diaspora. The confusion increases as political parties emphasize ideological notions of homeland, detached perhaps from personal experience but rooted in the past and in contemporary political events.

The land that is now the Republic of Armenia, or Hayastan, as Armenians call it, was previously a small, relatively forsaken corner of the ancient homelands (to be defined below). It declared a brief independence between 1918 and 1920 and then became part of the Soviet Union. Since 1991, with the collapse of the Soviet Union, it has been independent. It is, however, one of at least three parallel constructions of Armenian homeland. For those who live there, and increasingly, for many diaspora Armenians, it is "the homeland" today. It is a place where Armenian is spoken on the streets and heard in the opera and on television. Armenian schools, and the university, dance troupes, football teams, and choirs, are all pointed to with pride. It is regarded as a shelter, and also, in itself, as a delicate construction that must be protected. As Levon Avdoyan points out in the first issue of *Armenian Forum*, the importance of its survival is one of the few things that nearly all Armenians there and anywhere in diaspora will agree upon (Avdoyan 1998:14).

A second homeland is also called Hayastan: the ancient kingdom, the old territories embedded with a 2,500-year-old history, lands reaching from Dikranagert in Anatolia to Karabagh in the Caucasus. These have not been together under sovereign Armenian rule since 95 B.C.E., but encompass the ancestral homes of most of those now in diaspora. This is the homeland for intellectuals, activists, and, more generally, those more historically and politically inclined. A return to at least some of these lands (in particular Mount Ararat) has traditionally formed a major plank in the platform of the Dashnak party and the freedom fighters, or terrorists, who were active in the 1970s and early 1980s.

The third is a related but more intimate vision. Until recently the first question in a conversation between Armenian strangers was always "*Oor deghatsi ek?*," or "Where are you native?" In diaspora, the homeland is, or at least includes, an Armenian's own town or village of origin. Now, of course, that usually means the village of their ancestors' origin. This includes personal and collective memories of towns such as Kharpert and Adana, now in Turkey, and villages such as Kessab, in Syria, places that people wonder and care about and long to see. A number of books have been written about these towns—collections of customs, memories, descriptions of their social life and the accomplishments of the survivors. In the United States, fellow villagers or townspeople have created their own telephone directories, children's summer camps, and annual picnics, all of which help to continue the sense of belonging to a certain place already fostered within the extended family. To cite an example, from the 1982 Kessabtzi directory by the Rev. Vahan Tootikian: "We, the Kessabtzis, are the sons and daughters of an ancient and noble people. . . . We are the indivisible and inseparable part of that little territory, that 'Small Armenia' in the vast ocean of the Armenian Diaspora, which is called Kessab. . . . We are . . . (linked in family solidarity as kinsmen, rooted in the past). We have a bond with every other Kessabtzi no matter where or what" (Tootikian 1982:184).

Longing for Place

The varied customs and dialects found in different Armenian towns and villages of the Ottoman Empire have translated today into new differences of outlook, style, and linguistic ability in the more widespread diaspora. As in the past, Armenians often say that they feel most comfortable and have to explain less when they are with Armenians from their own diaspora countries. While I was doing fieldwork with Armenians in Cyprus and London, people often reminded me that they had come from varied backgrounds and their ties continued to stretch in different directions. One day as I sat with a group of men at their club in Nicosia, someone began, "This community is like a witch's brew. Everything is in it. The people are from everywhere and they are trying to extend their roots here. Look at me. Half of my family is in Hayastan and half are in America."

"Yes," added his neighbor, "I'm from Kharpert but my wife is from Adana, you see . . ." and others added their stories. Cyprus is not considered a homeland, but has become a well-loved home to its Armenian community—those who have chosen to remain. There, as in other places, Armenians have had to create a new community, and many elements, material as well as nonmaterial, go into this creation. The realm of the senses—the physical visual environment, foods, smells, and sounds—help to cement and pass on an attachment. Poems, stories, and anecdotes are also an important part of this mixture, helping to shore up and at times create a collective memory which serves to weave people together, at least for a time.

In this form, homeland is also often a utopian vision of paradise, something that might sustain a person in later years of insecurity and physical and psychological pain. The following is taken from a private memoir by Rebecca Hagopian:

Zeytoon—Paradise Lost

Today I am hearing the call of the past. The years of childhood. It shines as a bright light in the darkness of the past years. There are moments I want to be free from this weary, weak and old body. In my thoughts I am back in my home town in Zeytoon.

. . . The mountains misty and grand, the valleys green, the river flowing, The flock of goats resting in the shade of huge solid rocks, the shepherd boy with his flute, playing a young lover's song. . . . There is the walnut tree, the rope still hanging in its branches for us to swing on. . . . My sister Suran carving her initials on soft rocks (as if she knows she is going to leave her beloved homeland and die in an unknown place).

Here again, there are issues of longing and belonging. Again, the walnut tree anchors the scene, waiting for someone to come. There are references to both the author's own current physical distress and loneliness, and to past communal terror and loss. For Armenians, one particular event has bound and preoccupied the personal and collective imagination in this century: the devastating deportations and massacres of the late nineteenth and early twentieth centuries. In Cyprus (and other places in the Middle East), together with their Turkish and Greek neighbors Armenians have gone through more upheaval, loss, and displacement. The experiences of Armenians in Cyprus are also echoed in Renee Hirschon's portrayal of the Greek

refugees from Asia Minor settling in Piraeus (1989). There the past is a reminder of tragedy and loss but also an emblem of pride, continuity, and
strength. In their own words, Armenians relate that not only have they survived terrible pogroms, but they also can look beyond that to a glorious and
ancient past (as, for example, the first Christian "nation," and an early, distinctive alphabet). Like the Asia Minor refugees described by Hirschon, Armenians in Cyprus and around the diaspora have also found reasons for particular pride in their personal pasts or in the pasts of their old villages or
towns. Their histories embody behavior or values that they deemed worthier
than those of their non-Armenian neighbors, or even those of fellow Armenians from other areas.

People often brought up the subject of identity, both personal and communal. What does it really mean to be "Armenian"? They discussed how life
had been, how it should be, and, again, what was important to remember.
One way in which my own work was understood was as putting such memories on paper to preserve them for posterity, to keep them for the day when
the next generation(s) might be ready to listen—as surely they would,
eventually. While waiting for that day, older Armenians often voiced a wist-
fulness and concern similar to that witnessed by Jonathan Boyarin among
Polish Jews in Paris. He noted a "shortage of cultural heirs" in their newly
established community. Like their Jewish counterparts, Armenian children
have some information about their parents' and grandparents' lives—especially those parts that form the political memory—but these younger people
are selective, they are busy. Their interests and ambitions are aimed toward
the future. In a comment that is as applicable to Armenians as it is to the
Paris Jews with whom he worked, Boyarin adds, "Loss of homeland and family is a recurrent theme in Jewish popular memory, but the 'loss' of one's
children to a different cultural world, common as it may be, remains in large
measure an unalleviated source of pain" (1991:11).

Young people are often a source of tension for older people, an extension
of their dissatisfaction and uncertainty with their life decisions and the ways
their own lives have unfolded. David Kherdian, an Armenian American poet,
writes on this theme in "For My Father" (1971):

> Our trivial fights over spading
> The vegetable patch, painting the
> Garden fence ochre instead of blue,
> And my resistance to Armenian food
> In preference for everything American,

Seemed, in my struggle for identity,
To be the literal issue.

Why have I waited until your death
to know the earth you were turning
was Armenia, the color of the fence
your homage to Adana, and your other
complaints over my own complaints
were addressed to your homesickness
brought on by my English.

Each generation in diaspora worries that the next is not finding the right balance between accommodation of the host culture and assimilation into it (in Armenian, *jermag chart*, or white massacre). Nationalists take this further, as Kapferer points out, by reifying an idealized culture, extracting it from the "flow of social life," and establishing it as an object of devotion (1988:2). Culture is constantly changing, and not only individuals but various diaspora centers have, of course, developed in different ways. Each imagines the diaspora, the homeland, and the nation in particular ways. Similarly, they see the aims and methods of nationalism in widely different ways. The diaspora centers—loosely connected, relying on each other, sometimes criticizing or mocking each other, each rationalizing a certain (never the same) set of practices—share a common feature in that with each generation in place, diaspora becomes more comfortable and more a home in itself. Robert Mirak's *Torn Between Two Lands* focuses on Armenian emigration to America from 1890 through the World War I. The great majority of the descendants of those people no longer feel torn, and Anny Bakalian titled her contemporary study of American Armenians *From Being to Feeling Armenian* (1993). Western diaspora Armenians have set priorities in their own lives that are not necessarily shared by their Middle Eastern cousins, nor by the residents of Hayastan. Interestingly, this is not a one-way street—that is, toward straight assimilation in one place and purity in the other—and there are several areas in which this tension is played out.

The church, seen everywhere as a cornerstone and key symbol of Armenian culture, is itself highly contested. In the United States, where generations have now worked to build edifices, congregations, and particular divisions of communities, new waves of immigrants from the Near East and Hayastan are insisting that the language of the church (and its organizations) must be Armenian—and that those American Armenians who do not speak the language (the majority) are not really Armenian. The following quote is from a 1995 community survey conducted for the Armenian Church in America.[5] "Immigrants treat those of us whose families have been in the U.S. for a century as lesser people because we don't speak the language and/or we are from mixed parentage. Who paved the way for these people? Who built the churches they now control? What gives them the right to discriminate against us?"

Such issues of legitimacy and contested membership permeate the arena of work as well. The same survey asked Armenian Americans how they described themselves, given a number of options. "Hard-working" received the highest score (86 percent), followed by ambitious (79 percent). This attitude is taken as a given and is the subject of many family stories. When new immigrants come and are given what is seen as a "soft ride" by welfare agencies—or worse, try to slip into the cracks and live off the black market—European and American Armenians begin to froth: these people are not really Armenians! Ex-Soviet Armenians in particular are seen as guilty of playing the system and not really working. The idealization of residents of Armenia prior to their emigration, and the intense "disappointment" following their arrival in the West, echoes Markowitz's observations of changing mutual perceptions of Russian and American-born Jews in Brighton Beach (1993).

Changing Views of Armenia

A final contested area is the Republic of Armenia itself. Its independence has created a new focus for diaspora Armenians' imaginations, dreams, and hopes. In some ways independence is a rejuvenating force, in others, it is maddening and frustrating, as those who do visit or try to work there discover just how different the realms of ideas and patterns of daily life there actually are. Ten years ago, I asked a forty-year-old woman who had completed her university education in Hayastan whether she and her husband (another diaspora Armenian whom she met there) considered staying there or emigrating after they had lost their business in Cyprus in the war of 1974. "Oh no," she said, "we love it there, but they are very different from us— very Russian influenced. We are Middle Eastern." She added that if the people there were ever able to travel freely, she would certainly consider it. She and her husband, like others, still live in London, with no plans to move, and, indeed, many thousands of Hayastantisis are emigrating, mostly to Los Angeles. Armenians call this a "hemorrhaging," rather than a flow of migration.

In an earlier period, the ideological basis of the Soviet Union complicated the position of Hayastan as a diaspora focus. Its primary portrayal in diaspora was that of a national repository of culture and genes, waiting for an eventual release from foreign rule. The Soviet Union encouraged this and used it to attract diaspora goodwill and some aid—and to attract new immigrants through a "gathering in" program called *Nerkaght*. This program caused upheaval within families and communities, especially in the Near East. After the decisions were made, related questions and debates continued. Someone who did emigrate in the 1962 *Nerkaght* sent back a coded photo to warn other family members not to follow. One who later returned to Cyprus was bitterly disappointed by the experience and told me, "We were blinded by our love of Hayastan. . . . The people who didn't go can't understand what we went through." The experience was shattering for many, and yet those who later left Armenia were shunned as traitors by many of their former friends whom they rejoined in diaspora. For these people, nothing could be bad enough to warrant abandoning what was left of the homeland.

During my fieldwork, at a cultural event at Melkonian Institute, the Armenian high school in Nicosia, the annual guest teacher from Soviet Armenia gave a speech in which he damned the day the diaspora was formed. He pointed to the Melkonian itself as a superior personal identity to local ambitions (not Kibratsi or Kessabtsi, etc.), claiming that there was but one Armenian identity.

From the 1930s onward, but becoming especially dramatic during the cold war years, the two major diaspora political parties remained on either side of the homeland fence. The Ramgavars' attitude was generally admiring and condoning, while the more popular Dashnaks, who had ruled the short-lived independent state that preceded Soviet control, were much more critical of Soviet rule, planning for a future independent, free, and united Armenia. By the end of the 1970s, both sides had come to view Russia as a necessary protector, and thus independence was not greeted with unalloyed joy. It took some time to accept that, in fact, the system had imploded and Armenians had not brought independence on all by themselves. Then it became acceptable, even exciting, though worrying. The Dashnak side quickly warmed to the idea, especially as the new republic adopted symbols that the party had kept alive from the earlier republic, such as the tri-colored flag. After a turbulent relationship with the first administration, the Dashnak party is building a power base within the state but with considerably more difficulties than perhaps were anticipated.

Daphne Winland has observed that the independence of Croatia in 1990

was a catalyst for a similar process of revitalization, divergence, and transformation. Activists claim that independence has strengthened the unity
of the community, but Winland notes that certain differences and schisms
have been re-emphasized, taking on new form and meaning: "Boundaries
are being re-sited, but not destroyed" (1995:13). When, earlier in this century, Armenians became further dispersed, nationalists had insisted that
there was a particular way to be Armenian, glossing over the multiple layers
of identity which are taken for granted, and, indeed, make daily life possible,
for example, that one speaks the language, acknowledges the Apostolic
Church, marries another Armenian, seeks to be reconciled with history.
With the birth (or re-birth) of a nation/state there also is the rapid shaping
of the idea of one concrete homeland. Nationalism changes shape, both
within and without the state, and one can see a further narrowing and essentializing of identity. Winland finds similar developments in Croatia, where,
she writes, nationalist ideology does not recognize the "multistranded relationships" across borders nor the variety within the diaspora based on gender, generation, class, and regional affiliation (ibid.). For Armenians, such
ideology has the effect of distancing many people who consider themselves
to be part of the collective but also "different." There remain many ways of
unofficial belonging—and people may drift between public and private
realms. The shared memory of the genocide has united people and fed a certain sense of responsibility to the collective, to the past, and the future. Having been taught to behave as citizens of diaspora, with obligations to each
other and to a collective past, in recent years diaspora Armenians have increasingly been urged by their political, religious, and intellectual leaders to
also behave as potential citizens of the homeland, the Republic of Armenia.

Clifford Geertz has used the metaphor of culture as a guide, and ideology
as a map. In common with Israel and the Jews, Armenians growing up in diaspora have been shown the map and are now applying it to a new terrain,
occupying perhaps the same physical location but greatly transformed. In
the most radical cases, new orthodoxies and fanaticisms are being bred away
from the homeland and then transported there in a quixotic effort to "save"
the homeland from itself and its neighbors. One can again compare Armenia
and Israel, as well as parts of Eastern Europe. Does diaspora breed a particular kind of idealism without the constraints of responsibility and experience—a combination of naiveté, "rightness" (or self-righteousness), and violence? Apart from such radical cases, an equally important question can be
posed: should people in diaspora be allowed dual citizenship, holding passports from the homeland-state as well as their host country? Who really belongs? Thus far, the Republic of Armenia has required residency and exclu-

sive citizenship, the previous government (of Ter Petrossian) was at pains to point out the differences between the living experiences of the diaspora (anywhere) and the republic. The Kocharian administration, influenced itself by a diaspora political organization, has spoken of possible changes but has not as yet taken action.

For most in diaspora, the creation of an independent state does change the landscape, but symbolic identity, such as Bakalian describes in her book, and a looser self-definition and connection will continue to be the foundation of their "Armenianness." This brings us back to an important corner of the triangular relationship—that of the diaspora people to the various host cultures. Clearly the philosophies and legalities of the state in question have a decided influence, leaving Armenians in France with expectations and attitudes that are quite different from those of Armenians in the United States—or those living in Lebanon or Syria. How is one to be a "good, loyal citizen" of a particular country, with its own history and conjunction of peoples, an equal member of a pluralistic, democratic society, and also a "good Armenian"? How does one balance these roles: does one threaten the other? Can a democracy function with such fractured identities? Tölölyan writes that diasporas should not "apologize" for their hybrid identity but instead, "at its best the diaspora is an example, for both the 'homeland' and the 'host land' nation-states, of the possibility of living, even thriving in the regimes of multiplicity which are increasingly the global condition, and a proper vision of which diasporas may help to construct, given half a chance (Tölölyan 1996:7). Tölölyan and Cohen (1997) find a close "fit" (not causal) between globalization—the mobile, detached mode necessary to succeed in the contemporary world—and the characteristics of diaspora. Diaspora identity perhaps provides a connection otherwise missing in the modern, mobile world. However, another problem emerges as "proper" belonging, as Liisa Malkki points out, is seen to be rooted, like a tree, in the ground, not in metaphor, symbols, history, or even family. Thus, Malkki writes, there seem to be many who perceive refugees and diaspora peoples as somehow inherently "wrong" (1992).

Jonathan and Daniel Boyarin question the other corner of the triangle, the state/homeland, stating the creation of Israel was a subversion of a Jewish culture and not its culmination. Zionists saw diaspora as a "problem," as do some Armenian nationalists. The Boyarins see strength in the "diversity of communal arrangements and concentrations both among Jews and with our several others" (1993: 129). Indeed diaspora can be seen in this light as a borderless, stateless, free-floating—but nonetheless essentially meaningful—source of identity. Writing in *Prospect*, a British journal, Susan Greenberg echoes the Boyarins' concerns, asking whether Israel is "good" for Jews? She too answers with a provocative (even blasphemous) "no," wondering whether ethnic nationalism, when attached to a homeland which is a state, runs the risk of essentializing identity to the point that the more fluid and flexible identities found in diaspora are considered negatively or, worse, not to be in the running at all. Echoing Cohen, Greenberg also notes the advantages in diaspora of being connected and being marginal, a dynamic tension that encourages creativity. In an overwhelmingly mono-ethnic state, such as Armenia, the traditional multilingual skills and abilities to get along in a variety of other cultures will be lost. Greenberg worries that who is Jewish is being increasingly defined by those with particular plans for the state.

Conclusions

Armenians, like other peoples, disagree among themselves about interpretations and the relative importance of different components of certain issues, such as the homeland: where and what it is, how central it is, and whether the myth of return is a sustaining dream or a practical, if distant, reality. In an article in the 1998 edition of the *Kessabtzi Directory*, the author urges his compatriots to donate generously to a "community center" for the Kessab Education Association based in Los Angeles (Apelian 1998:200). This would physically resemble the "Library" back in Kessab, with its book-lined walls, canteen, and various social activities. The Kessabtzis may be an exception in the Armenian world in their continued tangible connections with the local homeland, but Armenians in diaspora continue to create new communities, on new terms, grounding themselves further in diaspora. A few are migrating to Armenia, but as yet not many have returned. Many Armenian homes bear a plaque with the following words by the California Armenian author, William Saroyan: "I should like to see any power in this world destroy this . . . small tribe of unimportant people . . . When two Armenians meet anywhere in the world, see if they will not create a New Armenia."

Of course, there is also the joke, repeated with variations among other ethnic groups, that those two Armenians will go on to create three competing organizations. Variety, as described earlier, provides flexibility but also frustration. The interpreter in *Calendar* was drawn ultimately to the more tangible space and identity apparently available in the state of Armenia. Whether or not it is one nation, as the slogans proclaim, or one culture, as the poet wonders, the new homeland, by its mere existence, changes the dynamics of the diaspora. It will continue to influence the ways in which Armenians elsewhere think about themselves. But the draw of internationalism, and the flexibility of diaspora, particularly in an era of increased ease of personal and financial mobility, is strong competition. The new homeland replaces the old, but so, too, in a continuing process, does the new diaspora replace the old.

REFERENCES

Adalian, Rouben Paul. 1989. "The Historical Evolution of the Armenian Diasporas." In *Journal of Modern Hellenism* 6:81–114.

Apelian, Vahe H. 1998. "K.E.A. Community Center: Is It Worth It?" In *Kessabtzi Directory and Yearbook*, pp. 200–202. Los Angeles: Kessab Educational Association.

Armstrong, John. 1982. *Nations Before Nationalism*. Chapel Hill: University of North Carolina Press.

Avdoyan, Levon. 1998. "The Past as Future: Armenian History and Present Politics." *Armenian Forum* 1(Spring):1–4.

Bakalian, Anny. 1993. *Armenian-Americans: From Being to Feeling Armenian*. New Brunswick, N.J.: Transaction.

Boyarin, Jonathan. 1991. *Polish Jews in Paris: The Ethnography of Memory*. Bloomington: Indiana University Press.

Boyarin, Daniel, and Jonathan Boyarin. 1993. "Diaspora: Generational Ground of Jewish Identity." *Critical Inquiry* 19:4.

Clifford, James. 1997. *Routes: Travel and Translation in the Late Twentieth Century*. Cambridge: Harvard University Press.

Cohen, Robin. 1997. *Global Diasporas: An Introduction*. London: UCL Press.

Egoyan, Atom, dir. 1993. *Calendar*. Toronto, Canada: Ego Film Arts.

Gaboudikian, Silva. 1985. "Walnut Tree." Trans. Diana Der-Hovanessian. In *Ararat* (25th anniversary issue) 26:1.

Geertz, Clifford. 1973. *The Interpretation of Cultures*. New York: Basic Books.

Gilroy, Paul. 1987/1991. *"There Ain't No Black in the Union Jack": The Cultural Politics of Race and Nation*. Chicago: University of Chicago Press (reissue).

Greenberg, Susan. 1998. "Jews Against Israel." In *Prospect* (June):12–13.

Hagopian, Rebecca. "Memoirs." Unpublished manuscript.

Hirschon, Renee. 1989. *Heirs of the Greek Catastrophe: The Social Life of Asia Minor Refugees in Piraeus*. Oxford: Clarendon.

Kapferer, Bruce. 1988. *Legends of People, Myths of State*. Washington, D.C.: Smithsonian Institution Press.

Kherdian, David. 1971. "For My Father." In *Homage to Adana*. Fresno, Calif.: Giligia Press.

Kugelmass, Jack. 1988. "Introduction." In *Between Two Worlds: Ethnographic Essays on American Jewry*, ed. Jack Kugelmass, pp. 1–29. Ithaca: Cornell University Press.

Malkki, Liisa. 1992. "National Geographic: The Rooting of Peoples and the Territorialization of National Identity Among Scholars and Refugees." *Cultural Anthropology* 7(1):24–44.

Markowitz, Fran. 1993. *A Community in Spite of Itself: Soviet Jewish Émigrés in New York*. Washington, D.C.: Smithsonian Institution Press.

Mirak, Robert. 1983. *Torn Between Two Lands: Armenians in America, 1890 to World War I*. Cambridge: Harvard University Press.

Pattie, Susan. 1997. *Faith in History: Armenians Rebuilding Community*. Washington, D.C.: Smithsonian Institution Press.

Russell, James. 1997. "The Formation of the Armenian Nation." In *Armenian People: From Ancient to Modern Times*, ed. R. G. Hovannisian, pp. 19–36. New York: St. Martin's Press.

Safran, William. 1991. "Diasporas in Modern Societies: Myths of Homeland and Return." *Diaspora* 1(1):83–99.

Tölölyan, Khachig. 1996. "Rethinking Diaspora(s): Stateless Power in the Transnational Moment." *Diaspora* 5(1):3–36.

Tootikian, Vahan, the Rev. 1982. *Kessabtzis U.S.A.-Canada*, pp. 184–86. Los Angeles: Kessab Educational Association.

Winland, Daphne. 1995. "National Independence and the Canadian Croatian Diaspora." *Diaspora* 4(1):3–29.

NOTES

This is an expanded version of an earlier paper, "Longing and Belonging: Issues of Homeland in the Armenian Diaspora," *PoLAR* 22(2) (1999). I am grateful to the anonymous reviewers of that journal for their suggestions. Another version was given at the Diaspora conference held in Beersheva, where questions and comments by other participants, especially Fran Markowitz, were very helpful. My thanks also to Razmik Panossian, Hratch Tchilingirian, and Peter Loizos.

1. A second Armenia/Diaspora conference was held in Yerevan in May 2002. Whereas the delegates attending the first conference were invited from the existing diaspora organizations, it was announced that anyone who wished could attend the second conference. This was an effort to meet the earlier criticism that only formal diaspora life was recognized, as well as an attempt to make new contacts for Armenia.

2. I am grateful to Razmik Panossian for texts and his translations of the speeches given at the 1999 Armenia/Diaspora Conference.

3. Adalian lists several Byzantine emperors of Armenian parentage, including Maurice (A.D.538–602), Heraklios (610), and Basil (867–86).

4. This is often called the "internal diaspora," in reference to the time when Armenia was part of the Soviet Union. When seen outwards, with Armenia as center, Armenians residing in the rest of the Soviet Union constituted the internal diaspora, while the rest were the external diaspora.

5. Issues and Answers, an anonymous postal survey conducted in 1995 among Armenians living on the east coast of the United States, targeted the 18–45 age group. It was commissioned by the Diocese of the Armenian Church in America with questions developed by lay members, and the results were tabulated by a independent professional research firm.

CHAPTER 3

A Community That Is Both a Center and a Diaspora: Jews in Late Twentieth Century Morocco

ANDRÉ LEVY

Introduction

During my first visit to the *Asile de Vieillards* (literally, "asylum for elderly people"), known to Moroccan Jews as "the Home," Miriam Tamsout, an elderly woman resident, noticing that I was a stranger to the local Jewish community, asked me in *darija* (Maghrebi Arabic): *"Fein tat'shkon fel fransa?"* ("Where do you live in France?"). I, taken aback by her intriguing assumption, responded that I live in Israel. She asked again, to make sure that I understood her query. I replied that I did understand. Then she asked if, at least, I had the sense "to make the papers" (i.e., to get a Moroccan identity card and a passport), which would ease my way to the desirable French passport. Again I had to disappoint her, and responded negatively. Astonished, she asked if I intended to return to Israel after completing my business in Morocco. When I replied yes, she soberly concluded: "This is no good. . . . One should live in Morocco and die and be buried in Israel!"

Of the various issues embedded in our exchange I will deal with two interrelated topics here. In practical terms, they are, first, the superior quality of life of Jews in Morocco in comparison to those in Israel; and second, the sacred status of the Land of Israel. Miriam's assertion touched upon a tension between the utopian and mythological vision of the homeland, on the one hand (a place to be buried in), and its unpromising socio-cultural reality, on the other (the low quality of life there). To put it slightly differently and from the vantage point of the "homeland," her statement exemplified the trouble that nation-states face when morally demanding that "their" exiles "come back" (e.g., Pattie 1994) or that they acknowledge their symbolic centrality. I would like to assert that this effort of nation-states/ homelands to call back their "lost sons" erodes their capacity to act as moral or symbolic centers. Moreover, this erosion risks (from the point of view of the self-proclaimed homelands) challenging their uniqueness as moral spaces. Pointing to these interrelated problems challenges a rather prevalent (though increasingly criticized) theoretical notion that I here call "the solar system model" of homeland-diaspora relationships. By this term I refer to the literature that depicts diasporic communities as constructing and cultivating longing for their symbolic center, which is often perceived as the cradle of their innermost being and their original homeland before dispersion. Concomitantly, diasporic communities are portrayed as fostering and nourishing values that originate from their singular homeland. These communities thus perceive themselves as structured symbolically like satellites circulating around their cherished "mother/father-sun" throughout history. It comes as no surprise then, that these studies claim that diasporic communities write their own historiography along the lines of the dream of return. For such theorists, these qualities represent the elementary features of diaspora (Cohen 1997; Safran 1991).

In this chapter I will join several of the scholars who have questioned the solar system model. The Boyarins, for instance, challenge the call Zionism made to refute diasporic existence by living in an independent Jewish nation-state (Boyarin and Boyarin 1993). Gilman, too, articulates that argument by criticizing "the imagined center which defines me as being on the periphery," noting in the same paragraph that: "Today, such a model no longer seems adequate for the writing of any aspect of Jewish history, including that of Zionism and of the State of Israel" (Gilman 1999:1).

These critical claims rely on post-colonial (and postmodern) thinking and provide important insights. One is the reluctance to accept as natural so-called facts constituted by hegemonic discourse coming from the homeland that encourages "desirable moral projects." I wish to proceed with this line of criticism by portraying the ambivalent relationships between homelands and diasporas. In order to criticize the elementary characteristics of the solar system model, I will employ vignettes from ethnographic work I have conducted among Moroccan Jews living in Casablanca during the 1990s. I will show how this unidirectional model is overly simplistic, and how it is challenged by the ambivalent attitudes of Moroccan Jews toward both their presumed homeland and their "exilic" space. These Jews, so I will show, propose to see their place in Casablanca not only as part of a global Jewish diaspora, but also as a homeland for a Moroccan Jewish diaspora.

Diasporas and Homelands

Some of the literature discussing the relationships between the homeland and its diasporas pictures historically constant and symbolically unidirectional relationships between two poles. At one pole we perceive the center, the focal point of longings, identifications, and aspirations. At the other end stand the various dispersed groups that maintain ties—sometimes strong, other times weak—with their symbolic center and amongst the other diasporic groups that identify themselves as belonging to the same center (see, for example, Safran 1991). Their very existence as a distinctive cultural group depends on the cultivation of these inter-communal ties. The dichotomous structure of the solar system model characterizes one end by utilizing concepts such as "eternity," "holiness," "myth," and "home," while the other end is described by concepts such as "temporality," "profanity," "contemporaneity," "alienation," and "guest."

Not only is this constructed dichotomy limited and limiting by being based on a relational comparison that overlooks the political role of the nation-states in nurturing this image, it also assumes fixity in these relations. It does so by attributing to the homeland characteristics that typically are drawn from mythological and religious spheres. In fact, all modern nation-states develop (sometimes religious, sometimes not) myths of national and sacred autochthony that naturalize the identity between people and place. Hobsbawm and Ranger put it clearly when claiming that "modern nations and all their impedimenta generally claim to be the opposite of novel, namely rooted in the remotest antiquity, and the opposite of constructed, namely human communities so 'natural' as to require no definition other than self-assertion" (1983:14).

Inclining to the mythological sphere is conspicuous when it comes to "traditional" types of diasporas such as the Jewish (compare Gurevitch and Aran 1994; Stratton 1997) or the Armenian (Pattie 1997). In the Jewish case, for instance, the space of the homeland gained the stature of holiness, of a sacred entity from which people were cut off due to a primeval sin or moral misconduct. That sacred domain—meticulously separated from daily profanity (and from which idioms of traditional homeland draw)—projects a sense of stability since homeland, the source of indigenousness, is perceived to be eternal.[1]

The dichotomy between the religious and the profane spaces itself reflects socio-cultural and political constructions in which peoples are either "out" of or "in" their place. This construction, produced by nation-state discourse, destabilizes notions of belonging to a space amongst those who "left" the presumed symbolic center. Within the dichotomy (between those who are "in" and those who are "out") is underlined a presumption that symbolic power lies exclusively at one end. In the heydays of nation-states, such dichotomy displays the triumph-of-the-center discourse that not only promulgates exclusiveness of belonging but also veils complex and more fluid relationships between socio-cultural groups and amongst different spaces. It also precludes simultaneity of indwelling and belonging to several spaces.

Yet the nation-state, as a phenomenon constructed as a "natural" and omnipotent entity, is under theoretical attack. For example, the growing writing about diaspora as a favorable space to deconstruct the nation-state (e.g., Levy 2000a) is rather flagrant today. Tölölyan mentions numerous reasons for the emerging critical discourse of diaspora and its widespread use amongst intellectuals (1996). I will not go into the details of his argument, but one of the most perceptible reasons for this critical writing is related to globalization, a process that involves a (relatively) free traffic of capital, including human beings as a labor resource. This intellectual agenda goes hand in hand with James Clifford's appeal a few years ago to divert the analytical focus from space to movement (1997). The need to focus attention on the movable character of human beings is particularly acute in the post-modern era. Postmodernity (or, alternatively, "supermodernity," to use Marc Augé's [1995] clever term) is characterized, among other things, by massive population movements motivated by pulling and pushing forces (like tourists, labor migrants, and so on), by the improvement of fast communication channels, and by the flow of ideas. The traffic of people, merchandise, and ideas — globalization, *tout court* — is deeply entrenched in the constitution of diasporas, since diasporas manifest a tension between "routes and roots." People leave their natal land (sometimes temporarily and sometimes permanently) and plant roots in other places. They seldom do so as distinctive cultural groups, while challenging *as such* the immovable picture so convenient to the discourse of the nation-state.

The study of diasporas stresses that these groups awaken feelings of nostalgic bonds toward the country that was left behind: "diasporas always leave a trail of collective memory about another place and time and create new maps of desire and of attachment" (Appadurai and Breckenbridge 1989:i). It also emphasizes that diasporas encourage feelings — even if imagined — of strong longings for their landscapes, their smells and sounds, as part of their constitution and maintenance as unique and exclusive group identities. Indeed, "the language of diaspora is increasingly invoked by displaced peoples who feel (maintain, revive, invent) a connection with a prior home" (Clif-

ford 1997:255). The sense of diaspora can be creative and politically motivated, as well articulated by Appadurai, who describes the establishment of
Khalistan as "an invented homeland of the deterritorialized Sikh population
of England, Canada and the United States" (1990:302). No doubt, this creative mechanism is not limited to diasporas, for it resembles the discourse of
nation-states. Benedict Anderson reminded us that all nations adorn themselves with a heroic and unique past that distinguishes them from others
(1983). The cultivation of a unique past is recruited for the needs of the present. Hence, although there is a constant preoccupation with the past it is
aimed at present needs. Therefore, diaspora, like nationalism, is not committed to "real" history. Its survival depends upon its ability to found and
enhance identification with "traditional" values that serve entrenched needs
in the present.

As already noted above, I wish to present my observations of Jews in Morocco and their attitudes towards their presumed symbolic "center" (Israel)
so as to question modernist premises regarding the successes of nation-states
(such as Israel) in maintaining their position as a symbolic center vis-à-vis
"their" diasporas. My focus is on the Jewish perspective *in* Morocco, and I
do not refer to the ways in which Jews who *left* Morocco perceive it as their
"new" state. I use these observations to rethink the assumed dominant position of a center-cum-homeland to establish uncontested narratives, but, I
hope, without getting onto the slippery route of ideological preaching. I will
demonstrate how the relationships between diaspora and homeland, or better, these very classifications themselves, may be fluid, historically conditioned, and even multidirectional. Moreover, I will show that a certain space
may be simultaneously a diaspora and a symbolic center. I discuss the theoretical meaning and nature of such possible venues. I use anthropological
methods in order to listen to minute, defiant voices coming from people living in so-called "diasporas," including their refusal to be categorized as marginal to the homeland. In addition to the ethnographic account that outlines
the complex relationships between a diaspora and its supposed homeland, I
also consider the emerging relations between the diaspora-cum-homeland
and its emergent peripheries. This situation is particularly intriguing since
in this case the peripheries demographically outnumber the self-proclaimed
symbolic center. Moreover, the members of the self-proclaimed homeland
accept the cultural domination of some of its new peripheries. Yet, the people
whose voice I bring here do not question the "binary system" (Foucault
1978) that precludes possibilities that transcend the bipolar construction of
"homeland" vs. "diasporas," as Gilman, for instance, contends (1999).[2] In
other words, although Moroccan Jews do not uncritically accept the "solar

system" model that Zionist Israel proposes and reject its "either/or" pre-sumptions, they do accept the ordering of the world into pairs of homelands and diasporas. This, as I will conclude, moderates their subversive attitudes towards Israel as the Center.

Let me turn now to a short description of the historical background that stood at the heart of the motivations to emigrate from Morocco. Hopefully, it will help to understand the processes that positioned Jews in their current situation vis-à-vis Morocco, Israel, and their other Moroccan diasporas around the globe. I will mainly focus on late historical development and show that the actualization of both Zionist and Moroccan national aspirations has generated historical and political processes and has reshaped the complex dynamics between Moroccan Jews and their homeland.

The History of the Jewish Community

Historical studies are uncertain of the date when the settlement of Jews in North Africa began. The first known document mentions a Jewish community some 300 years B.C. in Cyrenaica (see, for instance, Hirschberg 1974). Most of them, however, settled in Egypt. Throughout time, however, Jews slowly moved away from their base in Egypt toward today's North Africa (*ifriquiya*). This distancing from the Land of Israel did not preclude or deter contacts with it, since Jews, for instance, insisted on fulfilling their religious duty to make donations to the (first) Temple in Jerusalem. Hirschberg— probably the most prominent historian of North African Jewries—asserts that these communities flourished under the Roman regime to the point that the Roman historian Philo of Alexandria asserted that the Jews of Africa (in-cluding Egypt and sub-Sahara areas but excluding the areas west of Libya) numbered about a million souls. Hirschberg maintains that about one hundred thousand of them dwelled in the vicinity of Cyrenaica. After the de-struction of the first Temple, new waves of Jews moved towards Africa. Most of them *chose* to migrate, mainly because of the promising opportunities under Roman rule (Hirschberg 1974; Zafrani 1983).

I do not wish to get into a detailed diachronic account of remote times, but intend only to argue against the popularly held notion that most Jews were expelled from the land of Israel in one dramatic event. Rather, they gradu-ally moved away from it. With this emphasis I wish also to underline that one cannot understand the history of Jews in Morocco (or wherever, for that matter) without relating to broader political and socio-economic develop-ments in the region. Jews were part and parcel of these processes. They suf-

fered when local regimes were feeble and flourished when times were politically calm, so much so that their personal safety became a yardstick for political stability. Abu l'Qasim al-Zayyani, the historian of Morocco's Alawi
dynasty, described the security and serenity during Mulay Ismail's rule
by testifying that "even a woman or *dhimmi* could travel from Oujda to
Wadi Nul unmolested" (Stillman 1974:17). In the North African context
"*dhimmi*" refers to Jews, for they were the only group in that region that
was considered as a "tolerated" minority and hence allowed to maintain religious autonomy within bounded political, social, and symbolic constraints.
In practical terms, *dhimmi* status involved protection in return for submission *and* discrimination. Yet, submission and discrimination were practiced
differently throughout history under the Muslim world (*dar al-Islam*). Ba-
sically, as *dhimmis*—the non-Muslim subjects of the sultans and local pa-
trons—Jews suffered from several ritualistic humiliations and obligations.[3]

As a general pattern, it would be safe to assert that Moroccan Jews have
always had ambivalent relationships with their Muslim neighbors. These relationships included both a high degree of interchange and a tendency to
withdraw from contact. The relatively limited ethnography and unvaried
historical documentation of everyday life confirm this long-term and ambivalent split (Bashan 2000). Some scholars have described the manifestations of inclusion and exclusion as an intrinsic process related to differences
in daily religious practices (Ayache 1987; Flamand 1959; Hirschberg 1968;
Kenbib 1994), while others have understood them as a demonstration of the
Jews' low legal and social status as *dhimmis* (e.g., Bat-Yeor 1985). These differences aside, most scholars agree that Morocco's pre-colonial era was characterized by intimate and close socio-cultural interchange between Jews and
Muslims.[4]

The French protectorate (1912–52), to use the French euphemism for direct colonial rule, prompted dramatic changes in Morocco. One immediate
consequence was a massive flow of Muslims and Jews from small villages in
the hinterland to the larger cities.[5] Jews in particular wished to enter the urban spaces that French colonialists inhabited, as they aspired to benefit from
the egalitarian promise of French colonial discourse. Jewish enthusiasm for
the modernist promise brought about tensions between Jews and Muslims,
since the latter interpreted this attitude as a betrayal of Morocco's nationalistic dreams.[6]

Morocco's independence in 1952 brought about yet more rapid changes.
Jews felt these in particular because of Morocco's positive policy toward the
cultural and political idea of "Arabization" (Entelis 1989), Morocco's incli-
nation towards Islam (Bourqia 1987; Suleiman 1989; Tessler 1978), and the

steps taken by Zionist activists to encourage Jews to immigrate to Israel (e.g., Segev 1984). These interrelated factors did not leave much room for Jews to maneuver or redefine their position.[7] The establishment of the State of Israel had a particularly strong impact on the lives of Jews in Morocco and on the complex relationships between them and Morocco's Muslims: it appeared to offer a resolution of the political pressures affecting their lives (see Laskier 1990; Rosen 1968; Stillman 1991). Emigration seemed almost an inevitable solution to the attacks on their way of life, with Israel becoming the main target for this human flow. During the 1950s, practically every North African Jew had to make a conscious decision whether to stay put or to leave. Most Jews made the latter decision.[8] Morocco's Jewish population rapidly diminished. At its peak (in the 1940s) it numbered about 250,000; demographers estimate that at present the Jewish population in Morocco numbers at most five thousand persons.[9]

These developments heavily influenced the lives of those Jews who stayed, and jeopardized their relations with Muslims. French direct rule, for instance, broadened Jewish connections with Europe, which hitherto had been kept minimal. The opening of borders facilitated contacts with European Jews, and with French Jews in particular, who were committed to the missionary vision of modernization interwoven in the colonial process. The Alliance Israélite Universelle (constituted in Paris in 1860) was the main tool through which this "modernization" mission was carried out and spread to Morocco's Jews (Laskier 1983; Rodrigue 1990, 1993).[10] Israel's presence in Jewish lives more strongly contributed to a Jewish retreat from Morocco's socio-cultural landscape, since Israel's frequent involvement in Middle East violence raised feelings of insecurity among Jews.[11] At the same time, Israel's strong symbolic impact also provided the Jews with a model for their proper relationships with Muslims.

The Community's Organization Today

The well-rooted ethno-religious split between Jews and Muslims in Morocco is manifested and enacted nowadays in a unique way—the result of complex political forces that have reshaped and nourished the Jews' disengagement from Muslims. The massive emigration had a strong impact on the community's organization, which in turn influenced relationships with Muslims. Various Jewish institutional apparatuses were restructured to cope with the demographic dwindling and limit or stop the rapidly growing outflow. The strategy that eventually was adopted was to concentrate the Jewish population spatially in the name of efficiency. These institutions seek to maximize the service supply, which in turn even more crystallizes the trend of segregation.

"Le comité de la communauté" (the Jewish Community Council, henceforth the JCC)—the most prominent Jewish institution in Casablanca—takes care of the living, as well as the dead. The JCC, along with the *Ittihad* (Arabic for Alliance Israélite Universelle) and other educational systems, operates day care centers and elementary and high schools. The JCC supports institutions that are in charge of extracurricular activities such as the youth movements. It also partially and indirectly controls Jewish clubs. With its support, the community runs an exclusive Jewish health system and the Home (mentioned at the beginning of the chapter). This institution also takes care of the needy, providing various sorts of social and financial support.

The variety, scope, and intensity of services are impressive, even astonishing, keeping in mind the demography of the Jewish community. The range of JCC services grows as the number of Jews dwindles. This expansion of services contributes to the process of disengagement, for the institutions aspire to establish some kind of autarky. With its various satellite institutions, the JCC benefits from the partitioning walls between Jews and Muslims, since it eases the exertion of control over their constituency. This control is crucial, for without it the JCC risks the possibility that the community, as a unified entity, will dissolve. The more that individual Jews depend on the JCC services, the more they are reluctant to leave Morocco, and the more that the JCC grants services, the more likely it is that fear of the Muslims grows. Fear of the broader surroundings flows from this form of organization, since it contributes to the disconnection of Jews from greater Casablanca.

It is important to keep in mind that the JCC's educational system actively contributes to this isolation: Jewish youngsters learn French as a first language and Hebrew as the second, while Arabic becomes their third choice. It is no wonder that most Jews do not understand *fusha* ("classical" Arabic) and that most Jewish youth speak *darija* (indigenous "dialect") poorly. It is quite striking that practically all Jews (except a tiny layer of intelligentsia) do not watch the news on national TV, which is delivered in formal Arabic, not in colloquial dialect. They also cannot read street signs unless they are in French.

Self-confinement leads to great fears, and these fears encourage self-confinement. It is a vicious circle in which fear itself is confirmed and cultivated, and in turn accelerates the process of Jews disengaging from their neighbors and surroundings. These circumstances not only feed upon each other, they also are paradoxical. Fear leads to self-imprisonment, which leads back to fear, and this self-imprisonment makes people incapable of leaving. The more people rely on the JCC's generous services, the harder it becomes to emigrate, for they acknowledge that they will not get parallel privileges anywhere else, not even in Israel.

Jews cannot achieve absolute enclosure, of course. Not only are they too small a community to establish an autarky, they also find it impossible to altogether avoid Muslims on a day-to-day basis. Jews encounter Muslims on the streets, at coffeehouses, on the beach, as maids in their homes, as employers, counterparts, or employees at work, as neighbors, and so forth.

The current shape of disengagement has turned Moroccan Jews from an ethno-religious group into a diaspora. The complex processes with their organizational manifestations described thus far have drawn a strong demarcating and differentiating line between Jews and their place—Morocco. Jews in the late twentieth century became estranged from Morocco's people, from its politics, and, to a certain degree, even from its cultural architecture. Morocco, as a new nation-state, did not help in turning its Jewish population into an ethnic group, as it was unable to offer a shield from the effects of Zionism and the bloody conflict between Israel and the Arab countries around it. Yet, at the same moment that Jews became estranged from their country, Morocco also turned into a metaphoric place that contains and produces powerful symbolic representations, which, in effect, turn it to a "homeland."

In the sections that follow I focus on daily occurrences within a community that has begun to conceive of itself as both a homeland and a diaspora. I will present short ethnographic scenes to demonstrate the complex dynamics between the constructed dichotomy of periphery and center. I begin with a brief description of three instances of death and burial, since these demonstrate concretely and symbolically, and in a forceful way, the undermining of the feeling of belonging to Morocco. I then describe a bipolar attitude toward the assassination of a Jew, considering it as an event that exemplifies the position of Jews as a diaspora in Morocco and the questions that such a position poses. Towards the end of the ethnographic section, I present attitudes towards Hebrew and controversies over it as a prism through which one can examine the dispositions towards Israel, arguably the ultimate Jewish center that dominates its language. The debates about Hebrew exemplify how complex and fluid are the relationships between the constructed dichotomy "diaspora" and "homeland." These politically constructed concepts do not relate to concrete spaces (as burial sites) only, but to ideational and ideological topics as well.

Death, Burial, and the Absence of a Taken-for-Granted Space

Death and its ritualistic practices reveal the ways in which diasporic communities articulate their connections to their lands, as well as to their imagined homelands, since death is immersed in discourses that connect peoples to their soils (see Malkki 1997). Indeed, through death and burial practices Moroccan Jews constantly articulate attitudes and feelings of belonging to Morocco and Israel. Michel El-Hadad, for instance, often wondered aloud if he should transfer the bones of his long-dead father to Israel. He even consulted his rabbi, who recommended leaving the bones in peace.[12] Michel (like the elderly woman mentioned at the beginning of this chapter) hoped to constitute metonymic relations between himself, as his father's extension, and the Holy Land of Israel. Michel yearned to have his father's grave stand for him in Israel, and the Holy Land to be in him through his father. Interestingly, however, Rabbinical thinking postpones the constitution of such relations to Messianic days.

During the period of my main fieldwork I witnessed three cases of death.[13] Like any other unexpected death, the first case was tragic. A young Casablancan woman died in a car accident while traveling in Canada. Her parents brought her body back for burial in Casablanca. She was a member of an influential and affluent family, and Jews came from all over Morocco to attend her funeral. It looked as if about half of the community members came to share in the family's grief.

The second case was the death of an elderly woman who was buried in Casablanca's Jewish cemetery. Her fifty-five-year-old son—Mr. Joel Elkaim—was one of the few Jewish attorneys in the city. After his mother's death, Joel, who was single, remained in Casablanca alone. Feeling that he had reached a meaningful junction in his life, Joel expressed to me a wish to rethink his future plans. He revealed a desire to leave Morocco and consulted with me about the possibility of moving to Israel. He asked endlessly about the financial advantages of *Olim* (immigrants) to Israel, the social conditions, the cost of living, and the like. After a while he calmed down and stopped asking. He has remained until now in Casablanca.

The third death I witnessed involved a person in his forties who had long suffered from clinical depression. He was melancholic and constantly ill as a consequence of an unsuccessful suicide attempt he had made half a year before my arrival in Morocco. He died from a severe lung infection about six months later. His family held a short commemoration ceremony for him at Casablanca's Jewish cemetery and then flew to Israel to bury him there.

For the moment, these short scenes are aimed at demonstrating only one point: namely, all three relate to issues of space in diasporic context. More specifically, they are characterized by a need to consciously decide about the burial site. In the third case, for example, the parents decided to bury their son in Israel, but not because they wished to inter his body in the holy ground of Jerusalem, in accordance with Jewish tradition. In fact, the son was buried in a small northern town in Israel, where the parents planned to move. It is important to mention that, although more than ten years have passed, they still live in Morocco and do not show any signs of moving. Even in the first case, where it was obvious that the family wished to bury their daughter in Casablanca, they had to employ deliberate actions and take conscious decisions to bring their loved one to Morocco. Some of the participants questioned the parents' decision, for they speculated that the parents would eventually emigrate.

Apparently, belonging to a space does not necessarily or easily coincide with diasporic epistemology. Israel's very existence (as a concrete space and as a political entity) creates rapture and shakes the taken for granted in the sense of belonging to a space. It demands deliberate reference (be it positive or negative) to it, and thus the decision to bury a loved one raises the question of the locus. The realistic option that Israel radiates is the source of that schism. To this point, it would appear as if the so-called solar system model is quite appropriate. Yet, as we shall see, the schism, in its turn, generates the emergence of alternative and even competing interpretations of life in diaspora and questions the uniqueness of the "Center" as a symbolic source of moral and cultural legitimacy.

One Murder, Two Stories

One of the most fascinating stories about death and its relation to space came from two related young men. The first was Robert El-Nekawa's tragic story about his father's assassination, which he related to me as the murder of a Jewish employer by his Muslim employees. A few weeks later, I heard his

cousin Raphael's version. The differences in their versions illuminate the
linkage between death and space, death and belonging.

My conversation with the son, Robert, was conducted in Hebrew. He, like
Raphael later on, insisted on speaking to me in Hebrew. Robert's words came
out with difficulty, and not only due to language limitations. It was a painful
talk. I present here a short transcription from a long, convoluted, and tormented conversation, in which Robert told the story of his father's assassination. According to Robert, his father had a flourishing pesticide factory:

R. He was killed because of jealousy, not business . . .
A. Who was it? Muslims? Do you know the story? Where was it?
R. At the business . . . five years ago (1985) . . . well . . . see . . . here all
   (Muslims) are jealous. . . . it is a known fact . . . because a Jew . . . because . . . when you say "Jew," it means "rich." The word "Jew" itself
   stands for "a rich person." And when they speak amongst themselves,
   one says to the other: "Are you Jewish?" when meaning to say: "Are
   you rich?" You see what I mean?. . . . They had a certain plan. . . . They
   planned it.
A. How did the Jews here react?
R. They were scared. . . . All came (to the death commemoration) and . . .
   as soon as they realized that we were moving from Morocco to Israel
   . . . well . . . the people from the community (the leaders) understood
   that we say it is no good to live here in Morocco. You see?
A. You mean that by the very leaving you state that you don't like life in
   Morocco?
R. As a Jew you are dominant. You master people, and they (the leaders)
   are rich like us . . . and it also happened that they killed another Jew . . .
   a truly rich Jew. One came with a gun and shot him on the spot.
A. I see now what you wish to say. You say that by the very act of leaving
   you make some kind of critique against Jews.
R. It is a critique. But we did not mean to make a critique. We just wished
   to leave.
A. What did they say specifically?
R. They said: "Why do you leave? You have a flourishing business
   here . . ." But my mother did not wish to talk about it, or to discuss it.
   And our refusal to listen to their advice made the situation even worse.

According to Robert, the assassination of his father has one motivation.
There is nothing to explain here. He is laconic about it, especially when compared to the relative articulation about the friction with the community's
leaders. All my attempts to understand what happened in concrete terms

failed. The information regarding the assassination was poor: some employees had premeditated the execution of his father. The motivation was rooted in "classic" anti-Semitism—jealousy of the wealth and success of a Jew.

The cousin, Raphael El-Nekawa, offered a far more elaborate story. He also presented a different interpretation of the motivations behind the assassination. Raphael, who like Robert was twenty-five years old, told me the story while we were at a summer camp in the Middle Atlas. We were sitting together in the same room. After Robert left for his room, Raphael started immediately:

R. His father was very cheap. That's why he was killed. He refused to give money to an employee to buy a lamb for their *"fête de mouton"* (*'Id Al-Adha*—the feast of sacrifice). He refused to give him a lamb.

A. Why was he expected to give the lamb?

R. Jews always give a lamb as a present for the feast. It is a gift for the holiday. The Arab then asked for a loan and promised that he would repay the loan by deducting a certain amount of money from his salary for several months after the feast. Robert's father agreed, but he broke his promise and immediately deducted 200 dirhams each month. The Arab was very angry. His father was truly cheap, God forgive me. . . . He used to ride a motorcycle to his factory! He did not purchase a car or take a *petit taxi*! He also used to have a *baguette* with cheese so that he wouldn't waste time by going home to have a proper lunch. In that way he did not stop working. He did not take a break so he wouldn't lose money. Even Robert, the poor guy, didn't see a *centime* from him as a child. I remember that I used to lend him money.

A. How was he killed?

R. Look, Jews never—well . . . most of the time—lend their employees money for the holiday. They give the money as a gift to buy the lamb. And he not only refused to give it as a present, he deducted 200 dirhams each month, which is a lot of money for a simple worker in Morocco. So—you know what they did? His father used to sit at this desk that had many pesticide barrels on top of it. So, the workers put more and more on the wooden shelf . . . just above his head, until one day everything collapsed and fell on top of his head. He died instantly. Now . . . many times people from the community say to Robert that his father died because of a lamb!

Beside the idiosyncratic genres and flow of speech between the two relatives and friends (that have to do with the degree of involvement in the story), and besides the differences in individual temperament, there lies a contradictory interpretation of the story that is related to the ways in which diasporas and homelands are articulated. Robert, the son's victim, focuses on the Muslims' responsibility, which was driven by pure anti-Semitism. Raphael, on the other hand, almost overtly accuses the Jew, his uncle, who is driven by his own miserliness. These two stereotypical perspectives put the responsibility on two different, opposing poles. On the one hand, as indicated in the conversation, Robert and his family eventually left Morocco and immigrated to Israel; Robert himself came back to Morocco "to liquidate the family's businesses." It was during that period of time that I heard his version. Raphael and his family, on the other hand, remained in Morocco. Raphael utters a convincing explanation for staying (as against the decision of his relatives to leave). His explanation does not put the blame on the ultimate Other—the Muslims—for otherwise the feeling of personal control (e.g., Levy 1998; Levy 2000b) would be shaken or even shattered. Therefore, Muslims are not to be blamed for such a dangerously intimate and menacing event. On the other hand, Robert—in an embarrassingly easy way—weaves the event in the classical Zionist reasoning: it is not good for a Jew to live in the diaspora. Hence, they migrate to Israel.

Raphael constructs a story that supports a feeling of control and responsibility over his fate and destination. He structures a story which calls for conduct that plays according to local rules and is attuned and responsive to the hosting cultural environment. His story voices a call for a form of conduct that is interwoven within local culture; it calls for cultural understanding. Understanding grants control over unpredicted situations, and his story accepts the anti-Semitic discourse about Jews as pariahs. Robert, on the other hand, constructs a related yet antithetical story. As opposed to Raphael, he is brief and laconic. He does not elaborate or detail the story. He sticks to generic explanations—there is no personal story. We do not learn much about his father. There are no clear and definite spatial and temporal coordinates. He recounts a classical, almost mythological Jewish story that was told for centuries (mainly since the eighteenth century in England and in Eastern Europe). His father's impotence stands in total contradiction to Raphael's depiction of a rigid and tyrannical father. Even though it is not explicitly said, Raphael blame the father for his own death. He is responsible due to his improper conduct. The event, thus, is set in motion and driven by a Jew.

Perhaps unintentionally, both Raphael and Robert relate to diasporic life. They certainly comprehend their lives within this context. As in the three short opening ethnographic vignettes, which demanded a deliberate decision concerning the meaningful place of burial, so here too there is a diasporic story. By "diasporic story" I mean that questions regarding their belonging to a place are embedded in their discourse. The different stances of the cousins do not imply a disagreement regarding the basic fact that it is an ultimate diasporic story. That is why the family's decision to leave for Israel is not refuted or condemned by Raphael. Israel is the desired center for both of them. Raphael only wishes to stress that one could live peacefully and comfortably in exile, so long as one plays according to local cultural rules. The debate is over the prospects of living in peace in diaspora. Here lies the explanation for the different interpretation of the murder story. However, both interpretations differ from the death stories referred to earlier: Unlike the murder story, the former exposed a diversity of attitudes about the location of the meaningful space.

In conclusion, as long as death practices are involved it seems that the solar system model is a rather helpful way to understand lives outside the center, Israel, even though at some moments it is challenged. The unquestioned burial in Morocco, for instance, provides such a challenge, as does Raphael's version of his uncle's death. These contestations appear more clearly and rather more directly in the following ethnographic scenes that raise the theme of cultural or human mobility.

Emigration and Symbolic Centrality

The ambiguous attitudes of Moroccan Jews towards both Morocco and Israel are particularly illuminating when we listen to their reflections regarding migration to Israel, and witness the practicalities involved in such cases. We have already seen some of these ambiguities in the two versions of the murder story. Nevertheless, I wish to focus on emigration, since it risks bringing to demise the entire Jewish community in Morocco. I mainly refer to migration to Israel, since (as we have already seen) the latter poses existential and symbolic challenges for Jews. They also cannot avoid the gap between the (sometimes simplified) ideological rhetoric of longing for Israel, and the day to day struggles over collective and personal existence in Morocco.[14]

Paradoxically, however, instead of draining Morocco of its symbolic resources, emigration turned Morocco into a symbolic center that competes with Israel. Morocco became a *lieu de memoire* for the Jews who left it (Nora 1989), which, in turn made the Jewish community a center that retains its own diasporic communities. In their eyes they did not turn into an ethnic group in Morocco, but rather have established their own diasporic communities by contributing to processes that generate nostalgic feelings towards Morocco. It is important to note that this construction of reality is supported

by various indications that Jewish communities outside North Africa cultivate a collective—as well as a mythical—memory of the Maghreb. Joëlle
Bahloul's work, titled *"La maison de mémoire"* (The house of memory), for
instance, tells the story of the socio-cultural construction of memories of Algerian Jews living in France, of a house left behind (Bahloul 1996). Charlotte
Szlovak's film *"Retour a Oujda"* (Return to Oujda) tells the story of tourists
from France visiting their childhood districts in Morocco.[15] From Moroccan
Jews' perspective, Israel also is a base from which many travels are launched.
These "roots travels" from Israel (as well as France and Canada) that mix ha-
giolatric features with tourism intensify the feeling that the Maghreb is a focal point of admiration and longing. For example, in a trip from Israel that I
joined, travelers kissed the soil of Morocco after their landing in the country
that they had left some thirty years earlier (Levy 1997). Indeed, in many respects Morocco has become the "Center Out There" (Turner 1973).

What reinforces the perception of Morocco as an alternative homeland is
the symbolically meaningful but demographically negligible stream of Jewish immigration to Morocco. In the last few decades I estimate that no more
than fifty to eighty Israelis have migrated from Israel to Morocco. These Israelis (of Moroccan origins mainly) go back to Morocco to look for better
(usually economic) chances.

There seems to be a paradox at the basis of the transformation of Morocco from a "classical" diaspora into a diaspora that is also a center. Indeed,
the process that turned Morocco into a center has been caused by its demographic dwindling. In other words, it is emigration from Morocco that enabled the constitution of diasporic communities outside it. These new diasporic communities in time nurtured nostalgic feelings and romantic
attitudes towards their Moroccan diasporic-homeland.[16]

Jews living in Morocco realize that their community is small in number. Moreover, it is daily undergoing a demographic dwindling, and this
process is apparent to all. Their realization is crucial, since it affects the
epistemology of Jews in Morocco. Daily life is shaped by it. For example,
once a dispute broke out among teachers during a school break. Some complained about the inadequate behavior of one of the teachers. At this point
the vice-headmaster violently interfered, demanding that the discussion stop
at once. He was extremely aggressive. All of the teachers stopped immediately, stunned by his atypically violent intervention. Later, I saw him nerv-
ously wandering around in the schoolyard. He seemed troubled and embar-
rassed. He explained, half-excusing himself, that he was very anxious these
days. He was preoccupied, so he claimed, because he was about to leave Morocco. He said that he got an offer:

". . . to manage a Jewish high school in Black Africa. I was promised a lot of money. There is no future here. I don't understand why they discuss the problems we have with that teacher! What difference does it make? For there is no future here. How long we are going to stay here? So why all this mess? We don't have many bullets to shoot anyhow. We remained here to shoot the last bullets of our pistols, so why discuss a doomed future?"

The demographic threat poses a critical problem to the community as a whole when facing their diasporas in Israel, France, or Canada. The demographic inferiority that is far from being concomitant with their self-proclaimed symbolic centrality cannot be overlooked or ignored. The French journalist Gilles Perrault reviewed the long history of the cruelties of King Hassan's regime in his 1990 book *Notre Ami le Roi*. He details the king's violent political methods used against political "obstacles," such as the arrest of dissidents or the elimination of political opponents. Perrault did not spare any details about the arrests without charge and the "disappearance" of political rivals. No surprise then that the political atmosphere was charged. The national television reported political tension between Morocco and France. TV anchormen read endless letters sent from "loyal citizens," who protested against the support that Perrault got from France's politicians, especially from the then president's spouse, Mme. Mitterrand.[17] Jews worried that the need for his overt and orchestrated public support indicated that the king's throne was in danger, which, as in other historical moments, meant trouble for the Jews. However, they also felt a great relief when letters of support came from "their" diasporic communities. TV anchormen even read sections from a letter from Rabbi Meshash in Israel, formerly Morocco's chief rabbi. They highlighted Meshash's connection with Israel, mentioning that he was horrified by the book's distorted allegations and that he testified that King Hassan—like his father before him—treated the Jewish minority with great respect.[18] To their disappointment, many Jews noticed that the Montreal diaspora did not send a letter of protest like those of Israel or France: "now we are not important for Jews there," complained one with a sober acceptance. Indeed, many were distressed when realizing their marginality vis-à-vis their Canadian "branch," feeling that they had become negligible, redundant.

Nevertheless, their disappointment itself is telling, for it exposes the sometimes latent and sometimes overt high expectations regarding the centrality of the Moroccan homeland in the minds of its diasporic communities. Both expectation and disappointment point at the existential paradox mentioned above: the demographic weakening was the engine that generated the creation of the Moroccan Jewish diasporic communities and the transformation of Morocco into a homeland.

The examples that I have thus far given may appear to overstate the weakness of the self-proclaimed symbolic center due to demographic dwindling. Yet, it would be too simplistic to claim that this is the pervasive stance. Various manifestations of self-esteem and singularity of history were often expressed. One of the most fascinating examples is related to the attitudes towards Hebrew—the holy language that also is used in everyday life in Israel.

The Symbolic Location of a Language

My spouse, Sarah, is Israeli born, and when she was with me in Morocco she wished to work as a Hebrew teacher. To our naïve surprise, she had to overcome many unexpected difficulties. The administrators of Hebrew instruction had what looked to our Israelocentric eyes "peculiar" ideas regarding the ways in which one should teach this language, which were different from our notions. According to them, Hebrew is a holy language, and thus it should be taught without separating it from its cultural context and its historical significance as they see them. In other words, our transparent cultural context retrospectively became evident. Moreover, the other teachers doubted the standing of what we believed to be our cultural capital. In order to teach Hebrew, so she was told, one should know Halachic laws, *Midrash*, religious interpretations, religious rituals, practicalities and meanings of Jewish holidays, and so forth. They wished to ensure that Sarah was versed enough in these; that she could teach more than the language in "its narrow sense," as they saw it. She was accepted only after it was ascertained that she would do her best to follow this line.

That attitude was clearly articulated in a conversation conducted in Hebrew between the French chief supervisor of Hebrew instruction, and the Hebrew instructors of a prestigious Jewish high school (the ENH). The supervisor had come from France. Morris Levy, one of the most prominent ENH Hebrew instructors, claimed that it would be best if male instructors would teach Hebrew:

MORRIS LEVY: Our male instructors, as against women, possess a substantial knowledge of *limudei kodesh* (holy studies). Teaching Hebrew is not like any other common language . . . like we instruct French, for example. Hebrew has extremely deep cultural layers that encompass a multitude of Jewish studies. Female teachers—at least in Morocco—do not have these qualifications. Thus, they cannot serve as Hebrew teachers. We cannot, for example, confine ourselves to the pure analysis of its syntax. Hebrew is not something external, or foreign to us. We are deeply involved in it.

ANDRÉ OVADIA (another teacher): I totally agree. Tell me, André (referring to me), how do they teach Hebrew in your schools? Do they teach it as any other language? Is it . . . ?

The French supervisor, MOÏSE NAHON, interferes: Yes. That's the case in Israel. And I strongly believe that it should be so. We must teach its internal logic, its syntax, like any other language. And it is, after all, a common language! Here—in France we also teach the Bible (the Old Testament) that way. We treat it like any other text of fiction. We treat the historical facts with great caution and doubt. We certainly ignore belief . . . unlike you are doing here. We relate to it with universal analytical tools . . . like we treat a text written by Chekhov or Balzac, for instance. It is true that we have instructors who believe in these holy texts, and then they tend to relate to it like you do. But they have to clarify for their students that they believe in the text and that they treat it as holy. Then, it is clear to all that these teachers are deeply involved in the text.

All languages, of course, involve deep cultural meanings. In this controversy, these meanings are clearly apparent: Jewish teachers in Morocco are aware of the cultural project in which they are involved, and they are deeply engaged in it. But they also recognize that there are other competing ways to treat Hebrew. This was even more blatantly indicated during an argument between two Hebrew examiners, who came from France, and the local teachers. The examiners came to test the oral abilities of the students. Teachers claimed that the examiners were heavily influenced by the Israeli attitude towards Hebrew, and that they assumed that mastering a language means also possessing control over its oral aspects. The examiners, it is crucial to mention here, had lived most of their lives in Israel. The ENH teachers claimed that the examiners uncritically adopted the assumption that the ultimate test for orally mastering Hebrew is the ability to communicate with an Israeli. "Not only do I not have to accept such an assumption," claimed Morris Levy with passion, "but Israelis speak Hebrew incorrectly. They make many mistakes. Thus they certainly cannot stand as the standard against which one should measure oral capacities!"

In a different situation I heard an interesting distinction linked to this argument: "In Israel one does not speak Hebrew. One speaks Israeli!"

This argument, that rejects the imposition of the homeland (i.e., Israel), exposes a refusal to accept its symbolic domination regarding language. In this case, the center's effort to maintain exclusive legitimization as the standard-bearer of language is challenged. Language turns out to be a key device for cultural distinction. Morocco is, in the eyes of those Jews, a legitimate alternative and even a more genuine symbolic Jewish center. Like anti-Zionist ultra-orthodox Jews, they make a distinction between the State of Israel and the Land of Israel (see Boyarin and Boyarin 1993).

Yet, one should not overestimate this position, for the scene reveals that, in this case at least, it is a lost battle. Although not versed in Jewish Halachic laws and practices, Sarah was accepted as a Hebrew teacher. More important, the French examiners had the last word, since they are authorized by the French educational system to set the standard. Notice that the examiners embody a two-phase process: Israel sets the standard and delivers it to a powerful Jewish diaspora (France), and the latter is then qualified to test a minor diaspora—Morocco. This reverses a historical process that follows the line of the examiners' own personal history. I refer to the fact that they migrated from Morocco to Israel, and from there to France. The examiners are qualified to conclude that the Moroccan oral Hebrew is "archaic." Moreover, French (cultural) colonialism did not lose its grip. However, the teachers did not hesitate to voice their protest and dissatisfaction. Protest itself is a political practice that undermines hegemony and erodes legitimization through the very awareness of the dominant stance of Israel, and by the display of optional versions.

These scenes reveal yet another aspect with regard to the relationships between center and periphery. Immigration to homeland as well as its political "renewal" does not guarantee its becoming an uncontested symbolic center. Indeed, quite the opposite can happen (see Markowitz 1995). It is a hazardous enterprise. The political actualization of the utopian "dream of return" carries within itself the seeds of its refutation and disclaimer. For example, the decision to bring back to Morocco (and not to Israel) the body of the young woman who died in Canada manifests a conscious choice to bury the loved one where one plans to stay. Indeed, her parents do plan to remain in Morocco. So long as the "dream of return" is in the realm of millenarian aspirations, such a decision has no substantial implications. But when this dream becomes a tangible project due its political materialization, acts that might be seen as a declaration of a permanent stay in the diaspora operate to challenge the center. These acts are particularly challenging when it comes to a situation where the community is dwindling (like the Moroccan one).

Centers, Diasporas, Deaths, and Language

While the actualization of the dream of return carries with it the grains of its disclaimer, it also destabilizes life outside it. No wonder, then, that decisions regarding the burial sites were not taken for granted. The choice taken by the lawyer to remain in Morocco after his mother's death demonstrates that even after a long reflection the best choice for him was to stay. His hesitations position him somewhere in the middle, between two options. The parents who buried their daughter in Morocco mark one end in this continuum, while the parents who chose to bury their son in Israel stand at the other end. The latter choice indicates that this option is always present—a comforting idea for all Jews living in Morocco. But these parents did not actualize the option they chose for their son: they did not immigrate to Israel. They acted according to the advice of the elderly woman quoted at the outset of this chapter: "One should live in Morocco and die and be buried in Israel."

The decisions regarding the burial sites point to two related issues: the lack of taken-for-granted place on the one hand, and the different options given to Jews on the other hand. Both aspects undermine the two intertwined ends (or perhaps, twined concepts) involved: homelands and diasporas. This dual impact symbolically stands for the basic situation that Moroccan Jews experience nowadays—the situation of being simultaneously a center and a periphery.

The simultaneous appearance of a space as a homeland and as a diaspora is related to the emergence of the nation-state as a powerful political phenomenon. In this case, most Jews who live in Morocco feel estranged from the political Morocco while, at the same time, they are nostalgic about the ideational Morocco. They also feel longings towards the Land of Israel, but criticize the State of Israel. In short, both Morocco and Israel pay the price of the materialization of the vision of nation-state. In both cases Jews may escape into nostalgia. They reject the demand of the nation-state for an ultimate and unique loyalty that lacks flexibility, accepting multi-vocal links rather than spaces of life. The narrowness of the national project is rejected. Interestingly, nostalgia towards Morocco appears even if one is not migrating from it, while nostalgia for Israel appears even if one is not intending to

immigrate to it. This position does not dramatically undermine the imposition of the "binary system" of "homeland vs. diaspora" because it utilizes
the discourse of the nation-state. Yet, this position certainly proposes an alternative that situates Moroccan Jews in both ends of this dichotomy, and, by
implication cracks this construction, even if slightly.

A Few Concluding Words

At first glance, Casablanca's Jews perfectly fit the elementary features of
the solar system model. They perceive the Land of Israel as their sacred
homeland from which their forefathers were expelled and to which they will
eventually return (e.g., Abitbol 1981). These Jews appear to contradict the
utopian agenda articulated by the Boyarins' moral plea for a perpetual diasporic existence (Boyarin and Boyarin 1993) or Gilman's refutation of the
center-periphery model altogether (Gilman 1999). As I have claimed, they
speak about the return to Zion without challenging its Zionist (secular) interpretation and actualization. Morally, they reject Diaspora, seeing in it a
tragic outcome of the sins of their ancestors. Casablanca's Jews accept the
Torah's negative and punishing overtone regarding Diaspora, and approve
the demand to "go back" to Israel in order to amend the unhealthy diasporic
existence.

Nonetheless, as we witnessed through the ethnographic scenes, although
Moroccan Jews appear to fulfill the basic characteristics of the diaspora solar
system model, some fascinating and surprising features emerge as we take a
closer and more minute look. Morocco, *as an ideational entity*, has turned
into a new sort of a homeland. Yesterday's place of exile has turned into a sort
of a symbolic center. Hand in hand with this development, Israel became for
them a place that hosts "their" diaspora. Moroccan-born Israelis are perceived as their diasporic community. To put it somewhat differently, Morocco turned into a space for longings and nostalgia. In this respect, Morocco's position in their minds reassembles Israel's.

This symbolic reversal was dialectically synchronized with a paradoxical
change in the *imaginaire* of "Morocco" and "Israel." The former ceased to
be a "taken for granted" home, and became a "hosting" place. As long as
Jews perceived Morocco as an unquestioned habitat (other options not being
in their horizon), it was the place of exile and Israel was the exclusive
utopian homeland. But this picture significantly changed in 1948, when the
State of Israel was discursively conflated with the Land of Israel. Hand in
hand with this process, Moroccan Jews become estranged from their place of

birth as it was freed from its colonial regime and turned into a nation-state. The Moroccan state, committed to the "Arab cause," turned into a "hosting" place, but concurrently, although it appears paradoxical, the imagined "Morocco" turned into a desired homeland. Nostalgia for the places that "have been" and are no longer here enables the rejection, or at least the avoidance, of the demands of exclusiveness imbedded to the nation-state. In the Moroccan case it is especially intriguing, because Jews became nostalgic without physically emigrating from their land. An epistemological partition was erected between them and their place of birth.

Not only does this evolution seems perplexing and requiring further explanation, it testifies to the complexity of the concepts in hand—diaspora and homeland. By providing ethnographic scenes relating to this intricate situation I interpolated claims that challenge the rigid architecture of the solar system diaspora model. This rigidity is related, among other things, to the emergence of the powerful discourse of the nation-state. Nation-state discourse, like its diaspora twin, assumes a "natural" belonging of the majority of the state's citizens to their nation and territory, and demands exclusivity of belonging. In short, unlike the moral aspirations elaborated by the Boyarins, it appears that diaspora discourse emerges from nation-state discourse. Although diasporas do not deconstruct the capacity of the nation-state to impose the binary system—either "homelands" or "diasporas"— they can propose a place of refuge that provides the capacity to avoid the nation-state's demand for exclusivity and, in a limited way, erode the possibility of its imposition.

REFERENCES

Abitbol, Michel. 1981. *Contemporary North African Jewry.* Jerusalem: Shazar Library, the Institute of Contemporary Jewry, and the Hebrew University of Jerusalem. [Hebrew.]

Abitbul, Michael. 1986. "The Jews in North Africa and Egypt." In *History of the Jews in the Islamic Countries: From the Middle of the Nineteenth to the Middle of the Twentieth Century* [Part Two], ed. S. Ettinger, pp. 363–468. Jerusalem: The Zalman Shazar Center. [Hebrew.]

Adam, André. 1968. *Casablanca.* Paris: Editions CNRS.

Anderson, Benedict. 1983. *Imagined Communities: Reflections on the Origin and Spread of Nationalism.* London: Verso.

Appadurai, Arjun. 1988. "Putting Hierarchy in Its Place." *Cultural Anthropology* 3:36–49.

———. 1990. "Disjuncture and Difference in the Global Cultural Economy." *Public Culture* 2(2):1–24.

Appadurai, Arjun, and Carol Breckenbridge. 1989. "On Moving Targets." *Public Culture* 2:i–v.

Augé, Marc. 1995. *Non-Places: Introduction to an Anthropology of Supermodernity*. London and New York: Verso.

Ayache, Germain. 1987. "La minorité juive dans le Maroc précolonial." *Hesperis Tamuda* 25:147–68.

Bahloul, Joëlle. 1996. *The Architecture of Memory: A Jewish-Muslim Household in Colonial Algeria 1937–1962*. Translated by Ménagé C. Du Peloux. Cambridge: Cambridge University Press.

Bar-Asher, Shalom. 1981. "The Connections Between the Jews of North Africa and the Yishuv in the Land of Israel from the 18th Century to the Last Generations." In *The Jews of North Africa and the Land of Israel*, ed. S. Bar-Asher, pp. 5–8. Jerusalem: Beyachad. [Hebrew.]

Bashan, Eliezer. 2000. *The Jews of Morocco: Their Past and Culture*. Tel-Aviv: Hakibbutz Hameuchad. [Hebrew.]

Bat-Yeor. (Pseud.) 1985. *The Dhimmi: Jews and Christians under Islam*. Rutherford, N.J.: Fairleigh Dickinson University Press.

Bensimon, Agnès. 1993. *Hassan II et les juifs*. Tel-Aviv: Yediot Ahronot Books and Chemed Books. [Hebrew.]

Bilu, Yoram, and André Levy. 1996. "Nostalgia and Ambivalence: The Reconstruction of Jewish-Muslim Relations in Oulad-Mansour." In *Modern Sephardi and Middle Eastern Jewries: History and Culture*, ed. H. E. Goldberg, pp. 288–311. Bloomington: Indiana University Press.

Bourqia, Rahma. 1987. "State and Tribes in Morocco: Continuity and Change." Ph.D. dissertation. Manchester University, UK.

Boyarin, Daniel, and Jonathan Boyarin. 1993. "Diaspora: Generation and Ground of Jewish Identity." *Critical Inquiry* 19(3–4):693–725.

Clifford, James. 1997. *Routes: Travel and Translation in the Late Twentieth Century*. Cambridge, Mass., and London: Harvard University Press.

Cohen, Robin. 1997. *Global Diasporas: An Introduction*. Seattle: University of Washington Press.

Daure-Serfaty, Christine. 1992. *Tazmamart: une prison de la mort au Maroc*. Paris: Stoc.

David, Avraham. 1985. "The Connections Between North African Jews and the Land of Israel in the 15th and 16th Century." *Pe'amim* 24:74–86. [Hebrew.]

Entelis, John P. 1989. *Culture and Counterculture in Moroccan Politics*. Boulder, Colo.: Westview Press.

Flamand, Pierre. 1959. *Diaspora en terre d'Islam: les communautés israélites du sud-marocain*. Casablanca: Presses des Imprimeries Réunis.

Foucault, Michel. 1978. *The History of Sexuality*, trans. R. Hurley. New York: Vintage Books.

Geertz, Clifford. 1973. "Ritual and Social Change: A Javanese Example." In *The Interpretation of Cultures*, ed. C. Geertz, pp. 142–69. New York: Basic Books, Inc., Publishers.

Gilman, Sander L. 1999. "Introduction: The Frontier as a Model for Jewish History." In *Jewries at the Frontier: Accommodation, Identity, Conflict*, ed. S. L. Gilman and M. Shain, pp. 1–25. Urbana: University of Illinois Press.

Gurevitch, Zali, and Gideon Aran. 1994. "The Land of Israel: Myth and Phenomenon." *Studies in Contemporary Jewry* 10:191–210.

Hirschberg, Haïm Z. 1968. "The Jewish Quarter in Muslim Cities and Berber Arabs." *Judaism* 17(4):405–21.

———. 1974. *A History of the Jews in North Africa*. Leiden: Brill.

Hobsbawm, Erik, and Terence O. Ranger. 1983 *The Invention of Tradition*. Cambridge: Cambridge University Press.

Kenbib, Mohammed. 1994. *Juifs et musulmans au Maroc, 1859–1948. Contribution a l'histoire des relation inter-communautaires en terre d'Islam*. Rabat: Faculté des lettres at des sciences humaines.

Laskier, Michael M. 1983. *The Alliance Israélite Universelle and the Jewish Communities of Morocco, 1862–1962*. Albany: State University of New York Press.

Laskier, Michael M. 1990. "Developments in the Jewish Communities of Morocco: 1956–76." *Middle Eastern Studies* 26(4):465–505.

Levy, André. 1991. "Une grande Hillulah et une 'Atzeret Tshuvah': etude d'un cas." In *Recherches sur la Culture des Juifs d'Afrique du Nord*, ed. I. Ben-Ami, pp. 167–79. Jerusalem: Communauté Israelite Nord-Africaine. [Hebrew.]

Levy, André. 1997. "To Morocco and Back: Tourism and Pilgrimage among Moroccan-Born Israelis." In *Grasping Land: Space and Place in Contemporary Israeli Discourse and Experience*, ed. E. Ben-Ari and Y. Bilu, pp. 25–46. Albany: State University of New York Press.

Levy, André. 1998. "Controlling Space, Essentializing Identities: Jews in Contemporary Casablanca." *City and Society* (1998):175–99.

Levy, André. 2000a. "Diasporas through Anthropological Lenses: Contexts of Postmodernity." *Diaspora* 9(1):137–57.

———. 2000b. "Playing for Control of Distance: Card Games between Jews and Muslims on a Casablancan Beach." *American Ethnologist* 26(3): 632–53.

Malkki, Liisa H. 1997. "*National Geographic*: The Rooting of Peoples and the Territorialization of National Identity among Scholars and Refugees." In *Culture, Power, and Place: Explorations in Critical Anthropology*, ed. A. Gupta and J. Ferguson, pp. 52–74. Durham and London: Duke University Press.

Markowitz, Fran. 1995. "Criss-crossing Identities: The Russian Jewish Diaspora and the Jewish Diaspora in Russia." *Diaspora* 4(2):201–10.

Memmi, Albert. 1973. *Portrait du Colonisé.* Paris: Payot.

———. 1975. *Jews and Arabs.* Chicago: J. Philip O'Hara.

Nora, Pierre. 1989. "Between Memory and History." *Representations* 26: 7–25.

Ossman, Susan. 1994. *Picturing Casablanca: Portraits of Power in a Moroccan City.* Berkeley and Los Angeles: University of California Press.

Pattie, Susan. 1994. "At Home in Diaspora: Armenians in America." *Diaspora* 3(2):185–98.

———. 1997. *Faith in History: Armenians Rebuilding Community.* Washington, D.C., and London: Smithsonian Institution Press.

Perrault, Gilles. 1990. *Notre ami le Roi.* Paris: Gallimard.

Rodrigue, Aron. 1990. *French Jews, Turkish Jews: The Alliance Israélite Universelle and the Politics of Jewish Schooling in Turkey, 1860–1925.* Bloomington: Indiana University Press.

———. 1993. *Images of Sephardi and Eastern Jewries in Transition: The Teachers of Alliance Israélite Universelle, 1860–1939.* Seattle: University of Washington Press.

Rosen, Lawrence. 1968. "A Moroccan Jewish Community During a Middle Eastern Crisis." *The American Scholar* 37(3):435–51.

Safran, William. 1991. "Diasporas in Modern Societies: Myths of Homeland and Return." *Diaspora* 1(1):83–99.

Schwarzfuchs, Simon. 1985. "Between the Land of Israel and French Morocco, 1912–1914." *Pe'amim* 24:93–98. [Hebrew.]

Segev, Shmuel. 1984. *Operation "Yakhin": The Secret Immigration of Moroccan Jews to Israel.* Tel Aviv: Misrad Ha-Bitakhon. [Hebrew.]

Serfaty, Abraham. 1992. *Dans les prisons du Roi: secrets de Kenitra sur le Maroc.* Paris: Messidor/Social.

Stillman, Norman A. 1974. "Muslims and Jews in Morocco: Perceptions, Images, Stereotypes," pp. 13–27. Paper given at the Jewish Muslim Relations in North Africa conference, May 19, 1974, at Princeton, New Jersey.

———. 1979. *The Jews of Arab Lands: A History and Source Book.* Philadelphia: The Jewish Publication Society of America.

———. 1991. *The Jews of Arab Lands in Modern Times.* Philadelphia: The Jewish Publication Society of America.

Stratton, Jon. 1997 "(Dis)placing the Jews: Historicizing the Idea of Diaspora." *Diaspora* 6(3):301–29.

Suleiman, Michael W. 1989. "Morocco in the Arab and Muslim World: Attitudes of Moroccan Youth." *The Maghreb Review* 14(1–2):16–27.

Tessler, Mark A. 1978. "The Identity of Religious Minorities in Non-Secular States: Jews in Tunisia and Morocco and Arabs in Israel." *Comparative Studies in Society and History* 20(3):359–73.

————. 1988. "Moroccan-Israeli Relations and the Reasons for Moroccan Receptivity to Contact with Israel." *The Jerusalem Journal of International Relations* 10(2):76–108.

Tölölyan, Khachig. 1996. "Rethinking Diaspora(s): Stateless Power in the Transnational Moment." *Diaspora* 5(1):3–36.

Tsur, Yaron, and Hagar Hillel. 1995. *Les Juifs de Casablanca: Études sur la modernisation de l'élite politique juive en diaspora coloniale.* Tel Aviv: L'Université Ouverte. [Hebrew.]

Turner, Victor W. 1973. "The Center Out-There: Pilgrim's Goal." *History of Religions* 11:191–230.

Zafrani, Haïm. 1983. *Mille ans de vie au Maroc: Histoire et culture, religion et magie.* Paris: Maisonneuve et Larose.

NOTES

Previously published in *City and Society* (2001) 13(2): 247–72. Reprinted with permission.

1. Arjun Appadurai aptly determines that "natives are not only persons who are from certain places, and belong to those places, but they are also those who are somehow *incarnated,* or confined, in those places" (1988:37).

2. One explanation for this theoretical limitation might be rooted in the fact that diaspora discourse is well entrenched in national discourse.

3. For example, Jews were forbidden to ride horses (for these are noble beasts), to wear shoes in the vicinity of mosques, to wear colorful clothes, and to carry arms.

4. I should emphasize, however, that by using words like "intimate" and "close" I wish to evade idealization of these relations. Jews were, after all, a religio-ethnic minority under the rule of Islam.

5. For the impact of French colonialism on the demographic flow to Casablanca, see, for example, Adam 1968; Flamand 1959; Ossman 1994.

6. Albert Memmi expresses the tragic situation in which Jews were caught when describing the "double trap" of colonialism (1973, 1975).

7. Many historical documents and personal memoirs treat this period in the lives of Morocco's Jews. For a Zionist perspective of this activity, see Bensimon 1993; Segev 1984. For an attempt to present an uninvolved perspective see Stillman 1991:141–80, and for a multi-vocal perspective see Tsur and Hillel 1995.

8. Practically all the Algerian Jews immigrated to France, and about half of the Tunisian Jews. Only 25 percent of Moroccan Jews went to France. On the different options available to the North African Jews, see Abitbul 1986.

9. In fact, some claim that there are less than four thousand.

10. It is noteworthy that intervention was not limited to French Jews. For instance, British Jewish subjects of Moroccan origin (and perhaps others) lob-

bied for the visit of Sir Moses Montefiore in 1863. Montefiore visited Sultan Muhammad IV with a petition to moderate the burden of the *dhimmi* status. His request was not responded to favorably.

11. On Morocco's political commitment to the "Arab cause" see, for instance, Entelis 1989.

12. Incidentally, several Moroccan-born Israelis did transfer their parents' bones to Israel long after their deaths. Not only that, but also a member of the prominent Pinto family in Israel claimed that he transferred the bones of several holy descendants (*tsaddiqim*) presumably from Morocco to a small town in Israel (Levy 1991).

13. The death rate was rapidly dropping in those days, as the community was gradually vanishing. During the 1980s it dropped from ninety-two documented cases of death in 1980 to sixty-seven in 1990, a decline of 27 percent.

14. In fact, most emigration is to other countries. Moroccan Jews prefer France and Canada. Israel is only in third place, just ahead of the United States.

15. During a showing of the film in Jerusalem, the audience—most of whom were former residents of Oujda—could not stand aloof; they pointed their fingers towards the screen when sites of the town were shown and they laughed when faces were recognized. After the movie, the director was ready to answer questions, but instead people talked to each other trying to locate common acquaintances and past experiences. As the director later said, "it became a town gathering."

16. On these ambivalent attitudes from the Israeli perspective see, for example, Bilu and Levy 1996. From the French perspective see Bahloul 1996.

17. Indeed, following these orchestrated protests she postponed her visit.

18. On the political motivations of the Moroccan monarchy to underline good relationships with the Jewish minority and the moderate relationships with Israel, see Tessler 1988.

CHAPTER 4

Rethinking the Palestinians Abroad as a Diaspora: The Relationships Between the Diaspora and the Palestinian Territories

SARI HANAFI

Introduction

This article raises a series of questions regarding the taxonomy employed to understand the Palestinians living abroad, their identity, and their relationships to both the homeland and their host societies. Categorization, it should be recalled, is never neutral: the terms or concepts that are used not only provide an operational definition, they also shape the issues with regard to identities, personal and collective memories, and migration experience. For example, Luc Boltanski (1985) has shown how the creation of the category of *cadres* (executives and professionals) in France and its reference to specific social classes became the object of many manipulations on the part of the French unions. Thus, in addition to influencing the exchange of knowledge, the selected categories and notions also have obvious political implications.

For many reasons, the literature on Palestinians has extensively used the term "Palestinian refugees," and considers other notions such as "diaspora," "forced and volunteered migrants," or "Palestinians abroad" as inadequately stating or weakening the defense or "the cause" of this population. Moreover, the relationship between this population and the Palestinian territories or the historical Palestine is supposed to be "natural" and "primordial." However, since the beginning of the Oslo process, in 1993, we observe, as will be seen later on, the relative weakness in the relationships between the Palestinians abroad and the emerging Palestinian entity. This relationship is constructed and changed extensively, especially during the period of transition.

In this chapter, I first debate the problematic issue of the Palestinians abroad within the general trends of migration studies. I then examine the concept of "diaspora" in detail, particularly since it privileges as well as succeeds in emphasizing the relationships with the country of origin as a major element in the web of relationships that the forced migrant is able to establish. I go on to argue that the Palestinians abroad do not constitute a real diaspora, but rather a "partially diasporized people." This thesis is then examined by constructing a typology of three ideal-types: diasporized people, population in transit, and assimilated population. Finally, I develop an explicative model of the ongoing and unachieved diasporization of the Palestinian people. This model is based on two central points: the weak and fragile center of gravity of the Palestinian diaspora, and the recent crystallization of a Palestinian identity.[1]

Different Paradigms of Migration Studies

There are five main paradigms which dominate the field of migration studies and articulate between place, rooted identity, and transnational identity: assimilation, multiculturalism, transnationalism, diaspora, and cosmopolitanism.

The first paradigm, assimilation, is embedded in the theory of modernization which perceives the migrant as either an alienated agent seeking acculturation, integration, and assimilation in the host countries, or one who pathologically resists these processes. The culture of the host country is characterized as modern and universal relative to that of the immigrant's country of origin, which is considered to be local, traditional, and even primitive. For example, in a country like France, even if the official language recognized "integration," in practice and in the dominant sociological literature this really meant "assimilation" or some range of tolerance for difference. Assimilation, as Michel Wieviorka wrote, refers to the idea that "the universalism of individual rights is the best response to the possibility of discrimination which is inherent to any classification of people on a cultural basis"[2] (1998:894–96). The addition of tolerance "allows specificity in the private sphere and even in the public sphere provided that the requests, demands, even the visibility, are not the source of any difficulties"[3] (ibid.). In this regard the concept of "tolerance" asserts the centrality of what is called "Western culture." David Theo Goldberg argues that "tolerance" should best be considered to be a tool used by the colonial power to impose its laws and culture.[4]

In a country like France, this conception continues its dominance under the guise of "republicanism," even though some social scientists have sought to rethink the capacity of minorities or immigrants to sustain more than a single culture without feeling necessarily alienated and schizophrenic. It should be noted that this approach, which suggests a kind of multiculturalism and dual allegiance, has met with strong resistance from the scholarly community.

Multiculturalism, the second paradigm, was operative in Canada and the United States in the early 1970s, and later also became popular in Australia and Sweden. It finds expression in the social science literature, and also, even more significantly, in some of the policies adopted by these countries (Wieviorka 1998:884–86). Unlike cultural pluralism, multiculturalism grants recognition to the barriers produced by race and, therefore, posits a diversity of populations whose experiences of discrimination have given particular histories to peoples of color. The debate regarding multiculturalism commonly revolves around recognition, identity, and cultural difference, and tends to place an emphasis on "cultural injustice" rather than economic discrimination. Indeed, Charles Taylor has been criticized for assuming that rectifying cultural injustice would provide "significant leverage by itself to attack the structures of power that produce economic injustice" (Bashir 2001:11). In Canada, for example, there is a kind of integrated multiculturalism in the sense that there is no "separation between the cultural question and the economic question. Those primarily targeted by this policy are defined in terms of economic participation, and not only in terms of cultural difference" (Wieviorka 1998:884–86). In contrast, the United States experience indicates a different form, which can perhaps be termed "disintegrated multiculturalism." There the issues are seen not so much as cultural, but more as policies against social inequality based on racial discrimination. As Nathan Glazer (1997) has argued, affirmative action has "nothing to do with recognition of cultures. . . . It is about jobs and admissions."

Multiculturalism can be criticized on several grounds. First, it seeks to redress some of society's problems, but it does not directly attack the more rooted issues of the cultural and economic hegemony of some groups in relation to others. Historically, it can be seen as a response to the emerging cultural and racial minorities in North America, and a tentative approach to the issues of cultural difference. It was important for challenging the hegemonic culture in the United States, but over time it became a mere policy-oriented concept meant to counterbalance the marginalization of minorities and reduce the program of affirmative action. As Wieviorka formulates his critique: "the preconditions for multiculturalism are such that the problem is almost resolved before having been posed, or that it is based on the Utopia of a society which has already been capable of shaping its project" (1998:901).

The third paradigm analyzes the life experience of migrants in terms of transnationalism. The immigrant was perceived as participating in the cultural, social, economic, and political life of both countries: the country of origin and the host country. Moreover, transnationalism is an ongoing process of linkage rather than a single, unitary phenomenon. Existing between two worlds, however, does not necessarily indicate a transnational life-style; as suggested by Portes, Guarnizo, and Landolt, transnationalism is also rooted in extensive exchanges, new modes of transacting and the multiplication of activities beyond the national borders (cited by Grillo, Riccio, and Salih 2000:6). The importance of this concept is that it invites the researcher to maintain a global perspective on migration, and, in addition, to go beyond the classical conception of the nation-state in order to understand the immigrants' behavior. At the same time, what can be termed "transnational life experience" concerns not only the immigrant but also those who decide to return to their original homes (Basch et al. 1994:272). What distinguishes this paradigm from the others is that the nuanced nationalism of multiculturalism conceptually excludes political identification and participation in other national locations from those populations that are racially different.

In common with the other paradigms, transnationalism can be interpreted in different ways. As Salih (2000:7) argues, "while some see transnationalism as a counter-hegemonic process (Basch et al. 1994), other scholars see transnational migrants as the new postmodern *gastarbeiters* (Grillo 1998)." Some of the analysts who use this concept consider the existence of two states to which the migrant belongs as a condition of "the transnational life." I would argue that it is above all a feature of social behavior, and therefore a refugee migrant could also be involved in the political, economic, and social life of his/her home as well as in the host country. This is also the paradigm's weakness: no matter which interpretation is followed, the literature on transnationalism falls into the trap of generalization and tends to consider all immigrant experience as transnational by definition.

The fourth paradigm is the concept of diaspora. This paradigm stands in contradiction with the first one, assimilation, but is complementary to the second and third. The importance of this concept consists in its analytical power. It leads us to look at the connectivity between the ethnic and religious community in one particular place and the supposed same community abroad. The diaspora, in other words, is connected between the peripheries themselves and with the center as well. Connectivity means not only the possible "return to the center," but also continuous circulation and movement between peripheries and center. A good deal of research has been done regarding the economic and social networks established between individuals belonging to the same ethnicity. To cite a well-known example, Kotkin has made sweeping claims for the abilities and central importance of networking among certain diasporic groups. In his book *Tribes: How Race, Religion and Identity Determine Success In the New Global Economy* (1993), Kotkin traces the connection between ethnicity and business success—how in-group loyalties are becoming the driving force in the new global economy. These global tribes combine a strong sense of common origin and shared values—quintessential tribal characteristics—with two other critical factors for success in the modern world: geographical dispersion (within a global network) and the belief in scientific progress. Paradoxically, these two combine what liberals had wrongly thought to be intrinsically separate: ethnic identity and cosmopolitan adaptability. Kotkin maintains that in this new era, with the end of the Cold War and the reduced power of nation-states, these cosmopolitan groups will become more empowered and flourish. However, his concept of global networks is exaggerated, particularly in the sense that all of and ethnic group's members are connected and there is no room for the individual outside of his/her community.

Finally, the last paradigm, cosmopolitanism, is a long-sidelined concept recently reactivated by a wide range of social, political, and cultural studies theorists. It is currently presented by way of a new politics of the left, postulating alternatives for both the ethnocentric paradigm of assimilation and particularistic multiculturalism. Here, the migrant is not seen as attached to his/her rooted identity and not assimilated to the host-land identity, but open to world-identity. The *Oxford English Dictionary* defines cosmopolitan as "at home throughout the world or in many spheres of interest." Thus the cosmopolitism-like cultural hybridist concept turns into a reaction to the debate around the politics of identity. Timothy Brennan (1997) argues for a politics of positionality in which the value of nativism is not placed so much on where a person is born, but on how an individual is "situated in the place" and, most important, on his or her political position. Continuing this line of reasoning, in their discussion on the politics of non-identity, Edward Said and Jacques Derrida both claim that heterogeneity and hybridity come at the expense of identity and difference. Heterogeneity implies that homogeneity is not natural; rather it is politically crafted and fabricated for purposes of localizing and maintaining power (Bashir 2001:13).

Some key questions can now be raised concerning the application of these paradigms to the Palestinians abroad: How have the various host countries dealt with the Palestinians living among them? Which paradigm is most suitable as an approach to the situation of Palestinians abroad?

The assimilation paradigm has primarily been applied in two countries (Egypt and France) and in two quite different ways. In Egypt, the Palestinians' fragile status is partially the result of a kind of popular racism that has been leveled against them. Their own fear of isolation and marginality has pushed them to "become assimilated." It is probably accurate to say that the only Palestinians who speak with the exact accent of their host country are the Palestinians in Egypt. While the assimilation forces in Egypt are unorganized and essentially popular, in France they are more institutional and conform to the overall French system of Jacobean centralism. As shown in earlier studies, Palestinians, in common with other migrant communities, are also pressured into adopting a strategy of assimilation (Hanafi 2001a, 2001b).

With regard to multiculturalism, one can argue that this paradigm is appropriate only for Palestinians living in Western countries where Palestinian culture is markedly different from that of the majority. However, it may also be relevant to those Arab countries where the local culture and power structure can be said to inhibit cultural diversity. More generally, the problems of Palestinian refugees in the Arab world are not in the realm of culture, but rather in the economic arena. Just like the other immigrants working and living there, they are exploited by an economic system in which they are discriminated against and have few legal work rights. This is the case in Israel, Lebanon, and the Gulf States.

Transnationalism is a paradigm that challenges the classical concept of nation-state and, in our particular case, the relationship between Palestinian identity and the presence of Palestinian territory. As the transnational studies authors emphasize the economic aspects of migration and how transnational practice related to global capitalism and the accumulation of capital by its de-territorialization, here, in the Palestinian case, I will show how these practices have completely different meanings.[5]

The recycling of de-territorialized Palestinian capital reveals lines of fault in the international global market rather than beneficial workings of globalization. For instance, the geographical de-localization of Palestinian economic transactions can best be understood as improving the fragile legal status of the refugees, regardless of their wealth. As such, most of their investments reflect more of an economy of survival than the exercise of true political and economic power in the global economy and the world system. As Grillo, Riccio, and Salih argue, "Economic dislocation in both developing and industrialized nations has increased migration, but made it difficult for migrants to construct secure cultural, social and economic bases within their new settings (2000:19)." Therefore, transnationalism, whether in reaction to global capitalism or preceding its triumph (as in the case of the Senegalese communities in Italy), does not exhibit a straightforward relation to global capital (ibid.). The experience of Palestinians recruited through the UNDP's[6] TOKTEN (Transfer of Knowledge through National Expatriates) program shows that many of them come to Palestine because of their precarious situation in their host countries. Accordingly, their return expresses a model in which constrained people seek to improve their flexibility, rather than one of people with a straightforward choice between the country of residence and the country of origin.

My research among Palestinians indicates that transnational networks are not an expression of global capital; rather, they mainly constitute strategies of survival. In many transnational experiences around the world, for example the Chinese in the United States (Ong 1999:6), the quest to accumulate capital and social prestige in the global arena emphasizes and is regulated by practices favoring flexibility, mobility, and repositioning in relation to markets, governments, and cultural regimes. In the Palestinian case, however, this acquisition of capital disproportionally reflects a struggle for economic survival. While a New York businessman may not require expending more than a fraction of a second of his time on a million dollar transaction, thanks to the time-space compression enabled by new information technologies information (Harvey 1990), a transnational refugee in many Middle Eastern countries will most likely expend days on a much more modest transfer. In contrast with the euphoric tones of many recent transnational studies, my own research stresses the crucial importance of the particular class stratification that is linked to global systems of production. Accordingly, the cultural flows described by Arjun Appadurai (1996) involve not the entire population in question, but only a small segment. As Friedman (1997) argues, Appadurai ignores the political economy of time-space compression and gives the misleading impression that everyone can take equal advantage of mobility and modern communications and that transnationality has been liberating, in both a spatial and a political sense, for all peoples. What is missing from these accounts are discussions of how the disciplining structures—of family, community, work, travel, and nation—condition, shape, divert, and transform such subjects and their practices and produce moral-political dilemmas.

If the accumulation of foreign passports for some businesspeople is "a matter of convenience" and a "matter of confidence" in uncertain political times (Ong 1999:1), for almost all Palestinians residing abroad it is a matter

of survival. Not having a passport can render them immobile and force them
to live clandestine lives (Hanafi 2001b). For those who have never possessed
a passport, but have had to make do with a travel document, a passport signifies and allows basic connectivity to their family, as well as participation in
labor markets.

In contrast to the above, the diaspora paradigm takes into account the possibility of the Palestinians' transnational life abroad, and it also emphasizes
the importance of the multi-polar connectivity between the different peripheral communities, and between these and the Palestinian territories.
However, this connectivity is not necessarily real or evident. The dispersion
of a people, due to their forced emigration, is usually conceived as a source
of their transnational networks. Diasporas have also been viewed as contributing to the reshaping and emergence of new economic networks. For instance, the Palestinian-Israeli Oslo Agreement was seen as fostering the re-
establishment of local and international economic links after an extended
period of conflict. In this respect, the discourse on diasporic networks has
been overstated and almost mythic. Little attention has been paid to the absence of networks or to networks that were damaged or torn, disconnected as
a result of many factors (such as the impermeability of the inter-state borders, absence of relationship following a long period of separation, and so
forth). A careful examination of the Palestinian communities in their diaspora would show many forms of networks with varying degrees of institutionalization: familial networks that sometimes include a family council, village clubs which continue to be important (especially in the United States),
national and nationalistic-religious networks usually based on the different
popular organizations associated with the Palestinian Liberation Organization (PLO) or pro-Hamas. In addition, in both Europe and North America
one can also find active supra-national networks, such as Arab or Islamic religious networks, which include Arabs from many different national origins.

If the first three paradigms minimize the relationships between the migrant community and the host land, the advantage of the diaspora concept is
that it emphasizes these links, as well as the connectivity to the real or mythical homeland. Before turning to examine the extent of connectivity between
the Palestinian diaspora and its center, I raise the question of whether the
Palestinians abroad can be considered to be a diaspora. I will argue that the
dispersion of the Palestinian people has created a partial diaspora, and that
the Palestinians abroad continue to be an extremely fragile people.

Diaspora, Population in Transit, and Assimilated Population

Given the complexity of the Palestinians' status abroad, what concepts best express their present situation? An outline for useful classification can be found in the model suggested by Bassma Kodmani (1997), although the definitions used also differ from the original model. The classification is based on three ideal types that constitute a continuum within which the Palestinians can be said to be situated: diaspora, population in transit, and assimilated people.

DIASPORA

The concept of diaspora is used here in two different ways. First, it is employed in a generic sense, to conceptualize the study of the Palestinians as a temporary community settled in a number of host lands and longing for their homecoming. The second meaning is more analytical. A group of dispersed people, far from their homeland, can be considered a diaspora when it fulfills two necessary conditions: first, the group has an accepted legal presence in the host country, and second, members of this group are tied together by a variety of different networks which also link them to their real or mythical homeland. In the latter, members of the community are conscious of sharing a common identity.

For diasporized people, their identities refer to both homeland and host land and the relationship between these identities is not necessarily hierarchical. The quest for original identity need not be measured by their attachment to the homeland or the will to return. Many empirical studies about the refugees challenge the "idealized" and "nostalgic" image of voluntary repatriation home (Warner 1994:160). In the course of time, dispersal distorts the meaning of community and with it the memory of the homeland as well (Zureik 1997:80). Warner, like many authors of cultural studies who emphasize the transmigrants' cultural hybridity, argues that in a postmodern world the "politics of space" is transformed: in the past much of the communitarian argument focused on attachment to the land, while in the present, space has become more elusive and is not necessarily associated with any fixed locale, such as the refugee's original home (ibid.). Without adopting this extreme politics of non-identity, I would say that the diasporized people search for better socio-economic opportunities that are connected with their territorial identity or spiritual homeland. This means that the quest for a geographical position and a socio-economic basis takes into consideration the multitude of factors that are beyond the original group identity. As a result, the ontological question for the diasporized community becomes more "where am I" than "who am I."

It can also be argued that the more one is diasporized, the more one is able to transcend the identification between territory and nation: one considers oneself a Palestinian, among other identities, even if she/he lives voluntarily outside of Palestine. For some authors, the memory of a nation and the associated ego-conscience appears to continue to work even when they are in a "non-space" (*non-lieu*) (Ma Mung et al. 1998; Kodmani 1997). For example, when some diasporized Palestinians return to the homeland they develop an alternative view of homeland-nationhood: they may continue to maintain their allegiance to their host land in ways that are reminiscent of "a transnational life." In contrast to Kodmani's approach, diaspora need not be regarded as the negation of the notion of "refugee" (1997). To her, "diaspora" is how, through the manipulation of terms, the need for resolving the question of return and analyzing the population's integration in the host countries is set aside, while the term "refugee" means that this population and its return remains an issue to be resolved juridically. This polarization seems overstated. The category of "refugee" is more legal and administrative, while the category of "diaspora" is more sociological. The definition of refugee could clarify this distinction. According to the United Nation High Commission for Refugees (UNHCR), a refugee is any person who is outside the country of his nationality because he has or had a well-founded fear of persecution by reason of his race, religion, nationality, membership of a particular social group or political opinion and is unable or, because of such fear, is unwilling to avail himself of the protection of the government of the country of his nationality (Goodwin-Gill 1983:5).

Thus, a refugee remains a refugee even if she/he adopts the nationality of the host country, and even if she/he has acquired some resources or wealth.[8] The classification "refugee" is hence related to the condition of dispersion from the homeland and does not concern the juridical status or living standard in the host countries (Hanafi 2001b). "Diaspora" does not mean abrogating the necessity to change the Palestinians' situation outside their home country, but rather emphasizes the importance of analyzing the relationship between this population, their host lands, and their homeland.

The issues are, of course, filled with contradictions and dilemmas. If the Palestinians maintain a strong relationship with their homeland because of the ongoing Israeli colonial practices, it is also because their legal acceptance has not been fulfilled in the majority of Arab countries that have been their "hosts" (due to absence of civil rights in many of these countries and the

TABLE 4.1.
The Palestinian Refugees Registered at UNRWA (June 2000)

Region or Country	Number of Camps	Refugees Inside the Camps	% Refugees Inside the Camps	Total Number of Refugees
Jordan	10	280,191	18.4%	1,522,777
West Bank	19	157,676	26.5%	595,003
Gaza	8	451,186	54.9%	821,832
Lebanon	12	210,715	54.6%	385,925
Syria	10	111,712	29.2%	382,575
Total	59	1,211,480	32.4%	3,708,112

SOURCE: UNRWA, June 2000.

fragility of their refugee status there). While there are "diasporized Palestinians" in both North and South America and in Europe, the Palestinians in the Arab world have not accomplished their process of diasporization.[9] Instead, they have had to struggle for the right to work and reside there permanently. For this reason, Palestinians in the Arab countries, who also constitute the main population of Palestinians abroad, continue to be in a precarious situation.

POPULATION IN TRANSIT

The second ideal type can be termed a "population in transit." This type of population lives in a precarious juridical status in their host country, even though some may have attained a relatively high standard of living. According to UNRWA statistics (see Table 4.1), Palestinians living in refugee camps constitute about 32.4 percent of the 3,737,494 Palestinians residing in the countries neighboring Israel/Palestine. As Elias Sanbar (1989) has shown, this population is characterized by a condition of permanent liminality and a psychology of continuous transition.[10] Some among them wish to return to their village of origin or to the Palestinian Territories, while others wish to have the choice to stay in the host countries or to return. Their liminality is manifested both in their daily life in the camps, and in their economic activities as well, characterized by small projects or endeavors and diversification of investments in different fields and countries.

ASSIMILATED POPULATION

The third ideal type refers to what can be called "the assimilated population." This means the dilution of an individual into the host country's identity. In some cases and places, persons who, according to the common definition adopted by international organizations, are considered to be of Palestinian origin, choose not to identify themselves as Palestinians. Assimilation can be observed in Latin America, as demonstrated in many studies (Hanafi 2001b; Picard 1998; Gonzalez 1992) and, to a lesser degree, also in the United States. As is well known, this process is not necessarily irreversible: the sociological literature contains many instances in which the third and subsequent generations of assimilated emigrants embark on a quest to define their personal and collective identity. Nonetheless, at present these assimilated populations cannot be considered as part of the Palestinian diaspora.

This typology of Palestinians abroad (diaspora, population in transit, and assimilated population) is intended to indicate a dynamic process rather than describe a static, accomplished position. Diaspora culture is not a given, but is rather continually being constructed. Moreover, the reality is even more complex, since among these ideal types there are also different groups. For example, between "being in transit" and "being diasporized" there is another group, which can be defined "not-yet-diaspora." The Palestinians in Syria are an example of this last group: they are well integrated in the Syrian society, but Syria maintains their refugee status with temporary identity papers as well. In addition, the status of any given Palestinian population may change over time. This is essentially what took place among the Palestinians in the Gulf countries following the Iraqi invasion of Kuwait. The extreme vulnerability of these long-term migrants was made clear by the return of some 300,000 Palestinians to Jordan, the Palestinian Territories, and several other countries during the second Gulf War in 1990.[11] Finally, it should also be kept in mind, these different ideal types can "cohabit" alongside one another in the same country.

Palestinian communities abroad can also be seen as divided according to their time of arrival in the host lands (1948, 1967, etc.), and as a consequence of the differing political-legal statuses that their new host countries assigned them (deported persons, refugees, economic migrants, and so forth). In some instances, their specific geographical origin also plays a role. For example, in both Syria and Jordan nearly all of the Palestinians from Gaza were placed in a special status; these countries feared a large migration of Gazans, since they were formerly Egyptians, Egypt being a country which restricts the access of these refugees.

The classification of Palestinians abroad is not only based on their situation in the host country, but it is also linked to the homeland, in particular to their exodus or flight from Palestine-Israel. Three different categories can be distinguished in this regard.

The first category refers to those who migrated before 1948, mainly for economic reasons but also to escape from Ottoman military service. They migrated in particular to Latin America and North America, although some moved to various Arab countries as well. This population essentially lost its right to return to Palestine-Israel, because of various Israeli legal and administrative measures that hindered their return. Moreover, after the dissolution of the Ottoman Empire, many of these immigrants were without a passport with which they could return to Palestine. Consequently, the difficulties of their return transformed them into a forced migration, resulting in many of them becoming assimilated within their host countries.

The second category concerns the 1948 exodus of Palestinians, who also lost their right of return.[12] According to Palestinian historians and to a number of Israeli "post-Zionist" historians as well, Jewish paramilitary groups and the Israeli Army expelled this population.[13] This was a forced migration in the narrow sense: that is, these were expulsions and deportations of individuals and groups that were overpowered by superior forces and had no alternative except to flee. The Palestinians who left during the 1967 War (estimated at some 350,000 persons) are included in this category, and we must also add those who lost their residence rights by "being absent" during an Israeli census. For all of these persons it is fair to say that the act of leaving was more important than the location of their subsequent arrival. This forced migration was characterized by a lack of options; as Maurice Goldring and Piaras Mac Einri remind us regarding the Irish immigrants, what was important was not the place where the refugees went but the fact that they left the scene of war (1989:173).

The third category concerns Palestinians who immigrated for economic reasons, mainly to the Gulf countries, but to the United States as well. In contrast with the forced migrations, this voluntary migration is an individual migration, even though it is often not based upon individual decision. The family tends to act as a unit when it comes to migration decisions; it is the family member with the best chances of obtaining a well-paid job who is sent abroad. These economic migrants held on to their Palestinian/Israeli identity papers and travel documents that allowed them to return to the Palestinian Territories. In this sense, this category is distinguished by the migrant's ability to choose between a set of options, including the alternative to return to one's homeland. It is relevant to point out that some of these voluntary migrants to the Gulf were those who previously had been among the 1948 forced migrants (residents in the West Bank and Gaza as refugees).

The flow chart in Figure 4.1 summarizes general trends of Palestinian migration, with regard to period of time, type of migration, and relationship to

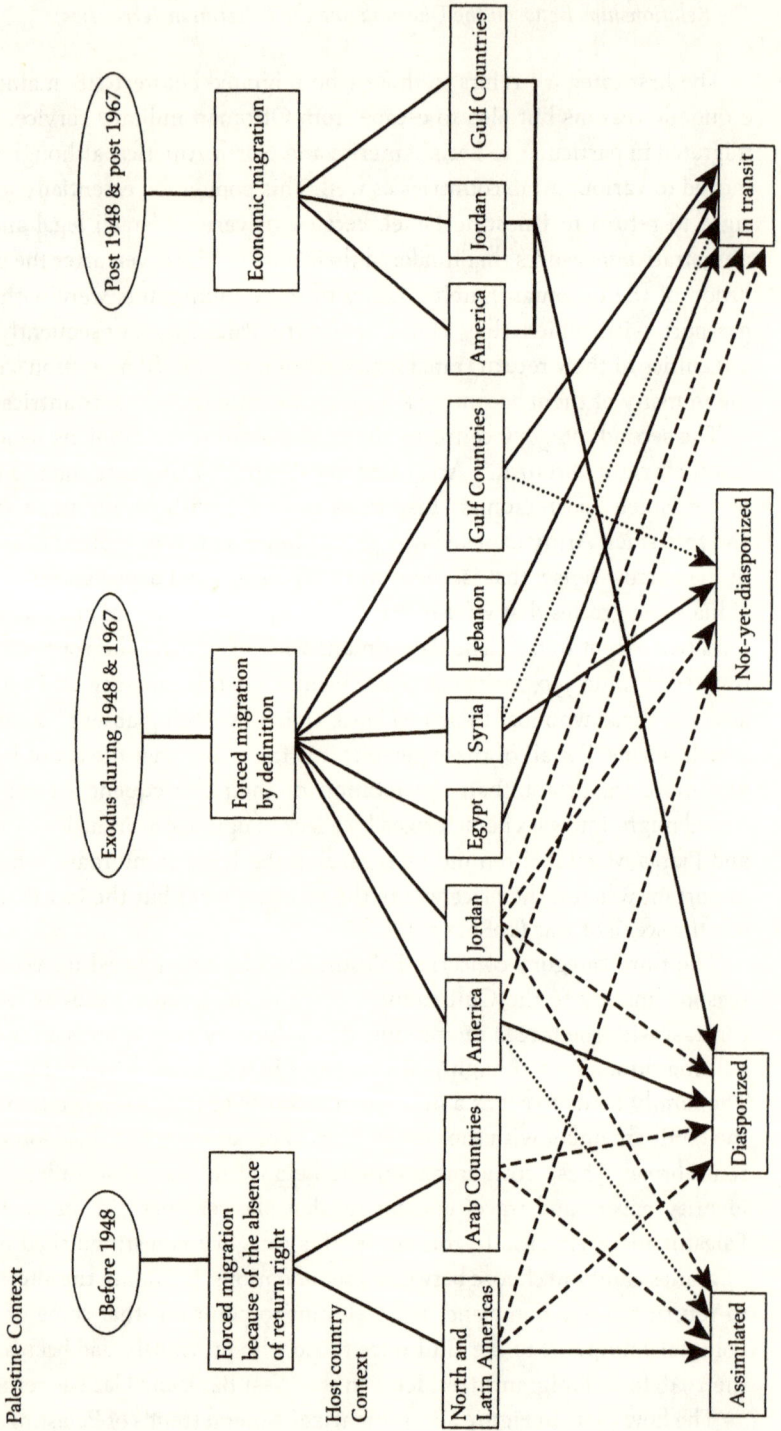

FIGURE 4.1.
Palestinians abroad.

both the "homeland" and the host countries. Several different conclusions can be drawn from the figure. First, the majority of Palestinians in North and Latin America and a portion of the Palestinians in the Arab countries who emigrated before 1948, can be classified as "assimilated." Their assimilation may be due to the long period of time that has ensued since their original emigration—their descendants are now fourth and fifth generation in the host countries (Picard 1998; Gonzalez 1992). The considerable distance between places, and the difficulties of travel during the early years of the last century, also aided in the severing of relationships between the overseas populations and Palestine. In addition, the relatively recent concept of "Palestinian identity" also facilitated their assimilation.

Second, having or obtaining citizenship is not necessarily a factor in the assimilation process. For example, Palestinians who fled to Jordan after 1948 and are now Jordanian citizens have not become assimilated. In fact, the apparent relationship between citizenship and assimilation was used as an argument against awarding citizenship to the Palestinian refugees. In my fieldwork in Arabic countries, the majority of my interlocutors distinguished between citizenship and nationality and they understood citizenship as a guarantee of minimal rights (civil and social, such as access to education, services, rights for mobility, permanent residency) as nationals. In many states in the Middle East, citizenship remains linked to nationality and noncitizens are in principle denied access to the public sphere defined by the state.

Third, in some instances the host countries legally absorbed Palestinian refugees in the sense that they allowed them the right to work as well as an open-ended resident permit. At the same time, however, this did not include citizenship or the possibility of institutionalizing their ethnic or communal life, as can be seen among the Palestinians in Syria.[14] Some of the Palestinians in Jordan also maintain a special status of "Jordanians." In these cases, the Palestinians can be considered as "partially diasporized" or "not yet diasporized."

Fourth, the weak diasporization of the Palestinians in Syria, Lebanon, Egypt, and the Gulf countries is also due to the continued conflict with Israel. Since Israel does not acknowledge the right of choice for Palestinian refugees and the possibility of some of them returning, this policy encourages the Arab countries to keep the Palestinian refugees in their present status quo.

Finally, from a numerical point of view, the Palestinians "in transit" constitute the most significant category. As can be seen in Tables 4.1 and 4.2, this

TABLE 4.2.
World Distribution of Palestinians

Palestinians of the Interior (Palestine / Israel) *	
West Bank	1,869,818
Gaza Strip	1,020,813
Residents of the West Bank and Gaza Strip	325,258
Israel	953,497
Subtotal	*4,169,386*
Diaspora Palestinians **	
Jordan	2,328,308
Lebanon	430,183
Syria	465,662
Egypt	48,784
Saudi Arabia	274,762
Kuwait and Other Gulf Countries	143,274
Libya and Iraq	74,284
Other Arabic Countries	5,554
American Continent	203,588
Other Countries	259,248
Subtotal	*4,233,647*
Total of the Palestinian Population in the World	*8,403,023*

*SOURCE: PCBS, Population Census, 1997
**SOURCE: Palestine 1948—50 years after Al-Nakba. Palestinian Diaspora and Refugee Center, Shaml estimation. See www.shaml.org.

category mainly refers to the Palestinians in the Arab world, with the exception of those in Jordan.

Conclusion: The Specificity of the Palestinian Diaspora

This final section turns to developing an explicative model of the Palestinians' "unachieved diasporization." Two central points are emphasized: the fact that the Palestinian diaspora has a weak center of gravity, and the relatively recent crystallization of a Palestinian identity.

A DIASPORA WITH A WEAK CENTER OF GRAVITY

A classic diaspora is defined by a *center of gravity*, which has two functions: it channels the flux of communications between diaspora members in different peripheries, while it also provides a location where members (especially family) can meet. The first function does not necessarily require a physical site; the meeting location might be a service provider or institution such as the National Jewish Fund for world Jewry, the Tunisian Base of the PLO for Palestinians, and the PKK in Germany in the Kurdish case. In regard to the second function, a physical, geographical location is a necessity and an important factor for communitarian (ethnic) economic transactions. Thus the center of gravity has nothing to do with the symbolic weight that represents a mythical or real homeland, but acts as a center for connecting members of the diaspora belonging to the same economic and social networks. In this respect, the historical Palestine continues to fill an important role in the imagination of the Palestinian diaspora, although not necessarily playing a role for everybody in connecting the members of Palestinian communities abroad. The Salomic Jews, expelled from Spain, who kept their house keys in exile to remember their home, did not go back even when Franco allowed it.

My research on Palestinian business people in the diaspora demonstrated the importance of a physical meeting place. A Palestinian originally from Nazareth (which kept its Arab population), for example, can have a very active economic network based in Nazareth capable of drawing those from Canada, the United States, or Australia for meetings with Palestinians who have remained in Nazareth. In contrast, Palestinians originating from Haifa (an example of a city in which the quasi-total of its Arab population was deported by Israeli forces in 1948) do not have access to such a network, due to the absence of remaining relatives there. Such inaccessibility to the territorial reference point effectively hinders the possibility of meeting. A Haifa family dispersed throughout Damascus, Montreal, Amman, and Abu Dhabi would have little interest in meeting in Syria, where only one member of the family lives. Those in Arabic countries may also find the cost of traveling to Canada or the Gulf prohibitive, long before the equally daunting dilemma of acquiring a visa ever enters into the discussion. These torn networks, due to the absence of territorial reference, are not exclusive to Palestinians. Such a network has also been studied in the case of Gypsies who migrated from Paris to New York. Williams (1987) reports that only a few years after this migration, the family relationships were broken.

The total inaccessibility of historical Palestine makes it impossible for it to function as a center of gravity (except for those who hold foreign passports or a permit to travel from the Palestinian Territories to Israel). Since this is the case, might the Post-Oslo Palestinian Territories play such a role? These territories would be considered as the "natural" center of gravity for Palestinians. A combination of factors, however, has prevented the Territo-

FIGURE 4.2.
A classic diaspora with center of gravity.

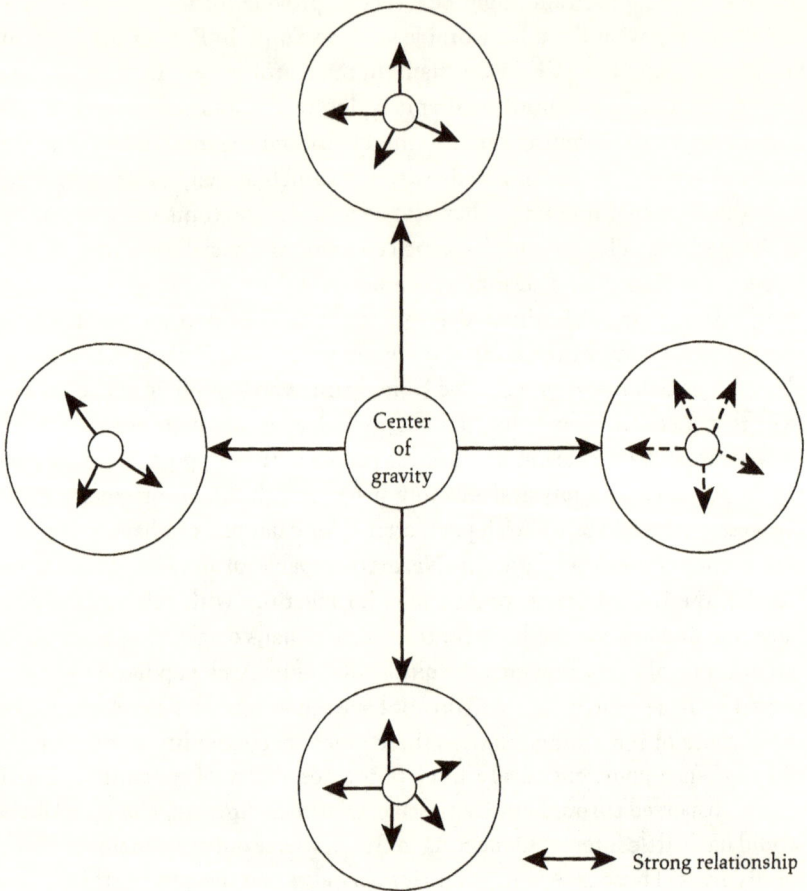

Strong relationship

ries from assuming this role (see Figures 4.2, 4.3, 4.4). The territories are not accessible to the majority of Palestinians abroad; in addition, many in the Palestinian diaspora have lost confidence in the Palestinian National Authority's (PNA) efficacy at state-building. Though the diaspora has played a major role in the nationalist issue and in supporting the PLO during 50 years of resistance, it consciously refuses to transform its role into that of a "Rothschild." Though willing to support the homeland economically and financially, the diaspora also seeks a decision-making role regarding the process of institution building. Here two nuances should be introduced. First, in the context of the second *intifada* (2000 on) the Palestinian territories obtained

FIGURE 4.3.
A diaspora without center of gravity.

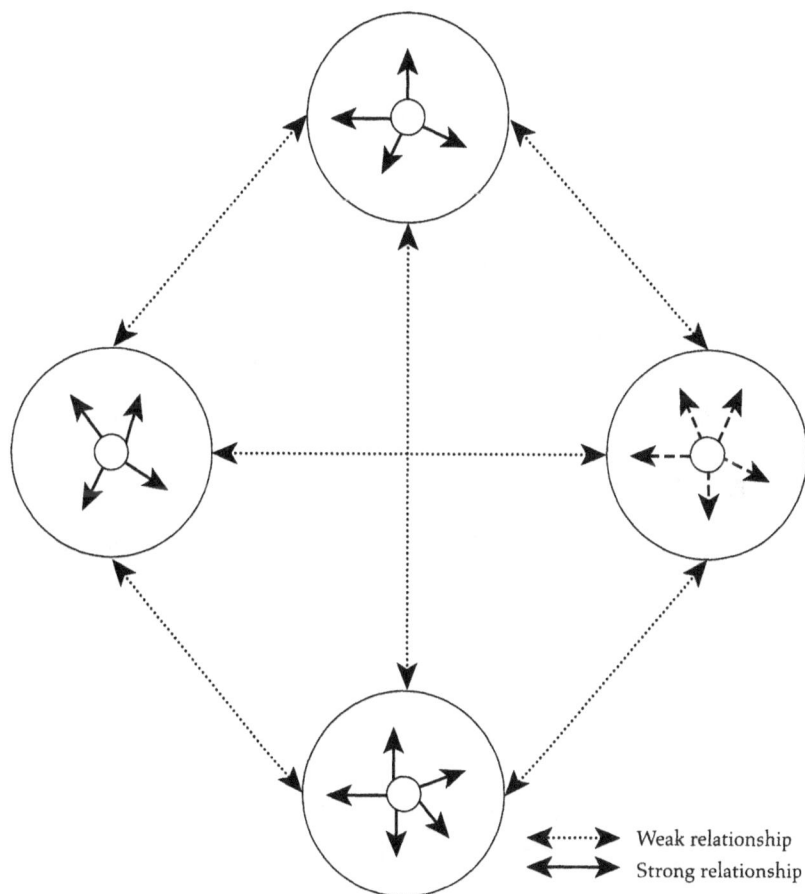

◄┈┈┈► Weak relationship
◄────► Strong relationship

some centrality: the lack of economic investment from the diaspora was compensated for by great solidarity with the population living under Israeli occupation and repression. This solidarity is manifested again by more connectivity on the level of family and village networks. Moreover, the PNA's image has since been rehabilitated and it has again become the center of Palestinian struggle. Even for the political opposition (e.g., Popular Front for Palestinian Liberation, Hamas, Islamic Jihad, etc.) whose leaders are historically located in Syria, the center of decision-making is in the Palestinian territories and not abroad.[15] The Palestinian security forces were no longer seen as gendarmes in the service of Israeli security. The second nuance concerns

FIGURE 4.4.
Palestinian diaspora with weak centers of gravity.

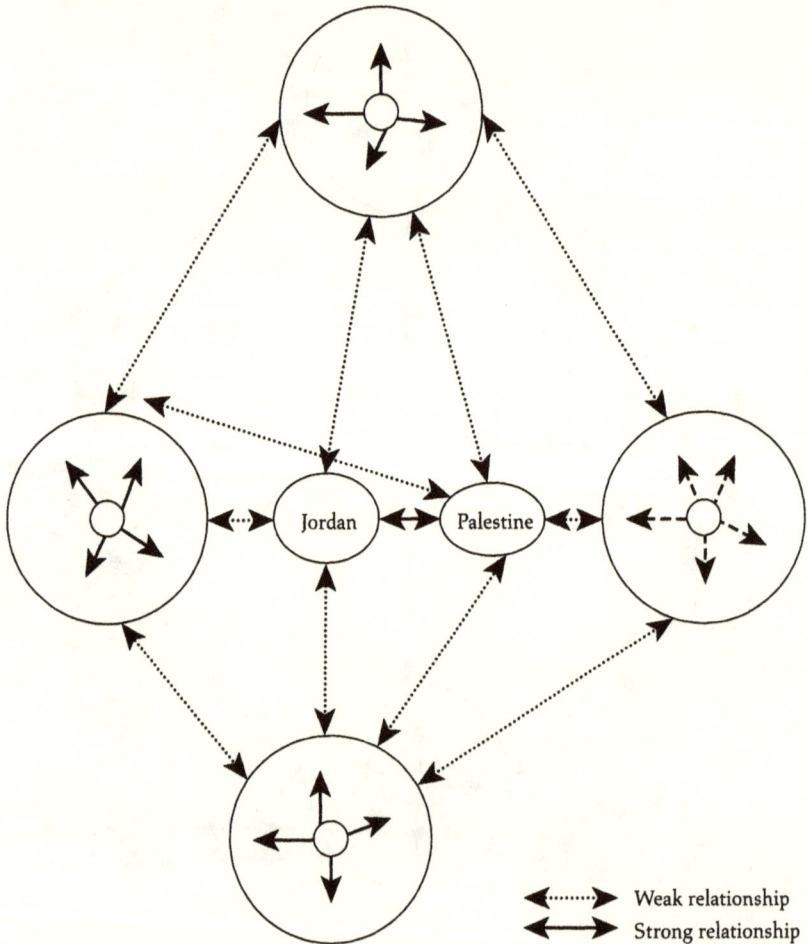

◀┈┈┈┈▶ Weak relationship
◀━━━━▶ Strong relationship

the different level of importance of the Palestinian territories as a center of
gravity. There is a notable difference between the Palestinians originally
from the West Bank and Gaza Strip, and those whose origins are in historical Palestine. The first group remained connected to each other because of
the greater accessibility of the Palestinian Territories. The majority of the
second group, however, have not been allowed, by Israeli Authority, to live
in the Palestinian Territories or even visit their place of origin.

Based upon my studies of Palestinian social and economic networks, I
suggest that Jordan could fulfill the role of a "small" center of gravity. Many

business people from North America and Latin America who were confronted with the unfavorable atmosphere in Palestine transferred their investments to the two countries which are closest to Palestine, Jordan and Egypt. Egypt, however, has until now had a negative policy towards the Palestinians living on its territory. Jordan might constitute a better candidate as the central node of Palestinian networks, since it is the only Arab country that has awarded Palestinian refugees citizenship and has a large Palestinian community. My study found that among the businessmen who decided not to invest in Palestine because of its political and economic situation, some decided to invest in Jordan instead.

However, this potential new center of gravity is actually weaker than the Palestinian Territories, and both would be likely to become even weaker, were they to compete with one another as rivals (see Figure 4.4).

A VERY RECENT PALESTINIAN-NESS

Although the construction of Palestinian identity began after the establishment of the British Mandate in Palestine, the crystallization of this identity —which occurred within a multi-layered context of space and time—is a relatively recent phenomenon (Khalidi 1997). The same can be said for Arab and Israeli identities, which emerged during the same period. Because of the relative tenuousness of this crystallization process, the state in the Arab world became a nationalizing state (*état nationalisant*). "After making Syria, Lebanon, and Jordan, . . . it must make the Syrians, the Lebanese, the Jordanians. . . ." as Bassma Kodmani has suggested (1997:217). The same of course could be said of Israel and the making of the Israelis. Thus, as Morawska argues in relation to Eastern Europe, we are far from a "civic-universalist type of nationalism which has relied in principle on voluntary-commitment and therefore flexible criteria of membership in the national collectivity, and on the legal-democratic, consensual process in resolving inter-group tensions" (1998:8). In our own case, and generally speaking, migrants are not encouraged to (and are often hindered from) declaring allegiance both to their countries of origin and to the host countries. (Hanafi 1997:13, 2001b). This fact informs us of the manner in which some Palestinians are assimilated into the new society, while others retain a sense of non-declared double identity, without adopting feelings of alienation or dissonance.

The weakness of the center of gravity of the Palestinian diaspora, along with the newly established Palestinian national identity, poses many complex questions regarding the specificity of the Palestinian case as diaspora. However, this does not suggest that the Palestinian diaspora is unique in comparison with other diasporas. One of this chapter's objectives is to move away from the mythology of uniqueness, which has characterized many of the previous studies of Palestinian refugees, and to achieve this result, I have examined the Palestinians abroad in the framework of many of the paradigms that are presently categorized in migration studies. This mythology relates not only to the Palestinian scholarly field, but also to a great deal of the research on Israel (Shuval 1998). Indeed, both Israeli and Palestinian scholars employ nomenclature which is overloaded with ideology and unspoken issues in such a way that it blurs the borders between research and policymaking.[16]

REFERENCES

Appadurai, A. 1996. *Modernity at Large: Cultural Dimensions of Globalization.* Minneapolis: University of Minnesota Press.

Basch, L., Schiller, G., Blanc, N., and S. Blanc. 1994. *Nations Unbound: Transnational Projects, Postcolonial Predicaments, and Deterritorialized Nation-States.* New York: Gordon & Breach.

Bashir, B. 2001. *Report on Multiculturalism for the National Center for Mediation and Conflict Resolution.* Ministry of Justice. Unpublished report.

Boltanski, L. 1985. *Les cadres.* Paris: Minuit.

Brennan, T. 1997. *At Home in the World: Cosmopolitanism Now.* Cambridge: Harvard University Press.

Eisenstadt, S. N. 1955. *The Absorption of Immigrants.* Glencoe, Ill.: Free Press.

Friedman, J. 1997. "Global Crises, the Struggle for Cultural Identity and Intellectual Porkbarrelling: Cosmopolitans versus Locals, Ethnics and Nationals in an Era of De-hegemonisation." In *Debating Cultural Hybridity: Multi-Cultural Identities and the Politics of Anti-Racism,* ed. P. Werbner and T. Modood. London and New Jersey: Zed Books.

Glazer, N. 1997. *We Are All Multiculturalists Now.* Cambridge: Harvard University Press.

Goldring, M., and P. Mac Einri. 1989. "La diaspora irlandais." In *Hérodote,* pp. 169–83. Paris: La Découverte / Maspero.

Gonzalez, N. 1992. *Dollar, Dove and Eagle: One Hundred Years of Palestinian Migration to Honduras.* Ann Arbor: University of Michigan Press.

Goodwin-Gill, G. 1983. *The Refugee in International Law.* Oxford: Clarendon Press.

Grillo, R. D. 1998. "Transnational or Postnational?" Unpublished paper presented at the University of Sussex seminars.

Grillo, R., Riccio, B. and Salih, R. 2000. "Introduction." In *Here or There? Contrasting Experiences of Transnationalism: Moroccans and Senegalese in Italy.* Falmer: CDE, University of Sussex.

Hanafi, S. 1995. "Palestiniens de l'exil, réfugiés et hommes d'affaires." *Libération* (Paris), March 25.

———. 1997. *Between Two Worlds: Palestinian Businessmen in the Diaspora and the Construction of a Palestinian Entity.* Cairo: CEDEJ for the French edition and two editions in Arabic: Cairo, Dar al-Mostaqbal al-arabi, and Ramallah, Muwatin.

———. 2000. "The Palestinian Refugees between the Truth and Five Illusions." *Al Hayat* (London), February 17. [Arabic.]

———. 2001a. *Reshaping the Geography: Palestinian Communities Networks in Europe and the New Media.* Cairo: CEDEJ.

———. 2001b. *Here and There: The Palestinian Diaspora from Social and Political Perspective.* Ramallah: Muwatin and Beirut: Institute of Palestinian Study. [Arabic.]

———. 2002. "Flexible Transnational Survival Practices of Palestinian. Transmigrants/Returnees, and Inflexible State Policies: Crafting the Palestinian Extra-territorialized Nation-State." Paper presented at the Third Mediterranean Social and Political Research Meeting, Florence.

———. Forthcoming. "Physical Return, Virtual Return: Palestinian Communities in Europe and the Homeland." In *On the Orbit: The Palestinian Communities in Europe,* ed. A. Shiblak. Oxford: University Press.

Hänsch, A. 1998. "Emigration and Modernity: On the Twofold Liminality and the Religious Responses to Liminality in Arab and Franco-Arab Literature of the 20th Century." Paper presented to the Conference on Self-Image and Image of the Other at the European University Institute in April in Florence.

Harvey, D. 1990. *The Condition of Postmodernity.* London: Blackwell.

Khalidi, R. 1997. *Palestinian Identity: The Construction of Modern National Consciousness.* New York: Columbia University Press.

Kodmani, B. 1997. *La diaspora palestinienne.* Paris: PUF.

Kotkin, J. 1993. *Tribes: How Race, Religion and Identity Determine Success in the New Global Economy.* New York: Random House.

Ma Mung, E., et al. 1998. "La circulation migratoire. Bilan des travaux," *Migrations Etudes* 84:12.

Morawska, E. 1998. "Intended and Unintended Consequences of Forced Migrations: A Neglected Aspect of East Europe's 20th Century History." Paper presented to International Migrations: Geography, Politics and Culture in Europe and Beyond in European University Institute, Florence, February 6.

Morris, B. 1986. *The Birth of the Palestinian Refugee Problem 1947–1949.* Cambridge: Cambridge University Press.

Naficy, H. 1995. "Diasporizing and Globalization: Iranians and Iranian Popular Culture." Paper presented to the Globalisation Conference in the CERI, Paris.

Ong, A. 1999. *Flexible Citizenship: The Cultural Logic of Transnationality.* Durham and London: Duke University Press.

Picard, E. 1998. "Les émigrants et leurs nations. Recompositions identitaires et nouvelles mobilisations des Arabes d'Argentine." In *Les Arabes du Levant en Argentine,* ed. M. Nancy and E. Picard. *Les Cahiers de l'IREMAM,* 11. Aix-en-Provence: IREMAM.

Salih, R. 2000. "Transnational Practices and Normative Constraints Between Morocco and Italy: A Gendered Approach." Unpublished paper presented at the First Mediterranean Social and Political Research Meeting, March 22–26, the Mediterranean Programme of the Robert Schuman Centre at the European University Institute in Florence, Italy.

Sanbar, E. 1989. "La diaspora palestinienne." In *Hérodote,* pp. 71–80. Paris: La Découverte / Maspero.

Schnapper, D. 1994. *La Communauté des citoyens.* Paris: Gallimard.

Shuval, J. 1998. "Israel in the Context of Post-Industrial Migration. The Mythology of 'Uniqueness,'" In *Roots and Routes: Ethnicity and Migration in Global Perspective,* ed. S. Weil. Jerusalem: The Magnes Press, Hebrew University.

Todd, E. 1994. *Le destin des immigrés.* Paris: Seuil.

Warner, D. 1994. "Voluntary Repatriation and the Meaning of Returning Home: A Critique of Liberal Mathematics." *Journal of Refugee Studies* 7(2/3): 160–74.

Wieviorka, M. 1998. "Is Multiculturalism the Solution?" *Ethnic and Racial Studies* 21(5).

Williams, P. 1987. "Les couleurs de l'invisible: Tsiganes dans la banlieue parisienne." In *Chemin de la ville. Enquêtes ethnologiques,* ed. J. Getwirth and C. Petonnet, pp. 53–73. Paris: CTHS.

Zureik, E. 1997. "The Trek Back Home: Palestinians Returning Home and their Problem of Adaptation." In *Constructing Order: Palestinian Adaptation to Refugee Life,* ed. A. Hovdenak et al. Jerusalem: Fafo, Institute for Applied Social Science.

NOTES

Previously published in *Hagar: International Social Science Research,* 4(1) (Spring 2003). Reprinted with permission.

1. This study is part of a larger research program about the social and economic networks of the Palestinian diaspora that I coordinated between 1995 and 2000 at the French Research Center in Cairo, the CEDEJ (Centre d'études et de documentation économiques juridiques et sociales), and Muwatin in Ramallah. See Hanafi 1997, 2001b. The typology employed here is based on 600 interviews of Palestinians in thirteen countries in the period between 1995 and

2000. This article is based on my research and surveys on Palestinians abroad conducted in Jordan, the United Arab Emirates, Egypt, Syria, Israel, Lebanon, Saudi Arabia, the United States, Canada, Chile, the United Kingdom, and Australia.

2. See, for instance, Emmanuel Todd (1994), who defends the goals of assimilation.

3. As an example of this trend, see Dominique Schnapper's *La communauté des citoyens* (1994).

4. David Theo Goldberg's lecture at the Van Leer Institute, Jerusalem, on September 4, 1999, entitled "The Power of Tolerance."

5. For more details about Palestinian transnational economic practices, see Hanafi 2002.

6. United Nations Development Program.

7. The Palestinian refugees did not benefit from the protection allocated by the UNHCR. They received services from United Nations Relief and Works Agency for Palestine refugees in the Middle East (UNRWA). This agency defines a Palestine refugee as "a person whose normal residence was in Palestine for minimum of two years preceding the conflict in 1948 in one of the countries where UNRWA provides relief."

8. This confusion between the legal status and socio-economic position of the category of "refugees" is relevant not only to the Palestinians. For example, when I wrote an article in the French newspaper *Libération* about the economic situation of the Palestinian in exile, the editor changed the title to "The Palestinian in Exile: Refugees and Business People" (Hanafi 1995).

9. See Picard 1998 and Gonzales 1992 for the situation of diasporized Palestinian and Arab community in South America, Hanafi 1997 for North America, and, finally, Hanafi (forthcoming) for Europe.

10. Concerning the general relationship between emigration, exile, and liminality, see the analysis of Anja Hansch (1998) regarding Arab and Franco-Arab literature, and also the analysis of Hamid Naficy (1995), which describes the liminal Iranian exile culture in the United States.

11. In fact, the five Arab nationalities whose governments have opposed the military option against Iraq adopted by the United States and its allies (the Palestinians, Yemenis, Sudanese, Iraqis, and Jordanians) have been subject to a real exodus from the Gulf States, along with many South Asians.

12. According to UN figures, the 1948 Arab-Israeli conflict displaced 726,000 Palestinians, who left Palestine/Israel for the Arab countries.

13. The birth of the refugee issue, and thus the motives of the Palestinian exodus in 1948, was for many years the subject of a highly charged debate between Palestinians and Israelis. If the Arabs consider the exodus as an expulsion from their land, the Israelis consider it voluntary migration resulting from the Arabs' appeal to their "brothers" to move to neighboring Arab countries.

A concealing thesis (which shows the process of expulsion has been occurring in many places) re-emerged with a new generation of Israeli historians such as Benny Morris (1986), Tom Segev, and Ilan Pappé.

14. However, since 1982, the Syrian government has not allowed the PLO to conduct any activities within its borders.

15. Concerning the Popular Front for Palestinian Liberation, for the first time the head of this organization lives in the West Bank. Since the second intifada, for the Hamas and Islamic Jihad, leadership from inside is more important than leadership from those living abroad.

16. While Israeli scholars did not employ the term "refugee" with regard to Jews—since they rejected the idea that Jewish immigrants would be categorized as refugees in their homeland—their Palestinian colleagues used only the term "refugee" in juridical and sociological works, reminding us that the Palestinians abroad "have to return home." Similarly, Palestinian scholars did not use the term "diaspora," since it was seen as replacing the category of refugees. Palestinians are seen as guests in the host countries, while the Israelis see the Jews as exiles in their countries of origin who feel a sense of homecoming upon immigration to Israel. If the choice of categories distinguishes the Palestinian scholars from the Israeli, they both share the perception that Palestinian and Jewish refugees, respectively, can be absorbed evidently and naturally in Palestinian territories and in Israel. The Israeli research focused, especially in the 1950s, 1960s, and 1970s, on the success of immigrant absorption and the associated social and psychological factors. The first book published by S. N. Eisenstadt, in 1954, was entitled *The Absorption of Immigrants*. For a critical point of view of Israeli migration studies, see Shuval 1998.

CHAPTER 5

Transmission and Transformation: The Palestinian Second Generation and the Commemoration of the Homeland

EFRAT BEN-ZE'EV

> It is not the literal past, the "facts" of history, that shape us, but images of the past, embodied in language.
>
> —BRIAN FRIEL [1]

For Palestinians, *Falastin* is a code used in varied contexts. It is present in political speeches, in prose and poetry, and in individuals' recollections of their village springs and wells, agricultural products, mountains, and plains. Its meanings change according to context, as do its alternative names. When talk is more official, it is often also *al-watan*, the homeland. When talk is more intimate, the homeland is also referred to by the actual place of origin— one's village or district name. Often it remains simply Falastin, the magic word that stands for everything for all generations.[2] It is its all-encompassing nature that enables each Palestinian to find in it his/her own meaning. This multiplicity and divergence of meaning is not merely an outcome of each individual's interpretation, but rather an outcome of specific group orientation. The attitude to Palestine is influenced by places of exile, by the fate of social classes (on these, see Bowman 1994), and it is exceptionally evident in the passage from one generation to the next.

For those who were actually uprooted, the lost homeland is concrete and palpable—a home and its dispersed family, a certain landscape and a plot of land. In contrast, for those born in the diaspora (meaning here any place outside of the village of origin, even within Israel's borders), the homeland has to be configured. Whereas the former have explicit memories that link their pre-1948 past to their present daily lives, the latter must commemorate rather than remember. Of course, the commemoration of the younger generation is based on the transmitted memories of the older. In the process of transmission, the dense autobiographic memory of those who remember the

homeland is thinned out, leaving the listeners, those who have not personally known Palestine, with sets of images that stand for the homeland. In this
chapter, I outline the position taken by members of "the second generation"
towards their parents' memories, and their perspective towards and commemoration of their villages of origin and their homeland.

In *The Sociology of Knowledge*, the classic collection influenced by the
World War I upheaval, Karl Mannheim argues that a generation becomes
an "actuality" not simply as an age cohort but through "a concrete bond,"
"created between members of a generation by their being exposed to the social and intellectual symptoms of a process of dynamic de-stabilization"
([1952] 1972:303). Renato Rosaldo, writing on Philippine Ilongot historical
rendering, further adds that the creation of a generational unity is an outcome not only of external structural conditions, but also of the shared interpretation and similar self-perception of its members: "When a number of
individuals reorient their lives in relation to certain historical events that
impinge upon them over a particular span of time . . . they emerge to a
greater or lesser degree as an identifiable group within their larger society"
(1980:111). Rosaldo, like Mannheim, argues that cohort "traits" become
more evident under shifting historical conditions (1980:112).

The members of the "second-generation" Palestinian cohort discussed
here, who were born in exile between the 1950s and 1970s, share a similar
structural setting despite their different places of exile. Their biographies
have been influenced by the harsh conditions of the early years in refugee
camps, and later, by the gradual emergence of political and military organizations during the 1960s and 1970s.[3] While the Palestinian deliberations and
practical choices in the 1960s and 1970s have previously been discussed
(Sayigh 1979; Harkabi 1979), this presentation considers the intergenerational dynamic and the emergence of the "second generation" as agents of
commemoration. Commemoration practices emerge as a generational response articulated under the conditions of intra-generational multivocality.

This discussion is based on fieldwork conducted among Palestinian families uprooted from villages along the coastal area of Mount Carmel. Fieldwork was conducted in Jordan, the Palestinian Territories, and Israel, mainly
between 1996 and 1998, though the author's relations have continued with
some of the interlocutors to this day. The discussion is biased towards the interpretations of the more educated interviewees. These interviewees were
not only more willing to meet me and exchange ideas, they also were exceptionally eloquent in explaining their critical outlook towards their past.

Becoming Transglobal

Randa was born in 1958 to one of the few families from the village of Tiret Haifa who managed to remain within Israel following the 1948 war, on land adjacent to their village. As she began talking she clarified this uniqueness, saying: "My parents did not leave the village on time," namely in the summer of 1948, when the "Israel Defense Force" captured Tiret Haifa and the great majority of its 5,000 inhabitants were uprooted and dispersed, mainly to Lebanon, Jordan, and Syria. In 1979, when the area where Randa's family lived and tilled the land on the outskirts of the city of Haifa was turned into an industrial zone, they were forced to move. This belated uprooting caused financial difficulties to her family of thirteen—parents, grandfather, and ten children—having lost their houses and sources of income. Despite the family's hardship, Randa was married in Haifa and completed a first and second degree in social work at the University of Haifa.

Randa's life history is atypical, for though she was born after 1948, she was brought up while her parents were still farmers (as in the "old times," before 1948) and she personally experienced the meaning of uprooting. This unusual history placed her in a position of being strongly attached to her parents, grandparents, and the peasant way of life, on the one hand, and yet able to reflect on the changes from her new place as an urban, educated Palestinian refugee, no longer living with her extended family, on the other. She recounted how, after the establishment of the State of Israel, her grandfather's Jewish partner tricked him into signing a document which was supposedly an exchange of land but actually was a yielding up of his land. Her grandfather, she said (while imitating the act), signed with his thumb. She further explained:

> I can say that I am angry with my family, with my grandfather, yet on the other hand, I look at it historically . . . at what the Turks and British have done, and people's ignorance. They did not study. The Jews came from Europe with everything that was there, with their education and class. They were different and had seen the large world while people here were sitting under trees. . . . It was different—the fact that someone can't even sign his name but signs with his thumb.

What Randa suggested implicitly was that, unlike her parents, she is educated and better understands the big world. Jihad, some years younger than Randa and also born to parents from Tiret Haifa, pronounced these points explicitly. Jihad was born in the early 1960s in Issefiyyeh, a Druze village not

far from the ruins of Tiret Haifa. He earned his first and second degrees at
the University of Haifa and worked as a high school teacher. Having previously heard from his parents of my research, he dropped by their home
while I was there in order to clarify a few points. He would not shake my
hand, for religious reasons, and was unwilling to be recorded.[4] He warned
me not to listen to his parents because, he asserted, their generation is naïve,
emotional, and irrational, unable to "read" world politics, and he offered two
pieces of advice. One was "Be objective!"—or at least aim at objectivity, and
the other was "See the macro!"—the long-term processes, not the micro,
short-term picture.[5]

The criticism of the generation of the parents (known as *Jil al-Nakba*,
"the Nakba generation") became even more apparent in the younger generation's examination of the actions the older generation undertook during the
1948 war. Nihad, born in the 1960s, a statistician whose family (uprooted
from 'Ain Hawd) found refuge in a West Bank refugee camp, commented on
the conduct of his parents' decision to withdraw from the village before it
was captured by the Israeli army. He said that even if he could comprehend
and accept his parents' account of the war, their thinking that they would be
able to return in a week or two, he still considers them "very simple." "They
shouldn't have left," he stated bluntly, and the implications for his generation were clear: "We will not be simple forever."

This contrast should be understood within the context of a wide educational divide between the Nakba generation and their children. Whereas
many of the women of the parents' generation are illiterate, and few of the
men ever reached high school, many members of the second generation
completed higher education (Tibawi 1956; Graham-Brown 1984). Hence, the
shift from one generation to the other is a shift from a predominantly oral
to a fully literate society. The narratives of the second generation are inter-
spersed with information gathered from newspapers and books. For instance,
when 'Abd al-Ghani, in his early thirties, was describing the events of the
1936–39 revolt in 'Ain Hawd, he noted that he knew the names of the rebels
from a book that he had read.

This literacy divide is further accentuated by the fact that, whereas the
parental generation grew up in a rural agricultural society, the second generation was born in towns and large refugee camps—that is, in urban envi-
ronments. Globalization affected the Palestinians in the diaspora; popular
literature and mass media, with their unifying images, were disseminated
through the circulation of books and newspapers, as well as the growing
availability of radios and later television.[6] The consequences of this diffusion—somewhat like the spread of print technology described by Benedict

Anderson for another time and place—in addition to the spread of literacy, altered the Palestinian situation and created a shared language that transcends locality.[7]

Not only were the members of the second generation exposed to transnational literature and images, their existence demanded that they too become transnational, acquiring what Weingrod and Levy have called "diasporic features." Palestinians are a "classic" diaspora, and yet they also embody postmodern features. Many have been uprooted from one place of exile to another. To give just two examples, tens of thousands who grew up in Lebanon have been forced to leave since the 1970s due to the civil war, the Israeli invasion, and harsh government working restrictions. Another case of mass uprooting is that of the tens of thousands of Palestinians who migrated to the Gulf States for better prospects of work, and yet never acquired citizenship there. Many were forced to flee following the 1991 Gulf Crisis. Palestinians are transitional and transglobal, mainly within the confines of the Middle East, but some even beyond it.

As an outcome of these movements, we can argue that some of the Palestinian second generation have more than one homeland. Indeed, even if Lebanon did not feel like a homeland to Palestinian refugees who were born there, some expressed yearning for it after they were forced to leave it. Tony Hanania, born of Palestinian descent in Lebanon in 1964 and currently based in London, describes in his first novel, *Homesick* (1997), his longing for Beirut from the distance of his boarding school in England. His second novel, *Unreal City* (1999), also deals with Beirut, though Palestine appears in it as a rather distant entity. In their introduction to this volume, Weingrod and Levy ask whether a place can be both a homeland and a diaspora, and here we find a striking example.

Transmission Disturbances

Many Palestinians of the second generation fit the traits that James Clifford (1997) attributes to key informants: they are hybrids, products and mediators of different places and cultures, incorporating both "the traveler" and "the native." Their biographies are accumulations of the "spaces in between" described by Levy and Weingrod in the Introduction. Firas, one such individual, embodies the combination of having been born in poverty yet having achieved a higher education, of being a traveler and a native, an insider and an outsider. He was born in Irbid's refugee camp (in the north of Jordan) in 1956 to a family from Tiret Haifa whose single room was shared by thirteen family members. He recalled the dripping ceiling in the winters, the biting cold inside the room, and the heater that leaked gas and "would kill everybody." However, as time went by, Firas's oldest brother, twenty years his senior, succeeded in business and the family's economic situation improved. Thanks to his brother's financial support, Firas completed a first and second degree in Jordan and then left for the United States, where he earned a doctoral degree and later became a university professor. Firas noted that he felt like an outsider to his own culture, having lived in the States for the last fifteen years. We met when Firas and his family came to Jordan on a summer vacation. Our meeting was in the home of Abu Majed, who had previously been Firas's university teacher and was a friend of his older brother.[8] The presence of Firas's teacher as well as his older brother triggered a lively discussion on the generational gap.

FIRAS: The old generation, they still have the memory of it [life in
              Palestine prior to the uprooting]. So they are not willing to
              give up. That's in their mind. . . .
              [Turning to Abu Majed] Abu Majed, I don't think they want to
              talk about it very openly?
ABU MAJED: They select.
EFRAT: What do they select?
FIRAS: For that particular story, they tell you the entire story, but
              they are not willing to continue telling stories if those stories
              . . . if those stories are not relevant for that particular setting.
ABU MAJED: [cannot be heard]
FIRAS: Things, they start coming back pretty quickly. So when they
              tell a story and they say—O.K., I don't want to talk about it.
              After they finish the story they say, "I don't wanna talk about
              it," so they change the subject. But if somebody starts [talking of the village or] if there is a joke [that reminds one of the
              village, they will talk of it]. Most of the stories they tell, it's
              about their social life, the way they used to function on a daily
              basis; what happened to them on a daily basis.

Firas feels distanced from his parents' old world, cognizant of the alterations that begin with the narrator; events are being reshaped and edited by the older people. Not everything is said, and he is precluded from understanding the elders. Sensing that the totality of their life cannot be transmitted, Firas feels that he is left with a puzzle that has missing pieces:

There is a story that my mom told me before I came here about the shepherd who was taking care of the sheep in the Carmel, [in] Wadi Falah or somewhere [around] there.[9] And she said: "Three guys tried to take three small sheep with them; to steal them. [It was] about two-three miles away from the group of sheep." She said: "Five minutes later, those sheep ran away from the thieves and came back" and I was laughing. You know, these are the types of stories they tell. And when I hear this, I start laughing and the way they look at it is from a pure religious point of view. You know, my mom said: "Because we paid *zakaa* [alms], because we paid *zakaa*, God told the sheep to come back and join the group."[10] So I was laughing. And she said: "Well, our neighbors didn't pay *zakaa* and thieves came and stole them and took them away." And I was just laughing and she thought I didn't believe what she was talking about.

Firas was not primarily concerned with the veracity of this tale. What seemed to preoccupy him was his distance from his mother's world. He recognized the cleft dividing him from his mother in terms of conceptualizing events in a rational versus a religious framework. Moreover, he was bothered by his unfamiliarity with the environment she was describing, since he had never visited the site of Tiret Haifa. As he stated earlier, the autobiographical recollections of his parents' generation were triggered by daily reminders and never delivered in their completeness; he kept discovering new details, "stories," as he termed them, which he never knew about the village:

EFRAT: Can you imagine what the village looked like?
FIRAS: Even imagining was pretty tough for me. You know . . . we did not . . . for example, in Jordan or anywhere, we did not live around cows and horses. So I don't know it. And their life was different; the lifestyle was different. So when they tell a story, it looks like it's a story—a story that I did not live. They lived it. . . . They tell about the sea, for example. My brother said: "when we used to go to school, you looked from the school window and the sea is there." So [I think] "Wow." We lived in Irbid and the only sea we've seen is the Dead Sea and you have to drive all the way down. . . . So when he said it, I said: "Wow, what kind of a childhood you had there."

The inability of the older generation to explain these childhood experiences to their children, and specifically the feeling of the Mediterranean Sea, is picturesquely expressed in Omar al-Qattan's film *Dreams and Silences*. The protagonist, a Palestinian uprooted from the Mediterranean city of Jaffa in 1948 who spent her life in refugee camps in Jordan, takes a trip with her son to the Dead Sea. While they sit on the seashore, her son asks her: "Is the sea there more beautiful?" and she replies: "There is no comparison. This is a dead sea, can't you see it? If only you could see the sea of Jaffa."[11]

Firas, in spite of his feeling of detachment, expressed his urge to learn and to draw from the older people—those who knew Palestine—what he could not gather through direct knowledge of the place. One of the aims of his vacation in Irbid was to bring together his children and his mother, so that her "stories" would take root in his children. His choice of the word "stories" for what he had learnt from his mother about the village can be illuminated by Walter Benjamin's assertion that a story is committed to memory if "its comprehension involves immediate integration into the experience of the listener" (in Andrew Benjamin 1989:123). The listener bears the story from there on, and its imprint is new and unique. The stories of Firas's mother were incorporated into his and his children's experience, albeit in a different context from what they had for his mother.

Some members of the second generation explicitly attested to a liberty—perhaps better termed a void—they have in adapting and redefining their link to Palestine. In *The Social Production of Space*, Henri Lefebvre argues that "groups . . . cannot constitute themselves, or recognize one another, as 'subjects' unless they generate (or produce) a space" ([1974] 1991:416). One option available, and only to some Palestinians, is to visit Palestine and the obliterated village in order to produce a common identity through the place.

The Village as Homeland?

A better understanding of village life becomes possible for second-generation refugees when they visit the village site with their parents. The "stories" become more tangible through the encounter with the relics—stone fences still erect, fruit trees, graveyards, or remnants of houses. Yet when Tareq described his travels to Falastin, he noted that the visit to the village site can create a dilemma. Tareq was born in 1967 in Jordan, completed a first degree at the University of Yarmuk in Irbid, and subsequently was stationed by the Jordanian Ministry of Education as a teacher in the southern city of Ma'an. While we were sitting on the second floor of an Irbid Café, he recounted how a couple of years earlier he and his father had traveled together to Palestine. On the day his father wanted to see the ruins of al-Tireh, Tareq refused to come along:[12]

> For me, it's a good dream in the past. It's my dad's country. And he was crying there [in a place not far from the village, where their relatives reside]

saying: "We used to go from here riding a donkey and bring some things from the fields and go back." And I said: "Well, no, I'm not going." I just told them "go" and they did that. I didn't want to see my father in pain, you know, maybe that's why I didn't go with him. But had I the chance to go there alone, with someone from my relatives there, I would.

However, a little later, Tareq related the same episode in a different manner: "As for the village, I went there [to Palestine] but I didn't go to the village because I thought that if I did, I would be too much related to it." Whereas in the first instance Tareq avoided his father's reactions to a visit, in the second he refrained from establishing a direct link to the village landscape. As transpired from our ongoing discussion that included an e-mail correspondence, Tareq was torn between maintaining some of his father's concepts of the village and establishing a new approach, and was bothered by his preoccupation with the past:

> I don't want to be living in the past. I think this is an Arabian principle or doctrine. They are living in the past. So O.K., we want Khaled bin al-Walid to come back to free Jerusalem and we want 'Omar Ibn al-Khatab and we want. . . . I mean, I am looking ahead for the future and I say, I don't look for the past as much as I expect more from the future to come.

Tareq was arguing not simply with a current Palestinian agenda, but with an age-old Arab legacy of nostalgia, mainly expressed as a literary genre (Meisami 1998). Linking this nostalgic discourse to political evaluations based on historical comparisons (such as the one made between the Crusaders and the Zionists), he wanted to free himself from certain pre-defined notions.

His younger brother, Hisham, who was present and yet silent during our Irbid Café talk, was irritated by this attitude. Hisham married young, and due to economic constraints he did not go on to higher education and currently worked in his father's butcher shop. He interrupted and rejected Tareq's unswerving dissociation from his parents, saying that "he who has nothing old, has nothing new" (*illi ma 'indosh 'atiq, ma 'indosh jdid*):

HISHAM: If you have children you will raise them to be Palestinians, to know about the village. . . . To raise our children to go back to Palestine, where they came from, where their grandfathers came from. You know, Palestine is their land; their right to go back. . . . Even if you ask Murad, my son, who is four years old, where are you from? He will say—I am from Palestine, from Haifa, from al-Tireh. . . . I taught him. I told him that you are Palestinian.

Your father is Palestinian, your grandfather is Palestinian. We
have a land in al-Tireh. We have a house in al-Tireh also. It's our
land and we are here nothing but "a refugee." . . . I want him to
go back in a political way, in a war way, in a peace way. In any
way it's possible.

The disagreement that surfaced between Tareq and Hisham is an instance
of what Karl Mannheim termed as *polar forms* within the same cohort. According to Mannheim, because the "location," in its abstract meaning, uni-
fies the entire cohort, the polar forms are still oriented towards one another
(1952:304–8). In today's terminology we would say that Hisham and Tareq
personify the multivocality within their cohort. Tareq's argumentation deserves further exploration because of its experimental nature—because he
seeks new forms of historical interpretation. Munir, older (b. 1953) and politically more experienced than Tareq, expressed Tareq's views evocatively. In
our first meetings he argued in a sweeping fashion against the Palestinian
fascination with history, echoing the popular proverb "What had passed,
died" (*illi fat mat*):

MUNIR: The truth is that I am not interested in the history of way back.
        I became interested only in 1978 [when he got personally involved
        in the fate of his village]. That's it. I didn't bother to inquire about
        things that happened earlier. No. I knew from here and there but
        it didn't attract me. Indeed, it is interesting but there are others
        who are preoccupied with it. . . . I wasn't a good pupil in history.
        I didn't like history, amongst other things that I disliked. All these
        *jabar*s (strongmen) and wars. He did this to him and the con-
        quests. He conquered this. And Turkey was here and then wasn't.
        It didn't appeal to me. The Battle of Yarmuk or any other battle.
        Why does it matter who won and who lost? Goliath and the
        Philistines, that's what they call it. Who cares? He hit him and
        finally, he killed him. What's all this nonsense. . . . I truly think—
        why should I care about them? If there was a war, it is finished.
        That's it. *Khalas.*

Munir personified a contradiction. On the one hand, he declared a dis-
like towards history; on the other, he also established a large classified and
computerized archive adjacent to his home, to which he dedicated many
hours. On another occasion he further demonstrated this dissonance. He
refrained from telling me stories of 1948, claiming that his knowledge was
limited since he had never been interested. Nevertheless, he asked me to tell

him what I had heard about the 1948 events in his village of origin and in its district.

Some time later, when I mentioned these contradictions to him, he acknowledged the inconsistency. What he had hoped, he said, was to achieve liberty from overriding conceptualizations of the past. He was rebelling mainly against two historical strands, one of which was the mainstream Zionist version created by the State of Israel. To demonstrate what he meant by this, he gave the example of the Jewish discourse that emphasizes a return to the holy land after two millennia. Such a discourse, he argued, compelled the Palestinians to respond and seek more ancient roots to prove their long-lasting attachment to the land. He also rejected the definitions imposed on him by the Jewish-Israeli state. Once he defined himself as someone who has been "Hebraized": *hit'avrateti*, he noted in his creative Hebrew. Such a stand was against the state's policy of maintaining the Arabs within their own separate identity enclave. Recently, while we were talking about Jewish and Arab perceptions of spaces, he commented that "Jewish Israel" wants to define him as a Palestinian in Israel, while he actually sees himself as an Israeli in Palestine.

The historicity that he opposed, though less vehemently than the preceding one, was that of his parents' generation. He was intolerant towards the old people's stories, claiming that they hold a "mythic-historical version of the past." Yet again, he was not uninformed of these mythic histories, of legends and proverbs passed in the family. Munir was trying, concomitantly, to preserve and transform traditional elements. For example, he detested the way his grandfather tried to control him after his father's death, yet at home he maintained patriarchic norms, making decisions regarding his wife's movements, his daughters' marriage, and his son's salary. His ambivalence, I propose, is a supplement to his (James) Cliffordian hybridity, exemplified in his biography, extensive political involvement, and perhaps most of all, his residence in the new village of 'Ain Hawd.

Munir's grandfather Abu Hilmi established the new village of 'Ain Hawd on his agriculture land, two kilometers east of the original village, shortly after the original 'Ain Hawd was depopulated in July 1948. As the years passed, the temporary shelters were turned into permanent homes, yet the State of Israel refused to recognize it as a village, denying it access to electricity, water supply, a sewage system, a paved road, or direction signs to the village. Meanwhile, Jews settled in the old village of 'Ain Hawd and turned it into an artists' village, giving it a Hebrew name that sounds like the Arabic one—'Ain Hod. Despite the difficult conditions at home, Munir completed an engineering degree at a prestigious Israeli institution, and in 1978 became involved in the struggle to win recognition for his village. When he discovered that the problem existed throughout the country, he established the Association of Forty, which united all of the unrecognized villages.[13]

The new village of 'Ain Hawd is another example of a place that is both a homeland and a diaspora. Its inhabitants daily witness their family's pre-1948 property in Jewish hands (since the old village is just below their new village), yet their pronounced struggle is for the recognition of their new village, not for a return to the old one. Indeed, they would be persecuted in Israel if they were to act in favor of the right of return. Yet there is something beyond fear in the choice they vocalize. It may be the daily encounter with the changes in their village of origin that makes them realize that a return would mean uprooting Jewish people; they may wish to settle for their current homes, for which they have struggled all their lives; what is more, the new village is on the family's aboriginal land, enjoying the aura of the old 'Ain Hawd, only two kilometers away. Even other ex-villagers who reside further away tend to perceive the new village of 'Ain Hawd as a "center."

Perhaps it is not accidental that Munir, who is offering a compromise in terms of the right of return, is also the most dedicated archivist. Putting the case in French sociologist Pierre Nora's terms, when history accelerates and takes over, causing a break with the past, few sites of living memory persist and preserve a sense of continuity. "Modern memory is, above all, archival," writes Nora (1989:13). When the older generation's conduct is rejected, when their lively memories are perceived as distant and difficult to grasp, when the homeland cannot serve as a center, the members of the second generation create other ways to remember.

Yet, as was already noted, the process is not smooth, and the responsive nature of commemoration is not only a reaction against the older generation but also a competition over content and method among members of the same generation. The heart of the issue here, much as in Michael Herzfeld's study of antiquities commemoration in Rethemnos, Crete, is "an intense argument over the definition—and above all the control—of history. Whose history is at stake? *Which* history is at stake?" (1991:53–54). Whereas Herzfeld's Cretan citizens compete with the Greek state, the Palestinians operate from different locations. The Palestinian state is too weak to create and disseminate dominant images through school curricula, state rituals, and other bureaucratic means. In this absence, Palestinian individuals and institutions throughout the world become memory agents who develop new mechanisms to condense the memory of the homeland.

Abstract Homelands

In her book *The Object of Memory*, Susan Slyomovics meticulously presents and analyzes the innovative ways in which Palestinians and Jews reproduce their past for the very same place, a place that we have already encountered, the pre-1948 Arab 'Ain Hawd and the newly established Jewish Israeli 'Ain Hod. Slyomovics focuses on the Arab-Jewish rivalry and shows the discourse and the means used by each side to present and justify its own version of the past. She shows, with great detail and penetration, the diffusion of memory practices, examining a variety of Palestinian memory sites such as privately and officially produced memorial books, maps drawn from memory, visits to the village site, the men's clubs established among diasporic Palestinian communities, and the poetry and prose created to commemorate and reconstruct the loss. Slyomovics is impressed by the memorial books genre, which "allows different kinds of chronologies to represent the passage of time." She dedicates a long discussion to 'Ain Hawd's memorial book, published as part of a series by Bir Zeit University, noting that

> In the case of memorial books, contributors-authors and readers overlap. They reconstruct pre-1948 Palestinian villages from fragments of oral history, folk history, personal narrative, photographs and kinship charts that also have a quality of the imagined, stretching back as they do to the twelfth century. All these memories and artifacts of memory embody a communal view of what might have happened in the past . . .
>
> The narrative voice that tells the tale in the memorial book presupposes that narrator and listener know the entire story in advance. The important point is that the memorial book allows different kinds of chronologies to represent the passage of time: the lore of a community, mythic time operating synchronically or diachronically, kinship charts for genealogical time, reminiscences of cultural life, and so on. (1998:28)

The major reason for the preservation of all these parallel chronologies is that they are an outcome of the tensions surrounding the reconstruction of a single community narrative. Their unification within a memorial book does not solve the disagreements.[14] Quite a few people of 'Ain Hawd, especially men who see themselves as carriers of history, disapproved of the memorial book on the grounds that it discussed the history of some family branches and neglected others, and that the people who were interviewed were unreliable. In addition, many did not like the memorial book literary genre—specifically, the inclusion of fables, tales, and information that bordered on gossip. One man said it was written in an "American" style. Others argued that some of the contents are not things to be registered in print. There is always much potential for strife when oral history is turned into literature (Shryock 1997). "What might have happened" is a contested terrain and different reconstructions do not necessarily fit together, nor do the readers necessarily agree with the contributors-authors.

Yet despite the internal disagreements, Palestinian commemoration has been prospering in the last decade, especially in three genres. I will mention them only briefly. The first is a sweeping fashion of collecting (and reading) written testimonies on the village, as the case of Munir epitomizes. This is, of course, linked to the educational revolution between the two generations that was mentioned earlier. Archival documents (such as lists of the families in each village from the late Ottoman time, British village censuses, old maps and correspondence of families with the authorities) are amongst the most sought after commodities. Bringing copies of these documents as a gift was one of the best ways to establish reciprocity between my interlocutors and myself. Nabil (born in the 1950s), of new 'Ain Hawd, asked for Von Muelinen's book on the ancient remains at Mount Carmel; Tawfiq (born in the late 1950s), also of 'Ain Hawd, showed me an old photograph of the women of Tantura, asking if I could supply him with documents on the massacre in Tantura for a newspaper article he was preparing. Some of the most dedicated collectors compile village ethnographies. These ethnographies, much as in the case of the memorial book discussed by Slyomovics, attract intra-communal criticism, yet they continue to flourish.

A second popular commemorative genre are Internet sites, both those dedicated to Palestine in general and those concentrating on specific villages. On these websites, ex-villagers and their descendants can establish social ties across borders that cannot be crossed, and post messages and photographs. To demonstrate the proliferation of this electronic medium in the last seven years: when I began the study on the Carmel villages in the summer of 1996, there were only five Web citations for the village of Ijzim. In the summer of 2004, there were 670.

The third prospering genre consists of films—amateur videotapes, documentaries, and fictional films. Amateur films made during visits to the obliterated village are taken back home, usually to a community distant from the village (e.g., in Jordan, Lebanon, or Syria), and screened to a crowd of family and friends. These settings trigger a lively nostalgic discussion, yet they too reveal the divergence of the memories of individuals who left the village half a century earlier, as well as the gap between the "remembered village" and the landscape as it is nowadays. A second category within this genre is commercial cinematographic productions, mainly documentaries. Tens of films have been produced in the last decade.[15]

This thriving wave of popular commemorations cannot be ascribed simply to the availability of new technologies. Even in their absence, archives and village ethnographies and memorial books could have been produced all along, yet they have blossomed only over the last decade. I would argue that the cardinal reason for their emergence is the generational shift. For the first generation of exile, the village and the locality always loomed as the main social framework. For those who had lived there, the village was a central point of reference, a palpable and fairly well framed environment. It is for the village that the first generation in exile longed, and it is the village to which they felt that they belonged. In contrast, the second generation has to recapture the past so that when voices fade away, there will be a permanently available record. To this end, new methods are developed and substitutes for a homeland are enveloped in books and viewed on television and computer screens.

REFERENCES

Benjamin, Andrew. 1989. "Tradition and Experience: Walter Benjamin's 'On Some Motifs in Baudelaire.'" In *The Problems of Modernity: Adorno and Benjamin*, ed. Andrew Benjamin, pp. 122–40. London: Routledge.

Bowman, Glenn. 1994. "'A Country of Words': Conceiving the Palestinian Nation from the Position of Exile," in *The Making of Political Identities*, ed. Ernesto Laclau, pp. 138–70. London: Verso. Also on the web: http://www.ukc.ac.uk/anthropology/staff/glenn/Laclau.html (August 2004).

Clifford, James. 1997. "Traveling Cultures." In *Routes: Travel and Translation in the Late Twentieth Century*, ed. James Clifford. Cambridge, Mass.: Harvard University Press.

Graham-Brown, Sara. 1984. *Education, Repression and Liberation: Palestinians*. London: World University Service.

Hanania, Tony. 1997. *Homesick*. London: Bloomsbury.

———. 1999. *Unreal City*. London: Bloomsbury.

Harkabi, Yehoshafat. 1979. *Hafalestinim mitardema lehitorerut* [The Palestinians from quiescence to awakening]. Jerusalem: Magnes.

Herzfeld, Michael. 1991. *A Place in History: Social and Monumental Time in a Cretan Town*. Princeton: Princeton University Press.

Lefebvre, Henri. 1991 [1974]. *The Production of Space*. Translated by Donald Nicholson-Smith. Oxford: Blackwell.

Mannheim, Karl. 1952. *Essays on the Sociology of Knowledge*. London: Routledge and Kegan Paul Ltd.

Meisami, Julie Scott. 1998. "Places in the Past: The Poetics/Politics of Nostalgia." *Edebiyat* 8:63–106.

Nora, Pierre. 1989. "Between Memory and History: Les Lieux de Mémoire." *Representations* 26:7–25.

Rosaldo, Renato. 1980. *Ilongot Headhunting 1983–1974: A Study in Society and History*. Stanford: Stanford University Press.

Sayigh, Rosemary. 1979. *Palestinians: From Peasants to Revolutionaries*. London: Zed Press.

Schudson, Michael. 1995. "Dynamics of Distortion in Collective Memory." In *Memory Distortion: How Minds, Brains and Societies Reconstruct the Past*, ed. Daniel Schacter, pp. 346–64. Cambridge, Mass.: Harvard University Press.

Shryock, Andrew. 1997. *Nationalism and the Genealogical Imagination*. Berkeley: University of California Press.

Slyomovics, Susan. 1998. *The Object of Memory: Arabs and Jews Narrate the Palestinian Village*. Philadelphia: University of Pennsylvania Press.

Tibawi, Abdul Latif. 1956. *Arab Education in Mandatory Palestine*. London: Luzac & Company.

NOTES

1. Brian Friel, quoted in the *International Herald Tribune*, October 2, 1987.

2. I use the terms "Falastin" and "Palestine" interchangeably: "Falastin" is used when describing from the Palestinian point of view.

3. See Rosemary Sayigh 1979 on Lebanon and Yehoshafat Harkabi 1979 on intellectual developments with regard to Palestine throughout the Arab world. In Israel, Palestinians organized in Arab political parties with difficulty, due to the state's prevention of the establishment of non-Zionist parties. In Jordan, Palestinians were armed until September 1970, when the Jordanian army crushed their militias.

4. Jihad's refusal to be recorded was exceptional. "I wish to write those things in my own book," was his pretext.

5. Michael Schudson writes that generally "there tends to be a loss of emotional intensity" along generational transmission (1995:348).

6. Before 1948, there were few radios in the villages, and all were owned by the wealthy and prominent men. Villagers would gather at these homes to listen together.

7. In a critique of Benedict Anderson, Glenn Bowman argues that it is not the mere existence of a text—a shared commodity—that creates a shared imagined community but the common subjectivity imagined through the text (1994:6).

8. Firas's elderly mother did not wish to meet me, and that is why we met in Abu Majed's home. I was told that she had sarcastically commented, "they

have chased us out of Palestine and now they are coming to search for us as far as Jordan."

9. Wadi Falah, literally meaning "the thriving valley," begins at the heart of the Carmel ridge, between the two Druze villages, and comes out of the mountain near 'Atlit Prison. Firas's family owned large plots in this valley, which was the southern boundary of Tiret Haifa's land.

10. Meaning either charity in general or an obligatory donation of food-stuffs required at the end of Ramadan, the month of fasting (*zakat al-Fiter*). To give *zakaa* is one of the "five pillars" of Islam.

11. *Dreams and Silences*, directed by Omar al-Qattan, Sindibad Films, London, 1991.

12. The interview with Tareq and his brother Hisham was conducted in English; hence, the language mistakes remain in the text.

13. The Association of Forty is so named because it was established forty years after the founding of the State of Israel. See its Web site: <http://www.assoc40.org/index_main.html>.

I use the term "unrecognized" for the village of 'Ain Hawd, although Israeli Minister of Interior Aryeh Deri officially recognized it in 1992. Since 1992 the bureaucracies involved, such as the local municipality, the National Parks Association, and The Jewish National Fund, have disagreed on the outline plan, and the village remains neglected.

14. In note 86, pp. 227–28, Slyomovics does briefly mention that Sharif Kanaana, co-author of the monograph on 'Ain Hawd, was aware of a disagreement that arose among the villagers following the compilation of the book regarding the family's genealogy.

15. Some of the themes of Palestinian films in recent years: the disintegration of families in Nizar Hasan's *Ustura* (1997); meetings between refugee children along the Israel-Lebanon border in Mai Masri's *Frontiers of Dream and Fears* (2001); visits to obliterated villages in Ra'anan Alexandrovitz's *The Internal Voyage* (2001); on 'Ain Hawd see Rachel Lea Jones's *500 Dunam on the Moon* (2002).

CHAPTER 6

Diasporization, Globalization, and Cosmopolitan Discourse

JONATHAN FRIEDMAN

One of the most common concepts currently in fashion among globalizing academics and intellectuals is "diasporization." It is in some ways the most obviously concrete manifestation of globalization itself, the movement of culturally identified peoples across the world. It is a direct expression of the globalization metaphor itself in all of its diffusionist connotations. Toynbee in his *Study of History* predicted that in the future worldwide diasporas would replace nation-states. Appadurai has recently made a similar statement (1996), and a similar diagnosis is made in innumerable postcolonial discourses of the future state of the globalized world. The notion of diaspora has a rather long and confusing history. In the Old Testament it is used to refer to Greek colonization. Later it was used to refer to the Jewish dispersal from the homeland Israel by imperial powers. It has been used to refer, following this definition, to all groups that define themselves as having been dispersed throughout the wider world by expanding state and imperial powers. Currently the word is often used to refer to all transnational social formations. Some would take issue with this and call for a restriction of the term to a more clearly delineated phenomena, and it might well be argued that the word has become uselessly diluted. I do not intend to enter into a discussion of definitions. I choose instead to use the term without defining it precisely, quite simply because it is not a theoretical term as such but part of the self-definition and definition of social phenomena by those who participate in them. What is crucial is that we are able to distinguish the enormous differences in the phenomena to which the term is applied. In what follows I shall be attempting to work out some of these differences and to argue for a slight change in focus in their comprehension.

A World on the Move?

It is commonly assumed that the world is on the move today in a way that was not the case in previous generations, and it is surely this that has meta-phorically extended the meaning of the term diasporic into new domains. This may indeed be the experience of many intellectuals and not least aca-demics (Friedman and Randeira 2004). Certainly global media and global tourism, via the increasing speed and cost-efficiency of transport, have made larger portions of the real globe accessible to increasing numbers. But the de-mography of movement is quite the inverse of the academic experience. It is of course true that global migration has been on the increase over the past decades and that this can even be characterized as mass migration. But this is not a new and certainly not an evolutionary phenomenon. Even if we ad-mit the existence of large-scale movements, it should be noted that mass migration does not mean that *everyone* is on the move. Less than 3 percent of the world's population is on the move in international terms. The over-whelming majority stay more or less put. Of course, populations may well be on the move within smaller or sometimes much larger state territories, however, as when one hundred and fifty million Chinese migrants consti-tute that country's "floating population." But this is largely ignored by those who argue that we are entering a new globalized era. International migra-tion is in fact a historically delimited phenomenon. It was at least as mas-sive at the turn of the last century as it is today. In fact, what is referred to as globalization is also a phenomenon of this type, reaching enormous pro-portions between 1870 to 1920, only to be reversed after that. The experi-ence of movement is something altogether different from the phenomenon of migration. It is constructed out of specific subjective experiences of things out of place of crossing borders, and this experience is primarily the experi-ence of those positioned in the upper reaches of society, where they can con-ceive of people and things circulating from above so that they are located within a particular field of vision. This vision can be the subject of media elaboration to such an extent that it may become institutionalized. One need only watch CNN's advertising for itself, or ads for Intercontinental Hotels, where one is at home anywhere in the world with a touch of cultural differ-ence to spice things up. It should be noted that the media operate to localize the global rather than to globalize the local. They bring the world into the minute spaces of individual living rooms and may imbue such spaces with an aura of globality, however virtual. The "globalization" of communication, then, implies the possibility of less, not more, movement, even among those whose access to such communication is instrumental in their lives. If such people are, nevertheless, more on the move than ever, it is not perhaps due directly to technological change. In her studies of global cities, Sassen has pointed out that even though transactions among multinationals and within such firms are increasingly carried out electronically, the personal meeting has become an ever more important instrument for cementing business relations. This accounts for the cultivation of certain urban centers, which are, of course, *localized*, as luxurious meeting places for executives.

It is the traveler-intellectuals who are the source for most of the current discourse of movement, with its boundary-smashing rhetoric of translocality, border crossing, de-territorialization, etcetera, terms that mirror CNN's self-image but do not add to our understanding of that image. The discourse of globalization as border-crossing in all senses of the word is part of the emergence of elite transnationalist identity, a positioning in the world, or rather above the world. The discourse expresses their own experience and not that of those whose existence they consume as objects in the formation of their own hybridized identities, an issue to which we return below. There is evidence that this kind of representation is not a mere intellectual product but is constitutive of a particular position. When, in 1998, Thomas Middelhoff, head of the media giant Bertelsmann, was asked about whether it was acceptable that a German firm controlled 15 percent of the American book market, he replied, "We're not foreign. We're international. . . . I'm an American with a German passport" (in McChesney 1999).

There is a crucial structural concern in the analysis of demographic movement. This is simply the requirement of fixity in order to define movement itself. Boundaries cannot be crossed unless they already exist. If *everyone* crosses boundaries, then they become empty categories in the political sense, but any consideration of the demographic realities entails that this is clearly not the case. In other words, the framing of movement implies the framing of the relation between those who move and those who do not. There is no de-territorialization without territory, and if the latter disappears as a category we are merely left with a larger category which defines the limits of movement. Movement between becomes movement within, and that spoils all the fun of being *trans-x*. The love of transnational, translocal movement is, paradoxically, the love of the borders that make it all possible. This accounts for the logical necessity of maintaining *roots* in order to define *routes*. And it is this distinction that is the basis of one of the more important theoretical discussions of the issue of diasporas. This paradoxical inclusion of place within movement as a practice of identity is one of the classical prop-

TABLE 6.1.

Elementary Forms of Movement and Collectivity*

	+ *roots*	− *roots*
+ DISPERSAL	Other referenced diaspora Jews (Zionists), Bosnians, Serbs, Greeks, Kurds, Indians, Muslim	Self referenced diaspora Gypsies, U.K. Blacks, certain orthodox Jews (Boyarin's model)
− DISPERSAL	National/indigenous identity closed nationalism or ranked multiethnicity	Modernist identity / citizenship open multiculturalism

*This is a simple cross tabulation of dispersal and rootedness which provides a preliminary classification of forms of displacement and localization. It is not an account but a preliminary partition based on the criteria used by many writers on the subject.

erties of the diasporic, even if, as we shall see below, there are cases in which origins may become insignificant, at least in certain historical conditions. Clifford makes use of a double set of distinctions in his well-known article on the subject, roots, and geographical dispersal. Table 6.1 is an attempt to capture the way in which the distinctions might be said to generate different kinds of identity. But the argument, as we shall see, can easily become self-contradictory.

Clifford's elaborate essay on diasporas deals with the contemporary popularity of the term and its related cultural studies cognates: travel, contact zones, creolization, and hybridity. He stresses the unifying principle of these discourses in their focus on movement, travel as opposed to fixity and closure. But these discourses are elite discourses, as Clifford also admits. They do not necessarily reflect larger realities than those whose experience and cultural politics they reflect. In his discussion of Gilroy's (1993) and the Boyarins' (1993) analyses of respectively the Black Atlantic and Jewish diasporas, he struggles through the problems of essentialism that these authors take as the central issue. Diasporas for both are creative counter-cultures of modernity and of purity. They hybridize their surroundings, the image being one whereby a population with culture C from X moves to Y and changes via its interaction with Y, producing a culture C_h, a process that continues over time and in open fashion. Continuity and change are combined. The word "transformation" would do well as a description. On the other hand, to privilege just diaspora culture in this way is to underprivilege the continuous change that goes on in all cultures where import routinely occurs. This is Lévi-Strauss' point in his (in)famous second discussion of ethnicity and race.

This stress on hybridity has a clear political dimension as well. Since diasporas are associated with the interstices of the global arena, situated in between essentialized entities, they represent a threat to such essentialisms. "The empowering paradox of diaspora is that dwelling *here* assumes solidarity and connection *there*" (Clifford 1997:269).

But this does not solve the problem as such, since diasporas in order to exist must also have a definite identity. Otherwise how are we to identify them? How are they to identify themselves? This is where the continuity/change paradigm is introduced. Now this can only confuse the issue. The fact that culture changes via, but not exclusively via, mixture says nothing about separation as such, which is a social issue and not one of cultural content. The threat of diaspora is not culture as such, but social differentiation, the potential of fragmentation of a larger unity. Thus, when the Boyarins assert that Zionism as a national essentialist ideology is destructive of Judaism as a diasporic culture, they state:

> Diasporic cultural identity teaches us that cultures are not preserved by being protected from "mixing" but probably can only continue to exist as a product of such mixing. Cultures, as well as identities, are constantly being remade. While this is true of all cultures, diasporic Jewish culture lays it bare because of the impossibility of a natural association between this people and a particular land—thus the impossibility of seeing Jewish culture as a self-enclosed, bounded phenomenon. . . . Jewishness disrupts the very categories of identity because it is not national, not genealogical, not religious, but all of these in dialectical tension with one another. (Boyarin and Boyarin 1993:721)

They go on to propose diaspora as a "theoretical and historical model to replace national self-determination" (p. 711). But in all of this liminality, identity seems to remain strikingly constant. The fact that Yiddish is a border language and perhaps a border culture does not imply a lack of social differentiation. For all the openness of Talmudic discussion and lack of reference to a return to Israel, there is always the distinction between Jew and Gentile. Yiddish culture is a culture of Jews, not of other people in their immediate vicinity. But the struggle to elevate the status of hybridity continues unabated. The distinction is "processual and nonessentialist" (Clifford 1997:275). In his discussion of Weinreich (1967) he argues that "difference, for Weinreich, is a process of continual renegotiation in new circumstances or dangerous and creative coexistence" (p. 276).

But all ethnicity involves exactly such processes! This was Barth's point many years ago. There is no way of arguing against classification by invoking other classifications. It is in the nature of the practice of classification that boundaries are created. No matter whether they are porous or not, they are still boundaries and still function to separate. Otherwise they cease to exist. It is for this reason that one suspects an ideological motive in the discourse of hybridity. One that stresses a model of continual transgression of borders, as if such a state could be maintained as a kind of permanent revolution. The facts of history and ethnography would seem to be otherwise. The content of social categories and group identities may indeed change, although there must remain a thread of continuity in order to be able to recognize the categories throughout all of this transformation. But the categories remain. Group identity remains and identity is bounded, by logical necessity. Otherwise it cannot be identified. And if it cannot be identified, well, then it doesn't exist as such. Modernism is a far more successful solution to the problem of cultural localization. One of the strategies of modernist identity is precisely the transcendence of culturally specific categories. But here it is a question of their replacement by the more abstract-universal categories of modernism itself: individual, citizen, class, and even nation-state, where the latter is emptied of its cultural content if this is at all possible.

I have argued elsewhere (Friedman 1997, 1998) that hybridity is an expression of a postmodern cosmopolitanism, one that is world-encompassing at the same time as it is culturally rooted. The latter is expressive of a genealogical mode of thought, where roots become mixed or intertwined as they become routes. The problem is that diasporic or transnational social worlds are not hybrid insofar as they maintain group identity. The latter would be impossible for their very reproduction. On the contrary such groups are some of the prime historical examples of strong ethnic identity and even homogenization, endogamy, endosociality, and symbolic closure. To take a bird's-eye view of such phenomena in order to raise them to the status of post-national solution is to confuse this sky-born perspective, the fact that diasporas are culturally creative and changing, with the social facts on the ground and the perspectives of the members of such groups.

Robin Cohen (1997) has taken a more sociological approach to the issues, one that, however, seems to assume a more concrete, almost institutional, existence for diasporas. The usual features that, as Cohen has argued, hang together by means of a chain of family resemblances are as follows:

1. Features
   a. Movement

  b. Homeland
  c. Solidarity among those dispersed
    1. Economic relations
    2. Relations of sociality
    3. Knowledge of
    4. Identification with

Now these features can be divided into two, material or even physical, the movement of people, the migration process itself, and the way the latter exists in the lives of those who move and those who do not but form the context of such movement. As we see in Table 6.2, Cohen divides diasporas into five types, which he characterizes by the metaphor of gardening.

The gardening metaphor could use some unpacking here. It expresses in fact a totally essentializing view of the process that conflates movement itself with culture. The movement of people and the derivative movement of culture are identified and classified into true species. But our argument is precisely the contrary, that diaspora formation is based in a process of identification and with the material and symbolic practices that are bound up with such identification. The above types disintegrate in the real processes of historical change if taken over a long enough period. Weeding can become transplanting or layering. Transplanting can become layering or, in the ancient world, even sowing, in the right conditions in which relations of power are reversed. As for cross-pollinating, it is not clear that this is ever the case in the social reality of ordinary people as opposed to the intellectuals who construct the categories of hybridity. And then all of these categories can be transformed via assimilation, that is, they can disappear into their destinations. So the status of the categories is not at all clear in theoretical terms. The problem here, as earlier, is the perspective of the observer. Much of the discussion of diasporas has been based on a misplaced concreteness, an objectification of movement in such a way that it is cultures that move and not just people. If we stay with the obvious fact of the demography of the situation, then all the rest is a question of the way in which people practice their movement in conditions where other people are also practicing receiving and sending people across borders. Faist's concept of "transnational space" (1998), which builds very much on the framework developed by Glick Schiller and Szanton-Blanc (1992) captures the social field in a most practical way, a social field characterized by cross-identifications by host states and sending states as well as migrant selves and local communities and a complex of different and contradictory strategies. In countering the use of the notion of diaspora he suggests the following: "Instead of stretching the term dias-

TABLE 6.2.
Five Types of Diaspora

Gardening Term	Type of Diaspora	Examples
Weeding	Victim/refugee	Jews, Africans, Armenians, Irish, Palestinians
Sowing	Imperial/colonial	Ancient Greek, British, Russian, Spanish, Portuguese, Dutch
Transplanting	Labor/Service	Indentured Indians, Chinese, Japanese, Sikhs, Turks, Italians
Layering	Trade/business/professional	Venetians, Lebanese, Chinese, today's Indians, Japanese
Cross-pollinating	Cultural/hybrid/postmodern	Caribbean peoples, today's Chinese, Indians

pora beyond its limits, it is more meaningful to speak of a *transnationalized and segmented cultural space*" (1998:241).

Faist characterizes such spaces as zones of multiple possibilities, from assimilation to the national host society to various combinations of private/public accommodations in which the home cultures play differential roles. These possibilities are not, of course, subject to free choice but are expressions of changing and variable circumstances for individuals as well as larger groups.

The Role of Identification in the Existence and Reproduction of Transnational Worlds

Transnational formations such as diasporas are the product of a complex of practices. They are not the result of mere physical movement. The evidence of this is clear from the transformation of diasporas into local ethnic minorities by means of re-identification, by the equivalent but opposite strengthening of transnational ties via transnational endogamy, which may go under the official rubric of "family re-unification," but is often better understood as "family formation." Assimilation has been the classic area of research in the migration literature in the United States, a process that combines powerful apparatuses of socialization and strong desires for re-identification, often the result of the change of status (and social mobility) that such identification entails. The intentional process of identification with the place of residence is often blind to its own consequences, that is, assimilation is always a dialogic process. The Jews of Frankfurt became painfully aware of this in the 1930s when they became increasingly the subject of discriminatory acts which they failed to understand, being able to re-categorize those who were subjected to Nazi discrimination into categories related to disloyal and anti-national activities. "So and so was not taken by the police because of his Jewishness but because he was a communist or traitor or misfit of one kind or another." It was only when things had already gone too far that the reality of the Nazi strategy became evident. The identifying actors and their changing intentionalities is a fundamental historical determinant of any transnational situation.

Diasporas are reflexes of global systemic relations. In the most general sense they can be defined as trans-state or, in the modern epoch, transnational social formations. While there may be, as noted by Cohen, differing conditions of their formation, they are social organizations in which recruitment, membership, and a series of group-based activities and identity are clearly established within a global network. The origins of diasporic formations are probably much less important than the way they are reproduced/practiced at any historical moment. It is not terribly interesting to try and distinguish the different forms as if they were species, since they themselves may change quite radically over time and may at any given time consist of several forms of organizational praxis. If transnational social formations can be taken as the most general category, all populations that maintain an identity X upon which a set of activities, cultural, social, and economic are elaborated, a diaspora as a subset would refer to all such organizations that maintained claims on a homeland and a historical relation of dispersal by descent from a historical homeland, real or imagined. Now all of this requires an active attribution of meaning to the fact of demographic movement. It is a construction, not an arbitrary one, but one that is always made and remade in a present. It is, then, a form of social identification and as such is part of a process in which there are several significant positions of identification. "Wandering Jews" were not created by Jews but by identifications of the former by various host societies, which become part of a general identity discourse that is available to Jew and non-Jew alike. This should not be understood as a constructivist position, except in a very particular theoretical sense. The constitution of social realities is bound up with identifications, which are in their turn embedded in material realties that exist in a dialectic of continuity and transformation. And of course, transformation is itself based on continuity, otherwise what is there to be transformed? Constructivism often overlooks the fact that people live in already constituted worlds and that they do not construct themselves *ex-nihilo*.

The kinds of categories that can be generated by the various practices of groupness in trans-state/transnational situations are sketched in Table 6.3.

The relation of identification to the process of transnational structuring always harbors a degree of rooting. This is a complex variable of course and it depends very much on circumstances, cultural strategies, and the way that they change over time. Thus all the groups in question can root themselves more or less intensively, even members of multinational corporations, and even mercenaries, which today are in fact organized as multinationals. The conditions of rootedness can be variable and these in their turn determine the degree of rootedness. On the other hand, certain types of organization are defined by their rootedness. These are mafias, diaspora I, and colonies. The others are dependent upon circumstances. Thus diaspora II groups can become rooted in periods of ethnification, just as ethnic minorities and mercenaries. On the other hand, transnational corporations are organized around not becoming rooted, especially if they are truly transnational and not merely multinational. This may not be an easy task to carry out. In a leading multinational French engineering firm, which was one of the first to invest in multiculturalism, recruitment from the global arena did not, as planned, create increased circulation while maintaining ties to home countries. A large number of the recruits met and married and established families in one or another country where they were temporarily established and became rooted in their new localities, refusing the idea of return.[1] In the same way, the formation of mafia organization can occur in almost any transnational population, and mafias can be more or less rooted with respect to homelands depending on the particular historical context.

Another crucial aspect of transnational practices is the issue of levels of integration. It is important not to assume that the group, identified externally, is a unitary formation, a corporate entity. Many transnational phenomena are primarily organized at the family or community level. Migrant members of a village maintain and develop economic and social relations with that particular village and not necessarily with the homeland as a whole. This is one of the most common research findings from studies of migrant communities from Turkey and the Middle East. So the relation between the actual operating units in transnational relations and the categories of iden-

TABLE 6.3.

Categories Generated by Various Practices of Groupness in Trans-State/Transnational Situations*

Transnational Group	Diaspora I	Diaspora II	Mafia	Colony	TNC	Mercenary Global Services	Immigrant Ethnic Minority	Tourist	Cosmopolitan
PROPERTIES									
Group identity	+	+	+	-(+)	-	-	+	-	+
Roots	+	-	+	+	(+)(-)	-	(+)-(-)	-	-
Economic organization	+	+	+	+	+	+	-	-	-
Social organization	+	+	+	+	-	-	(+)-(-)	-	-

*These terms need some clarification. Group identity refers primarily to the identification of a strong collective sense of self. The term *social organization* refers to the existence of internal organization within the transnational population. Characteristics such as hierarchy, the use of violence, and the kind of economic organization are left out here although they are absolutely relevant in distinguishing between different types of grouping. The purpose of this simplified chart is primarily to provide a basic set of distinguishing features and not to describe the precise nature of any of the groups. It is in no way meant to be all-inclusive but merely to exemplify.

tity which are employed by host societies, and even by transnationals themselves, needs to be dealt with in a precise manner.

In other words, the categories that we have discussed here are not meant to fix particular populations in particular classifications. On the contrary, our principal argument is that it is the practice of the transnational that constitutes any particular form of community and that such practices change over time. That even transnational corporations can tend to form communities of a certain type has been documented, and it is certainly one of the available models for such organization.

Cultures of Movement

The relation between practices of identity has also been discussed in terms of the social organization of movement itself, the way in which space is strategically organized into life processes. Samoans are spread out over the entire world, perhaps more than any other single population, and it has been suggested by anthropologists such as Epeli Hau'ofa and recently Marshall Sahlins that this is a specific cultural organization of the movement of people in which rhizomic practice is part of the basic structure of life. The latter, like many other Polynesians, understand their relation to the world not in terms of "islands in the sea" but as a "sea of islands," in which the ocean does not separate but joins. The reproduction of social life is not restricted to local resources but extends to a much wider region. This has generated a situation that, from the outside, is described as the ease of migration, but which from the inside, is not migration at all, but movement within a larger common world. The degree to which this can be applied to the modern situation of widespread labor migration is not clear to me and many have raised doubts. In any case, the reasons for movement today are vastly different than in the past, but there is an interesting practice of space, so to speak, that is invoked even in the contemporary situation. There are numerous cultures of travel and migration, such as those of certain Middle Eastern trading groups in the past and present. The specificities of this kind of relation to the larger world must be more carefully explored, but it is clear that the notion of life space is not restricted to the territorial state. This may be true for Palestinian and other merchant communities, for example, as well as for Polynesian peoples, and it is not only salient but crucial for the now increasingly documented Chinese transnational communities. The latter are a population of at least 25 to 50 million people who are active in the political and economic life of the home country, accounting for the major portion of all foreign investment in

---

China. Studies of Chinese diasporic formations have demonstrated the degree to which they tend to be closed, tightly organized, often stratified, and even endogamous in a broad sense (Ong 1999). This is difficult to reconcile to the notion of hybridity. Of course new elements enter into the lives of transnationals, but, as we have suggested, they are absorbed and enclosed within community relations. It is also the case that such communities become class stratified in interaction with their surroundings. The Hakka Chinese of Tahiti represent a history of such social differentiation, with those who remained at the bottom of the social scale becoming increasingly "Tahitian" or local, and in this sense creolized, while those at the top becoming increasingly cosmopolitan but socially Chinese (Trémon 2000).

That the maintenance of transnational organization requires a high degree of group control is illustrated by the example of a certain Hakka Chinese family living in Sweden. This family, "originally" from India, has branches in Southern China, India, Northern Europe, and the United States. This particular family, like many of the others, is in the restaurant business. They are extraordinarily well adapted to Swedish society, and they maintain a very low profile in contrast to other minorities, such as Arabs, that are very much engaged in cultural politics. The woman learnt Swedish as part of the national effort at integration, whereas the man in this particular family was very much isolated as the chief cook in his own establishment. He could understand but not speak Swedish after many years. The children went to school, and the eldest daughter caused a crisis that highlighted the diasporic strategy. She had become so integrated into her local society that she was not only fluent in Swedish, but refused to learn to write Chinese. She had her own social life with its own priorities. There was great consternation, especially in reaction to the language issue. Her mother was herself keen on living a Swedish life, but she had little leverage in this situation. A family reunion was called in New York and kin arrived from all parts of the world. It was decided that the local relation had to be severed. The family moved to another small city further north in the country, leaving a cousin to manage the old restaurant. The daughter was forced to learn to write her native language and the praxis of the diaspora was upheld. The mother was brokenhearted at having to leave the community in which she had rooted herself, but she understood that she had no choice in the matter.

The specificities of this conflict demonstrate more than the strength of a transnational ethnic or family strategy, they also highlight the zones of conflict. In a world in which imperial cities were organized into enclaves, such a conflict might not have arisen, since the possibilities of integration into *another* local world would have been almost inconceivable. But in the context of the nation-state the situation is vastly different. In any case, these are real conflicts that should not be reduced, as in the transnationalist ideology referred to above, to a moral issue. Thus, for a typical example of the latter:

> ... To understand homes in this way—as being synonymous with Durkheimian notions of solidary communities and coercive institutions in microcosm—is anachronistic, and provides little conceptual purchase on a world of contemporary movement. . . .
>
> ... People are more at home nowadays, in short, in "words, jokes, opinions, gestures, actions, even the way one wears a hat" (Berger 1984:64). "Home" in Bammer's words, "is neither here nor there. . . . rather, itself a hybrid, it is both here and there—an amalgam, a pastiche, a performance" (1992 xi). Or else, in a reactionary refusing of the world of movement, one is at home in a paradoxical clamoring for "particularisms": in a multiplicity of invented "primordial" places for which one is perhaps willing to kill and die. (Rapport and Dawson 1998:7)

This is precisely the normative expression to which I referred earlier, chastising anachronistic, reactionary illusions and desires for place and a completely celebratory vision of people on the move. In this particular example the anthropologists are arguing for a broad shift in anthropological epistemology, much like Clifford, to a framework based on movement rather than place. It is quite extraordinary to witness the extremes to which what is clearly a self-identity can be imposed upon other people's realities: "Palestinians are more worried about getting Israel off their backs than about the special geographical magic of the West Bank" (Appadurai 1996:165).

In the author's personal vendetta against the obvious evil of the national, he does whatever he deems necessary to define it away, to expel the idea of place. Noting that what he calls "trojan" nationalisms are orchestrated by transnationals,[2] he believes that nationalists, localists, ethnics engaged in violent assertion, don't really know what they are up to. While he is aware that identities can become aggressive in certain periods, he has no global grasp of why so many in certain periods and not in others. On the contrary, he seems to think that this is a question of evolution toward a new, globalized world. Here of course the fact that the people that we actually study seem to be engaged in the same things that some of us poor reactionary anthropologists are describing is a problem to be denied. Where such a realization does occur, it leads to the most self-contradictory acts of denial. Thus: ". . . Anthropologists' obsession with boundedness is paralleled by the ways in which the people they study try to deal with seemingly open-ended global flows" (Meyer and Geschiere 1999:3).

So, not only have *we* got it wrong, but the people we study have also got it wrong! The error here lies not in the interest on movement, but in the poverty of its conceptualization. No one actually lives in movement, not even traveling executives and salesmen, since their traveling cannot be said to characterize entire lives. The movement to which these anthropologists refer is always movement between or among locations. Otherwise there is no way to describe the movement as such. This is a trivial point, but it needs, unfortunately, to be made. That people can make their homes in transnational contexts, as the Hakka described here do, does not imply that they are "dwelling" in movement. On the contrary, they are reproducing a set of relations across spatial boundaries that bind themselves into definite worlds. And all of this bounding, not fluidity, is the source of structural incompatibilities and real conflict in their lives.

The Interface of Transnational Practices and Territorial Political Fields

We have suggested several times that transnational relations are parts of a larger whole, the state systems within which they operate. The diasporic, as Clifford stressed, may be better suited to imperial pasts than to the nation-state present. Rather than simply evaluating relative compatibility, it is more important to gain a purchase on the actual articulation between the social fields of nation-states and transnational formations. It is clear that potential contradictions are generated by the structures involved. The nation-state is constituted on the basis of a common project and a common identity with that project that is usually highly culturalized. It is also based on an elaboration of social organization around the relation between people and the state. Roots are the principal means of defining the territory and the combination of the disintegration of sub-state political forms of kinship and community sodalities are powerful historical forces in the formation of a new state-based identity. The latter leads to an individualization that is the basis of nationality, where identification is based on the formation of a state-based investment of the subject, a level of represented cultural commonality that enables a new kind of community sentiment. The latter is of course riven by other kinds of difference, especially class, but it has certainly demonstrated its effectiveness in acts of mobilization for war. In fact, class politics itself has been driven essentially on nationalist grounds, in which the We of "We the people" is the subject of the nation. The national political sphere is one defined as made up of individuals and not of groups and the entire legal edifice of such states expresses the issue of rights and duties in terms of individual subjects. This is clearly in contradiction with the existence of any subgroups that might form communities within the nation, irrespective of whether they are indigenous or immigrant. It also enforces a dynamic in which individualization and integration are pitted against the maintenance of group strategies.

The question of relation to home lands or home countries has been elaborated upon in recent studies of European suburban immigrant zones. There is a great deal of variation here, not least in the intergenerational changes involved in identification. The simplest division can be said to be that of the maintenance versus the rupture of the relation to a foreign place. But this in its turn is also quite variable. In one recent thesis on the subject (Schiff 2000), a dichotomy is suggested between the practice of local entrenchment and the practice of spatial otherness. In a *cité* north of Paris, Asian immigrants were commonly more connected to a homeland and for that reason not really part of the place. Their strategies were based on adaptation to the local situation, but the latter was primarily a resource within an enclave whose goals extended far beyond the locality or even the nation, and constituted an ultimate "working relation" between two or more points in the global arena. These people were not de-territorialized but dually or even multiply territorialized. They were classified by the host society as *merely* immigrants and low ranked in terms of the linked categories of class and residence, as people of *les banlieux*. But they themselves did not participate directly in this classification, since their own life plans were located within a world defined by the transnational group usually at the level of the extended family. The second or later generation descendants of immigrants from North Africa and to some extent the Middle East, as well as new immigrants who had experienced failure in France, began to categorize themselves, or take on an identity in which their position in the larger society became more politically salient. They were at the bottom, they were discriminated against and they began, paradoxically, to identify as part of the larger society. Their identity became more localized at the same time as, for youth at least, it became more multicultural, since territory began to override origins. They were simply the population of the *banlieu, les banlieusards*, a new multicultural minority, reproducing and identifying the larger social category used to classify them. Among youth groups here one may even speak of a hybridization of sorts, insofar as the local culture assimilated and elaborated elements from different origins (this is course is a general phenomena of all cultural production), but what is interesting is that it is not the sense of mixture that dominates but the homogenizing identity of spatial or territorial closure. If the cultural origins of this group were diverse, their identity was unitary. A youth of French origins from the ghetto is no ordinary Frenchman. He may speak Arabic fluently and understand a good deal of the activities of other cultures simply by having been brought up together with them. His identity is that of the place and not of his national origins. This is ambivalent, of course, and throughout a life cycle, identity choices are made according to individual interest, changing environment, and social mobility both up and down. Thus the positions within the larger social field remain relatively stable with respect to the movement of individuals through the cultural categories that they generate. And these positions are themselves generated by the structure of the state or national society and not by some transnational formation. *Banlieusards* defined themselves in stark opposition to first generation transnationals in ways that simply extended the opposition of national/foreigner. They became, in this sense, a real status group, emically, within the French national structure, more similar to a culturally specific underclass than to an ethnic group.

Pluralist empires such as the Ottoman and even the Habsburgs were organized in terms conducive to the relatively autonomous, if hierarchical, accommodation of transnational and other minority communities. This is a very general issue in the understanding of the global that is not often clear in current theoretical discussions in which the nation-state is described as under siege by the forces of transnationalization (Appadurai 1996), in which a new world of diasporas is predicted as a new historical era. In this closet evolutionist understanding, the nation-state is primarily understood as "the local" expressed in terms of the national. Globalization is interpreted as an externally orchestrated wave of the future to which the nation-state will inevitably succumb. This needs to be deconstructed. Who are the relevant actors? What are these forces that are supposedly external to the nation-state? The position adopted here is that the very formation of the nation-state was itself a global systemic phenomenon, a concentration and localization of capital accumulation and political control within a larger global field. Its European history was also one of the fragmentation of larger imperial formations. The nation-state is not a product of diffusion in this approach but an artefact of real global processes that take on distinctive local forms. This argument echoes in different terms the thesis of Elias concerning the formation of European states. In this sense the nature of the trans-state sphere is structurally bound up with that of the state sphere. This logic can be seen most clearly in the contrast with the Ottoman or Habsburgs. If imperial orders, or even absolutist states and feudal kingdoms, are structured in such a way that enclaves are not only compatible but constitutive of their political arenas, the nation-state tends, in its identification of the state with a particular community, to exclude such plural organization. Even here, however, I would insist on the variability of such structures over time. The fragmentation of empires can take the form of the localizing of community and the formation of strong ethnic sodalities. It might also be the case, as we shall argue here, that nation-states can transform themselves into more absolutist or even imperial formations as in the tendencies present today in the European Union. This would imply a movement toward a more plural organization, one that is tendentially evident in the current transformation of European states.

I suggest, then, that diasporas cannot be assessed in themselves, since their formation and reproduction are systemically related to the larger worlds that they inhabit. For the world of nation-states, we might suggest the following cyclical pattern. In periods of expansion a number of phenomena can be said to coincide. The state tends to nationalize and thus to homogenize.[3] It tends to individualize its population via the dissolution of regional and local sodalities, a violent process of intervention including persecution, prohibition, criminalization, and new forms of socialization. This process is strongest in periods of the formation of imperial hegemony. In such eras there is a decline in cultural difference. Diasporas, where they exist, tend to be transformed into localized ethnic minorities under assimilatory pressure. The evolutionary model of integration of immigrants which developed in the United States in the first half of this century is based on a movement from immigrant community with strong diasporic connections, to an economic integration of the second generation, where ethnic communities may still maintain themselves in social terms, to a gradual assimilation of individuals into the host society, transforming real ethnicity into symbolic ethnicity (Gans 1979). The validity of this model may however depend on the period of expansion in which it was produced. This might account for the genuine surprise of ethnic researchers in the early 1970s at the ethnic identity that had made a powerful re-entry into the political arena after years of predictions of its immanent demise. The very history of ethnic discourse is revealing here. In the 1950s and 1960s assimilation or integration into the host society was considered progressive. More recently the movement from homogeneous nationality to multi-culturalism has been understood as the true progression of world history. In both periods the progressive is identified as that which is in some sense the obvious direction of change. In fact there is a clear reversal in which assimilation is replaced by differentiation, by a dis-assimilation or cultural fragmentation. The increase of interest in diasporas is part of the interest in multi-culturalism in general.

And this interest is a reflection of the changing balance between forces of
state integration and fragmentation. This does not imply that the state is becoming weaker, although there has been a very long economic crisis of the
state finance, its virtual bankruptcy in the West, followed by a contraction
and retrenchment of state functions. This process might be called the de-
nationalization of the state. The latter has become more of an instrument of
global capital accumulation than a welfare machine. This is a process of lift-
off: the state ascends into the stratosphere of Trilateral Commissions and
Davos cocktails while the nation is left behind and chastised for its increasing xenophobia and backward anti-immigrant attitudes. The formation of
the European Union shows clear tendencies to the formation of a superstate
with a low level of representativity and accountability. If there is a tendency
to the absolutization of the nation-state and the formation of larger regional
institutions reminiscent of former imperial orders, then we should expect
that conditions for the emergence and reproduction of diasporic social formations are excellent.

This cyclical pattern might well account for the different models of integration and multiculturalism that have appeared in the past century. While
there was massive migration in the first part of the twentieth century, there
were clear differences in the relation between migration and the nation-state
in for example France and the United States. In the latter the category of ethnicity was practically non-existent, and while the percentage of immigrants
was equal to that of the United States, assimilation was assumed to be natural, so that one was either not French or French. Membership in the French
nation implied the self-evident necessity of becoming French, although this
also provoked some heated debate at the beginning of the Century. That
is, other cultures were not recognized as such within national borders, i.e.
as ethnicity. In the United States, migration led to a major debate between
proponents of multiculturalism and assimilationism. Even here, however,
assimilation became the dominant policy from the 1920s on, but with a
stronger tendency to the formation of subnational minorities. Thus there
was a tendency for diasporic relations to become national ethnic minority relations even though there was a general tendency, much more pronounced
in France, toward assimilative integration.[4] The current phase, from the
1970s on, represents an inversion of the previous tendency, a fragmentation
of separate cultural identities within the larger state. This has occurred in
France as well as the United States, where it began earlier. The fact that it has
occurred in a strongly republican France as well indicates the power of the
forces at work. The opposed tendencies involved in this historical movement
are on the one hand homogenization and on the other heterogenization. The

former tends toward the production of egalitarianism, which in polities such as the Swedish welfare state leads to the equation of equality with identity, in the sense that being equal means being *identical*.[5] The latter tends toward the production of hierarchy, in which difference is the norm. Difference, in the sense of the freedom to be different, easily merges with actual social differentiation, in which inequality is acceptable and even laudable.

The increase of ethnically differentiated labor markets in the United States, and more recently in Europe, is an example of this kind of process. The new textile industry in California is highly stratified ethnically, and the economy of the state as a whole follows suit. The transnational wage relations that are established by Asians and Central Americans are part of the very functioning of this differentiated labor market. This is a market that might seem highly questionable by the standards of labor union ideology, but in a world of neo-liberal globalization, union ideology is a thing of the past, and even an expression of racism. But then ethnically stratified labor markets were also assumed to be a thing of the past, or at least an aberration, most recently in the organization of colonial and plantation economies. As the nation-state becomes, to varying degrees, a plural society, the relation between the social space of the territory and that of potential migrants changes significantly. In highly capitalized markets, ethnic differentiation generates the production of a labor force. The global cities that are emerging in many developed and even less developed countries are fueled by a supply of immigrant workers who fill definite niches in the urban economy. These are not necessarily only the poorest, although the latter are certainly the majority. Engineers, doctors, and other high-end transnational populations have begun to fill niches, the most salient being, perhaps, Silicon Valley in California. The discussions surrounding the recruitment process have focused on the nature of the potentials of the global market and the labor market bottlenecks of nation-states.

The increasing differentiation of social worlds is an aspect of that transformation of the global arena referred to as globalization. This differentiation is driven by the increasing dominance of "cultural" identification over previous modernist (also cultural of course) forms of social classification in which the core figures were class, citizenry and the abstract individual, and a strategy of social development based on the desire for control by national, or territorially identified, populations over their conditions of existence. With the fragmentation of the national sphere and the promotion of political classes to higher cosmopolitan realms, the national project has lost its State, and commoner identification is being sought elsewhere, in rooted identities, national, immigrant, indigenous, but also regional, religious, and sexual. In this emergent world, the transnational or diasporic is clearly on the rise, and in an important sense it is primarily the expression of the ethnification of global demographic movement.

Not Just the Nation-State: Historical Cycles of Diaspora Formation

It might be suggested that the kind of global transformation in the conditions of identity formation discussed above is applicable in different configurations to earlier historical periods. Certainly the emergence of nationalisms in the wake of the decline of both the Habsburg and the Ottoman empires is also the production of diasporic identities, the latter usually linked to the process of nationalization itself. Thus Zionism, Armenian and Kurd identities, even Greek diasporic identity (which began somewhat earlier) can be traced to the processes of fragmentation of the Ottoman empire. That this is not just a contemporary phenomenon is borne out by research in ancient history. Thus the emergence of Jewish identity in which diaspora was crucial during the Hellenistic era is also related to the process of imperial dissolution. While all the minorities of Hellenistic Alexandria were identified by geographical origin, they were also defined as Hellenes, citizens of the empire, similar to British subjects (Modrzejewski 1993:76), but this situation changed during the decline period which saw the rise of what can be described as national movements, such as that of the Maccabees in Judea.

> As detected through the process of revival of national anthroponymy, more especially through the taste evinced for Biblical names, the Jews of Egypt have thus been imperceptibly moving from the situation of an ethnic group settled in an alien milieu to a diaspora community, drawing its vitality not only from its numerous relations with the "metropolis," but also from an inner strength. The shift moreover implied the growing awareness of a particularism, that is, the formation of a diaspora situation perceived as such.
> (Honigman 1993:125)

In other words, diasporas, like other ethnic phenomena, are historical processes involving the practice of identification as well as a set of social, political, and economic practices that are implied in group formation. Whether this identification crosses extant political boundaries or not is not crucial for understanding the nature of its emergence. The nation-state cycle described above moves from a period of cultural centralization/marginalization as hegemony is achieved to a re-emergence of cultural identities as hegemonies fragment. This kind of pattern can be said to characterize earlier empires as well, even if the fragments that emerge in periods of hegemonic decline need not take the form of nation-states. It should be noted, however, that there are family resemblances of a transhistorical nature here, insofar as a singular logic linking territory (place) and people seems to become salient.[6]

Conclusion

Globalization and diasporization are both products of a major reconfiguration in the global system, one that has also led to indigenization, ethnification, and the emergence of globalizing elite identities based on the ideology of cosmopolitan hybridity. Globalization has not invaded the domain of the nation-state. Rather, the nation-state has transformed itself increasingly into a plural state in which multiculturalism is competing to become the dominant ideology. It would be an exaggeration to suggest that the state is the cause of the current situation. Globalization is, as we have argued elsewhere, a process related to declining hegemony in which there is a rapid decentralization of capital accumulation in the world, one that accompanies the rise of new economic zones and potential hegemons. However, the state is clearly a major actor in the globalization process, rather than its unwilling victim. It is the state that has created the legal and political infrastructure for many of these processes. It is easier to grasp the importance of the state-as-actor by envisaging the contemporary state as an apparatus whose function is increasingly to attract capital. Now the process of decentralization of accumulation entails that the state may indeed have to adapt itself to new conditions, but this is always a double process, one, in this case, where there is no politics of opposition, only a single way to get things done: a Third Way, a *Neue Mitte*, a *voie unique*. It is in this sense that globalization within the world system is generated from within the state itself, a state that tends in such periods to become a political class for itself. The discourse of cultural globalization, which is in very large measure about the global diffusion of culture, via commodities, information, and the movement of people with their "cultures" in their baggage, is itself part of this global change and needs to be analyzed as an ideological or positioned normative discourse. I have suggested that no understanding of diasporas or any other transnational formations can be achieved without accounting for the ways in which such groups emerge and are reproduced. This necessitates making distinctions among different positions from which meaning is attributed to the world. The celebratory representation of movement by elites may not necessarily correspond to the representation of those who inhabit the lower classes of transnational movement. And these representations and experiences, as well as the social conditions that generate them, are themselves historically variable. It is crucial that demographic movement in itself implies nothing about the social form that it takes, a form that is, of course, culturally as well as historically specific. We have nonetheless suggested that there are some common patterns implying that the emergence and disappearance of transnational formations are dependent on the cycles of growth and decline of global hegemonies.

The current infatuation with the diasporic is, in the terms set out here, an ideological reflex, the experience of a certain segment of the elite, the experience of flying, of becoming cosmopolitan and being able to afford it. Real transnational populations and diasporas are, as we have suggested, not multicultural experiments, not hybrid formations. They are, on the contrary, relatively closed entities that practice closure in order to maintain themselves, and which, even if they assimilate new elements from their surroundings, are strict in the maintenance of their identities. These identities are not necessarily forms of resistance to the nation-state, not for those economically based transnational organizations that play such an important role in the contemporary world. Nor are they harbingers of a brave new world of cultural freedom. They are very much products of the state of the global system today, in which globalization and the transformation of state societies are systemic constituents. I would even venture to suggest that cosmopolitans also tend, as they have historically, to form relatively closed transnational groups, visiting the same international hotels, consuming the same foods, wines, high-end culture, speaking the same cultural codes, and even intermarrying. There are of course numerous hierarchical levels within this group, and there is a marked segregation of true blues from wannabe cultural elites. But there is a common participation in a similar set of social projects, and it is people slightly lower down on the scale who are often the most enthusiastic producers of cosmopolitan discourse. The only difference between transnational elites and those in the lower half of the social order is that the former tend to characterize themselves as open, which, as we have argued, is a well-conceived self-misrepresentation of their own social reality. The latter may well be open with respect to national borders, but it is relatively closed as a world of elite social life, interaction, and a limited number of local venues, meeting places for those of the same "kind" (Friedman 2004).

I have sought throughout this discussion to displace current usage of nouns to that of verbs in the description of transnational and diasporic phenomena. I have suggested that it is the practice of transnational relations and relations of identification which should be the locus of analysis. The emergence, reproduction, and demise of such relations can best be understood if they are construed as parts of larger global systemic fields within which both state formations and transnational formations emerge and disappear.

REFERENCES

Appadurai, A. 1996. *Modernity at Large*. Minneapolis: University of Minnesota Press.
Bammer, A. 1992. "Editorial." *New Formations: Journal of Culture/Theory/Practice* 2(2):1–24.
Berger, J. 1984. *And Our Faces: My Heart, Brief as Photos*. London: Writers and Readers.
Boyarin, Daniel, and Jonathan Boyarin. 1993. "Diaspora: Generation and the Ground of Jewish Identity." *Critical Inquiry* 19(4):693–725.
Braudel, F. 1984. *The Perspective of the World*. New York: Harper & Row.
Clifford, J. 1997. *Routes: Travel and Translation in the Late Twentieth Century*. Cambridge, Mass.: Harvard University Press.
Cohen, R. 1997. *Global Diasporas: An Introduction*. London: UCL Press.
Faist, T. 1998. "International Migration and Transnational Social Spaces." *Archives Européennes de sociologie* 39(1):213–42.
Friedman, J. 1997. "Global Crises, the Struggle for Cultural Identity and Intellectual Pork-Barreling: Cosmopolitans, Nationals and Locals in an Era of De-hegemonization." In *Debating Cultural Hybridity*, ed. P. Werbner. London: Zed Press.
———. 1998. "Transnationalization Socio-Political Disorder and Ethnification as Expressions of Declining Global Hegemony." *International Political Science Review* 19(3).
———. 2004. "The Dialectic of Cosmopolitanization and Indigenization in the Contemporary World System: Contradictory Configurations of Class and Culture." In *A Companion to the Anthropology of Politics*, ed. D. Nugent and J. Vincent. New York: Blackwell.
———, and Randeira, S. 2004. *Worlds on the Move: Globalization, Migration and Cultural Security*. London: Tauris.
Gans, H. 1979. "Symbolic Ethnicity: The Future of Ethnic Groups in America." *Ethnic and Racial Studies* 2(1):1–20.
Gilroy, P. 1993. *The Black Atlantic: Modernity and Double Consciousness*. Cambridge, Mass.: Harvard University Press
Glick Schiller, N., and C. Szanton-Blanc, eds. 1992. *Towards a Transnational Perspective on Migration: Race, Class, Ethnicity and Nationalism Reconsidered*. New York: New York Academy of Sciences.
Harvey, D. 1989. *The Condition of Postmodernity*. Oxford: Blackwell.
Hau'ofa, E. 1993. "Our Sea of Islands." In *A New Oceania: Rediscovering Our*

Sea of Islands, ed. Epeli Hau'ofa, Vijay Naidu, and Eric Waddell, pp. 4–19, 126–39. Suva: University of the South Pacific, School of Social and Economic Development.

Honigman, S. 1993. "The Birth of a Diaspora: The Emergence of a Jewish Self-Definition in Ptolemaic Egypt in the Light of Onomastics." In *Diasporas in Antiquity*, ed. J. D. Cohen and Ernest S. Frerichs, pp. 93–127. Brown Judaic Studies, no. 288. Atlanta, Ga.: Scholars Press.

Lévi-Strauss, C. 1985. "Race and Culture." In *The View from Afar*. Oxford: Blackwell.

McChesney, Robert W. 1999. "The New Global Media: It's a Small World of Big Conglomerates." *The Nation*, November 29:4–6 (http://www.thenation.com/doc.mhtml?i=19991129&s=mcchesney).

Meyer, B., and P. Geschiere. 1999. "Introduction." In *Globalization and Identity*, ed. B. Meyer and P. Geschiere. Oxford: Blackwell.

Modrzejewski, Joseph M. 1993. "How to Be a Jew in Hellenistic Egypt." *Diasporas in Antiquity*, ed. Shaye J. D. Cohen and Ernest S. Fredrichs, pp. 65–91. Brown Judaic Studies, no. 288. Atlanta, Ga.: Scholars Press.

Ong, A. 1999. *Flexible Citizenship: The Cultural Logics of Transnationality*. Durham: Duke University Press.

Rapport, Nigel, and Andrew Dawson. 1998. "The Topic and the Book." In *Migrants of Identity*, ed. N. Rapport and A. Dawson. Oxford: Berg.

Sassen, S. 1991. The Global City: New York, London, Tokyo. Princeton: Princeton University Press.

———. 2000. *Cities in a World Economy*. Thousand Oaks: Pine Forge Press.

Schiff, C. 2000. "Situation migratoire et condition minoritaire. Une comparison entre les adolescents primo-arrivants et les jeunes de la deuxieme génération vivant en milieu urbain défavorisé." Ph.D. diss. Ecole des Hautes Etudes en Sciences Sociales, Paris.

Trémon, A-C. 2000. "Les Hakka en Polynésie Francaise: Constructions identitaires et relations interethniques." Ph.D. diss. Ecole des Hautes Etudes en Sciences Sociales, Paris.

———. 2002. "The Chinese in French Polynesia." Unpublished ms.

Weinreich, Max. 1967. "The Reality of Jewishness Versus the Ghetto Myth: The Sociolinguistic Roots of Yiddish." In *To Honor Roman Jakobson: A Collection of Essays*. The Hague: Mouton.

NOTES

1. Personal communication from an employee of a leading French engineering firm.

2. But what then are we to make of the large number of nationalist movements of the nineteenth and twentieth centuries that engaged transnationals

on a major scale, such as those in China and Greece. But then it is typical of ideological thinking that it suppresses those realities that would contradict it.

3. "Homogenization" here is not akin to the notion of "essentialization," in which identical subjects are produced by a state that aims at total cloning of its population. This notion is the basis of the claim of essentialism, but it is not the real meaning that authors such as Gellner had in mind. Homogenization concerns the establishment of a common set of public values, a homogeneous public sphere of political action and communication. It is not about totalized subjects, but about shared values.

4. The United States, a "racial formation" from the period of slavery, was never a totalizing assimilation machine like France, and it might even be suggested that the nature of the assimilation process was very different. What was assimilated to was much more a set of explicit values than a deeper or more complete cultural homogenization. This is a complex problem that has rarely been dealt with in comparative terms, so it rests here as a suggestion for future research and analysis. It does, however, serve to remind us that terms such as "integration" and "assimilation" need to be unpacked, since we all too often assume that they mean the same thing in all situations.

5. The Swedish word *likhet*, with cognates in Danish and Norwegian, means "equal" but also "sameness."

6. And it is, of course, true that other forms of identity—ethnic, religious-based, regional—are also common in our nation-state system, forms that are not simply reducible to the latter.

PART TWO

Changing Homelands and National Identities

CHAPTER 7

Commemoration and National Identity: Memorial Ceremonies in Israeli Schools

AVNER BEN-AMOS AND ILANA BET-EL

Introduction

Commemorative acts simultaneously exist in the past, present, and future, a fact that makes them powerful events and, in turn, helps to mold national identity. Commemoration, first and foremost, refers to a common past with which the entire community can identify. It makes no difference whether this past is real or imaginary. So long as the members of the nation believe in its existence, and so long as they believe it belongs to them, it constitutes one of the important components of national identity. In the late nineteenth century, the French historian Ernst Renan wrote about this subject in his well-known essay "What Is a Nation?"

> The nation, like the individual, is the culmination of a long past of endeavors, sacrifices, and devotion. . . . A heroic past, great men, glory (by which I understand genuine glory), this is the social capital upon which one bases a national idea. . . . One loves in proportion to the sacrifices to which one has consented, and in proportion to the ills that one has suffered. . . . Where national memories are concerned, griefs are of more value than triumphs, for they impose duties, and require a common effort. (Renan [1882] 1990:19)

Renan's understanding of the emotional power of mourning will guide us later in the chapter, but we must first examine the dimension of the "present" in acts of commemoration. For Renan, the present constituted "the desire to live together" shared by all the members of the nation. But such desire cannot exist without the prior existence of a feeling of "togetherness." Commemoration, which takes place simultaneously in various places, is one of the proven means by which this feeling can be created. Benedict Anderson noted that the modern nation is dependent on a scientific outlook that presupposes a homogeneous sense of time through which the nation advances as one unit (1991:24). The simultaneous existence of all the members of the nation is dependent on a uniform calendar of hours and dates by which the nation marks its important events. Citizens participating in a commemorative event taking place at a certain location can therefore be confident that all other members of their nation are participating, at the same time, in similar commemorations taking place in other locations. That is how an imaginary national community is formed, a community whose members do not know each other personally yet are still convinced that they have much in common.

The "future" is also present at the commemorative event, because it embodies a promise that only the national community can fulfill. This promise is part of a "quasi social contract," which exists between the citizen, who is expected to sacrifice his life for the fatherland in times of danger, and the nation, which promises him immortality in return (Morin 1970:56). Thus, the citizen, conscious of his mortality, can be consoled by the possibility that even after his death he will continue to exist in the nation's collective memory as a glorious figure. The commemorative event is one of the means by which the inclusion of the dead hero in the national memory is ensured, and it acts as a form of "proof" that the nation truly fulfills its part of the contract. The mortal individual's feeling of transience is contrasted with the nation's pretension that it will exist forever, which symbolically helps the individual to overcome death—a pretension which is, of course, groundless.

The memorial ceremonies that take place in Israeli schools every year are examples of such commemorative events, and being an integral part of the centralized, established education system enhances their effectiveness. This chapter will analyze the contribution made by these ceremonies to the formation of Israel's national identity, both as events that occur simultaneously, and thus strengthen the community's bond, and as commemorative events, representing a past common to the entire nation. The ceremonies to be analyzed are the three annual ceremonies that commemorate modern historical events and are of central importance to the history of the Jewish people and the State of Israel: the Holocaust and Heroism Day ceremony; the Memorial Day ceremony, dedicated to those who fell in Israel's wars; and the Jerusalem Day ceremony.

These memorial days are, first and foremost, national events, and the ceremonies held in schools have, accordingly, the same national meaning. However, as an integral part of the school system they have received a pedagogical and psychological "added value." The information transmitted during a memorial ceremony complements the regular curriculum, and at times replaces it, while the emotional dimension of the ceremony remains no less important. The participating students are exposed to powerful images of bereavement, suffering, sacrifice, and heroism, which cannot but make a deep impression upon the adolescent mind. The ceremonies also have an accumulative effect: they are repeated year after year, at the same season, with only minor changes. The chances are great, therefore, that a graduate of the Israeli educational system who has spent twelve years in it has participated in about twenty-four such ceremonies. These ceremonies become for the students a kind of "natural phenomenon," representing eternal truths that cannot be questioned (Moore and Myerhoff 1977; Handelman 1990).

The ceremonies under study are those held in the state-run public education sector, which includes, since its establishment in 1953, over two-thirds of Israel's students (Elboim-Dror 1985:85).[1] We based the chapter on a large body of literature written between 1948 and 1998 on school ceremonies, including official publications, scripts of pageants, texts read during performances, and newspaper reports. In addition, we used material gathered during observations of forty-two ceremonies held between 1990 and 1998 in elementary, middle, and high schools throughout the country.[2] Despite the length of the period under study, we do not intend to discuss how the ceremonies have changed over the years.[3] Instead, we wish to present their major characteristics, those which have helped mold national identity and have remained relatively stable. With that said, to understand the principal components of Israel's ceremonial tradition, a short discussion of the historic circumstances leading to its formation is necessary.

The Formation of the School Ceremony Tradition

National memorial ceremonies have been held in Jewish schools in Palestine since the late nineteenth century as part of the educational efforts of the Zionist movement, which strove to create a "new Jewish man," radically distinct from a "Diaspora Jew." The model of the new man was embodied in the figure of the *halutz* (pioneer): a proud farmer with a collectivist attitude, making do with little, ready for self-sacrifice, working to "redeem" the land (Firer 1985:152–61). In fact, one of the basic Zionist tenets was the "negation of the Diaspora," which meant that the period of exile had acquired negative connotations. According to this view, due to their lack of sovereignty, the existence of the Jews was abnormal and defective during that time, whereas in the periods of the First and the Second Temples, they had been full of strength and vigor. Zionist identity was thus dependent upon creating an opposition between itself and the previous phase of Jewish history, while emulating the earlier phase of that history—a move typical of modern revolutionary movements that reject the immediate past in favor of a more distant one (Raz-Krakotzkin 1993, 1994).

The organization that sought to develop a system of school ceremonies was the National Fund Teachers' Association, a voluntary body founded in 1927, whose goal was to advance Zionist education in schools (Ichilov 1993: 40–68; Siton 1994). The underlying assumption of the association was that ceremonies would enable it to reach students not only through their intellect, but also through experiences that would affect all the senses. The teachers argued that the attempt to build a different kind of Jewish community in Palestine, away from the Diaspora, required speedy formation of a new tradition. They believed this could be achieved mainly through the young generation that—in contrast to its parents—was not chained to the past.

Most of the ceremonies that took place in the period before the establishment of the state in 1948 were held within the framework of traditional Jewish holidays. In the pre-state period they were imbued with an agricultural-national significance while their traditional/religious origin was blurred (Leibman and Don-Yehiya 1983:48–55). At the same time, the Jewish community in Palestine began to develop a new tradition of ceremonies based on modern "national" dates which included the "birthday" of the Jewish National Fund (19th of the Jewish month of Tevet) and the anniversary of Theodor Herzl's death (9th of Tamuz). But these two dates remained at the margins of the new system of holidays, and only Tel-Hai Day (11th of Adar), which inaugurated the tradition of collective memorial days, attained central importance (Shapira 1992:141–56; Zertal 1994; Zerubavel 1995).

This memorial day commemorated the death in battle of Joseph Trumpeldor and his comrades at Tel-Hai on March 3, 1920, transforming them into model figures—pioneers and heroic fighters—with whom students were to identify. The Teachers' Association, together with other organizations such as the Histadrut (General Workers' Union) and Zionist youth movements, anthologized, published, and distributed to schools special brochures containing songs, stories, playlets, and general guidelines for the organization of the ceremony. The celebration of Tel-Hai Day included most of the motifs of the national memorial days created after the establishment of the state: heroism and self-sacrifice, the struggle of the few against the many, and the relationship between death, commemoration, and national revival. Furthermore, the basic elements of Memorial Day ceremonies—their solemn atmosphere, the pageantry, and the educational agenda—were already manifest in the 11th of Adar rites. Tel-Hai Day became, in fact, a model for the national Memorial Day ceremonies, which eventually usurped its position among school ceremonies.

After the establishment of the state, memorial days were marked mainly in schools belonging to the state educational system, which had replaced the voluntary, pluralistic, and politicized pre-state system. The educational content hardly changed, but the new system was more homogeneous and centralized, which allowed for better control of teachers and students (Carmon 1985:135–46). Since the state assumed responsibility for all facets of education, the Teachers' Association was pushed aside, transforming it from an independent body into one subordinated to the Ministry of Education and Culture and to the Jewish National Fund. The two faces of the new state—on the one hand, a political system with democratic features, and on the other hand, the embodiment of a nation—caused a split in the manner in which the future citizens were shaped. While citizenship was studied at school as a "universal" subject, related to theoretical questions of government and society, commemorative ceremonies became the principal means through which the values of "love of the fatherland and loyalty to the State of Israel"[4] were inculcated. These values were also instilled through the study of school disciplines such as history and geography (Firer 1985; Bar-Gal 1993); however, these subjects were usually taught according to the general principles of each discipline, and the patriotic values did not occupy a central place. In contrast, memorial ceremonies were integrated into informal activities, such as daily tours and visits to museums, which extended Zionist education outside the classroom.

National memorial days gradually took their place in the calendar during the state's first twenty years, and the first to be officially celebrated was Memorial Day. At first it was integrated into Independence Day celebrations, but in 1951 it was established as a separate event, to be celebrated on the 4th of Iyar, the day before Independence Day. The decision regarding the date was the result of a compromise between various official bodies that were in charge of military commemoration, but in retrospect this choice had deep symbolic meaning; binding mourning and victory together became a uniquely Israeli phenomenon. Officially, Independence Day was more important than Memorial Day: the former was a national holiday, set in law since 1949, while the latter became a national day of mourning only in 1963. But expressions of grief, both private and public, which encompassed large sections of the Jewish population, together with the difficulty of developing a tradition of joyous celebrations, made Memorial Day an event that gradually overshadowed Independence Day (Azaryahu 1995:19–35, 138–63; Don-Yehiya 1988).

Already on the first celebration of Independence Day the Ministry of Education demanded that schools observe the day with ceremonies commemorating the fallen soldiers. During the 1950s, official circulars of the ministry helped to create a standardized form of the event. Because schools were closed on Independence Day, they had to commemorate both the victory in the 1948 war and the fallen soldiers the day before. Since two distinct ceremonies could not be held within such a short time, the same event had to commemorate the two faces of independence, but the structure of the ceremony emphasized grief over the death of the soldiers at the expense of the joy of victory.

Holocaust Day was established officially in 1951, through the legislation of "Holocaust and Ghetto Uprising Day" law. The choice of the date (27th of Nissan, after the holiday of Passover) meant that the Holocaust was commemorated through the memory of the Warsaw Ghetto uprising, which began on Passover 1943. But the day's particular place in the Jewish calendar, five days after the end of Passover and a week before Independence Day, also separated it from the other Jewish days of mourning. Another reason for choosing this date was that it could be incorporated into the school calendar, thus enabling mobilization of the students for the purpose of the commemoration. Despite this official sanction, Holocaust Day remained a marginal event during the 1950s, due to the complex attitude towards the survivors of the Holocaust—a mixture of feelings of superiority towards the Jews of the Diaspora, shame in that they went like "sheep to slaughter," and guilt over the meager help offered to them. Furthermore, Holocaust survivors, who wished to be integrated as fast as possible into the new society, were not inclined to talk openly about their past. Accordingly, schools dealt sparingly with the Holocaust in both formal and informal education. At the time, no school ceremonies were held on Holocaust Day, but on that day teachers were required to discuss issues of the Holocaust and heroism for an hour, using special brochures containing testimonies and memoirs that were published by the Ministry of Education and Yad VaShem institute.[5]

The status of Holocaust Day changed in the early 1960s following two events. The first was the passage of the "Holocaust and Heroism Day" law (1959), which decreed, among other things, the sounding of a siren to mark the beginning of the day, the closure of places of entertainment in the evening, and the holding of memorial ceremonies in army camps and schools. The second event was Adolph Eichmann's trial in Jerusalem in 1961, which riveted public opinion, and after which it became impossible to ignore the Holocaust as a central chapter in the history of the Jewish people. The central place of Holocaust Day was also evident in the education system. Since 1963 schools have been required to hold yearly Holocaust Day ceremonies which followed the model of Memorial Day ceremonies. In the same year the Ministry of Education introduced for the first time a school program, which was destined for elementary and high schools, and whose subject was Holocaust and heroism. The program was to be taught around Holocaust Day, which indicated that the intellectual aspect of the subject was secondary to its emotional dimension (Yablonka 1994; Keren 1985; Segev 1991; Friedlander 1990; Young 1990).

The third memorial day, Jerusalem Day, was the last of the national memorial days to become an official celebration, and was also the least important.[6] The day was fixed for the 28th of Iyar, to commemorate the conquest of the eastern part of the city during the Six Day War (1967), yet the law did not stipulate any specific form of commemoration. The celebration of Jerusalem Day developed therefore gradually, during the late 1960s and early 1970s, as a local initiative of the Jerusalem municipality and other government agencies.[7] The Ministry of Education instructed schools to mark Jerusalem Day after 1971, but it had been celebrated sporadically prior to that year. The manner of the commemoration was similar to that of Holocaust Day in the 1950s. Teachers were asked to discuss with their students the meaning of "liberated, united, Jerusalem, capital of the State of Israel,"[8] either in the classroom or in general assemblies. The Jerusalem Day ceremony was further developed during the 1992–93 school year, when the capital and its history became the education system's central theme for the year. Special ceremonies were held in many schools, but this was not followed by the creation of a tradition of commemorative events. The position of Jerusalem Day remains secondary in comparison with the other memorial days, not only because it has not been given official status, but also because the Ministry of Education has been unsuccessful in imbuing it with a unique character.

The special brochures issued by the ministry for the 1993 Jerusalem Day expressed the tension between two primary components.[9] The date of Jerusalem Day (28 of Iyar) points, first, to the city's conquest during the Six Day War and underlines the particular meaning of the event for the Jewish people ("The Temple Mount is in our hands"). But the celebration is supposed to have also a universal dimension, by emphasizing the "dilemmas that arise from the co-existence of different cultures, religions and nationalities in the united city which is a spiritual symbol for all of them."[10] However, the tension between these two components remained on paper only; in the actual Jerusalem Day ceremonies, the particular, nationalist aspects had the upper hand. The ceremonies commemorated the soldiers who fell in the 1967 battle for Jerusalem and were not very different from those of Memorial Day. The universal dimension, which was too abstract, and could not serve as an emotional focal point, was suppressed. As a result, the Jerusalem Day school ceremonies were unable to take root.

The position of the memorial days in the Jewish calendar resulted from various considerations, such as the date of the event to be commemorated, pressure of interest groups, and dates of nearby holidays. Finally, a compact cycle of national holidays was formed, beginning at Passover and ending with Jerusalem Day, which gave meaning to the history of the Jewish people and the state of Israel as it unfolded in the spring. The use of the Jewish calendar to determine dates of memorial days placed them in a wider cultural context, and created a connection between the traditional Jewish holidays and modern "secular" commemoration. The journalist Doron Rosenblum claims that this period has become a "series of educational experiences" and suggests that "because of [them], spring has become in Israel a type of a national Memento Mori." [11] However, the scheduling of memorial days in this season may lead to a position that interprets them as signifying renewal that comes after death, in a never-ending chain of destruction and rebirth. This is also the basic mythical pattern lying at the basis of the history of the Jewish people: the movement between the Diaspora and the Land of Israel, identical to the movement between destruction—or a threat of destruction—and redemption, and between servitude and liberty (Walzer 1993; Handelman and Katz 1990:198–99).

The story of the exodus from Egypt, told in the Passover ceremony, embodies this pattern in its ancient manifestation. The other memorial days express it in relation to the history of the twentieth century. Holocaust Day commemorates, accordingly, the modern attempt to exterminate the Jewish people, and the Warsaw Ghetto uprising is the heroic spark that will be ignited again in the Land of Israel. Memorial Day commemorates the victims that needed to be sacrificed in order to achieve the long-awaited liberation, which is then celebrated on Independence Day. And Jerusalem Day represents yet another stage in the realization of independence and the progress toward complete redemption. The establishment of the State of Israel and the expansion of its borders are represented as the sole goal toward which Jewish history strives, and the only conclusion that can be deduced from the attempts to destroy the Jewish people in the Diaspora.

This mythical pattern was to be found also in the education system, as in the "From Holocaust to Revival" curriculum created in 1975, and intended to "deepen in our students' hearts the feelings of belonging to the nation and the state." [12] But the pattern was above all manifested in the three commemorative ceremonies, which separately and together signified a historical progression, from destruction to redemption. Despite the unique circumstances of their creation, these ceremonies had much in common. This was to be seen, first and foremost, in the structure of the events, which was one of the means by which the ceremonies were infused with meaning. This structure also enabled the creation of a connection between school ceremonies and national identity.

The Structure of the Ceremony

The anthropologist Don Handelman claims that official ceremonies in modern industrialized, bureaucratized states are based on the principle of addition and multiplication of identical elements, and reflect the state's ability to mobilize large quantities of manpower and material resources. Only in this way can these ceremonies create the required effect and convey the desired messages. The military parade in Moscow's Red Square during Soviet rule was for him a good example: large numbers of identical soldiers and motorized weapons passed in procession in front of the leaders.[13] The school memorial ceremony was, by comparison, a modest event, but when we examine the educational commemorative effort in its totality it becomes apparent that it too followed the same principle of multiplication, which, in this case, worked through reproduction in space. The Ministry of Education's modern bureaucratic apparatus, which not only coordinated educational activities, but also distributed educational material, contributed to the reproduction of memorial ceremonies in two ways: through the simultaneous celebration of similar memorial ceremonies in most schools, and through creating similarities between the three different memorial ceremonies. But such reproduction was not mechanical, like the one that—according to Walter Benjamin—brought about the loss of the holy aura surrounding the unique work of art. It was, rather, a reproduction that maintained the sacredness of the event (Benjamin 1969). Every one of the ceremonies was unique, unfolding in particular time and place, allowing its participants to "touch" the sacred dimension of the nation's values. In addition, there was no single, original, "authentic" ceremony which was reproduced by the other ceremonies, but a general model that generated similar ceremonies (Ben-Amos and Ben-Ari 1995).

The general model allowed the organizers of the ceremony a significant amount of freedom, as we learn from a circular sent to all schools on the first celebration of Independence Day. It states that the Ministry of Education regulations constitute "an obligatory framework for the school's celebration, a framework that every school will fill with the content that seems to it fit for the occasion." The framework included, in this case, coming to school in holiday attire, raising the national flag—a symbol of national unity ("No symbol or slogan is to be added to the flag"), and a rigid timetable, according to which the ceremony would begin at 10 A.M., and would stop "exactly at 10:45," in order to hear a speech by the Minister of Education, Zalman Shazar, "which will be broadcast (by radio) to all the children of the country." The ceremony would then end with the singing of the national anthem, *Ha'Tiqva*.[14] Like the framework, the overall meaning of the ceremony and even the feelings of the students were predetermined: "the beginning of the fulfillment of the longings of generations, the joy over the acquirement of freedom and national independence, reward for daring acts of heroism, and compensation for the suffering and sacrifices of the nation."[15]

During the 1950s, other elements were added to the Memorial Day ceremony, and it got its permanent format, which remained unchanged into the 1990s. With the encouragement of the Ministry of Education, schools began constructing memorial corners and monuments to their graduates who had fallen in the War of Independence, inviting their families to the ceremonies.[16] In these schools, the ceremonies were held alongside the monuments, and names of the dead, usually engraved on the monument, were read aloud during the event, in the presence of the bereaved families.[17] The relationship between the schools and the families was strengthened in 1954, when delegations of students began to put flowers on soldiers' graves in military cemeteries. Furthermore, a connection was formed between school-time and national-time by the siren which marked the commencement of Memorial Day and created a two-minute "frozen" moment in time throughout the country, affording communion with the memory of the fallen (Azaryahu 1995:153–57). Beginning in 1958, the siren was set at 10 A.M., and most schools used to begin their memorial ceremony with these two minutes of silence, thus synchronizing the educational and national schedules.

Other symbolic actions that became integral parts of the memorial ceremony included the lighting of a memorial candle or torch, the lowering of the flag to half-mast, an honor guard of students, and a march in front the monument saluting the fallen soldiers.[18] Very often the participants were treated like soldiers in a parade, being required to stand alternately at ease and at attention, thus imparting a military quality to the ceremony. The outcome was the creation of an equation between bereavement, the state, the army, and the education system.

Holocaust Day ceremony acquired many of the characteristics of the Memorial Day ceremony not only because the latter took shape first, but also because of the similarity between the main themes: bereavement, sacrifice, heroism, and resurrection. The basic structure of the ceremony was fixed rather early, in 1963. It included, like the Memorial Day ceremony, a siren sound at the beginning, the lowering of the flag to half-mast, and the lighting of six candles (in memory of the six million victims).[19] Other elements of the ceremony that have been added since then also increased the similarity with Memorial Day: arriving to school in blue and white holiday attire, the military dimension of the event, and ending the ceremony with the singing of *Ha'Tiqva*. In one ceremony, held in a high school in the southern part of Israel in 1994, the singing of the anthem was preceded by a quasi-military parade of students, similar to the parade held in front of the school's memorial during the Memorial Day ceremony.

Yet the structure of Holocaust Day ceremony was, on the whole, less rigid and more dynamic than that of Memorial Day. While the latter took place against a background of continuous violent confrontations between the State of Israel and the Arabs, and reflected a relatively stable conception of Israeli-Arab relations, Holocaust Day commemorated a unique event, whose memory was influenced by the changes in Israeli society. Thus, for example, a new kind of ceremony appeared in some schools in the 1990s: it was based on the experiences of delegations of students who had gone on a visit to the Nazi concentration camps in Poland (Segev 1991:451–68; Keren 1998). These ceremonies included oral testimonies by students or the screening of films documenting their visits. Yet, even with these additions, the basic framework of the ceremony remained the same, and its meaning did not change.[20]

Jerusalem Day ceremony, the "youngest" of the three school ceremonies, was also the least codified. It lacked the symbolic gestures related to bereavement and mourning, though many of the texts referred to battles that took place in Jerusalem during the War of Independence and the Six Days War—texts similar to those read at Memorial Day ceremonies. In addition, the Jerusalem Day ceremony took place in the same locations as the other ceremonies: in the schoolyard, near the memorial to the fallen graduates, or in the school gymnasium, where the Holocaust Day ceremony was usually held. These locations, where the memorial ceremonies took place year after year, took on a special meaning, which was later conferred on other ceremonies as well.

The structure of the memorial ceremonies was a sign that they did not belong to the mundane realm of schooling, but to the sacred realm of national identity. These were extraordinary events, based on order, discipline, and a clear hierarchy, which rendered them especially authoritative (Moore and

Myerhoff 1977; Goffman 1974:58). Their authority also derived from the main speech, which was usually delivered by the principal or one of the teachers, defining for the students the meaning of the event. The speech was an integral part of the symbolic action of the ceremony, which had an important function: expressing the movement of the Jewish people from destruction to redemption. Certain elements of the ceremony represented the pole of destruction and mourning: the lowering of the flag to half-mast, lighting of memorial candles, and reading of the names of the fallen soldiers. Other elements symbolized the opposite pole, that of recovery and resurrection: the military aspects of the ceremony, which emphasized the role of the Israel Defense Forces (IDF) as a tool of redemption, the parade of students, expressing power and determination, and the singing of "Ha'Tiqva," which testified to of Israel's status as a sovereign nation. In addition, the very possibility of holding such ceremonies without interference was a further testimony to the fact that the nation had successfully made the transition from servitude to freedom.

Aside from these symbolic gestures, the memorial ceremonies included songs, recitations, and dances that formed the heart of the event, and belonged to a theatrical genre known in Hebrew as *masechet* (holiday pageant). This type of didactic theater originated in the Proletkult movement of the Russian Revolution, and was also used by the German communists in the period between the two world wars. It was brought to Palestine by socialist Jewish immigrants from Eastern Europe, and became popular among the youth movements and the kibbutzim prior to the establishment of the state. One could also often encounter it at various official mass gatherings and political meetings (Ophrat 1980:200–224; Mally 1990). The holiday pageant assumed various forms, but it was usually based on short plays with a uniform narrative structure, telling the story of the resurrection of the Jewish people with the help of a narrator, a choir, actors, and an orchestra, who were directly addressing the audience.

Beginning in the 1950s, the stature of such pageants declined as a result of their overly didactic nature. The education system preserved them because they suited the needs of schools, but the structure of the pageants was modified. Instead of using a single text by a certain writer expressing a coherent worldview, they were made of a collage of prose pieces, poems, and songs drawn from a variety of sources such as books, letters, and diaries. But despite the diversity of sources and authors, the pageants did not create a polyphony, reflecting diverse views and perspectives (Bakhtin 1981). Though the Ministry of Education allowed schools to choose the texts and decide upon their order of appearance, it edited and published special brochures which included a selection of texts and model ceremonies.[21] These brochures, which reflected the official point of view, simplified the organizers' role, and contributed to the creation of a limited repertoire of texts that appeared in most ceremonies. Even so, the similarity between pageants was an indication of a wide consensus, at least among the teachers who organized the ceremonies, concerning the meaning of Jewish history.

At times, however, texts that deviated from the official version of the national past were presented in the ceremonies, but even they could not change the consensual meaning of the events.[22] The symbolic gestures that opened and closed the ceremonies created a framework that encompassed the pageant—like a Chinese box that contained another, smaller one—and determined the overall meaning of the various texts (MacAloon 1985:258–60). In addition, texts were not presented by title or by author's name, but anonymously, one following another in a way that obscured their uniqueness and created a continuing textual flow.

While the symbolic gestures were relatively simple, the texts presented during the pageants were multi-layered, and contained a great deal of information that conveyed the characteristics of the national identity—the ceremony's "protagonist." This identity did not represent a historical reality reflected in the texts, but was rather an imaginary construct that guided the organizers and served as a model for students. The analysis of this construct requires us to pay close attention to the texts heard during the pageants.

Texts and Identity: "Only to Tell of Myself Did I Know"

The basic assumption informing any act of commemoration is the existence of a multi-dimensional identity: those being commemorated were identical among themselves, and were free of inner conflicts; we, the commemorators, are the same, that is, unified among ourselves; the commemorators are identical to those whom they commemorate; in the future the commemorators will always be the same (Ozouf 1983). In order to emphasize this common identity, one needs to emphasize those elements that underline similarities and ignore those that point to differences. As Renan has observed: "The essence of the nation is that all individuals have many things in common, and also that they have forgotten many things" (Renan [1882] 1990:11). The reconstruction of the past (of those who are commemorated) and the description of the present (of the commemorators) in the ceremonies could not display the entire historical gamut, but only a limited range of phenomena. A gap was thus created between the information that the student received in history and civic lessons and the information presented in memorial ceremonies.

True, the information received in the classroom was often one-dimensional and distorted (Podeh 1997), but the historical picture presented in the ceremonies was even more simplistic. The effect of the ceremonies was stronger because of their emotional dimension and repetitious nature. When students reached the upper grades of junior high or high school in which the history of the twentieth century was studied, their image of the national past—an image that was difficult to change—had been already formed.

Every type of identity, whether personal or collective, needs the "other" in order to fashion itself against it. The nation, too, as big as it may be, is always limited in its scope and strives to differentiate itself from other nations and groups that do not belong to it (Connely 1991:1–15; Anderson 1991:7; Tajfel 1981). Israeli national identity is no different, in principle, from other national identities, and like them it was formed through a long, complex process in which the "other" was used to define the collective "self." Due to space limitations, we cannot address this issue at length, but only analyze how the distinction between the self and the other was elaborated at school memorial ceremonies, and how it contributed to the formation of a national identity.

This distinction was based on a set of oppositions, in which the first member represented the collective self and the second stood for the other, such as Jews/non-Jews, Zionist Jews/Diaspora Jews, Israelis/Arabs, Ashkenazim (European Jews)/Sephardim (Oriental Jews), men/women (Raz-Krakotzkin 1993, 1994; Piterberg 1995; Lentin 1998; Kimmerling and Moore 1997). This was not a consistent and clear-cut binary system, but a series of vague, imprecise differences, partially overlapping each other, emphasized or ignored in accordance with changing ceremonial circumstances. Often only the collective self was represented in the texts, while the other was conspicuously absent. This was the result of the nature of the commemorative event, in which it was possible to focus only on those factors that constituted identity, and to do so in such a fashion as to present a one-dimensional world where the self existed alone, without any reciprocal relationship with others.

The most basic definition of the collective self in the ceremonies is that of "The People of Israel," which appears in the *Yizkor* (Remember) prayer that opens both the Holocaust Day pageant ("The People of Israel shall remember the sacred communities in the Diaspora, which were uprooted, destroyed and obliterated . . .") and the Memorial Day pageant ("The People of Israel shall remember its sons and daughters, who gave their lives in the struggle for the establishment of the state, and the soldiers of the Israel Defense

Forces . . ."). This "People" is a communal body with flexible contours, vaguely defined both in time and space. It can be imagined as the Jewish People living in the Diaspora for many generations, as the Hebrew nation returning to its land in the twentieth century, or as a combination of both.[23] The command to remember, which appears in Avraham Shlonski's poem *Neder* ("Vow") ("I made a vow: To remember all, to remember—and forget nothing"), defines for the participants in the ceremony their role: to secure, through commemoration, the future existence of the nation. The texts that later appear in the pageant detail and illustrate the *Yizkor* prayer, which outlines in general terms the content of the commemoration, without changing the meaning of the event.

Who is the other that confronts the People of Israel and contributes, by the way of negation, to its definition? In the Holocaust Day pageant, which often includes prose pieces with detailed historical information, there is no doubt as to its identity: "the Nazi oppressor" or "the German" is the figure responsible for the terrible tragedy, and is also the enemy against whom the ghetto fighters rebelled. The Memorial Day pageant, on the other hand, includes more poems than prose, and focuses on the grief and mourning of families and friends of the fallen soldiers. These texts do not usually contain a direct reference to the enemy, and the circumstances of death remain unknown. Arnon Lapid, for example, describes at the beginning of his reminiscences, "Invitation to Cry," his meeting with his friend Uriel on the morning of a battle, "a few hours before he fell," and describes the plans they made for the future. After this introduction he suddenly skips forward in time: "At noon his body too lay, covered by a blanket, near the field hospital."[24]

Putting the emphasis on the collective self and its suffering blurs the differences between the enemies, and creates a parallel between the Nazis and the Arabs as enemies who both wish to destroy the People of Israel (Zuckerman 1993). The reading in Memorial Day pageants of prose pieces written in the context of the wars that Israel has fought since 1948, without noting the circumstances and the dates of the writing, obliterates the unique features of these wars, and gives the impression that what is described is the same war that repeats itself again and again. The unique features are further obscured by the emphasis on the grief of those who remained alive, as in Avraham Halfi's poem, *Tkhila Bokhim* ("At First We Cry") (Miron 1992: 193–95). Dead soldiers appear in these texts as passive victims of a war that is taken for granted and that broke out without apparent reason. This image is opposed to the Zionist aspiration to play an active role in history—which is eventually fulfilled with the establishment of the state of Israel. In this way, the actions of the state become an undisputed given, with no mention of the political controversies that surround them (Shapira 1992; Ginosar and Bareli 1996).

In contrast to the passivity attributed to the soldiers, the Holocaust Day pageants emphasized the actions of the ghetto fighters, as commemorated in the second half of the official title of the Memorial Day ("Holocaust and Heroism Day"). The opposition between Diaspora Jews, who went "as sheep to slaughter," and active Zionists, who successfully fought for the establishment of the state, created a situation whereby Israeli society commemorated the only group it could identify with: those who fought the Nazis, and especially the Warsaw Ghetto fighters. They were compared to the fighters of Masada, the defenders of Tel-Hai, and the soldiers who fought in 1948, whose tales of their bravery were told in great detail in the memorial ceremonies (Zerubavel 1994).

One such tale was the letter, written on April 23, 1943, by the commander of the Warsaw Ghetto uprising, Mordechai Anilewitz, in which he summarized the achievements of the fighters: "My life's final aspiration has been fulfilled. Self-defense became a fact. Opposition and revenge were a reality. I am happy that I was among the first Jewish fighters in the ghetto."[25] Another popular letter, written by the paratrooper Opher Feniger, who fell in the battle over Jerusalem in the Six Day War, illustrates the Zionist "lesson" of the Holocaust. Feniger sent the letter to his girlfriend in 1963 after reading *The Dollhouse*, a book on the Holocaust by K. Cetnik, and after visiting Prague and the Holocaust Museum in Kibbutz Lohamei Ha'Getaot. His conclusions were unambiguous: "I feel that out of all the horror and helplessness, there arises in me a great force and a will to be strong; strong unto tears; strong and sharp like a knife; quiet and terrible . . . Never again to be led to slaughter" (Carmon and Oron 1975b:88). This was the only piece read in Holocaust Day pageants in which the name of the author, his role, and the circumstances of his death were mentioned, due to the assumption that mentioning them would give his words special force.

Alongside the distinction between Israelis (superior and proud) and Diaspora Jews (inferior and low-spirited), there was a distinction between Jews of European extraction (Ashkenazi Jews) and Jews from Muslim countries (Sephardic Jews). As opposed to school curricula and history textbooks, this distinction was not explicit in Holocaust and Memorial Day ceremonies (Ben-Amos 1995). However, the central place occupied by the victims of the Holocaust and the fallen soldiers in the national identity, together with the Sephardim's inability to take an active part in the commemoration, made them marginal even in the domain of official memory. The Holocaust took place, after all, in Europe, and despite the destruction of Sephardic communities, such as that of Salonica, and the threat posed to North African Jewry, it was, first and foremost, a tragedy of European Jews. Thus, for example, when students were required in 1955 to complete a "witness form" as part of the Yad VaShem's project to register "the names of the victims of the Holocaust and heroism," the Sephardic students were unable to take part.[26] As a result, the writers of the school program "Jewish Vitality in the Holocaust" maintained that they were "aware of the difficulty of arousing interest in and understanding of the Holocaust among Sephardic students." They also feared that the widespread opinion that "only Ashkenazi Jews were killed" contradicted the ideology of the "common destiny of the Jewish people" (Carmon and Oron 1975b:2, 7). In addition, the selections read in Holocaust Day ceremonies mentioned only the experiences of European Jews. Only the music of Yehuda Poliker and Ya'akov Gilad *Efer VeAvak* ("Ashes and Dust") (1988), whose songs were often performed in Holocaust Day pageants, added a Sephardic element to the ceremonies (Gavish 1998:208).

Like Holocaust Day ceremonies, Memorial Day ceremonies made it difficult for Sephardic students to identify with those who fell in the wars. The structure of Memorial Day commemoration took shape in the early 1950s, and the heroes of the ceremony were the soldiers who fell in the War of Independence. Despite the fact that the number of Israel's war casualties has tripled since then (rising to about nineteen thousand), this structure has remained almost unchanged. Most of those commemorated among the dead soldiers of the 1948 war belonged to the elite of Jewish society: native-born, well-educated, and well-connected (Sivan 1991). The various features of the commemoration reflected Israeli culture, which was formed in that period, combining European elements with "native" Hebrew practices into a unique, novel structure (Even-Zohar 1980; Almog 1997). The immigrants from North Africa who arrived in the 1950s and completely changed the demographic balance in Israel remained for many years outside the political and cultural elites in Israel. They had, therefore, no influence on the shaping of Memorial Day ceremonies. Even in the 1990s the genre of the *masechet* continued to dominate the ceremonies, and most of the readings were pieces composed in relation to the War of Independence by such writers and poets as Nathan Alterman, Hayim Guri, and Hayim Hefer, who operated within the new Israeli cultural tradition. The pieces that were added afterwards to that repertoire, by writers such as Ehud Manor, Nathan Yonathan, and Naomi Shemer, belonged to the same tradition. Although Ashkenazi hegemony had broken down in many domains of Israeli society, Sephardic culture was still considered populist and inferior. It could not, therefore, enter the sacred realm of military commemoration, which required a solemn and serious attitude (Bourdieu 1979).

The gender aspect of Israeli identity, as expressed in the memorial ceremonies, did not obey—unlike other aspects—the dialectics of presence/absence, but relied on differences between the various modes of presence. Like other political bodies, modern nations—and the Israeli nation among them—made use of the metaphor of the family in defining themselves (Hunt 1992; Raz-Krakotzkin 1991). This metaphor transforms the nation into a familiar entity, with which one can easily identify. However, it also contains a clear division of roles between men and women, typical of modern society in which nationalism emerged. This division placed men at the head of the family and women in a secondary position of wife and mother. However, at times a more equitable relationship formed within the imaginary family. This is why one should pay close attention to the gender dimension of the ceremonies, and also note the differences between Holocaust Day and Memorial Day.

One of the central texts of the Holocaust Day pageant making use of the family metaphor is *Nizkor* ("We Shall Remember") by Abba Kovner. The poem opens with the command "We shall remember our brothers and sisters," which creates solidarity and equality across gender boundaries. Kovner then lists the victims who are to be remembered, specifying "families of man" that belong to "the Jewish people": "the elderly . . . the mother . . . the young girl . . . the infant . . . the man . . . the woman . . ." However, when he describes those who resisted the Nazis, Kovner uses only the masculine pronoun: "and they (men) are those who fought back, disregarding the danger." [27] Nevertheless, the emphasis on the act of resistance did not result in exclusive recognition of the role of men. Female figures such as Tzvia Lubetkin, one of the leaders of the Warsaw Ghetto uprising, and Hanna Senesh, the parachutist sent to Europe by the Jewish community in Palestine, were accorded an important place in Holocaust Day ceremonies.

The attitude to "heroism" began to gradually change after the Yom Kippur War (1973), and, as a result, also the attitude towards gender in the context of commemoration. The anxiety provoked before the war by the military threat undermined Israeli society's self-confidence and narrowed the mental gap between it and Diaspora Jews. The new attitude, and the decline in the importance of the soldier as a Zionist hero, led to an increased emphasis on the suffering of the victims, with greater attention to daily life in ghettos and concentration camps. New figures were added to the pantheon of those meriting commemoration: women, children, and especially girls. A typical piece was Anda Amir Pinkerfeld's *Buba Sarina* ("Sarina the Doll"), which told the story of Lea, a four-year-old who took her doll to the concentration camp, drawing comfort from it. Holocaust Day ceremonies presented, then, a complex image of gender roles: women and children—usually grouped together—had a prominent place among the passive victims, whereas among the fighters, who continued to play an important role in the ceremonies of the 1990s, one could find both men and women.

Memorial Day ceremony, on the other hand, presented a one-dimensional image of gender roles, in which there was clear division between women and men. This distinction was based on the division of labor within the IDF, in which all combat soldiers, and therefore almost all casualties, were men. However, this division was not a "natural" one but was based on a cultural conception that viewed women and territory as male assets, which the men had to defend (Berghahn 1981; Yuval-Davis 1997:93–115). The IDF's central role in Israeli culture and society gave birth to a situation in which its particular gender concepts influenced all of society, finding expression in, among other places and events, Memorial Day ceremonies (Ben-Eliezer 1995; Kimmerling 1993; Feder and Ben-Ari 1999). True, a reading of the two central texts used in the pageants reveals equality along gender lines. The official version of *Yizkor* ("Remember") calls on the "People of Israel" to remember their "sons and daughters"; the heroes of Nathan Alterman's *Magash Ha'Kesef* ("Silver Platter") are "a young woman and a young man" who sacrificed their lives for the fatherland (Miron 1992: 63–87). But both these texts were written in the period of the War of Independence, before the IDF's elaboration of the distinction between men (fighters, strong, superior) and women (non-combatants, weak, inferior). A piece typical of gender divisions was Hayim Hefer's poem *Misdar Ha'Noflim* ("The Parade of the Fallen Soldiers"), written after the Six Day War, which describes the dead soldiers forming ranks "with manly steps, strong and tanned . . . brave like lions, daring like tigers . . ."

The key description of the relationship among male soldiers, and between them and their social surroundings, was "camaraderie." The connection between the male friendship ideal and nationalism was formed in Germany in the early nineteenth century, during the wars of independence against Napoleon's armies (Mosse 1985). Previously, friendship among men had been valued as superior to sensual, heterosexual love because of its intellectual dimension. The war added a military dimension to it and related it to the love of the fatherland.

Such romantic conceptions are to be found in a wide variety of pageant texts, from the Biblical lament of David over Jonathan, through Azariya

Merimtchik's letter about his friends who fell in a battle of the 1948 war ("They were my brothers. I loved them all! All of them!!!"[28]), to Naomi Shemer's song *Anachnu Shneinu Meoto HaKfar* ("We Are Both From the Same Village"). The most important text, one that deals in its entirety with this subject, is a poem written by Hayim Guri and set to music by Alexander Argov, *Ha'Reut* ("Companionship"), which has become one of the most popular songs of the pageants (Miron 1992: 246–51). In the poem, Guri ties together friendship among men, the death of soldiers, and the commemoration of the fallen, expressing the connection between destruction and resurrection in the lines: "A love sanctified by blood / You will bloom among us again." Although these texts belong to separate genres, they all share a dual function: to demonstrate equality among brothers in arms, in a way that suggests the absence of hierarchy among the members of the nation; and to exclude women from this masculine group, because of their inability to take part in the "fighters' brotherhood."

But though they were excluded from the group, women continued to play important symbolic roles in Memorial Day ceremonies. Their special position—outside the world of men, but within the nation—turned them into the principal addressee of the discourse of friendship. A typical example is the letter from a paratrooper read at a Memorial Day pageant held at a high school near Tel Aviv in 1994. The paratrooper tells his mother about a friend of his who was killed, and ends the letter with the words: "Mom, if one day my commanders come to your home, wounded and in pain, regard them as my partners. . . . Remember: I was one of them. I believed in my way—which was also theirs." The ending alludes to the principal role of women, for which they must prepare themselves: to carry the weight of bereavement, as mothers, widows, or daughters, and personify the nation mourning its sons.[29] While Memorial Day pageants did include texts written by bereaved fathers, most presented the painful, feminine point of view and transformed the "family of the bereaved" into a collective body devoid of men (Viztum and Malkinson 1993). Thus, for example, the grief of a teacher, a mother who had lost her soldier son, was at the center of a Memorial Day ceremony held at a high school in the southern part of the country in 1994. The teacher opened the ceremony with a speech in which she defined Memorial Day as an event that combined private grief and public sorrow and united Israeli society. Afterwards she read a poem about her longing for her son, written after his death. In another Memorial Day ceremony, held in 1993 in an elementary school in the southern part of the country, a girl student who had lost her father read a letter that she had written, in which she expressed grief but also pride in his death "for the fatherland." While males, as soldiers, were directly identified with the nation, women were dependent upon men in order to form a (bereaved) identity of their own, which allowed them to become part of the nation.

What is the meaning of the deaths of the victims of the Holocaust and the soldiers who died in war? Did they indeed die "for the fatherland," or for another purpose? Or, perhaps their deaths had no meaning? Since there was no way to ask the dead, the answer was provided by the commemorators who took them under their auspices: they had died to assure the lives of those who commemorated them, in other words, the nation, the fatherland, the state, and the People of Israel, which became a single abstract body during the ceremonies. But this answer was still too general, and the pageants gave the deaths a more succinct meaning through selected texts written by or in the name of those who fell. The Zionist "lesson" of the Holocaust, which has been transmitted in history textbooks (Firer 1989), was imparted in Holocaust Day pageants as well by describing the fighting in the ghettos as a link in the chain of Jewish heroism that led all the way to the IDF. Even texts of a different kind, dealing with women's and children's daily struggle for survival, which could have been given universal meaning, received a particular, Zionist meaning. The structure of the ceremony and at times the teachers' speeches emphasized the message that only the existence of the state and its army could prevent the Jews from becoming helpless victims once again.

Memorial Day ceremonies imparted Zionist meaning to the deaths of soldiers through another rhetorical device that was absent from Holocaust Day ceremonies: the words of the "living-dead." The soldier who continued to act and speak after his death—half-dead, half-alive—was a common figure in the poetry of the War of Independence, and was the protagonist of two poems that became the principal texts in the Memorial Day pageants: "*Magash Ha'Kesef*" ("The Silver Platter") by Nathan Alterman and "*Heene Mutalot Gufoteinu*" ("Here Our Bodies Lie") by Hayim Guri (Hever 1986). Although this figure later disappeared from "serious" poetry, it continued to appear in "lower" literary genres such as the popular ballad,[30] and it was part and parcel of Memorial Day ceremonies. The figure provided comfort to the bereaved through its continued existence—albeit symbolic—after death, which suggested revival and renewal even in the midst of grief. The authority granted those who had made the ultimate sacrifice was mainly used to give meaning to their deaths. Alterman's poem is explicit ("We are the silver platter upon which you were given the Jewish state"), whereas in the words of Guri's living-dead soldiers we find a kind of apology ("We did not betray, look, our weapons are with us, emptied of bullets"). Both poems justify the death of the soldiers in the name of the national struggle.

The recitation of these poems by students soon to be enlisted into the army added a dimension missing from the written texts to the ceremony. Just as the role of women was to bear the burden of bereavement in the memorial ceremonies, the role of men was to be sacrificed in war, and to talk to us—the living—from their place among the angels ("Sorry, but we had to / we won the battles and now we rest").[31]

Instead of Conclusion: Subversive Commemoration

Using the figure of the living-dead soldier does not necessarily imply that his sacrifice for the values of the community that had sent him to battle was justified. Archibald MacLeish's poem "The Young Soldiers Who Died," which was included in several Memorial Day pageants, gave its protagonists a voice, but they refused to take a stance, claiming that it was for the living to give meaning to their deaths.[32] However, memorial ceremonies can also express a critical stance towards the official commemorative discourse, either by attributing alternative meanings to the deaths of the soldiers or by shifting the attention to other victims. As Michel Foucault points out, there are no relations of power without resistance, and the latter can be especially effective since it appears in the locations where power is applied (Foucault 1980:142).

The field generating the most explicit resistance to official commemoration was plastic arts, which adopted the same tools used by the commemorators to offer a different reading of the national past. We cannot offer here a complete overview of the works that strove to undermine the official commemorative tradition, but three examples would suffice to delineate the main characteristics of this subversive approach.

In three exhibitions that were held during the 1990s in Tel Aviv—by Nir Nader and Erez Harudi, Gili Meizler, and Meir Gal[33]—the artists incorporated objects and symbols belonging to official commemoration while changing their meaning and disassociating them from their "natural" context (Weiss 1998). Nader and Harudi created a kind of a military memorial site in the gallery, with a clear separation between the audience and the "families of the heroes." Meizler exhibited items that he had purchased at the shop of the Armory Corps memorial in Latrun. Gal presented copies of plaques with street names that commemorated military units, heroic battles, and fallen soldiers (Director 1997). These artists used a variety of artistic media and styles, but all criticized the way in which the state had taken control of private grief in order to turn it into a public affair and harness it to its own goals.

While the artists formulated their criticism from the "outside," using an ironic mode of discourse, the schools that organized alternative memorial ceremonies presented a more "internal"—though no less critical—stand. The need to hold ceremonies on the official day of the commemoration, to respect the general instructions of the Ministry of Education, and to offer students a clear "lesson" led these schools to organize events that sought to produce sympathy with groups that, until then, had not been represented in the ceremonies. It was no coincidence that the two Tel Aviv schools which organized such ceremonies were on the margins of the educational system: Ankori, a private high school for students who had dropped out of the state educational system, and Kedma, a high school in the poor HaTikva neighborhood in Tel Aviv, which was established to promote Sephardic culture. Each school introduced changes in both Holocaust Day and Memorial Day ceremonies; they had a role in the same historical narrative, and any change in the one required a change in the other. The Ankori Holocaust Day ceremony in 1993 was based on a text written by its principal, Israel Perez, in which the visit of the students to the concentration camps in Poland was described as a combination of shopping trip and nationalistic indoctrination. The Memorial Day ceremony held in 1994 included monologues by teachers who had fought in several wars and told of their horrors.[34] In the 1995 Holocaust Day ceremony performed at Kedma High School an additional, seventh, candle was lit in memory of those who were killed but were not commemorated in the official ceremonies: Armenians, Gypsies, Blacks, Indians, and homosexuals. The Memorial Day ceremony that year was based on readings taken from Sephardic sources, and also included a documentary movie about Shimon Ifargan, a resident of the town Ma'alot and a member of a Moroccan family, who fell in the 1982 war in Lebanon.[35]

The intense public debate which followed these subversive events, particularly in the wake of the exhibition by Nader and Harudi and the Holocaust Day ceremony at Kedma,[36] testified to the centrality of the memory of the Holocaust and the mourning over the fallen soldiers in Israeli society. Any deviation from the official meaning given to these events was considered as undermining national identity, and a sacrilegious act. The meanings of death and collective identity were, thus, related to each other, and only a change in one could bring about a change in the other.

REFERENCES

Almog, Oz. 1997. *The Tzabar: A Portrait.* Tel Aviv: Am Oved. [Hebrew.]

Anderson, Benedict. 1991. *Imagined Communities: Reflections on the Origin and Spread of Nationalism.* London: Verso.

Azaryahu, Maoz. 1995. *State Cults: Independence Celebrations and the Commemoration of the Fallen.* Sede Boker: University of Ben-Gurion in the Negev. [Hebrew.]

Bakhtin, Mikhail. 1981. "Discourse in the Novel." In *The Dialogic Imagination: Four Essays,* ed. Michael Holquist, pp. 259–422. Translated by Caryl Emerson and Michael Holquist. Austin: University of Texas Press.

Bar-Gal, Yoram. 1993. *Fatherland and Geography in 100 Years of Zionist Education.* Tel Aviv: Am Oved. [Hebrew.]

Ben-Amos, Avner. 1995. *Impossible Pluralism? European and Eastern Jews in History Curriculum in Israel.* In *Education Toward the 21st Century,* ed. David Chen, pp. 267–76. Tel Aviv: Ramot-, University of Tel Aviv. [Hebrew.]

Ben-Amos, Avner, and Eyal Ben-Ari. 1995. "Resonance and Reverberation: Ritual and Bureaucracy in the State Funerals of the French Third Republic." *Theory and Society* 24(2): 163–91.

Ben-Amos, Avner, and Ilana Bet-El. 1998. "Ceremonies, Education and History: Holocaust Day and Memorial Day in Israeli Schools." In *Education and History,* ed. Emanuel Etkes and Rivka Pheldahi, pp. 457–79. Jerusalem: Shazar Center. [Hebrew.]

Ben-Eliezer, Uri. 1995 *Through the Gun Barrel: The Formation of Israeli Militarism 1936–1956.* Tel Aviv: Dvir. [Hebrew.]

Benjamin, Walter. 1969. "The Work of Art in the Age of Mechanical Reproduction." In *Illuminations,* ed. Hannah Arendt, pp. 217–51. Translated by Harry Zohn. New York: Schocken Books.

Berghahn, Volker. 1981. *Militarism: The History of an International Debate.* Warwickshire: Berg.

Bourdieu, Pierre. 1979. *La distinction: critique sociale du jugement.* Paris: Les Editions de Minuit.

Carmon, Arik. 1985. "Education in Israel—Issues and Problems." In *Education in an Evolving Society,* ed. Walter Akerman, Arik Carmon, and David Zuker, pp. 135–46. Tel Aviv: Ha'Kibbutz. Ha'Meuhad and the Van Lear Institute. [Hebrew.]

Carmon, Arik, and Yair Oron. 1975a. *Jewish Vitality in the Holocaust: The Aims of the Program and Recommendations for Activities.* Jerusalem: Ministry of Education and Culture. [Hebrew.]

———. 1975b. *Jewish Vitality in the Holocaust.* Jerusalem: Ministry of Education and Culture. [Hebrew.]

Connolly, William. 1991. *Identity/Difference: Democratic Negotiations of Political Paradox*. Ithaca: Cornell University Press.

Director, Ruti. 1997. "Meir Gal: I Have a Lover in the Commando." *Studio*
85:69–72. [Hebrew.]

Don-Yehiya, Eliezer. 1988. "Festivals and Political Culture: Independence Day
Celebrations." *Jerusalem Quarterly* 45:61–84.

Doshkin, Alexander. 1961. "What Do We Do to Bequeath the Lessons of the
Holocaust?" In *Teaching the Holocaust in Schools: Discussions and Deliberations*. Jerusalem: Ministry of Education and Culture. [Hebrew.]

Elboim-Dror, Rachel. 1985. "Determining the Educational Policy in Israel."
In *Education in an Evolving Society: The Israeli System*, ed. Walter Aker-
man, Arik Carmon, and David Zuker, pp. 35–116. Tel Aviv: Ha'Kibutz
Ha'Meuhad and the Van Lear Institute. [Hebrew.]

Even-Zohar, Itamar. 1980. "The Growth and Formation of Local and Native
Hebrew Culture in Israel 1882–1948." *Cathedra* 16:206–61. [Hebrew.]

Fargo, Uri. 1984. "The Consciousness of the Holocaust Among Israeli Students." *Newsletter for the Study of the Holocaust* 3:172–89. [Hebrew.]

Feder, Edna, and Eyal Ben-Ari, eds. 1999. *The Military and Militarism in
Israeli Society*. Albany: SUNY Press.

Firer, Ruth. 1985. *Agents of Zionist Education*. Tel Aviv: Ha'Kibutz Ha'Meuhad and Sifriat Poalim. [Hebrew.]

———. 1989. *Agents of the Lesson*. Tel Aviv: Ha'Kibutz Ha'Meuhad.
[Hebrew.]

Foucault, Michel. 1980. *Power/Knowledge: Selected Interviews and Other
Writings, 1972–1977*. New York: Pantheon.

Friedlander, Shaul. 1990. "The *Shoa* Between Memory and History." *The Jerusalem Quarterly* 53:115–26.

Gavish, Ofer. 1998. "Songs on the Psychiatrist's Couch—Songs of the Holocaust Written in Israel." In *Hidden Memory, Public Memory: The Image
of the Holocaust in Israel*, ed. Yoel Rapel, pp. 197–214. Tel Aviv: Ministry
of Defense and Masua. [Hebrew.]

Gilboa, Amir. 1953. *Morning Songs*. Tel Aviv: Ha'Kibbutz Ha'Meuhad.
[Hebrew.]

Ginosar, Pinhas, and Avi Bareli, eds. 1996. *Zionism: Contemporary Polemic*.
Sede Boker: University of Ben-Gurion in the Negev. [Hebrew.]

Goffman, Erving. 1974. *Frame Analysis*. New York: Harper & Row.

Handelman, Don. 1990. "Introduction." In *Models and Mirrors: Towards an
Anthropology of Public Events*, ed. Don Handelman, pp. 1–81. Cambridge:
Cambridge University Press.

Handelman, Don, and Elihu Katz. 1990. "State Ceremonies in Israel—Remembrance Day and Independence Day." In *Models and Mirrors: Towards an
Anthropology of Public Events*, ed. Don Handelman, pp. 191–233. Cambridge: Cambridge University Press.

Hever, Hanan. 1986. "The Living Live and the Dead Are Dead." *Siman Kria*
19:188–95. [Hebrew.]

Hunt, Lynn. 1992. *The Family Romance of the French Revolution*. Berkeley:
University of California Press.

Ichilov, Orit. 1993. *Civic Education in a New Society, Palestine — State of
Israel*. Tel Aviv: Sifriat Poalim. [Hebrew.]

Ilan, Dan, ed. 1990. *The Holocaust and Heroism Day Ceremony*. Jerusalem:
Ministry of Education and Culture. [Hebrew.]

———. 1991. *Memorial Day to the Fallen in Israel's Wars*. Jerusalem: Ministry of Education and Culture. [Hebrew.]

Keren, Nili. 1985. "The Influence of Opinion Makers, on the One Hand, and
the Study of the Holocaust, on the Other Hand, on the Evolution of Pedagogical Discussion and Holocaust Curricula in High Schools and Informal
Education in Israel Between 1948 and 1981." Ph.D. diss. The Hebrew University of Jerusalem, Jerusalem. [Hebrew.]

———. 1998. "A Voyage to Mold the Memory—Student Tours to Poland."
In *Hidden Memory, Public Memory: The Image of the Holocaust in Israel*,
ed. Yoel Rapel, pp. 93–100. Tel Aviv: Ministry of Defense and Masua.
[Hebrew.]

Kimmerling, Baruch. 1993. "Militarism in Israeli Society." *Theory and Criticism* 4:123–40. [Hebrew.]

Kimmerling, Baruch, and Dahlia Moore. 1997. "Collective Identity as Agency
and Structuration of Society: The Israeli Case." *International Review of
Sociology* 7(1):25–49.

Laor, Yizhak. 1995. "'Those Sending You to Death Cry for You, Who Are
Going to Die': Dan Miron's Great Poetry and National Poetry." In *We
Write You Fatherland: Essays on Israeli Literature*, pp. 192–223. Tel Aviv:
Ha'Kibutz Ha'Meuhad. [Hebrew.]

Leibman, Charles, and Eliezer Don-Yehiya. 1983. *Civil Religion in Israel: Traditional Judaism and Political Culture in the Jewish State*. Berkeley: University of California Press.

Lentin, Ronit. 1998. "To Reconquer Silent Territories—Israeli Women Writers
and Film Makers as Daughters of Holocaust Survivors." In *Hidden Memory, Public Memory: The Image of the Holocaust in Israel*, ed. Yoel Rapel,
pp. 169–95. Tel Aviv: Ministry of Defense and Masua. [Hebrew.]

MacAloon, John. 1985. "Olympic Games and the Theory of Spectacle in Modern Societies." In *Rite, Drama, Festival, Spectacle: Rehearsals Toward a
Theory of Cultural Performance*, ed. John MacAloon, pp. 241–80. Philadelphia: Institute for the Study of Human Issues.

Mally, Lynn. 1990. *Culture of the Future: The Proletkult Movement in Revolutionary Russia*. Berkeley: University of California Press.

Miron, Dan. 1992. *Facing the Silent Brother: Studies in the Poems of the War
of Independence*. Tel Aviv: The Open University and Keter. [Hebrew.]

Moore, Sally, and Barbara Myerhoff. 1977. "Secular Ritual: Forms and Meanings." In *Secular Ritual*, ed. Sally Moore and Barbara Myerhoff, pp. 3–24. Assen: Van Gorcum.

Morin, Edgar. 1970. *L'Homme et la mort*. Paris: Seuil.

Mosse, George. 1985. *Nationalism and Sexuality: Respectability and Abnormal Sexuality in Modern Europe*. New York: Howard Fertig.

Ophrat, Gideon. 1980. *Land, Man, Blood: The Myth of the Pioneer and the Cult of the Land in Settlement Plays*. Tel Aviv: Cherikover. [Hebrew.]

Ozouf, Mona. 1983. "Peut-on commémorere la révolution française?" *Le Débat* 26:161–72.

Piterberg, Gabriel. 1995. "The Nation and Its Narrators: National Historiography and Orientalism." *Theory and Criticism* 6:81–104. [Hebrew.]

Podeh, Eli. 1997. *Against the Embarrassment and for the Cover-up: The Israeli-Arab Conflict as Reflected in History and Civic Education Manuals in Hebrew, 1953–1995*. Jerusalem: The Hebrew University. [Hebrew.]

Raz-Krakotzkin, Amnon. 1991. "Political Family and the Politics of the Family." *Politica* 39:18–21. [Hebrew.]

———. 1993–94. "Exile Within Sovereignty: A Critique of The 'Negation of the Diaspora' in Israeli Culture." Parts 1 and 2. *Theory and Criticism*. 4:23–56; 5:113–32. [Hebrew.]

Renan, Ernest. [1882] 1992. *Qu'est-ce qu'une nation?* Paris: Presses Pocket.

———. 1990. "What Is a Nation?" In *Nation and Narration*, ed. Homi Bhabha, pp. 8–22. London: Routledge.

Segev, Tom. 1991. *The Seventh Million: The Israelis and the Holocaust*. Jerusalem: Keter. [Hebrew.]

Shamir, Ilana, ed. 1989. *Monument*. Tel Aviv: Ministry of Defense. [Hebrew.]

Shapira, Anita. 1992. *The Sword of the Dove*. Tel Aviv: Am Oved [Hebrew.]

Shelhav, Ya'akov, ed. 1971. *Anger and Ardor: Readings For Holocaust and Heroism Day*. Jerusalem: Yad VaShem. [Hebrew.]

Siton, Shoshana. 1994. "The Contribution of the Teachers' Union of the JNF to the Creation of Zionist Ceremonies." *Proceedings of the 11th World Congress of Jewish Studies*, pp. 235–42. [Hebrew.]

Sivan, Emanuel. 1991. *The 1948 Generation: Myth, Portrait and Memory*. Tel Aviv: Ma'arakhot. [Hebrew.]

Tajfel, Henri. 1981. *Human Groups and Social Categories: Studies in Social Psychology*. Cambridge: Cambridge University Press.

Vinitzky-Seroussi, Vered. 2001. "Commemorating Narratives of Violence: The Yitzhak Rabin Memorial Day in Israeli Schools." *Qualitative Sociology* 24(2): 245–68.

Viztum, Eliezer, and Ruth Melkinson. 1993. "Bereavement and Commemoration: The National Myth's Double Face." In *Loss and Bereavement in Israeli Society*, ed. Ruth Melkinson, Shimshon Rubin, and Eliezer Viztum, pp. 231–58. Jerusalem: Ministry of Defense. [Hebrew.]

Walzer, Michael. 1993. *Exodus from Egypt as Revolution*. Tel Aviv: Papirus. [Hebrew.]
Weiss, Meira. 1998. "Bereavement and Subversion: A Critique of the Commemoration of the Fallen Soldiers." In *Molding the Memory*, part B, pp. 182–89. Tel Aviv: Aschola. [Hebrew.]
Yablonka, Hana. 1994. *Strange Brothers: Holocaust Survivors in the State of Israel 1948–1952*. Jerusalem: Yad Ben-Zvi and the University of Ben-Gurion in the Negev. [Hebrew.]
Young, James. 1990. "When a Day Remembers: Performative History of *Yom ha-Shoa*." *History and Memory* 2(2):54–75.
Yuval-Davis, Nira. 1997. *Gender and Nation*. London: Sage.
Zertal, Idit. 1994. "The Martyrs and the Saints: The Formation of a National Martyrology." *Zmanim* 48:26–57. [Hebrew.]
Zerubavel, Yael. 1994. "The Death of Memory and the Memory of Death." *Alpayim* 10:42–67. [Hebrew.]
———. 1995. *Recovered Roots: Collective Memory and the Making of Israeli National Tradition*. Chicago: University of Chicago Press.
Zuckerman, Moshe. 1993. *Holocaust in the Sealed Room: The Holocaust in the Israeli Press During the Gulf War*. Tel Aviv: self-published. [Hebrew.]

NOTES

Previously published in *Between "I" and "We": The Construction of Identities and Israeli Identity*, ed. Azmi Beshara, pp. 129–51 (Tel Aviv: The Van Leer Institute and Hakibbutz Hameuchad Publishing House, 1999) [Hebrew].
We would like to thank the Spencer Foundation and Tel Aviv University's Basic Research Fund for the funding of this study. We would also like to thank Roni Reingold and Yael Kafri for their help in gathering material.

1. There is no exact statistical information on the number of schools that regularly hold commemorative ceremonies, but sample studies held between 1960 and 1982 indicate that over three-quarters of schools commemorated Holocaust Day with a ceremony, and it can be assumed that those schools also held ceremonies on Memorial Day. See Doshkin 1961:8; Fargo 1984:172.

2. Of the ceremonies we observed, twenty were performed on Memorial Day, eighteen on Holocaust Day, and four on Jerusalem Day. In addition, we held interviews with principals and teachers who organized the ceremonies and with students who participated in them.

3. For a history of memorial ceremonies in schools, see: Ben-Amos and Bet-El 1998.

4. From the State Education Law (1953). Quoted by Carmon 1985:140.

5. General Director Circular, Ministry of Education and Culture, Jerusalem, March 21, 1957, pp. 2–3 [Hebrew].

6. Another national memorial day is in memory of Yizhak Rabin, established by a law enacted on July 18, 1997. For information on this day, see Vinitzky-Seroussi 2001.

7. The Jerusalem Day Law reached a first vote in the Knesset on September 3, 1998 but was never fully approved.

8. General Director Circular, Ministry of Education and Culture, Jerusalem, May 1, 1974, p. 4. [Hebrew].

9. "The Central Subject for the 1992–1993 School Year: Jerusalem, Ministry of Education and Culture, Special General Director Circular," June 1992 [Hebrew]; "The Central Subject for the 1992–1993 School Year: Jerusalem—Pedagogical Material, Plans and Studies, Ministry of Education and Culture, Special General Director Circular," October 1992 [Hebrew].

10. "The Central Subject for the 1992–1993 School Year: Jerusalem," pp. 3, 9.

11. Doron Rosenblum, "The Cruelest Month," *Ha'Aretz*, March 30, 1993 [Hebrew].

12. "General Director Circular, Ministry of Education and Culture, Jerusalem," March 6, 1975, p. 4. [Hebrew]. On this subject, see also Firer 1985: 166–81.

13. Handelman contrasts these rituals with those of small tribal societies, based on a complex "script" of exchanged roles. See Handelman 1990:22–48.

14. Baruch Ben-Yehuda, Education Department, Director Circular, 26 Sivan, 5709, no. 111/155/6730 (The Jewish Education Archives, file 1.161).

15. The Ministry of Education even considered having a uniform program for the school ceremonies, in an attempt to transform the holiday into a regular pedagogical object. See Azaryahu 1995:63.

16. Baruch Ben-Yehuda, Education Department—Director Circular, 24 Tishrei, 5711, no. 11/4/216 (The Jewish Education Archives, file 1.61). After the Six Days War, the Ministry of Education published a special pamphlet with examples of and recommendations for various commemorative acts that schools can initiate. See *I Will Remember Them* (Tel Aviv: Ministry of Education and Culture and Ministry of Defense, 1969) [in Hebrew].

17. For photos of sixty-two memorials built in schools, see Shamir 1989.

18. The Ministry of Education did not officially require schools to perform these acts, but they were mentioned in brochures published for Memorial Day, and became an inseparable part of the ceremony. See, for example, *20th Anniversary of the State of Israel, A Teacher's Guide for Educational Activities* (Jerusalem: Ministry of Education and Culture, 1968) [Hebrew].

19. "General Director Circular, Ministry of Education and Culture, Jerusalem," 23/7, March 11, 1963, p. 3.

20. A Holocaust Day ceremony held at a Tel Aviv high school in 1995, which included the screening of a movie about a student trip to Poland, began with the sounding of a siren and ended with the singing of the national anthem.

21. These brochures were also published by other official bodies, such as the Ministry of Defense, education departments in municipalities, and various commemorative bodies. They were distributed directly to schools and also sent to pedagogical centers, municipal libraries, and Yad-Lebanim institutes (local memorial centers for fallen soldiers). See, for example, Ilan 1991; Shelhav 1961.

22. Poems with an anti-war stance which criticized the cult of the fallen, such as Amir Gilboa's "And My Brother Is Silent" (Gilboa 1953:18), were often included in Memorial Day ceremonies, but neither the organizers nor the audience found them inappropriate (Miron 1992:329–34; Laor 1995).

23. Memorial Day's main text, *Yizkor* (Remember), exists also in a religious version, which is identical to the secular one except for the opening: it uses "God will remember . . ." instead of "The people of Israel will remember." State schools tend to use the secular version, which appeared in the brochures as "version b" (Ilan 1991:48). Replacing "God" with "The people of Israel" indicates the emphasis put by Zionism on the nation as an active historical agent.

24. The text originally appeared in *Shdemot*, no. 53, and became one of the most popular texts expressing soldiers' grief over a comrade who had fallen in battle. Arnon Lapid, *Hazmana LeBechi* ("Invitation to Cry"), in *The Silver Platter*, ed. G. Ron-Peder and A. Carmon, p. 29 (Jerusalem: Ministry of Education and Culture, n.d.) [Hebrew].

25. See the letter in *The Holocaust and the Revolt* (Tel Aviv: Ha'Histadrut Ha'Klalit, 1964), p. 40 [Hebrew]. The similarity between the ghetto rebels, the fighters of Massada, the defenders of Tel-Hai, and the soldiers of 1948 was noted by Chief of Staff David Elazar in a speech during the Holocaust Day ceremony in Kibbutz Lohamei Ha'Getaot in 1973, which is included in both Holocaust Day and Memorial Day pageants (Ilan 1991:16–17).

26. "General Director Circular, Ministry of Education and Culture, Jerusalem," 15 (3), October 23, 1955, pp. 1–2. Another form of commemoration from which Sephardic students were excluded was the school museum, which includes pictures of family members who perished in the Holocaust (Ariela Azulay, "The Never-Ending Attempt to Commemorate the Holocaust," *Globes-Friday*, July 22, 1994, [Hebrew]. See also Rafi Aharon's article, in which he recalls his difficulties, as a son of parents born in Yemen, to identify with Holocaust commemoration in his school (Aharon, "Holocaust—but from the Margins," *Ha'Ir*, April 6, 1994, [Hebrew]).

27. Quoted in *The Holocaust and the Revolt*, p. 10.

28. Quoted in *The Silver Platter*, p. 27.

29. The Hebrew language, as a gendered language, reinforces the gender distinctions through feminine words such as *moledet* (fatherland) and *uma* (nation), which are associated with birth and motherhood. On the other hand, *gibor* (hero) has the same root as *gever* (man).

30. Poems such as "And My Brother Is Silent," by Amir Gilboa, and "Rain in the Battlefield," by Yehuda Amichai, which make a sharp distinction between the living and the dead, constituted a departure from the tradition of the living-dead figure that was common in the poetry of the 1948 war. This figure appears again in Hayim Hefer's poem *Misdar Ha'Noflim* ("The Parade of the Fallen").

31. "The Parade of the Fallen."

32. The song is included in "Memorial Day Ceremony, Prime Minister's Office, Jerusalem," 1968, p. 19 [Hebrew].

33. The exhibitions were (1) Nir Nader and Erez Harudi, "Photography in the Confession Box," curator, Ariela Azulai, Bugrashov Gallery, January–February 1993; (2) Gili Meizler, "The Tendency to Concentrate on the Details," curator, Meir Gal, Limbus Gallery, November–December 1994; and (3) Meir Gal, "I Have a Lover in the Commando," curator, Ami Steinitz, Ami Steinitz Gallery, May–June 1997.

34. Ran Reznik, "Benetton Auschwitz," *Ha'Ir*, April 16, 1993 [Hebrew]; "Let the Twelfth Grade Student Remember the Bodies," *Ha'Ir*, April 13, 1994 (in Hebrew).

35. Ran Reznik, "The Principal Who Recommends a Little Bit of Hashish," *Ha'Ir*, April 20, 1995 [Hebrew].

36. Yaron London, "A Smile with a Shudder," *Ma'ariv*, February 5, 1993 [Hebrew]; Zahara Ron, "Holocaust Against Holocaust," *Ha'Ir*, April 28, 1995 [Hebrew].

CHAPTER 8

Shifting Boundaries: Palestinian Women Citizens of Israel in Peace Organizations

HANNA HERZOG

My study deals with women who are in search of their social identity in a situation of protracted national and gender conflicts. The theoretical starting point of the research is that identity is not a given, but a phenomenon that emerges, flourishes, and changes in varying social contexts. Identities are never uniform or one-dimensional. They are constructed and structured within a complex array of social discourses, practices, and social positions that cross-cut and affect one another. Social identity is a road sign, a trajectory, and temporary positions in socio-cultural-political-economic fields. As such, identity is not only open to change—it lacks any essential existence, and its components do not necessarily include uniformity. Differences and contradictions exist simultaneously (Hall 1990; Hall and Du Gay 1996).

The research follows the growing body of work that combines the large historical narratives of national, class, and gender subordination and oppression with local narratives that contextualize women's experiences in historical, sociopolitical, and cultural conditions (Fraser and Nicholson 1989). Women's social experiences reveal that they are not defined only by structure; rather, women as social agencies search for their own ways to survive and/or shape their social worlds. Political identities are shaped in a never-ending social process of construction and reconstruction of social selves (Cockburn 1998; Fraser 1997; Routherford 1990; Yuval-Davis 1997). Empirically, this chapter analyzes the ways in which the marginality of Israeli-Arabs in general, and women in particular, trickles down into peace organizations, and how women as social agencies choose, operate, resist, and/or subvert this imposed structure of marginality.

Situating Women in Palestinian History

The history of Palestinian women in Israel has not been researched deeply. Yet, there are some works that throw light on Palestinian women's past and enable us to situate their unique experience (Cockburn 1998:108–28; Herzog 1999b; Mar'i and Mar'i 1991; Sharoni 1995). Prior to 1948, although marginal in their own communities women belonged to the Arab majority. Palestine was their homeland and the taken-for-granted base of their social identity. After 1948 life in the State of Israel conferred Israeli citizenship on these women but also imposed a double national boundary: between them and their people in the West Bank and Gaza Strip, and between them and Jewish society within Israel. Following the establishment of Israel in 1948 and until the mid-1960s, Israeli Palestinians, who were then under military rule, were largely restricted to their own localities. They were allowed to leave their place of residence only by special permit. These state-imposed restrictions referred to the entire Palestinian population in Israel, but for women it was an addition to their traditional restrictions. The outcome of the 1967 war brought about a renewed encounter between those sections of the Palestinian nation that had been separated nineteen years earlier. This meeting between and subsequent interaction among Palestinians from both sides of the Green Line revealed the barriers that had sprung up in the interval, some of them due to legal definitions but mostly the result of each community's different experience. In addition, in 1987 the *intifada,* or Palestinian uprising in the occupied territories, opened many new frontiers for political activity among women. Dialogue, protest, and help groups have emerged, and they have led to new bases of meetings between Jewish Israelis, Palestinian Israelis, and Palestinians in the Occupied Territories. Palestinians, who were excluded from the dominant Israeli discourse that identifies civic virtue with military virtue, have in some instances been incorporated in peace organizations where they discovered the "virtues of liberal citizenship" and the political right to organize (Peled 1992). How have women confronted these social changes, and in what ways, if at all, did these changes influence and affect their social identities?

The question of women's national and citizenship identity cannot ignore their status and identity within their own community. Sami and Mariam Mar'i (1991) have shown that changes in the status of Arab women are intimately intertwined with intra-community processes engendered by the Arab-Israeli conflict. With the establishment of the State of Israel, virtually all of the political and organizational institutions of Palestinian society collapsed, its economic structure was shaken to the foundations, and the social order crumbled. In the first two decades of the Israeli state, Palestinian men became vulnerable due to loss of livelihood, lengthy absences from home (to find work), displacement within a foreign culture, encounters with Jewish women whose behavior they could not fathom, dependence on Israeli authorities, and threats to their national identity. Traumatized, Israeli-Palestinians clung to their traditional culture. In this sense the Arab-Israeli conflict has given the Palestinian family a boost beyond the traditional cultural sources, ensuring that women's inferior status is preserved within the community as well. Political marginality and barriers to integration in Israeli society make the Palestinian family the locus of social solidarity and nationalism. The central concept of family honor added an additional dimension. Insecurity produced greater social supervision over women: indeed, control of women became the yardstick by which Arab society measured its resilience and distinctiveness (Shokeid 1980). Upholding traditional values underscored the community's selfhood vis-à-vis the Jewish society, and was a way of displaying identification with the surrounding Arab world. Women were given the role of preserving and transmitting the culture, and, in turn, the community's ethnic identity was strengthened by defending their honor (Hasan 2004; Kanaaneh 2002).

Ibrahim (1993) describes how, under the claim of upholding family honor, Palestinian women work in cucumber fields under the watchful eyes of men—who, or course, also relieve them of their wages. Radical adherence to tradition finds expression in the phenomenon of murder of women for family honor, which has persisted during the rule of Israeli law. According to Arab tradition, close family members (father, brother, uncle, or son) are allowed to punish, and even to murder, a woman who is suspected of immodest sexual behavior. According to Hasan, the term "family honor" actually serves as a kind of fortress wall behind which are mustered all the forces that restrict women's freedom, keep them economically and socially inferior, and attempt to perpetuate—both by ideological means and through coercion, including murder—the prerogatives of male privilege (Hasan 2002).

Israeli authorities encouraged these tendencies to insularity and the reinforcement of traditional family patterns. In many cases this encouragement has been an unintended consequence of the security frame. Seeing the Palestinian citizens as a security threat, the state kept them under efficient, tight control (Lustick 1980). Although this control was subsequently loosened, it has far from disappeared. By recognizing the heads of local *hamulot*, or clans, as representatives of the Palestinian community as well as mediators between the Israeli-Palestinian public and the government, the state created defined channels of communication through which they were able to maintain effective rule (Al-Haj and Rosenfeld 1990). Competition among these local headmen made them vulnerable to divide-and-rule tactics, and the system also neutralized various attempts at nationalist organization. The result was reinforcement of the traditional clan structure, and the superior status of sheikhs and notables. The system also prevented any direct, effective approach by ordinary Palestinians to Israeli government agencies. Women paid the highest price for this form of rule; most strikingly, they were unprotected from the custom of murder to "preserve family honor." Many Israeli-Palestinians also link "traditional identity" with "national identity." As a result, men's privileges represent the "Palestinian" way, entailing the suppression of women and a preference for tradition over nationalist or democratic values (Hasan 2002:71). In addition, the prevailing masculine mindset among the Jewish authorities who interact with the Palestinian population helped blind the latter to the heavy price paid by the community's women.

The Military Government that was imposed upon the Palestinians in Israel formally ended in 1966. Nevertheless, both formal and informal restrictions on their integration into the labor market continue to exist, and these have produced a relatively high rate of unemployment. With the continuing aspiration to increase standards of living in order to raise family incomes, pressure has grown to send more Palestinian women into the labor market. Due to scarce employment opportunities in their villages and their low levels of education, many of these women enter the unskilled market. Consequently, many women work for low pay in an economy subject to fluctuations and/or seasonal work (e.g., agricultural employment). Above all, the market is under male control (Ibrahim 1994). At the same time, there has also been a general rise in the level of education among Israeli Palestinian women. This has given them access to new areas of employment, such as teaching, law, welfare, and social work. Still, tradition remains a potent constraint on Palestinian women—the preference is for them to work in the village. The still-limited employment opportunities then thrust women into competition with men, a contest in which the latter generally prevail. Teaching, for example, which in the Jewish sector is considered a "female" occupation, is a field dominated by males in the Israeli-Palestinian sector.

Women, particularly those who are well-educated and have entered the labor market, predominate among those who have found their way to women's organizations. Although traditionally perceived as the preservers and transmitters of tradition, women have more recently become agents of social

change (Mar'i and Mar'i 1991). The adoption of modern ways of life undermines the traditional family structure. Until 1967 these processes were
identified with assimilation into the Jewish society, and therefore they generated fierce opposition. However, following 1967 and renewed contacts between Palestinians on both sides of the Green Line, awareness of women's
equality ceased to be a "Jewish" problem which had infiltrated the Israeli-
Palestinians arena, and became a general problem for the entire Arab nation.
Indeed, this was a watershed in terms of building Israeli-Arab identity as
Palestinians. These new developments improved women's standing within
their society but also disturbed the Israeli authorities, who looked askance at
the growth of Palestinian identity. Until recently, they were pleased that
Palestinian women remained at home and did not enter the public sphere,
particularly politics (Mar'i and Mar'i 1991). Ironically, the Jewish authorities' interests intersected with the interests of the conservative forces in the
Arab community—both sought to preserve women's traditional, unequal
status.

This intended or unintended Israeli state support for traditional social
forces proved counterproductive when it sought to intervene or promote
particular policies. For example, authorities sometimes found themselves
stymied in trying to apply the Compulsory Education Law to young Palestinian girls. The girls' fathers often had a different agenda. Some sought to
place their daughters in the labor market as soon as possible, and to "marry
them off young." Others wanted them at home to run the household and
look after the younger siblings so that their mothers could work. The government's attempts to introduce family planning, which might ease women's
family burden, also encountered sharp resistance in the name of tradition.
What is more, the Palestinian community claimed that the Israeli state
wanted to reduce the birth rate among Palestinians as a means of national
control and suppression. Again, women paid the price. Yet, at the same time,
women have often looked at the situation differently: the fact that they are
considered the prime carriers of the traditional/national identity locates
them within the Palestinian collectivity, even if this entails marginalization
and dependence (Espanioly 1994; Hasan 2002; Kanaaneh 2002).

It is probably fair to say that more Palestinian women have in recent years
sought to carve out an independent road. After acquiring education and a
profession, they refuse to abide by family marriage arrangements, prefer-
ring to choose their spouses themselves. This can be socially costly: for example, some women "exile" themselves to Jewish locales to pursue an independent way of life, cutting themselves off from their community but not
finding acceptance from their Jewish environment. Life in the shadow of "se-

curity" fears means that it is more difficult for Palestinians to find an apartment to rent or a place to work, not to mention the difficulty of developing
social networks and close relations with Israeli Jews. In other instances, some
women remain single since they refuse to compromise, or else because there
are few men willing to marry a woman who deviates from the norm. Still
others eventually give up their independence, marry, and return to their village, where they resume the traditional functions of mother and wife (Herzog 2004).

The "peace arena" has been a sphere within which women could carve
their own way. At the end of 1989, the number of peace groups in Israel was
close to 170. Palestinian women took part in many of them. The role of Israeli Palestinians in these organizations, and the way this activity affected
their identity, has not been widely studied. While peace activities of Palestinians in the West Bank and Gaza Strip have been thoroughly researched
(Hasso 1998; Jad 1990; Peteet 1991; Pope 1993; Sharoni 1995; Strum 1992),
and the volume of studies on Jewish women's peace activity has also grown
(Azmon 1997; Chazan 1991; Emmett 1996; Helman and Rapoport 1997;
Sharoni 1995; Svirsky 1989), research on Israeli Palestinian women's peace
activities has begun only recently (Emmett 1996; Herzog 1999b).

To sum up briefly, marginality is the major social experience of Palestinian-
Israeli women. They are part of a minority population that does not enjoy
full civil equality, and hold the lowest positions in gendered-ethnic stratified
political system. Even on the research level their social world and life experiences have long been neglected. Participation in peace activities is an experience that is simultaneously inclusive and exclusive. My argument is that
the "peace arena" is a multi-dimensional situation that allows us to follow
Israeli Palestinian women's voices, and to see the ways in which they negotiate their gender, national, and civil identities.

The Study Method

The study is based on fifty open-ended, in-depth interviews with Israeli
Palestinian women that were conducted during 1995. The sample includes
women who were members of either one or several peace organizations.
Some were members of womens' organizations only, while others were active in both women's and general peace organizations. The women in the
sample came from different geographical regions of Israel, and also from
both rural and urban settings. The interviewees varied in their religion, age,
education, and marital status. The intention was to reach a broadly diverse

selection of women. However, no claim is made that this group constitutes a representative sample, since the number of interviews is too small to claim statistical representation or to venture statistical generalizations.

Half of the interviews were conducted in Hebrew, and the other half in Arabic. The interviews were carried out by trained Jewish and Palestinian research assistants. All the interviewees knew Hebrew very well, and the decision regarding the language in which to conduct the interview was taken randomly. By interviewing in both languages we sought to obtain a wider range of women's voices. Interviewing in Arabic enabled unmediated ties between interviewees and interviewers. It also created a closeness and intimacy that in turn allowed a discourse which did not sidestep political issues or stringent criticism of the dominant Jewish society. On the other hand, due to their distancing effect the interviews held in Hebrew generated discussions focusing on issues that, according to internal community norms, may not be spoken about (for example, relationships between women and men before or outside of marriage). The Palestinian society in Israel is a closed community, with a dense network of acquaintanceships and with strong social control. There always are fears that the community might hear about the interviewee's opinions. In retrospect, the interviewed women did voice such concerns, and it transpired that there was a foundation to this methodological perspective. Several issues connected with internal criticism, particularly regarding sexual harassment and women's status, were raised more openly in interviews conducted in Hebrew by a Jewish interviewer.

The in-depth interviews enabled the researcher to thoroughly probe the variety of women's social worlds and life-experiences. The interviews, which lasted from two to five hours, uncovered a rich, highly diverse, and multidimensional universe. Only a small portion of these findings are considered in this chapter. In fact, my aim here is to highlight the less expected and less known views that are expressed among Palestinian women.

Peace and Equality

Cockburn (1998:127) claims that the women's peace movement created a three-way process of dialogue between Israeli Jewish women, Israeli Palestinian women, and Palestinian women in the West Bank and the Gaza Strip. While dialogues are considered to be a path for mutual understanding on the way to conflict resolution, it would be a mistake to assume that they are by definition conducted under equal conditions and on equal footings.

A striking finding is that although peace movements aim to enhance co-existence, they failed to achieve this within their own organizations. The asymmetric relationships of the Israeli-Palestinian conflict are reflected in encounters between Jewish-Israeli women and Palestinian women from the West Bank and the Gaza Strip in women's peace organizations (Sharoni 1995). Moreover, social cleavages that exist in Israeli society also penetrate into the peace movement (Cockburn 1998:139–55; Emmett 1996).

Many of the Israeli peace organizations consist of Jews only, while others have a Jewish majority and mainly ignore Palestinian Israelis. Conversely, organizations where the majority of the activists were Palestinians tended to play up the presence of Jews in their leadership (Herzog 1997). Israeli-Palestinians felt deprived even in the women's peace movement. As one interviewee reported:

> A major women's peace organization advertised for a salaried chair. I saw
> their ad in the paper and I said to someone who works with me, What do you
> think about this. He said, Great, apply. I told him they wanted a Jewish direc-
> tor and an Arab coordinator.
>
> Interviewer: Did it say so explicitly?
>
> The Palestinian woman, smiling: It wasn't stated, they didn't say so. They
> wanted a number two who spoke Arabic, who knew Arabic. But what do you
> think? I knew it all along, but I applied anyway because I was unemployed at
> the time, but I wasn't chosen. In the end the coordinator was also a Jewish
> woman who knows Arabic.

The peace arena again confronted the women with experiencing social distancing and inequalities. Israeli Palestinian women expressed a sense of an unbridgeable divide between Jews and Palestinians citizens of Israel. As one activist says, "I was beyond the pale," always being made to feel that "I don't belong." She noted that she is "active in many political organizations of the left and in peace organizations. But there are few close social relationships, and for many of the Arabs I know who work with Jews, all such ties disappear altogether. Instead, the social relations are bounded within the national 'market.' "

Although activity in the peace arena enabled women to become part of the political discourse and brought them closer to Jewish and Arab males, it has not given rise to closer social relationships.

Another interviewee described her experience as follows:

> Since 1987 I have felt that there is more activity, including women's activity.
> There is a support for my people's struggle. More and more women are tak-

ing part. I also began to get involved, to get to know different organizations, to attend meetings. But at some stage the Arab women began to feel out of place in the joint organizations. In the women's groups the initiative came from the Jewish women. They asked the Arab women to join. There were a few Arab women in every organization. The Arab women were decoration, for the media.

Experiencing marginality leads some women to reconsider their cooperation in joint Jewish-Arab organizations: "We were not made part of the decision making process. Arab women lacked experience and did not know the rules of the game. They were pushed to the sidelines. Recently young Arab women have been leaving the joint organizations and setting up their own groups."

Israeli Palestinian women not only complained about the way their voices were muted by Jewish women, but also by Palestinian women from the occupied territories: "They used us as interpreters, and if they were able to converse in English we were really not needed." Or, "They call us a bridge to peace, but a bridge is something you step on, you don't march hand in hand across it."

Another woman painfully described the attempt to silence the voices of Palestinian Israeli women and said she yearned to make her own voice heard:

The Palestinian women from the [occupied] territories consider themselves and refer to themselves as though they are the true and authentic Palestinians. . . . But they take a completely different attitude toward Palestinian Israeli women who carry an Israeli ID card and can stammer a few words in Hebrew, like me. They refer to themselves as though they embody the tragedy and are the heart of the tragedy because they are suffering. They are the ones that have to confront armed Israeli soldiers. I don't say they have no problem. . . . But they do not know what our struggle is, what we are fighting against. . . . Their problem is much more obvious and acute, and also violent; the truth is that their problem is much clearer and much more painful. Perhaps our pain is less then theirs . . . but that is all relative. . . . But this point of view they convey, that they feel things in the clearest possible way. . . . To them I am half-Jewish, to them I just copy Jewish women. . . . But they are very wrong to take that attitude . . . not only toward me personally, I am talking about everyone. What I mean is that we did not develop only because the Jews "cultivated" us—the whole world is developing . . . As individuals, we have the right to choose our own course of development. We are not talking about roads and houses. . . . this is our inner subject, involving culture, education, and knowledge.

Nevertheless, Palestinian women don't speak in one voice. In some cases, a feeling of attachment to Jewish women prevailed, in others alignment with Palestinian women was stronger. For some women the involvement in peace activity was self-empowering, a feeling of doing work that was both meaningful and egalitarian: "We worked together, Jewish women and Arab women." And, "There is pleasure in doing. In Neled [Hebrew acronym for Women for Coexistence, the meaning of which is 'we give birth'] I feel no problem about being an Arab."

In the peace arena these women, in contrast to those quoted above, felt that their voice was equal to that of other women. Some of these women expressed a sense of the common voice among women that transcends national borders: "For me the most important thing is the encounters with other women, both Jews and Palestinians. The encounter itself is important, even if there is no special subject to talk about. You know, a meeting with women. Here [in the village] there are no women I can talk to, all you can talk about is cooking and laundry."

Another woman said, "I feel close to Jewish and Palestinian women from the [occupied] territories because all of us are mothers and have sons to worry for."

Gender Identity

The quotations above indicate that some women identify with other women on the bases of womanhood, while others prefer to emphasize their common fate as mothers. These differences reflect the contrasts that exist in the women's peace movement in Israel. While Women in Black, for example, insisted on their identity as women, rejecting any attempt to identify them as mothers (Helman and Rapoport 1997), others intentionally mobilized their motherhood as their base for political protest (Azmon 1997). Some women also join the peace movement as a result of their social and feminist activities: "Education is the most important target for me. To educate women. Being active in women's organization in Acre brought me to the peace activity as well." And another woman: "I am first and foremost a feminist." For some women, membership in a peace organization was framed in national and civic terms and had no gender significnace.

Does women's solidarity necessarily lead to feminist identity? To which kind of feminist identity? Many studies have indicated that feminist positioning leads to the conclusion that there is a deep connection between national conflicts and women's inequality (Herzog 1998; Sharoni 1995; Yuval-

Davis 1993). Activity in women's peace organizations very often leads to the emergence of feminist awareness, as women realized through dialogue groups and exchanging of information that there is an inextricable link between sexual violence against women and the military violence of the state (Cockburn 1998:128). Nevertheless, not all women who are active in peace movements are feminists (Chazan 1991; Emmett 1996), and those who are don't necessarily agree on their perception of feminism.

> Cooperation isn't enough for me, nor the fine words I hear morning, noon, and night, and those impressive slogans . . . For example, I have problems in cooperating and working jointly with the feminist movement. I very often hear it claimed there that we—the Arab women and the Mizrahi women— have a common struggle against the Ashkenazi establishment. I don't see the issue in that way. . . . we Arab women sometimes agree with Mizrahi women on specific issues, but we have common problems with other social cross-sections, sometimes with lesbians as oppressed women. But my problem as a woman—with every Jewish woman—is the national question, no matter whether she's Ashkenazi, Mizrahi or lesbian. There are also Arab lesbians, that's not the point, the point is the national aspect. She is a woman who served as a soldier, or else her husband or brother is in the army. Her son isn't in the army because he's Mizrahi or Ashkenazi, but because he's a Jew. I don't see how one can separate national issues and feminist/women's issues. I cannot identify with all Jewish Israeli women. Or with every shade of opinion in women's frameworks and organizations in the Jewish sector, I simply can't. I can be a partner with Israeli women from the Israeli left, who can distinguish my existence. And you always have to remember that, even within the left, there is a patronizing approach, a sense of superiority and paternalism. . . . but at any rate, there is a minimal option for communication: but if a religious woman settler talks to me about women's status and rights, I simply don't believe her, and don't believe in her. Because I can't make a separation between values.

While from the above citation it is clear that national bonds are seen to come before feminist bonds, national affiliation does not necessarily assure "feminist sisterhood." The following citation, a criticism of the uni-national feminist organizations, is relevant to this point:

> The women leaders of uni-national feminist and Arab organizations are domineering and condescending. . . . One of the problems I have in communicating with Arab women is that I can't relate to them on an egalitarian level, nor can they relate to me in that way. They're accustomed to being

subordinate to someone, or to being above someone else. . . . there's no attitude of equality. . . . Arab women have high political awareness which is relatively good compared to that among Jewish women, but . . . they don't accept criticism. . . . In the bi-national organizations I belong to, such as Women to Women, I can connect with them, I don't feel I'm rejected or unaccepted because I'm an Arab woman. . . . In Women in Black, though, I did experience some conflict. . . . the Arab women at the Feminist Conference were simply chauvinists.

Feminist identity also enables some women to cross national boundaries. A woman who identified herself as a feminist described her situation as follows:

The truth is, those meetings [with Palestinian women from the occupied territories] moved me . . . and I very much admire the Palestinian women, and admired them even more after those meetings. But you know what, I sometimes felt that some of them were nitpicking and superficial. . . . they expected us to come up with a solution for each one of their problems. And it's only us who can change the entire Israeli reality. Sometimes we raised concrete proposals for change, for even a minimal improvement. . . . but they couldn't relate to the concrete issues. It bothered me that they spoke in slogans, and they aren't practical.

To the interviewer's question concerning who she felt more connected to at the tri-lateral meeting—the Palestinian side or the Israeli side—the respondent answered:

Truthfully?! The Israeli [side]. I don't know why, but strangely enough, I experience my Israeliness there. What happens is that I always introduce myself as a Palestinian, but there I feel more Israeli, in terms of how they think, the level of awareness, the style and pattern of living, and altogether, I think and talk at another, totally different level. A different way of thinking, [another kind of] understanding, and perception. That is, my identity, the things I think about, my opinions contain more and more Israeli features. . . . I feel that it's easier for me to communicate with and relate to what a Jewish woman or an Arab Israeli woman says than what a Palestinian from the territories says. They are more abstract, and especially so in feminist terms. And that's what's vital for me—the feminist side.

The role of gender identity is also discussed in the context of gender relations. When a woman enters the public sphere she looks for the support of her family and her spouse: "I am very progressive in my thinking, at least in this sphere, compared to most women, but I still needed the support of a man. I have to admit: first it was my father and now my husband."

As found in other studies in regard to Jewish and Palestinian women (Abu Baker 1998; Herzog 1999a) such support may help women to overcome normative obstacles, but it also entails a dimension of partnership and even recognition of women's changed status. The interviewee just quoted was invited to several international conferences as a representative of the Arab women in Israel. She related:

> On my last trip [to a peace convention], I wanted him [her husband] with me because I had found it difficult on the previous occasion. I wanted him to be there very much, to have the experience, to go through the experience of . . . of . . . being the main person invited to a conference, to see the pleasure it gives me and how much I can contribute to my society, which is also his . . . . Well, I understand that this is hard for him as an Arab man, but within two days he fit in very well . . .

The move into the public sphere is more than self-empowerment. It is also a means for altering traditional conceptions, at times transforming the relations between men and women. The peace arena provided an experience of equality not only vis-à-vis other women but also in relation to men, including Israeli Palestinian men.

For some women, gender inequality within the Palestinian community came under sharp criticism: "Even though we are an oppressed people, we are also a people that oppresses its daughters. . . . When I was young I asked myself all the time why my brother has to be my enemy?"

National Identity

Activity within the peace organizations intensified the contacts between Palestinian Israeli women and Palestinian women from the occupied territories. What was the impact of this encounter? The variety of responses that this question elicited shows that, just as there are different voices among Jewish women (Emmett 1996), the views of Palestinian Israeli women also cannot be termed monolithic or one-dimensional.

Many of the interviewees defined themselves as Palestinians, and saw their activity in peace organization as part of their national struggle and their national loyalty. "First and foremost I am Palestinian," was a common response. At the same time many expressed a split and negotiated identity:

> I find myself in between them, I mean between the one and the other. When
> I sit with a Palestinian woman from the [occupied] territories I can under-
> stand her and empathize with her and understand her, I find my true self
> with her. That is the plus we have, we "inside" Palestinians of '48. I have a
> very good understanding of—I won't say 100 percent—but 98 percent of the
> inner nature and the psychology of Palestinian women. And I understand
> 100 percent the inner nature and the attitude of [Jewish] Israeli women. I
> have both sides. . . . Sometimes I understand them and grasp their situation
> better than they realize. . . . I can find my true self either here or there. . . .
> But I am also alienated. . . . I feel solidarity and warmth, closeness, identifi-
> cation with the Palestinian women from the [occupied] territories, but intel-
> lectually, or in debates and dialogues I find myself close to the Israeli women.

In this case and others, there is a sense of feeling connected to both Jewish and Palestinian women, but ultimately these interviewees reveal the
inner division and alienation that result from these different contacts and
loyalties.

These last quotations, like others, attest to the attempt by Palestinian Israeli women to forge their own autonomous social identity, separate from
the Jewish Israeli but also, in large measure, distinct from the national development of the Palestinians in the West Bank and the Gaza Strip. The
quest for an autonomous identity is seen in the same speaker's description of
the strong but ambivalent relationship she has with Jewish women—but
also with Palestinian women from the occupied territories:

> I could definitely support their viewpoints, but in fact they are much stron-
> ger, they have the strength, the possibility, and the ability to themselves far
> better than I can. They simply don't need me. . . . I could not speak either in
> their name or in the name of Israeli women . . . It is not good to be in the
> middle. . . . The women's movement in the [occupied] territories is part of a
> national liberation movement that is seeking political independence, and only
> at the margins is there a struggle for women's liberation. My struggle is com-
> pletely different. . . . I do not see myself leaving the Galilee one day to go and
> live in the [occupied] territories. My struggle is taking place in my home, to
> improve my status as a minority and as a woman.

Between Gender Inequality and National Inequality

Women choose alternative ways to express their identity. Some decided to
join bi-national feminist groups in order to struggle with gender inequality.

For others, national inequality superseded gender inequality and they preferred uni-national organization:

> One aspect of peace is equality, and equality is incompatible with dependence on the Jewish establishment and on the Jewish society in general.

> I do not rule out cooperation between Jewish and Arab women, on condition that it takes into account my mentality and my problems. . . . Our real need is for uninational groups of Arab women, because that is the only way it will be possible to cooperate with Jewish women's organizations. That kind of cooperation is at a completely different level.

Palestinian activist women experienced frustration both within their own communities in terms of gender inequality, and also within feminist organizations in terms of national identity. The following remarks by an activist emphasize this point. After completing her studies, she returned to the village, where her work with women provided a tremendously fruitful experience.

> The problem with work in the village . . . [is that] the men, and this is always my feeling, want to grab all the cards, meaning that they will run things while I do the dirty work. . . . It's true that this is not just characteristic of the Arab sector, but it is very pronounced [there]. So I joined feminist organizations—and I discovered that my interests [as a Palestinian] were pushed into the corner.

Women are constantly involved in making decisions and choices—such as the deliberate choice to join joint Arab-Jewish or separate national peace organizations. Many of the conversations evoked a feeling of alienation, even of despair: "I am tired already, I don't have the strength to fight the whole world on every front." Many women spoke of their desire "to do" and "to try hard." However, "doing" and "trying hard" are channeled into different paths that become foundations for alternative definitions of citizenship and identity.

Being an Equal Citizen

Although Palestinian women positioned themselves in the Palestinian national community, many of them simultaneously draw a borderline between the Israeli Palestinian community and the Palestinians in the territories.

I draw a clear line, clear boundaries, between the outcome of the 1948 war and the outcome of the 1967 war. Those are two separate files as far as I am concerned, and I belong to the 1948 file. I have plenty of problems, but they are different problems, and my methods of work and activity are different from those of the people in the [occupied] territories.

I think I have to make my voice heard, like other voices in the country. . . . My struggle on behalf of the Palestinians in the [occupied] territories is part of my circle of identity as a Palestinian woman, and my struggle to improve my status in Israel is part of my Israeli identity. I have a minority status and I want to improve my situation as a minority within the state.

And in another version: "My dream is that the Arabs in this country will be active and effective citizens."

Palestinian women citizens of Israel see their activity in peace movements as part of their struggle to gain new rights and give substance to existing ones. For them the resolution of the conflict between Israel and its neighbors is inextricably linked to the relations between Jewish Israelis and Palestinian Israelis. As they see it, the peace process will not be complete until they obtain full equality within the state of Israel and within their own community: "What is peace?" a woman activist who heads a Jewish-Arab center asked rhetorically. "I always say about peace that first of all you need peace at home, first you need domestic peace. What does that mean? That first we have to talk about it inside Israel, the Jews and the Arabs in Israel. . . . Without equality there is no peace." Such expressions reflect the process of Israelization of Palestinian Israelis. It indicates the thrust toward integration among Israel's Arabs and the concomitant demand for civil equality (Smooha 1990). Though women disagree whether the road to equality should be paved by uninational or binational organizations, they do share the aspiration for equality and integration within Israeli society.

These interviews with women peace activists support the view that the claims for alternative definitions of peace, as well as the creation of uninational organizations, are a challenge to the existing patterns of organization and also a trenchant criticism of the persisting inequality between Jews and Arabs. Nonetheless, these women considered themselves as integral members in the peace movement. The resolution of the conflict between Israel and its neighbors is inextricably linked to the relations between Jewish Israelis and Palestinian Israelis. For Israel's Palestinian citizens, the peace process will not be complete until they obtain full equality.

Concluding Remarks

Palestinian Israel women are situated on shifting social, political, and normative borderlines where social boundaries are being redefined and social relations rearranged. Their location on the periphery of each of the social categories that demarcate the boundaries of identity and social affiliation has
the effect of heightening the tension that exists between and within gener-
alizing and binding group definitions. Such tension is found at a structural
level in state and institutional structures, at the social level in the community, and at the personal level within each individual. For Palestinian Israeli
women, the categories by which their identity could be defined—equal citizenship, a sisterhood of feminists, national affiliation, and local-community
belonging—are shattered in every case. In each category they find themselves perched on the borderline.

Contextualizing women's narrative and rendering their cultural and historical specificity illuminates the singularity of their social position, which
shapes a different voice—one that is openly defiant toward the Jewish society but is also critical of its own community. While membership in peace organizations includes them as active citizens it also marginalizes them. As
women they are marginal vis-à-vis the men, and as Israeli-Palestinians vis-
à-vis the other partners: Jewish members of the peace organizations and the
Palestinians in the territories.

Though most of the interviewees positioned themselves in the Palestinian national community, they simultaneously draw a borderline between the
Israeli Palestinian community and the Palestinians in the territories. Within
Israeli society Israeli-Palestinian women attempt to define a small local collectivity operating within the community of Israel's Palestinian citizens and
within their own native village or place of residence. These attempts confront them with their inequality in a patriarchal male society and lead to the
examination of gender boundaries, gender identity, and gender roles.

For them, peace is not only peace between states or representative of
states but also between the state and its citizens, and between the citizens
and their communities. Peace is not gender neutral. Peace means equality,
including gender equality. Whereas the dominant discourse emphasizes
work in joint organizations as an expression of equality, many Palestinian
women proposed an alternative—multicultural discourse—and hence reflected on the demand for work in national and/or gender-separate organizations as an expression of equality and mutual recognition and respect. This
is a call of defiance vis-à-vis the patterns of dependence and paternalism that

were prevalent in the Israeli society, and that have also trickled down into the peace movements. Their discourse of identity emerges as they negotiate the dominant Israeli perceptions of citizenship with the traditional national and gender definitions of the practice and roles of Palestinian women today.

REFERENCES

Abu Baker, Khawla. 1998. *A Rocky Road: Arab Women as Political Leaders in Israel*. Ra'anana: The Institute for Israeli Arab Studies.

Al-Haj, Majid, and Henry Rosenfeld. 1990. *Arab Local Government in Israel*. Boulder, San Francisco, London: Westview Press.

Azmon, Yael. 1997. "War, Mothers, and Girls with Braids: Involvement of Mothers' Peace Movements in the National Discourse in Israel." *Israel Social Science Review* 12(1): 109–28.

Chazan, Naomi. 1991. "Israeli Women and Peace Activism." In *Calling the Equality Bluff: Women in Israel*, ed. B. Swirski and M. P. Safir, pp. 152–61. New York: Pergamon Press.

Cockburn, Cynthia. 1998. *The Space Between Us: Negotiating Gender and National Identities in Conflict*. London and New York: Zed Books.

Emmett, Ayala. 1996. *Our Sisters' Promised Land: Women, Politics, and Israeli-Palestinian Coexistence*. Ann Arbor: University of Michigan Press.

Espanioly, Nabila. 1994. "Palestinian Women in Israel: Identity in Light of Occupation." In *Women and the Israeli Occupation — The Politics of Change*, ed. T. Mayer, pp. 106–20. London and New York: Routledge.

Fraser, Nancy. 1997. *Justice Interruptus: Critical Reflections on the "Postsocialist" Condition*. New York and London: Routledge.

Fraser, Nancy, and Linda J. Nicholson. 1989. "Social Criticism Without Philosophy: An Encounter between Feminism and Postmodernism." In *Feminism/ Postmodernism*, ed. L. J. Nicholson, pp. 19–38. New York: Routledge.

Hall, Stuart. 1990. "Culture Identity and Diaspora." In *Identity: Community, Culture and Diaspora*, ed. J. Rutheford. London: Lawrence & Wishart.

Hall, Stuart, and P. Du Gay. 1996. *Questions of Cultural Identity*. London: Sage.

Hasan, Manar. 2002. "The Politics of Honor: Patriarchy, the State and the Murder of Women in the Name of the Family Honor." *The Journal of Israeli History* 21(2): 1–37.

Hasso, Frances S. 1998. "The 'Women's Front'—Nationalism, Feminism, and Modernity in Palestine. *Gender & Society* 12(4):441–65.

Helman, Sara, and Tamar Rapoport. 1997. "Women in Black: Challenging Israel's Gender and Socio-Political Orders." *British Journal of Sociology* 48(4): 682–700.

Herzog, Hanna. 1997. *Geography of Peace: Palestinian-Israeli Women and the Map of Peace Organizations.* Tel Aviv: Golda Institute.

————. 1998. "Homefront and Battlefront and the Status of Jewish and Palestinian Women in Israel." *Israeli Studies* 3(1): 61–84.

————. 1999a. *Gendering Politics — Women in Israel.* Ann Arbor: University of Michigan Press.

————. 1999b. "A Space of Their Own: Social-Civil Discourses Among Palestinian Israeli Women in Peace Organizations." *Social Politics: International Studies of Gender, State and Society* 6(3): 344–69.

————. 2004. "'Both an Arab and a Woman': Gendered Racialized Experiences of Female Palestinian Citizens of Israel." *Social Identities* 10:53–82.

Ibrahim, Ibtisam. 1993. "The Cucumber Pickers." *Nogah* (26):34–37. [Hebrew.]

————. 1994. *The Status of the Arab Women in Israel.* Jerusalem: Sikkuy, The Association for the Advancement of Equal Opportunity. [Hebrew.]

Jad, Islah. 1990. "From Salons to the Popular Committees: Palestinian Women, 1919–1989." In *Intifada: Palestine at the Crossroads,* ed. J. R. Nassar and R. Heacock, pp. 125–41. New York, London: Praeger.

Kanaaneh, Rhoda Ann. 2002. *Birthing the Nation — Birthing the Nation — Strategies of Palestinian Women in Israel.* Berkeley, Los Angeles, London: University of California Press.

Lustick, Ian. 1980. *Arabs in the Jewish State.* Austin: University of Texas Press.

Mar'i, Mariam M., and Sami Kh Mar'i. 1991. "The Role of Women as Change Agent in Arab Society in Israel." In *Calling the Equality Bluff — Women in Israel,* ed. B. Swirski and M. P. Safir, pp. 213–21. New York: Pergamon Press.

Peled, Yoav. 1992. "Ethnic Democracy and the Legal Construction of Citizenship: Arab Citizens of the Jewish State." *American Political Science Review* 86(2): 432–43.

Peteet, Julie M. 1991. *Gender in Crisis: Women and the Palestinian Resistance Movement.* New York: Columbia University Press.

Pope, Juliet J. 1993. "The Emergence of a Joint Israeli-Palestinian Women's Peace Movement during the Intifada." In *Women in the Middle East: Perceptions, Realities and Struggles for Liberation,* ed. H. Afshar, pp. 172–83. London: Macmillan.

Routherford, Jonathan. 1990. *Identity: Community, Culture, Difference.* London: Lawrence & Wishart.

Sharoni, Simona. 1995. *Gender and the Israeli-Palestinian Conflict — The Politics of Women's Resistance.* Syracuse, N.Y.: Syracuse University Press.

Shokeid, Moshe. 1980. "Ethnic Identity and the Position of Women Among Arabs in an Israeli Town." *Ethnic and Racial Studies* 3(2): 188–206.

Smooha, Sammy. 1990. "Minority Status in an Ethnic Democracy: The Status of the Arab Minority in Israel." *Ethnic and Racial Studies* 13:389–413.

Strum, Philippa. 1992. *The Women Are Marching — The Second Sex and the Palestinian Revolution*. Brooklyn, N.Y.: Lawrence Hill Books.

Svirsky, Gila. 1989. "Women in Black." *Present Tense* 52–53.

Yuval-Davis, Nira. 1993. "Gender and Nation." *Ethnic and Racial Studies* 16:621–32.

———. 1997. *Gender and Nation*. London, Thousand Oaks, New Delhi: Sage Publications.

NOTES

This study on Israeli Palestinian women in the peace movement was supported by the Tami Steinmetz Center for Peace Research, Tel Aviv University; The Harry Truman Research Institute for the Advancement of Peace, Hebrew University, Jerusalem; Israel Foundation Trustees, and The Golda Meir Institute at Tel Aviv University.

I am thankful to Kamilia Badar-Araf, Gili Avrahmi, and Dina Roginsky for their meaningful contribution to this study.

CHAPTER 9

From Ethiopian Villager to Global Villager: Ethiopian Jews in Israel

LISA ANTEBY-YEMINI

Introduction

This chapter examines levels of identity construction among Ethiopian Jewish immigrants who are now living in Israel. Ethiopian Jews previously lived as peasants and artisans in the Ethiopian highlands. After they were recognized as Jews by the Israeli Rabbinate in 1975, the first massive migration to Israel began in the 1980s, mainly from the northern regions of Ethiopia. The second wave of migration took place in May 1991, when the Israeli government airlifted more than 14,000 persons from Addis Ababa to Tel Aviv as part of a secret rescue operation dubbed "Operation Solomon." Today, the Ethiopian community in Israel numbers more than 80,000 people.

The goal of this chapter is to examine how this population of Ethiopian villagers are today becoming not only Israeli citizens but also "global villagers," members of both Israeli culture and world culture, articulating and reconstructing local and global identities in the context of their new nation-state. We begin by considering various mechanisms of re-establishing a feeling of "home" in a new environment, the first level of reconstruction of personal identity and re-creation of locality. Second, we explore the formation of an Ethiopian ethnic identity as the group integrates as citizens of their new country and constructs a national Israeli identity. Third, we analyze the processes by which an Ethiopian-Israeli transnational identity is being formed, and also trace the emergence of a new Black diasporic identity based on models of global culture.

These topics will be examined against a theoretical and methodological background that raises questions concerning the framing of this research. How does the study of immigrants who are constructing national, transnational, and global identities "fit in" with the classical models of anthropological research, and more so, with the rich literature on migration studies in Israel? What new epistemological frameworks can best account for these new domains of knowledge? In this sense, this chapter seeks to propose a new approach for studying migration in Israel that includes issues of de-territorialization and displacement, citizenship and ethnicity, transnational and global cultural forms.

Reconstructing Locality and Identity

During their first months in Israel, the Ethiopian immigrants experienced a phase of harsh de-socialization as most of their social networks, cultural patterns, religious rituals, and communal organization collapsed. In such a case, how does the anthropologist carry out fieldwork with people who are no longer living in their original environment, do not speak the language of their host country, and whose social, political, religious, and economic structures have been deeply transformed? How can she understand the internal differentiations, gender relations, power hierarchies and social distinctions as the group encounters a totally new setting? How is she to distinguish the degree to which the present social organization relates to "traditional" constructs, how it is influenced by the host society, or whether the initial phase is best understood as a "temporary migration situation"?

Writing an ethnography of a displaced population and a fragmented culture surely challenges the frameworks of "classic" anthropological practices. However, one way to understand some of the social and cultural reconstructions at play in the new country is to focus upon the specific processes of identity formation and locality production. In all societies, constructions of identity and difference are essential components of social organization, and these always have a spatial dimension. Indeed, with regard to migrant and migrating groups, recreating a sense of locality is often one of the first steps towards reconstructing identities.

Ethiopian immigrants in Israel were able to re-create new patterns of social organization and identity formation rapidly. One of their first identity constructs was related to reconstructing locality and giving meaning to their temporary "homes" in an absorption center. We will examine the ways in which a "local" identity developed, and how an Israeli spatial unit gave rise to new identities that functioned as categorizing elements for making internal distinctions and for various other social purposes. At the level of the entire community, similar mechanisms recreated a new spatial identity related to the territory of residence in the host country. In addition, the Ethiopian Jews' dwelling places also became markers of social identity, paralleling some of the territorialization processes formerly used in the culture of origin.

These two sets of examples demonstrate how Ethiopian Jews who migrated to a foreign environment, and were moved into strange, unfamiliar housing conditions, nonetheless rebuilt their spatial and social borders and re-established a new sense of locality and identity.

A NEW DWELLING: PRODUCING LOCALITY

Most of the 14,000 Ethiopian Jews who were airlifted from Addis Ababa to Israel in May 1991 were temporarily settled in various hotels, holiday resorts, *kibbutzim*, and absorption centers. When I began my fieldwork with several Ethiopian immigrant families in Jerusalem, they were living in a sixteen-floor high-rise building that formerly had been a five-star hotel. The immigrants I became acquainted with lived in one hotel room, or sometimes two rooms if they had a large family. In the narrow space of the long corridors, they found themselves lodged together with other newcomers who neither belonged to their own kin group nor originated from their village in Ethiopia. In general, the majority of families occupying the same floor had never lived together, yet in a matter of days they came to make up a kind of heterogeneous group, first and foremost on a regional basis. Similar to other migrant groups described in the literature, these Ethiopian Jews were a concentration of people that had been "accidentally regrouped." For example, in her research on Hutu refugee camps in Tanzania, Malkki (1995) refers to the population of her anthropological field site as "accidental communities of memory," that is, groups who share a transitory memory and experience that unites them by chance in the same refugee camp. In our case, too, the Ethiopian immigrants did not form an "ethnologically recognized" community; on the contrary, several hundred newcomers were arbitrarily housed in one building, whereas in Ethiopia they had been scattered in more than four hundred villages. Moreover, we must also keep in mind that we are dealing with de-territorialized individuals who are seeking, while living in a transitory situation, to redefine, in their new relations of neighborliness and intimacy, concepts of dwelling and notions of home, borders between public and private space, social networks, and community structures.

Re-creating a sense of community was not an easy task, not only since the newcomers originated from different parts of Ethiopia but particularly because the familiar figures of authority from the immigrants' village were not always present in the absorption center. For example, because there were no *qesotch* (the religious and spiritual leaders in Ethiopian Jewish life) living at the hotel, many adults complained that they could not consult with them as they would have done in Ethiopia. There also were a number of elders (*shmagellotch*), recognizable by their horsehair whisks and white shawls, who, on the model of the meetings held in Ethiopian villages, participated in the large gatherings held in the hotel lobby to discuss various problems of life in the absorption center (Weil 1997a). In addition, a "council of elders," composed of five *shmagellotch*, was established and charged with resolving internal quarrels among the immigrants. However, these were not necessarily the elders whom the immigrants knew. As Kaplan observes concerning spatial dispersion in Israel: "Traditional leaders whose influence was exercised on a determined region find themselves often relatively cut off from their old supporters" (1990:175–76). Tracing the processes by which new networks of power and decision were reconstituted indicates how the newcomers began to re-establish a certain "locality," and to think of themselves as a "community of Ethiopian immigrants" in the hotel.

For the Ethiopian immigrants living in the hotel-turned-absorption-center, the process of reterritorialization and re-creation of the "local" had to adapt to the spatial configurations of their new dwelling. In a short time, certain behaviors clearly revealed how new social groupings based on spatial divisions came into being. For example, I noticed that the inhabitants of the ninth floor (whom I visited the most) stayed with one another in the hotel, and even ate together at the large tables in the dining hall. Furthermore, the children of the ninth floor always played together and hardly mixed with the children of the other floors. In addition, during an incident where a young man had a fight with his mother and decided to move to the fifteenth floor, all the neighbors came to watch him "moving out" of the room he shared with his mother. They complained that "he will not be a resident of the ninth floor anymore!" And, in fact, this "change of address" transformed his status into that of "resident of the fifteenth floor," as he was later called.

This feeling of a "community of residence" given by the spatial unit of the floor confirmed the emergence of a social entity based on this new organization of space. The borders of belonging were the stairs separating the floors. In brief, the construction of a collective identity in this unfamiliar territory was based on the floor as a spatial and social reference point.

This identity construct also translated on the verbal level, and was neatly illustrated in the linguistic practices employed by the hotel's occupants. The Ethiopian immigrants had quickly learned to announce in their native tongue, Amharic, the number of the floor on which they lived. The Hebrew word *koma*, "floor," was immediatly adopted to designate these spatial divisions, even though there is an Ethiopian term, *foq*, that signifies both "floor" and "building." The latter word, however, was only used in reference to the entire building and not in its more restricted sense, which the newcomers seldom had to use. The Hebrew loanword *koma* illustrates the adoption of a new vocabulary that translates an unfamiliar practice of space which had no equivalent in their original culture. To the extent that it became a referent to localize and categorize other co-residents, this term also codifies a social space. For example, I heard my friends mention in conversations and stories "the people from the ninth floor" (*yäzätänänna koma säwotch*), a classification they still use today when talking about their days in the absorption center. The floor number thus attributed a label to the group and established a correspondence between toponym—a place name—and *anthroponyme*—an individual's name. Interestingly, these mechanisms of territorial constructs predicted the social organizations that later appeared in the locations where the immigrants eventually settled.

A NEW *AGÄR*: RE-DRAWING TERRITORIES OF IDENTITY

The strategies used to construct the notion of "home" and to define belonging to a place as "locals" became more clear when the Ethiopian immigrants began leaving their initial dwellings and traveling around their new country. Indeed, they rapidly began traveling by public transport to various places in Israel in order to visit relatives and to attend celebrations such as marriages and funerals. Since the immigrants are exceedingly mobile and spread over much of Israel, they gradually established a new geography of their spatial environment. This was completely mental, however, since hardly any of the adults had ever examined a map. They held what can be called a "nongraphic" image of their new country, in which geographical localization and distances between places belonged to the domain of the experienced and the traveled.

When I asked some of the immigrants I knew to situate their village in Ethiopia, they referred mostly to the number of hours or days that it took by foot to reach a large town such as Gondar, a regional center such as Debark, or a large market like Azezo. In Israel, travel from place to place lasted only a few hours. When I enquired about the trips some of the adults took around the country, instead of using units of time or distance, almost everyone described the length of the trip by the price of the bus ticket (kilometers were completely ignored). Worknesh, for instance, told me she lived "far" from her sister because it was "two shekels and a half to take the bus to her house." An old lady who lived in the north of Israel once told me she had to take four buses to visit her children in the area of Rehovot. When I asked how long it took, instead of giving me the time she traveled (something like five hours), she simply said it had cost 55 *brr*, the Ethiopian currency she calculated in instead of Israeli shekels.

In toponymic discourse, travels and enunciation acts constitute a discursive series within a narrative whose function, Michel de Certeau (1990) tells us, is to transform spaces into places. For the Ethiopian adult population in Israel, the geography of their new homeland is summed up by the names of different temporary housing sites (called *karavanim* in Hebrew) and towns where other Ethiopian immigrants reside. This stock of place names reflects a selective knowledge that draws a specific cartography of the Israeli landscape regardless of whether these places are significant or not on a national level. The location of some large Israeli towns where no Ethiopians have settled may sometimes remain unknown or at least unfamiliar to them. Making use of this spatializing practice of the toponymic language, one can also observe how the notion of "locality" is reconstructed and how the network of Ethiopian Jewish communities in Israeli has become reterritorialized. For example, when Ethiopian Jews meet in the street or in a bus, they invariably ask in Amharic: *"Yet näw agäreh?"* (where is your "country"?) in the same way that they used to enquire about one's home region in Ethiopia. In the Israeli context the question concerns the temporary housing site or the town where one lives, and thus, the families I knew always answered: "Hulda *agär*" or Hulda "country," Hulda being the name of the temporary site where they lived for a number of years. This amounts to considering these localities as an Ethiopian "home" territory, what in Amharic is called an *agär*.

As Levine explains, *agär* signifies more than just a place of dwelling. It designates a "home" or even a "homeland," and all those who reside there are considered to be allies, whereas those beyond one's *agär* are looked upon with suspicion bordering on hostility (1974:49–52). The adoption of Israeli toponyms demonstrates the spatial logic and processes of local identification that continue to be applied in the new country in order to restore the territories of identity and, at the same time, of otherness. This can be seen in the ways that spatial identity expressions used in Ethiopia (such as Dembya *säw*, i.e., "a person from Dembya") are transposed upon the new Israeli reality. For instance, the first time that I visited Tesfay's sister in Rehovot, she screamed out with joy: "Hey!! Here come the people from Hulda!" (*Arrrah!! Hulda säwotch yämetallu!*)

We have been examining two localizing strategies that are primarily processes of reconstructing place, locality, community, and identity in a situation of de-territorialization and displacement. Given the new conditions of neighborliness in the hotel, the Ethiopian immigrants sought to re-create on each floor a group identity that came close to or paralleled that of a neighborhood. On the scale of the country, the use of indigeneous categories such as *ägar* demonstrates the complex mechanisms of re-territorializing their landscape of origin into the landscape of Israel. These spatial practices are fundamentally identity practices—that is, ways of negotiating new identities in a foreign setting. As Appadurai remarks: "The many displaced, deterritorialized, and transient populations that constitute today's ethnoscapes are engaged in the contruction of locality, as a structure of feeling, often in the face of the erosion, dispersal, and implosion of neighborhoods as coherent social formations" (1996:199). The Ethiopian immigrants' production of locality is mainly a construction of identity and difference in a host society where they are confronted by the double tension of becoming Israelis and also remaining Ethiopians.

Reformulating Ethnicity and Citizenship

Israel can be seen as an example of what Kimlicka (1995:6) calls a "polyethnic state" (where cultural diversity emerges from immigration) as well as a "multinational" state (where cultural diversity arises from the incorporation of previously self-governing cultures into a larger state). In this sense, Ethiopian immigrants to Israel become at the same time Jewish nationals (as opposed to Arab Israelis, for example) as well as an ethnic and cultural group among Israeli Jews of different origins. Furthermore, as opposed to immigrant groups in many other parts of the world, Ethiopian Jews presumably benefit from "optimal conditions" to integrate into their host society: they receive full citizenship rights upon arrival, and as Jews "returning to their homeland" they are encouraged to "melt" into Israeli society and identify with the ethno-religious nationality of their new state. However, as Jews deemed the "same" as the host population because of a common Jewish heritage, yet often perceived as "other" because of their physical and cultural features, the immigrants' reconstructions of identity and difference pose a number of complex theoretical questions.

What do the immigrants do when faced with the "other-self," that is, the Israeli Jew who is thought to be so close in the imaginary but appears so distant in reality? How do Ethiopian Jews, who had considered themselves "identical" to the locals, reformulate their own ethnicity? What are the signs of "otherness," and how are the boundaries of the group redefined? How do they become Israeli citizens when at the same time they develop ways of being "different"? These questions also require examination of how Israeli society treats these immigrants, who are considered to be part of their "own people" and yet turn out to be such an "exotic" alterity. Indeed, the meaning of absorbing "black Jews" challenges the racial definition of who is Jewish. Thus, issues of ethnicity and citizenship among Ethiopian Jews bring to the fore the paradox of the "ingathering of the exiles" (*mizug galuyiot*) into one national and cultural identity and the growing pluralist trends in Israeli society.

We begin by first examining how the Ethiopian immigrants emphasize their "sameness" and their shared identity with the Jewish people, becoming "good citizens" and constructing a new identity as "true Israelis," sometimes at the price of judaizing their practices or inventing traditions. In addition, we consider how the immigrants simultaneously stress their "difference" and their otherness as opposed to the host society, constructing an ethnic identity as "Ethiopians" and creating symbolic boundaries through linguistic patterns, foodways, religious rituals, and social networks.

ISRAELI CITIZENS

For generations the Ethiopian immigrants dreamed that they would one day reach the Promised Land and live in Jerusalem. When the dream did come true for many of them, they were ready to give up everything to become "Israeli" and integrate into their "ancestral homeland." They almost immediately identified with the Jewish people and the Israeli population, who, in turn, welcomed them warmly with presents of food, clothes, and toys. In a short period of time both children and adults began entering Israeli society through the channels of schools, army service, employment, politics, and their reliance on health, legal, and welfare institutions. Analyzing these patterns highlights the different ways in which the newcomers became citizens of the nation-state, as well as how they gradually constructed their new identity as Israeli citizens.

For the younger generation, the educational system represents their first formal socialization experience. During their first year in Israel, all of the Ethiopian children were sent to schools and boarding schools belonging to the state religious network (*mamlakhti-dati*). More recently, a growing number of Ethiopian students also began attending secular schools (*mamlakhti*). Hebrew often becomes their most fluent language, and even among themselves the majority of children and teenagers prefer to speak Hebrew rather than Amharic. Even though in their scholastic achievements (as measured by grades and test scores) they still score poorly in comparison with the Israeli average, various after-school programs designed for Ethiopian students attempt to diminish the "learning gaps." In addition, affirmative action and government grants offer opportunities to further their higher education. Overall, throughout their schooling Ethiopian students acquire an Israeli identity that in most cases is emphasized by a religious schooling education.

In common with other Israelis, Ethiopian men serve their compulsory army duty for three years, and some also sign on to stay in the army for several additional years (*keva*). Until recently, young women either were exempted on religious grounds or chose instead to fulfill "national service" (*sherut leumi*). Like many of their Israeli counterparts, a growing number of Ethiopian women now also choose to serve in the army. Even though discrimination and racist treatment have sometimes been reported, on the whole the army experience appears to strengthen their Israeli identity and increase their feeling of belonging to the Israeli nation (Shabtay 1995). With time, more and more soldiers of Ethiopian origin have died, and these losses make the families feel that they, too, share the burden and the pain of other Israeli families who lost their children in combat.

Adults normally attend a ten-month *ulpan*, or intensive Hebrew language class, and this experience also gives insights into Israeli culture and Jewish traditions. Since most of adults were either craftspeople or peasants in Ethiopia, a range of vocational training programs was offered to them. The majority of men have found employment in low-skilled positions, joining the Israeli workforce side-by-side with foreign workers, Arab Israelis, Russian immigrants, and Palestinians from the West Bank and Gaza. Those who are unable to work or are unemployed receive pensions or unemployment payments, and mothers get children's allowances. Like all Israeli citizens, the immigrants are eligible to benefit from national health insurance and municipal social services, linking them to the Israeli welfare state.

However, the clearest expression of their use of citizenship rights is the way Ethiopian Jews have participated in Israeli civil society and political life. For many, their right to vote was initially used when, in 1992, they voted en masse in the first national elections that took place following their arrival. With no prior experience of citizenship in a democratic state, this was the first time that they voted in free elections as citizens of a nation-state. Although they have not formed their own ethnic political party (in contrast with the Russian immigrants, whose sheer number in Israel in part explains their organizing Russian parties), many Ethiopians have tended to support national and religious parties and platforms and cast their votes on the right of the Israeli political spectrum. In this sense, it may be said that they have integrated into the political system first and foremost as Israeli citizens— they use their civic rights to inscribe themselves politically in Israeli society rather than to develop a political conscience based on ethnic membership.

Their ideological positions on issues of national security and the "peace process" also show that they express views close to some sectors of the Israeli public. For example, Worknesh often told me: "We cry every time an Israeli soldier is killed. And when we see images on television of a bomb attack, we cry. Why does our government want to give land to the Arabs? The Arabs are not good, they are not good people." This sense of shared destiny and common suffering enables the new immigrants to feel part of and identify with the nation. This, in turn, heightens their identity as Jewish nationals, as opposed to Israeli Arabs and other non-Jews.

On the national level, Ethiopian Jews rapidly built a tight network of associations and organizations; according to Weil (1997a) over a hundred Ethiopian organizations exist, which assist community members to defend their rights in such fields as education, culture, and welfare. They have also successfully staged strikes and large demonstrations, often under the auspices of their own umbrella organization, the United Organization of Ethiopian Jews. In this sense, Ethiopian Jews who previously lacked any formal communal structures or community-wide leaders are now organized as Israeli citizens who are able to claim their rights and bring about group mobilization in times of crisis. Concurrently, a new group of young, charismatic secular leaders has also emerged. For example, the first Ethiopian Jew, Addisu Messale, was elected to the Knesset in 1996, and a number of others were appointed to key positions in government ministries and agencies. Although they currently do not have a representative in the Knesset, their strong communal organization constitutes an important ethnic lobby. Furthermore, at the local level, Ethiopian Jews have influence in towns with high concentrations of Ethiopian voters, and some have also been candidates in various municipal elections. In becoming organized as an ethnic pressure group, they also acquire citizen identity.

In contrast with the differential political and cultural demands voiced by other minority groups, such as Israeli Arabs, for instance, Ethiopian Jews do not have specific cultural claims that would result in "differentiated citizenship." However, as Kimlicka (1995:4) has pointed out with reference to other countries, the preferential treatment that they have received in areas such as housing subsidies (see below) or affirmative action in higher education may lead to the claim to permanent differentiation in the rights or status of group members. Kimlicka also remarks that group-differentiated rights for minority cultures may inhibit the development of a broader, shared identity; yet, in this case, Ethiopian Jews develop a strong affiliation with Israel and, in general, "strive for equality as Jews" in a Jewish state (Weil 1997b).

While Ethiopian Jews have formulated a strong Israeli-Jewish national identity, they also have sought to reconstruct an Ethiopian ethnic community
within the framework of their new nation-state. After their first phase of de-
socialization in the absorption centers, they began to revive social and cultural practices that were crucial in the definition of identity and the formation of an ethnic community, or *edah*, in Israel.

Language is often the most visible marker of difference and ethnic identity in migration situations. The majority of Ethiopian Jews continue to use
their native tongue, Amharic,[1] even though the second generation mainly
speak Hebrew. For the most part illiterate in their native language, the adult
population still has difficulties with second-language acquisition and Hebrew literacy competence. The availability of "indigenous media" in the
Amharic language enables them to maintain their own linguistic space. A
daily two-hour Israeli radio broadcast in Amharic features news, community
information, interviews, Ethiopian music, and explanations of current issues
such as health problems, political topics, and government policies. In addition, a weekly television program in Amharic deals with general topics that
are part of the Ethiopian Jews' daily life in Israel—the army, the educational
system, and so forth. In recent years, an Amharic language exam was introduced by the Ministry of Education for the matriculation exam (*bagrut*) that
students take at the end of high school. Finally, the Ethiopian movie videos
that circulate among the immigrants and the quasi-rituality with which they
are watched also reinforce the group's ethnic identity (Anteby 1999a). In this
way, modern media help to maintain the vitality of Amharic, and this also in
part explains why most of the adult population has little need for Hebrew.

Another feature of Ethiopian ethnic identity is connected with food.
Shortly after leaving the absorption center, the Ethiopian Jews re-established their traditional foodways with their own flavors and smells, practices,
and symbols, commensality rules, and ritual laws. Women once again began
preparing *enjära*, a sour pancake that constituted the staple food in Ethiopia,
as well as different varieties of *wät*, a stew that accompanies this bread. Ethnic stores that sell food products imported from Ethiopia are flourishing in
towns with a large Ethiopian population. *Enjära* continues to be served as a
sign of hospitality to visitors and is also used as a gift within social and kinship circles (Anteby, 1995). Like Tesfay, the majority of adults who still eat
enjära daily claim that "it is good for you."

Meat is another sign of ethnic membership. Most adults who immigrated during Operation Solomon, in 1991, still refuse to buy or eat Israeli kosher meat. Instead, an elder or a *qes* ritually slaughters an animal that is usually purchased from a nearby *kibbutz*. If it is a large animal, it may be slaughtered on the premises of the *kibbutz* and the meat then brought back to the elder's home, where it is either prepared for a specific ceremony (wedding, funeral, birth celebration, religious festival) or simply divided among the households who contributed to buying it. Smaller animals like lambs and chickens are bought alive and then prepared outside of the house. The reason for maintaining this separate slaughtering practice was explained to me by Gebayo: "Israelis do not kill the animal in the proper way." To this day, separate slaughtering is one of the most fiercely kept practices, thereby demonstrating its political, religious, and ethnic value (Anteby 1995). Indeed, preserving the core diet of *enjära* and *wät* (prepared by women) as well as continuing the traditional practice of ritual slaughter (performed by men) are strategies to maintain a distinct ethnicity in a new environment.

Living in an Israeli urban setting also challenges the immigrants' construction of ethnic identity. At the neighborhood level, most Ethiopian Jews have been able to recreate their community structures. Housing is the key element in forming or maintaining communities. In 1994, a government housing policy was launched to help Ethiopian immigrants purchase their own apartments. A state agency offered subsidies to buy a home (up to $90,000 for an average family of five, plus interest-free loans for larger amounts, to be repaid over a period of twenty-eight years). This plan applied to certain towns specifically selected for their "strong neighborhoods" and middle-class population. The goal was to avoid spatial segregation and large concentrations of Ethiopian Jews in remote places, such as development towns situated in the peripheral areas. In fact, groups composed of kinsmen often wanted to reside in the same neighborhood, street, or even building, and significant numbers of families ended up living in the same areas.

The most obvious links between Ethiopian neighbors are woven through coffee ceremonies (*bunna*), and in a short time clearly defined groups were re-established who drink coffee together several times a day. As noted previously, meat-buying groups were also constituted by households who share the costs of an animal slaughtered by an elder or a *qes* in the neighborhood. Other forms of mutual aid have been set up among Ethiopians Jews. These include informal rotation credit associations for savings and loans (called *qubye*, but also known as *eqqub*) composed of more than a dozen members, which are organized on a neighborhood basis; and mutual assistance associations, which are primarily burial groups (*edder*) that lend chairs, rent buses, and provide money for food and drinks at funerals. Through these patterns, they have recreated traditional forms of village organizations in urban Israeli neighborhoods, and these frameworks also maintain their ethnic identity.

The religious and ritual life of Ethiopian Jews has drastically changed since they discovered that the forms of Judaism observed in Israel varied from their own practices. Many religious festivals were unknown to them, and the rituals surrounding the life-cyle and purity laws were quite different from their own. In addition, the religious authority of the *qesotch* is still at the center of an ongoing debate between the immigrants and the Rabbinate, which claims that because of their unfamiliarity with rabbinical law (*Halakha*), Ethiopian religious leaders cannot perform marriages and burials. In these circumstances, how can one preserve a unique religious tradition as well as assimilate into mainstream Israeli Judaism?

In fact, it seems that most adults continue to celebrate festivals specific to Ethiopian Jewry, such as the *Segd,* or the celebrations on the fortieth or eightieth day after birth (for a male or a female infant, respectively). While weddings seem to be celebrated in Israeli style, there always is an "Ethiopian" part of the celebration, usually taking place throughout the night. Funerals, however, continue to be one of the deepest expressions of the group's ethnic specificity. They are still performed in traditional style (with wailing, dancing, hundreds of participants, and a large feast) and include as well specific mourning rituals and a cycle of commemorations (*täzkar*). Finally, the purity laws, especially regarding women, are still partly observed, even though spatial isolation of women and taboos on contact have largely disappeared (Anteby 1999b). The community's religious leaders have maintained their role and continue to pray in Ge'ez, the liturgical language of the Ethiopian Jews, during holidays and life-cycle celebrations. Confronted with a new language of prayer (Hebrew), plus a new corpus of texts and new religious rites, most Ethiopian adults choose not to adopt them, constructing a symbolic border between themselves and other Jewish Israelis. It is interesting to note that Lewis points out the same paradox concerning Yemenite Jews in Israel: "The practice of Judaism is a major ethnic boundary marker between the Yemenites and their Jewish neighbors and fellow citizens. On the one hand it differentiates them; on the other it results in an intensification of interaction and sentiment within the group" (1989:138).

To sum up, through the continued use of their own particular linguistic features, foodways, social and economic networks, religious rituals, and life-cycle ceremonies, Ethiopian Jews have preserved group boundaries and developed a strong ethnic identity. These features of cultural ethnicity also enable us to observe what the immigrants are willing to relinquish in order to "become Israelis," and what they are reluctant to give up. However, doing so poses some additional questions. Does the fact that their primary relationships (neighborhood, friendships, and marriage partners) continue to be ethnically homogeneous lead to social and cultural segregation? Has their grouping in what essentially are segregated neighborhoods also isolated them from mainstream Israeli culture? Does their concentration in unskilled labor and high rate of unemployment label them as an "occupational underclass"?

Indeed, some researchers have argued that what characterizes the community is "marginalization" at different levels (Weingrod 1995). As we have already seen, they also develop various modes of belonging to the nation-state. The group's boundaries are also constructed situationally, and the difference between "Ethiopian" and "non-Ethiopian" is often superseded by the distinction between "Israeli" and "Arab," the prominent other in Israeli national identity. These reconstructed identities are at the same time ethnic and national, ensuring Ethiopian Jews full membership as citizens of the state as well as membership in an ethnic community (*edah*). These also are strategies that allow them to fully enter Israeli society—that is, by behaving as "ethnics," they are also becoming "Israelis."

Indeed, in the Israel of the end of the last century, there were various ways of negotiating ethnicity. During recent decades, the previously dominant "melting pot" model of immigrant "absorption" has been challenged by an increasingly legitimate "new ethnicity" (Cohen 1983). Pluralistic patterns arise today in Israeli society as immigrants maintain aspects of their ethnic heritage in dress, food, and religion while they also participate within the public institutions of the dominant culture. Thus, as Weingrod (1985) has shown in a number of studies on immigrant groups in Israel, cultural assimilation and heightened ethnicity are quite compatible trends. Yet the situation is still more complex: as we shall see, most young people do not eat Ethiopian food, do not participate in neighborhood networks or religious rituals, and speak less Amharic. They, in turn, find other ways to construct difference, and develop signs of otherness in which the interplay between ethnicity and race holds a growing and central role.

Encountering Transnationalism and Globalization

By immigrating to Israel, the Ethiopian Jewish community not only adopted Israeli citizenship and became acquainted with numerous other Jewish ethnicities, it also met with broader spatial horizons of cultural production and

234   *Anteby-Yemini*

identity construction. The first trips Ethiopian Jews made back to Ethiopia, as well as their constant exposure to global culture, have led to a new range of transnational practices as well as a growing awareness of belonging to a "colored minority" in their host country. These new processes of ethnic and racial transformation need to be seen together with the development of national identity and the re-creation of Ethiopian ethnicity. Transnationalism and globalization were encountered soon after nationalism and ethnic pluralism, and consequently widened the possibilities of reconstructing their identities.

From a theoretical point of view, the anthropologist needs to deal with two different problems. First, how does one go about studying the "traveling culture" of a displaced population that is beginning to make return trips back to its country of origin and develop transnational practices? How should one describe the "imported Ethiopian culture" that is currently emerging in Israel? Can a transnational identity emerge for Jewish immigrants who are supposed to have come back to their ancestral homeland? How is the image of the original "home," Ethiopia, reconstructed? A second point is the difficulties in identifying the influence of global culture, mainly when it is conveyed through electronic media. How should one look at an immigrant group that is exposed to identity models transmitted by "virtual" communities? Taking a slightly different twist, how does one compare Ethiopian immigrants with Black diasporas, when the migration process is characterized by the special meaning of the "return" of a Jewish population to its homeland?

The models Ethiopian Jews are discovering in Israel point to the emergence of new ethnic identities that are based on cultural constructs formerly unknown. First, we will examine the emergence of an "Israeli-Ethiopian transnational identity" that is forged through new links with Ethiopia and the flow of material goods and cultural references from urban Ethiopian society to Israel. Second, we will explore the recent emergence of a Black diasporic identity that is modeled on global constructions of race and ethnicity. These new identities create racial and ethnic boundaries that add intricate dimensions to the cultural and social lives of Ethiopian Jews in Israel.

AN ISRAELI-ETHIOPIAN TRANSNATIONAL IDENTITY?

Many adults I know have traveled back and forth to Ethiopia, sometimes making several trips. It is interesting to note that even if they did not wish to return to live in Ethiopia, and despite the fact that there is no longer an Ethiopian Jewish community left there, the immigrants wish to travel to their country of origin. Some are like Fanta, who took a trip after completing his army service with his cousin, a student on a university break. In another instance, family members traveled back together, sometimes for "fun and leisure" and sometimes to seek cures for health problems or to bring back various plants and remedies. In addition, a growing number of young entrepreneurs make regular business trips to import Ethiopian goods. Needless to say, this new mobility creates strong links with their country of origin, and compels a population that had rarely left its native villages to rethink geographical space and integrate transnational subjectivity in its spatial constructions.

The preferred destinations are Addis Ababa, the capital of Ethiopia, and Gondar, a large city in the north. Travelers rarely return to their native villages; as Fanta explained, "Why should I go to the village? My friends can come and visit me in Gondar." In a sense, the visitors from Israel are not returning to their former "homes" but rather to a "reconstructed and imaginary home." As Appadurai would put it, this yearning for Ethiopia is a "post-nostalgic" phase: a process of "re-indigenization" is taking place, in which Ethiopian Jews are behaving as urbanites who have emigrated from the capital and not from their actual Ethiopian highlands villages. This reinvention of locality and a reappropriated urban culture make Addis Ababa into their new ethnic landscape.

The Israeli visitors come as "rich Westernized Ethiopians" bringing a flavor of modernity, affluence, and a First-World aura. Like others, Fanta stayed in the city's hotels, enjoyed Addis Ababa's night life, and eagerly consumed the goods and leisure industry that the city offers. This transition in class status, from peasant to wealthy tourist, is a proof that Ethiopians have succeeded in Israel, and offers a rewarding self-image that is not always enjoyed back home in Israel. Feeling like tourists for the first time also heightens their sense of Israeli identity: as Fanta proudly announced, "I stayed in a hotel in Addis for one month; it's so cheap for us Israelis!"[2]

When someone arrives back in Israel from a trip to Ethiopia, all the family members and neighboring Ethiopian households come to welcome the traveler and see what he brought back. For example, everyone gathered around Fanta when he arrived from the airport. Opening his suitcase, he took out several white cotton dresses that elder women still wear and plastic bags filled with various spices, including hot pepper powder (*berberre*); everyone became excited when he opened another bag that contained *gesho*, a plant used in making the traditional Ethiopian beer, *tälla*. The last bag of herbs was for Alaka Abraham, a healer, who had specifically asked him to bring back these plants for his remedies. In addition, Fanta showed everyone cassettes of the latest popular songs in Addis Ababa and also circulated videotapes of Ethiopian movies and music.

A growing number of Ethiopian Jews are importing goods to Israel— clothes, jewelry, tapes and video cassettes, incense, and food products such as special leaves, spices, and *tef* flour, the main ingredient for the Ethiopian *enjärä* bread. These young entrepreneurs have begun setting up "ethnic businesses," traveling around the country in vans to neighborhoods with large concentrations of Ethiopians Jews, or simply supplying to stores (owned by Ethiopians or Israelis) which sell these ethnic products. Others, like Fanta, sell the items often purchased at the Mercato, the main market in Addis Ababa, to neighbors, friends, and family members. He told me: "it pays back at least twice the costs of my trip."

While participating in Ethiopian urban culture is mainly a male experience, those who do not travel become consumers of this popular culture through the "cultural traffic"—the narratives, behaviors, and even identity models that the travelers bring back, adapt, and spread in Israel. One can see this influence in the way apartments are decorated, often modeled after those of the Addis Ababa bourgeoisie, as well as clothing styles and eating habits. Furthermore, the stories of the trip and the descriptions of Addis that the travelers relate in great detail enable those who remained in Israel to reconstruct images of the "home country." The circulation of videotapes and music cassettes from Ethiopia, and in particular the landscapes seen in the movies, are alternative ways of re-envisioning the homeland from their Israeli living rooms (Anteby 1999a).

The spread of Ethiopian popular music is perhaps the best example of cultural flows between Ethiopia and Israel. Large numbers of adults living in Israel listen to Ethiopian popular music that combines disco beats with specifically Ethiopian melodies and Amharic words. Unknown as such to the older generation, who never listened to these tunes in their villages, Ethiopian popular music is now being adopted and re-appropriated by the Ethiopian community. The music is spread in several ways—by Amharic broadcasts on Israeli public radio, by music cassettes and videos brought back from Ethiopia, as well as through concerts where Ethiopian singers perform. These singers, often Christians from Ethiopia, are sometimes invited to perform at weddings, and some famous singers also appear at Ethiopian night clubs in Tel Aviv.[3] These major sites for performance and consumption of urban Ethiopian music indicate the extent to which it has become an important ethnic marker and means of identification. Indeed, these exchanges of commodities between the two spaces are key elements in the construction of an Ethiopian-Israeli transnational identity.

What is more, these flows of goods and people also enable the circulation of new identity models. Through their contact with the African urban culture of Addis Ababa, certain Ethiopian Jews became aware of alternative racial constructions. The most striking feature that many travelers pointed out is that, in contrast to their lives in Israel, during their stay in Ethiopia they no longer felt that they were a racial minority. This cross-cultural experience of skin color challenged their construction of race and bestowed on the visitors a different self-image and a new racial identity. While visiting in urban Ethiopia they can be seen to be in what Homi Bhabha has called a "third space": "These 'in-between' spaces provide the terrain for elaborating strategies of selfhood—singular or communal—that initiate new signs of identity, and innovative sites of collaboration, and contestation, in the act of defining the idea of society itself. It is the emergence of interstices—the overlap and the displacement of domains of difference—that the intersubjective and collective experiences of *nationness*, community interest, or cultural value are negotiated" (1994:1–2). Through Ethiopian Jews' simultaneous participation in several different racial systems, their concepts of race became altered, and they also discovered new constructions of Self and Other. Once again, this process has a number of complex and somewhat unexpected dimensions.

A BLACK DIASPORIC IDENTITY?

Ethiopian Jews never thought of themselves as "blacks" until they arrived in Israel.[4] Like Fanon's example of African students arriving in Paris and suddenly facing their "blackness" (1952:125), Ethiopian Jews immigrating to Israel experienced an even more powerful revelation, since they had thought of themselves as belonging to the Jewish people. Furthermore, as Fanon reminds us: "wherever he goes, a negro will remain a negro"—that is, a black person cannot escape the category "black" in the eyes of a white man (1952: 140). And, in fact, Ethiopian Jews are in a way rediscovering their blackness, or *négritude*, growing more aware of their black identity among the Israeli population. The racializing of the Other, in Fanon's terms, can be seen in the feelings of prejudice and discrimination some Ethiopian Jews experience in school, in the army, in the workplace, or in public spaces where skin color continues to be a marker of difference. During my research, Ethiopian Jews often told me they were called "*shrorim*" (blacks) by other Israelis, and some said they had been insulted by being called "*kushi*" (nigger).[5] On the other hand, Ethiopian Jews, including those who have lived in Israel for as long as two decades, still use the Amharic word *färänj* (white people) to designate non-Ethiopians. For example, sixteen-year-old Alamu, who goes dancing in an African discotheque in Tel Aviv, explained to me that there are no *"färän-jim"* there. Recently, the Amharic broadcasts on the Israeli radio have used the word *"netchotch"* (whites) for naming the Israelis, a clear increase in the awareness of race and the use of the Western hegemonic black/white racial discourse.

For the Ethiopians, racial consciousness came to its height following the disclosure that the blood donations of Ethiopian immigrants were discarded. This brought to the fore new political uses of blackness. The issue erupted in January 1996, when 10,000 Ethiopian Jews demonstrated in Jerusalem against what has been since coined "the blood scandal" (*parashat ha-dam*). They held banners and screamed: "We are Jews just as you are," or "Even if we are Black, our blood is also Jewish." From these slogans, we can see that they wished to be recognized as Israelis and as Jews, at the same time denouncing the racist discrimination that made them feel as if they were "second class citizens" (Weil 1997b). The use of a rhetoric of racial discrimination, social inequality, and color prejudice, often modeled on the race discourse in the United States, turned inter-ethnic relations in Israel into inter-racial relations. As Ethiopian Jews became aware of their blackness, they also became aware of the "politics of identity" and the constructions of a "Black diaspora," models they observed by being exposed to global culture.

This shift in self-identification is especially apparent among a minority of the younger generation, who have begun to adopt Afro-American models and international symbols associated with Black youth subcultures. These youngsters are beginning to dress like urban black youth on the model of American inner cities and to adopt rastafarian patterns. Certain adolescents, such as Alamu, often wear woolen "rasta hats" with green, red, and yellow colors (that also are the colors of the Ethiopian flag), and some wear jackets with the image of Bob Marley on the back. Hairstyles such as crew cuts or dreadlocks are being adopted, and some women use beauty products imported from the United States to treat their hair. Teenagers also go dancing in night clubs in Tel Aviv where reggae and Ethiopian and West African music are played. These "black music genres" represent Afrocentric cultural expressions that the Ethiopian youth re-appropriate as a music culture of their own and through which they are able to identify with a wider Black community.

In addition, they are also influenced by Afro-American identity models conveyed through the media and through global youth culture. For instance, together with his brothers and sisters Alamu regularly watches American television series (such as the *Bill Cosby Show*) where Black Americans are portrayed as affluent, modern, and Westernized. Cable channels such as MTV also spread a youth culture where blacks often are the leading stars. Like those of many of his friends, Alamu's room is covered with posters of black singers, including Michael Jackson (considered here to be "black"). These images not only allow world culture to enter their apartments and give them a sense of other places, cultures, and lifestyles, they also offer Ethiopian Jewish viewers new identity models and global constructions of race. In Appadurai's terms, electronic media offers resources for the construction of imagined selves and imagined worlds as an everyday social project: "The work of the imagination, viewed in this context, is neither purely emancipatory nor entirely disciplined but is a space of contestation in which individuals and groups seek to annex the global into their own practices of the modern" (1996:4). The media provide large repertoires of images and narratives for the young Ethiopian viewers; belonging to this "virtual" MTV culture corresponds to what Appadurai defines as a characteristic of modernity, namely, the *imagination as a social practice.*

The problem of identifying with a Black transnational culture as an "imagined community" is relevant to the situation. If one follows Benedict Anderson, a nation is defined as an *imagined* community because "the members of even the smallest nation will never know most of their fellow-members, meet them, or even hear of them, yet in the minds of each lives the image of their communion" (1983:6). In the same way that Anderson explains how novels and newspapers "provided the technical means for 'representing' the *kind* of imagined community that is the nation" (ibid.:25), one might argue that television and video cassettes play the role of creating an "imagined black community" for Ethiopian Jews in Israel. Just as Anderson sees print capitalism as a means "for rapidly growing numbers of people to think about themselves, and to relate themselves to others, in profoundly new ways" (ibid.:36), we can consider that the new audiovisual media have the same function among Ethiopian immigrants, leading to a new form of imagined global community of Blacks around the world. However, identification with Blacks remains in the realm of the virtual and the imaginary, since there is hardly any contact between Ethiopian Jews and other black groups living in Israel (e.g., the Black Hebrews and African foreign workers), except perhaps in certain African night clubs. This, in turn, poses the question of whether a certain portion of Ethiopian Jews truly adopt a "Black" identity, or mainly use it as a form of situational ethnicity.

Of course, one might think that Ethiopian immigrants do not have other ethnic options than identifying as blacks since their skin color immediately distinguishes them from the rest of the Israeli population, and also since their identity as Jews has been severely damaged by continuing conflicts with the Israeli Rabbinate. Many studies have shown that skin color influences the formation of ethnicity and has different consequences for the racial identity of non-white immigrants. In our case, the question of the self-presentation of Ethiopian Jews as blacks and their ascription as such by Israelis is particularly complex since we are also dealing with a population that immigrated to Israel because they were considered Jewish. Yet precisely since Ethiopian immigrants are also Jewish and Israeli, they can choose not to identify as blacks. In fact, on the whole the older generation chooses not to adopt such identity constructs.

Identification with the Black experience in the United States bestows a new status on a significant portion of Ethiopian youth, and thereby becomes a strategy of Goffmanian-styled self-presentation. For some Ethiopian teenagers, belonging to a global Black urban and youth culture can be seen as an answer to the social exclusion that they feel in Israel. As cultural differences between them and their Israeli peers become minimal—they share the same food, go to the same schools, serve together in the army, and speak the same language—the process of "ethnicization" of color turns "blackness" into a marker of ethnic identity. As noted earlier, the signs of Ethiopian ethnicity maintained by their parents (in foodways, language patterns, neighborhood networks) are not adopted by most of the younger generation, and they turn to other strategies in order to establish their own ethnic identity. Their Black ethnicity can be seen as a socially and politically constructed "new ethnicity," originating in global identity models and situationally used. This trend provides a means of inventing, negotiating, and contesting blackness in an Israeli society perceived by them as White, and may represent the main strategies of differentiation from the host population.

Conclusions

The processes analyzed in this chapter contrast sharply with previous patterns of immigrant absorption in Israel. Ethiopian Jews are able to fully participate in Israeli life without the de-socialization and re-socialization stages of the 1950s and 1960s. In this era of cultural pluralism, they have been able to reconstruct an ethnic community and maintain a strong Ethiopian identity while at the same time participating fully in Israel's civil society and be-

coming active Israeli citizens. In addition, as a result of transnational practices new identities are constructed from the models offered by Ethiopian urban culture, turning Addis Ababa into what Appadurai defines as an
"ethnoscape." A second set of identity references are based on a Black global
model of racial constructs and an "imagined community." This corresponds
to Appadurai's "mediascape," that is, the repertoires of images and information and the cultural flows produced and distributed by newspapers, maga-
zines, television, and film.

This does not mean, however, that global flows—mediascapes and ethnoscapes—have a more important role than locally based national identities.
The interplay between the local Israeli context, the former society of origin
and the global dimension of "world culture" should not be interpreted as a
sign of failure of Ethiopian Jews' absorption. On the contrary: it shows that
de-socialization did take place as some of the former religious and social
structures collapsed and new lifestyles were imposed; but re-socialization
and "integration" entailed not only modernization, urbanization, Westernization, and Israelization, but also adoption of broader cultural norms that
previously were unknown in Israel and Ethiopia. Some researchers may
maintain that these new forms of identification stem from a "culture of resistance" or represent a "counter-culture" at the margins of Israeli society.
Indeed, some Ethiopian Jews feel like "second-class citizens," excluded from
the main centers of power and subject to racism and discrimination. However, I suggest that these trends may well represent a new form of participation in Israeli society which combines Israeli and global identities. Integrating into global culture may be yet another way of integrating into Israeli
society and culture.

These new ways of constructing, reconstructing, inventing, and changing
identities challenge the views of classic anthropology that considers cultural
models as spatially bounded in specific places. As Appadurai and others have
shown, "groups are no longer tightly territorialized, spatially bounded, historically unselfconscious, or culturally homogeneous" (1991:191). Ethiopian Jews' new identifications, whether at the local, national, transnational,
or global level, are one example of today's shifting and multi-sited identity
constructs. Indeed, if Ethiopian Jews are re-establishing locality in the Israeli
environment, formulating Israeli citizenship as well as an Ethiopian ethnicity, re-inventing their "home" culture and adopting global black symbols,
this requires the anthropologist to rethink the concepts used for studying migrant populations and sites of cultural production. The "hybrid location" of cultural value, as Bhabha (1994) observes, leads to new ethnicities

connected to transnational communities and global identities; yet at the same time, it also enables Ethiopian immigrants in Israel to re-ethnicize their Ethiopianness as well as develop their Israeliness.

More particularly concerning migration studies in Israel, we need to re-situate the study of Jewish immigrants into a broader theoretical framework that takes into account transnational practices and global identity constructs. Immigration to Israel has often been conceptualized as a linear and permanent movement from the country of origin to the Promised Land, where assimilation (the proverbial "melting pot") into the new society would inevitably follow. If Israel was seen as a special case in migration studies, mainly due to its "mythology of uniqueness," this seems less and less appropriate today, as new immigrants increasingly display the same attributes as migrants to Western countries (Shuval and Leshem 1998). We have tried to show that the way Ethiopian Jews reconstruct their identities and ethnicities, as well as the manner in which they articulate the relation between the local, the transnational, and the global in many ways resembles experiences of migration and de-territorialization among other displaced populations in the world.

REFERENCES

Anderson, Benedict. 1983. *Imagined Communities: Reflections on the Origin and Spread of Nationalism*. London and New York: Verso.
Anteby, Lisa. 1995. "Alimentation, différenciation sexuelle et identité ethnique chez les Juifs éthiopiens en Israël." *Information sur les Sciences Sociales* 34(4):633–62.
———. 1999a. "Of Names, Amulets and Movies: Some Patterns of Oral, Written and Non-verbal Negotiation Among the Ethiopian Jews in Israel." In *The Beta Israel in Ethiopia and Israel: Studies on Ethiopian Jews*, ed. T. Parfitt and E. Trevisan Semi, pp. 201–08. Richmond: Curzon Press.
———. 1999b. "There's Blood in the House: Negotiating Female Rituals of Purity Among Ethiopian Jews in Israel." In *Women and Water: Menstruation in Jewish Life and Law*, ed. R. Wasserfall, pp. 166–86. Hanover, N.H.: Brandeis University Press.
Appadurai, Arjun. 1996. *Modernity at Large: Cultural Dimensions of Globalization*. Minneapolis: University of Minnesota Press.
Bhabha, Homi. 1994. *The Location of Culture*. London: Routledge.
Cohen, Eric. 1983. "Ethnicity and Legitimation in Contemporary Israel." *Jerusalem Quarterly* 24:21–34.
de Certeau, Michel. 1990. *L'invention du quotidien*. Paris: Gallimard.
Fanon, Frantz. 1952. *Peau noire, masques blancs*. Paris: Seuil.

Kaplan, Steve. 1990. *Les Falashas*. Turnhout: Brepols.

Kimlicka, Will. 1995. *Multicultural Citizenship: A Liberal Theory of Minority Rights*. Oxford: Clarendon Press.

Levine, Donald. 1974. *Greater Ethiopia*. Chicago: University of Chicago Press.

Levy, André. 1997. "To Morocco and Back: Tourism and Pilgrimage Among Moroccan-born Israelis," in *Grasping the Land: Space and Place in Contemporary Israeli Discourse and Experience*, ed. E. Ben-Ari and Y. Bilu, pp. 25–46. Albany: State University of New York Press.

Lewis, Herbert S. 1989. *After the Eagles Landed: The Yemenites of Israel*. Boulder: Westview Press.

Lomsky-Feder, Edna, and Tamar Rapoport. 2000. "Visit, Separation, and Deconstructing Nostalgia: Russian Students Travel to Their Old Home." *Journal of Contemporary Ethnography* 29(1):32–57.

Malkki, Liisa. 1995. *Purity and Exile: National Cosmology Among Hutu Refugees in Tanzania*. Chicago: University of Chicago Press.

Salamon, Hagar. 1997–1998. "Transformation of Racial Consciousness: From Ethiopia to the Promised Land" *Jerusalem Studies in Jewish Folklore* 19–20:125–46. [Hebrew.]

Seeman, Don. 2000. "The Question of Kinship: Bodies and Narratives in the Beta-Israel-European Encounter (1860–1920)." *Journal of Religion in Africa* 30(1):86–120.

Shabtay, Malka. 1995. "The Experience of Ethiopian Soldiers in the Israeli Army: The Process of Identity Formulation Within the Military Context." *Israel Social Science Research* 10(2):69–80.

Shuval, Judith, and Eliazer Leshem. 1998. "The Sociology of Migration in Israel: A Critical View." In *Immigration to Israel: Sociological Perspectives*, ed. J. Shuval and E. Leshem, pp. 3–50. Somerset, N.J.: Transaction Publishers.

Weil, Shalva. 1997a. "Changing of the Guards: Leadership Among Ethiopian Jews in Israel." *Journal of Social Sciences* 1(4):301–07.

———. 1997b. "Religion, Blood and Equality of Rights: The Case of Ethiopian Jews in Israel." *International Journal on Minority and Group Rights* 4:397–412.

Weingrod, Alex. 1985. *Studies in Israeli Ethnicity: After the Ingathering*. New York: Gordon & Breach.

———. 1995. "Patterns of Adaptation of Ethiopian Jews Within Israeli Society." In *Between Africa and Zion: Proceedings of the First International Congress of the Society for the Study of Ethiopian Jewry*, ed. S. Kaplan et al., pp. 252–57. Jerusalem: Ben Zvi Institute.

NOTES

1. A smaller group of Ethiopian Jews speak Tygrinya, too.

2. Israeliness is similarly put forth by young Russian immigrants in Israel going back to Russia (Lomsky-Feder and Rapoport 2000). Levy (1997) also observes how Moroccan-born Israelis discovered their Israeliness in travels back to their native Morocco and how the reversal of patron-client relationships between Israelis and Muslims gives way to manifestations of superiority and use of Israeli idioms of power and affluence by the visitors.

3. This re-appropriation process can be compared to a certain extent with the phenomenon of *raï* music among Franco-Maghrebi youth in France who adapted Algerian popular tunes to a modern beat.

4. They thought all Jews were dark-skinned like them until their encounter with the first European Jew, Joseph Halévy, in the nineteenth century, who convinced them that he was a "white Falasha"; cf. Seeman 2000. See also Salamon 1997–98 on skin color in the Ethiopian and Israeli contexts.

5. For Ethiopian Jews, this represents a double insult, since they did not consider themselves as "black" in Ethiopia, this color being associated with a specific racial group, the Barya, who used to be slaves in Ethiopia; cf. Salamon 1997–98.

PART THREE

Between Homeland and Diaspora: Spaces of Interaction

CHAPTER 10

Ethnicity and Diaspora: The Case of the Cambodians

IDA SIMON-BAROUH

Global migrations, and in particular those taking place in the latter part of the twentieth century, raise many questions regarding the culture of both individuals and collectivities who have migrated across the world. They also pose no less important issues regarding the culture of the host populations, especially in nation-states such as France where the close coincidence of the majority culture based upon a presumed national homogeneity and citizenship is typically taken as the model of reference. In this chapter I propose to explore the meaning of the concept of culture as it applies to immigrant collectivities. More particularly, my specific reference are those persons commonly classified as "Cambodians," most of whom immigrated to several countries in Europe, North America, and Australia during the past quarter-century.

Before examining the specific instance of "Cambodians" in France, it is important to briefly review the main directions taken in recent studies of Cambodia and "Cambodians" overseas. The complex problems that confront refugees from Southeast Asia in Europe, Australia, and North America has been a topic of interest among national and local-level policy makers, as well as among psychiatrists, historians, sociologists, and anthropologists. To cite some examples, historians have analyzed the Khmer Rouge regime of the 1970s within the broader context of Cambodian history, and there have also been historical studies of "native politics" and the French colonial administration. Taking a more individual and personal perspective, there are a number of autobiographies describing life during and after the Khmer Rouge period, and also depictions of what has been called the "odyssey of the boat people."

Sociologists and anthropologists have mainly focused their research on the refugees' resettlement and their integration into the various host societies. Studies by sociologists have often dealt with topics such as economic integration, entrepreneurship, and the formation of small businesses. Several sociological studies concentrate upon the so-called "Chinese" from Cambodia, Laos, and Vietnam, and they examine their construction of networks as well as their social integration (sometimes called "insertion") as this develops primarily through their childrens' participation in local schools and the resulting changes in identity as well as greater proficiency in language. Generally speaking, with the exception of the so-called Chinese, these surveys have typically considered "Southeast Asian refugees" as a single social category.

In contrast, studies by anthropologists tend to focus upon a specific collectivity, and they trace the migration experience over time of various communities (such as Cambodians, Hmong, Lao, and Vietnamese) and the group's subsequent resettlement in a Western host country. These studies proceed by first describing the historical context that led a specific group to immigrate to a particular place, and then go on to consider the social and political contexts that characterize their new lives. They may also include a survey of the collectivity's "cultural background" in their place of origin, and then examine their relationships with members of the host society. Some researchers phrase their analysis in terms of "culture" and "culture change," while others choose to emphasize "ethnic relations."

Overall, with the exception of the Chinese and the Hmong (perhaps because they appear "more exotic" than other Southeast Asian refugees), little attention has thus far been given to the concept of "diaspora." Even though previous studies may make mention of links with the "land of origin," or with the real or supposed "homeland," this topic has only rarely been developed and analyzed. For example, although the word appears in the title of a recent book (Nancy J. Smith-Hefner's *Identity and Moral Education in a Diasporic Community: Khmer American*), the term "diaspora" itself does not appear in the Index.

This poses an interesting series of issues: a fairly large number of "Cambodians" presently live overseas, but is this in itself sufficient to characterize them as a "diaspora"? What are the links between what can be characterized as "Cambodian culture" in Cambodia itself, and "Cambodian culture" (or "Cambodian cultures") outside of Cambodia as these are produced and transmitted in different places and widely contrasting situations? How can we describe them without caricaturing and thereby distorting their distinctive realities? In order to be defined as a "people in diaspora,"[1] a people scattered across the world needs a belief in a common origin as well as links that transcend their dispersion.[2] Do we find among the "Cambodians," wherever they live, such elements of culture that resist social change and that are common to them? Does the name given to a dispersed people *ipso facto* justify its designation as a "diaspora"?

These surely are complex questions, and they form the major focus of this chapter. Before proceeding to examine these issues, let me first clarify what will be meant by "culture." "Culture" is used here in its anthropological sense: that is, those ways of being, thinking, and acting which are transmitted from one generation to the next, and that are at the same time open to change and consequently are transformable. In this sense the concept of culture refers to *social heritage* and should not be taken to be an essentialist interpretation. Moreover, this conceptualization helps us understand the process of ethnic relations, particularly within the French context. As a consequence of the multiple interactions between migrant groups and various other collectivities—including the majority population—the concept of "culture" indicates how immigrant collectivities contribute to the diversification of the homogeneous nation-state and to its internally differentiated organization. In so doing, the immigrant collectivities passively (only because they are there) and actively (by dint of their own will and desire to succeed) take part in the new political and moral definitions that are given to particular nation-states. These definitions are based on a more or less applied ideology of respect for different cultures (but, once more, we must know what meaning we give to this word), and to equality among all of the nation's citizens. This is, of course, the project of multicultural politics. These processes also provoke new questions, perhaps more philosophical ones, that are closely connected with on-going ethnic coexistence.

These are among the many topics that emerge from my own lengthy fieldwork among small groups of Vietnamese, Cambodians, and their children who have made their home in France. Over time I observed their progressive acculturation and acquisition of French citizenship.[3] Even though they have been living in France for many years and have full legal or formal citizen rights, they continue to be perceived—and, alas, studied by some sociologists and geographers—as "Asians," "Chinese," or "Indo-Chinese"—the old category terms used during the decades of French colonization in Southeast Asia. These generalized forms of classification reinforce the perception of them as a homogeneous group, and may even lessen the cultural complexity that characterizes their lives. In fact, under certain conditions they may actually encourage such a homogenized vision of themselves. In so doing, they legitimate its use within the dominant global society as well as among other minority groups.

This chapter is developed around three major themes. First, I examine the meaning of "Cambodian" both within and outside of Cambodia. Are the people who are called, and who also name themselves, "Cambodians," really Cambodians? What does "being a Cambodian" mean? Second, I consider the perspective of ethnicity: what are the ways in which one "becomes a Cambodian" in the migratory situation? Third, in reference to particular Cambodian *cultural focuses*—that is, practices that are uniquely Cambodian—is it possible to define the meaning of "Cambodianity" as these are becoming fashioned and expressed in the dispersion?

On Designation: Who Is Cambodian?

The word "Cambodian"—what in French or English usually designates either the inhabitants of Cambodia, or those who having left their country live in another place—in reality has different meanings depending on the situations or contexts of reference. Let us examine its use in Cambodia and in the dispersion.

Cambodia, which for nearly a century (1863–1953) was a French protectorate in Indochina, is a multi-ethnic and a plural society.[4] It is principally made up of a politically and demographically dominant majority group, the Khmer (they compose 90 percent of the population) and a number of minority groups considered as either "foreigners" (the Vietnamese) or "an assimilable people" (the Chinese) or "hyphenated nationals" (the Cham or Khmer-Islam). Other groups include the Khmer Krom, or "Khmer of the lower side," which refers to the population living in what is now southwest Vietnam, on territories annexed during the nineteenth century by the Vietnamese; and the Khmer Loeu, or "Kmer of the upper side," mountain dwellers who live apart from the rest of the rural and urban populations on the high plateau bordering the eastern sections of the country. With the exception of this latter group, the various "communities" differentiate each other by their own particular occupational specializations. Moreover, in addition to this broad, general stratification, an internal social hierarchy also exists within each particular stratum.

The Cambodian language distinguishes between "Khmer" and "citizen of Cambodia." The situation is complex. While each Khmer in Cambodia is a "Cambodian," the mere fact of having Cambodian identity papers does not necessarily designate membership in the "Khmer people." On the contrary, formal identity papers also list specific ethnic memberships (for example, "Cambodian citizen with Khmer nationality," or "Cambodian citizen with Chinese nationality," and so forth). Religious membership (Buddhism is the official state religion of Cambodia) is also listed on a Cambodian citizen's identity papers. Moreover, the Cambodian language clearly differentiates between "nationality" (in the sense of "people" or "ethnic group") and "citizenship" as a Cambodian. In this fashion it strongly underscores the hierarchy established between the Khmer, who claim to be the original "historical people," and all of the other citizens of the Cambodian state.

If there is a specific word to designate the country as a political entity (Kampuchea = Cambodia), Cambodia in the phrase "going to Cambodia" or "living in Cambodia" is rendered as *srok Khmer*, which means "the country, the earth, of the Khmer people." These linguistic designations express the perception that the inhabitants of Cambodia have of themselves: a people differentiated within an ethnic system of stratification, demarcated more or less according to population group and historical period. With regard to the Chinese who live in Cambodia, the distinctions are quite subtle. The extent of racial mixture with the Khmer people is reflected in the language: "entire Chinese" refers to persons who arrived first and have not intermarried with Khmer; those who are racially more mixed (the "half-breed") are called "Khmer cut with Chinese"; after generations of intermarriage, they may become Khmer. In a kind of continuum from the first Chinese who came to Cambodia and their descendants, they change from the state of "raw" Chinese ("uncooked," as it is said in the Khmer language), to being "half-breed" and then, finally, to becoming "absorbed" as Khmer.

A close look at their ways of life reveals a complex interweaving of cultural references and changing identifications which shift according to circumstances. For example, the Khmer, who are Buddhists, usually burn their dead, while the Chinese typically bury the dead. This cultural feature is relatively obvious, and there are many more subtle distinctions and mixtures.[5] Take the instance of a woman dressed in a Cambodian skirt, her hair cut traditionally according to the style or custom of women of a certain age, speaking the Khmer language as she honors the dead of her family, whose names, written in Chinese, appear on the tablets of the ancestors' altar behind their photos. Such instances of syncretism can also be seen in the celebrations of the Chinese and Cambodian New Year. An individual may go to the Chinese pagoda for some of the celebrations, and then, moments later, continue on to the *watt*, the Buddhist space where the temple, the monks' houses, the schools, and so forth, are located. Attending these festivities at practically the same moment is not experienced as a contradiction, but rather as being complementary. To sum up briefly, all of these and many other forms of behavior are taken to be "normal," but they also are noted and taken into account as Cambodians continuously classify each other.

Over time some of the "half-breed Chinese" may become "Khmer people," and thereby be absorbed into the majority group. However, persons who are Vietnamese are designated as *"Youen,"* a pejorative expression meaning "aliens," and are generally excluded from entrance into the majority Khmer. They are Cambodian citizens, and yet even following their marriage with Khmer they are still perceived and categorized as Vietnamese. They periodically have been persecuted, attacked physically, and even killed.

This form of ethnic plurality was maintained in Cambodia until 1970. The Khmer, the "founder people" or "historical people," justified their dominant position by claiming their presence in the land from "time immemorial." In seeking to legitimate themselves as *the* people of Kampuchea, they placed emphasis upon four topics or themes: first, their own mythology, which presumably attested to their aboriginal place in the land; second, archeological projects, which also were meant to indicate their archaic presence; third, the establishment and reproduction over time of cultural patterns that were taken to be "authentically Khmer"; and finally, their continued presence as the majority group, tightly linked to their land, and the relative absence (until then) of immigration to other places. The other ethnic collectivities were perceived either as minorities who migrated long ago to Cambodia (the Chinese), as an invading people (the Vietnamese), or as the remnants of an ancient past. This nationalist schema was, of course, similar in many ways to others constructed elsewhere.

The ethnic distinctions between those who are "Cambodians" has also been maintained in the dispersion. It is reinforced by the remembrance of two deep crises: first, the ethnic violence perpetrated by the so-called "Republicans" (supported by the United States) during the *coup d'état* against Prince Sihanouk in 1970, and second, with even more deadly force, after the Khmer Rouge, or Communist Khmer, seized power in the period between 1975 and 1979. The national question on *khmerity* became crystallized in the course of these two lengthy, bloody events. In the first crisis, the Republicans attacked and pursued the Vietnamese. During the second, the Khmer Rouge hunted and often massacred both Vietnamese and Chinese, since they maintained that, with their evil pursuit of money and their minds already subverted by American imperialist ideology, their very presence would "pollute" the construction of a legitimate social system. It was claimed that they would spoil the Khmer race, which had to be purified, and violence was considered a legitimate means to build a new basis on which the Khmer nation-state (that is, the ethnic-state) would be constructed. Indeed, violence was believed to be the way to bring about the revival of the state's legendary glory.

Driven by these extreme beliefs and ideologies, what had been a pluralistic, integrated society became a state based on racial principles. In the intervening years, the ethnic and other distinctions have not disappeared, neither in Cambodia itself nor among those living in the dispersion. Closely linked with political affiliation, they continue to be among the key bases of identification among Cambodians wherever they live.

This brief background review has emphasized processes of national inclusions and exclusions. For the nationalist militants, it created a kind of majority arrogance. These attitudes found expression not only in everyday life in Cambodia, but also among Cambodian groups abroad. Having fled the country in 1975, after the "murderous utopia" of the Pol Pot regime, the exiles and refugees now live scattered in a number of countries across the world. In their *stricto sensu* application of the communist doctrine, the Khmer Rouge hermetically sealed the boundaries, "cleaning away" (following the mournful expression which, sadly, has become all too common) all those who were suspected of "worldly knowledge" and "capitalist leanings," clearing the towns in order to presumably benefit the government's agricultural works, applying the principle of equality to its final mad realization in hundreds of thousands of deaths,[6] and, as a result, creating a large movement of refugees to neighboring Thailand, their initial place of settlement.

The census that was then conducted in order to make preparations to send them elsewhere registered the refugees with regard to their country of origin and citizenship. Officials of the Office of the United Nations High Commissioner for Refugees therefore listed those who had fled to Thailand as "Cambodians," and settled them there in Cambodian refugee camps. This is a critical point. The persons who subsequently arrived in France, the United States, Canada, and various other countries were called "Cambodians" and listed as "Cambodians" in the various official statistics. Consequently, the persons that an anthropologist first encounters when he/she seeks to define his/her population are presented as "Cambodians."

A quarter-century has passed since they initially fled from Cambodia. In time, the refugees became citizens of the countries where they settled, and their children also were born as citizens of those countries. Even so, they are still perceived as "Cambodians" or, at the least, as "Asians." Members of the immigrant generation also call themselves "Cambodians." In the second generation, they have various ways of naming, perceiving, and identifying themselves. Who are they, and, more important, how have they become "who they are"?

On Ethnicity: Can One Be, Can One Remain, a
Cambodian — and How — in the Dispersion?

It is not possible in this brief chapter to describe the richness of everyday life and the relationships of persons (both the immigrant generation and their children) who more or less find their "common origin" in Cambodia. Instead, I will focus upon several particularly significant examples that best illustrate what can be called the "cultural foci" of Cambodians living in the dispersion.

The passage of time operates for the Cambodians in much the same way as it does for other migrant collectivities. That is, over time they quickly pass from a more or less accurate cultural reproduction of their previous lives to a wide range of new expressions and continuing acculturation. Of course, this simple-sounding scheme varies widely depending upon the age of the immigrants when they arrive in their new land, and, in addition, according to the composition of their families (that is, whether they arrived alone without family members, or if their families include two or three generations as well as collateral relations). The adults and older persons are likely to "remain Cambodians," and believe that they mainly continue their lives without any change from their former ways of being, thinking, and doing. However, for the youngsters who were born in France or who arrived when they were infants or young children, the realities of life are much more complicated.[7]

As we study and come to better understand them, it becomes possible to perceive the gap between what the "Cambodians" themselves feel, live, and experience, and the ways in which they are represented by the dominant majority culture. A significant difference exists between their own repeated crossing through relatively porous "ethnic boundaries," and the tendency of the dominant group to define them in a more or less unchanging fashion. In fact, the "Cambodians" often are depicted as retaining a kind of "traditional homogeneity" that they themselves do not necessarily recognize, but at times are able to exploit for their own purposes.

These processes of change are extremely complex. There are a variety of different factors at play—the often confusing cultural pressures that socialization exerts on both young and old; the sometimes dialectically opposed interests and pressures of the collectivity (the immediate family as well as other Cambodians); the constant pressures of the dominant society; and finally, the exercise of personal choice and free will. To be sure, these are not new questions or issues, and yet there are also no clear models or answers.

The major reason lies in the difficulty of being able to understand and then to properly analyze what Bastide has termed the "intertwining of civilizations."[8] What this means is that collectivity by collectivity, situation by situation, it is not always possible to comprehend how the various contacts and interactions, as well as their re-interpretations and identifications, all take place together. While, for the immigrant generation, the schema of changes more or less follows the classic "race relations process,"[9] it looks quite different for their children, for whom the cultural constructions have different meanings and are experienced in quite different ways. We can illustrate these processes by briefly considering the Cambodians' links with Cambodia, and also with their varied expressions of Buddhism.

Cambodians' Relations with Cambodia?

In considering how Cambodians in the dispersion tend to view Cambodia, one must recall that, by and large, the immigration is recent and began less than thirty years ago.[10] This is a critical fact, basic to understanding their situation, and it should be kept in mind throughout this presentation.

Overall, it can be said that how persons view and otherwise relate to Cambodia varies according to their age and legal status. For the elders, the first generation of immigrants who were born there, for them to assert their continuing links to and interest in Cambodia is no problem. Their ties are relatively tight and unbroken, and in some instances they at times still appear to live in the drama of their former lives. In contrast, the identifications and connections of the youngsters, who were born or brought up in France, are quite different. Their knowledge or image of Cambodia is essentially constructed from their family discourse, or from videos and films about Cambodian life. While there are many different subtle expressions of these links to the past, in a general way four different types of relationship can be identified: sentimental recollections, family support, compassionate solidarity, and national and political engagement.

SENTIMENTAL RELATION TO CAMBODIA

Among those born and reared in Cambodia, to be a descendant of the fabulous builders of Angkor (ninth to twelfth centuries A.D.), and hence to be anchored in history and art lends a feeling of status and pride. Beyond this sense of honored descent, their relationships to Cambodia are complex, built upon happy memories that also are blurred by suffering and death. After all, Cambodia was in times past famed for the sweetness and softness of its life.

This legendary reputation is confirmed by memories that spring out suddenly in discussion or in dreams and thoughts. There are instants in which flashes of memory recall the sight of a good dish cooked by a traveling merchant on the pavement of the streets, the smell of fine fragrances, the sight of bright colors and varying hues, a sudden movement outside that brings back those special sounds which are linked to particular settings, a summer rain that evokes memories of childhood games played outdoors in the midst of hot tropical showers. Even though one cannot truly share these rich, nostalgic reminiscences, they somehow are imparted to the youngsters, who, although they have never been to Cambodia, progressively build their own imaginary images of the past. In this sense Cambodia is first attached to affect, to the ungraspable, the impalpable, and in so doing reveals a culture that gives shape to the depth of the unconscious.

SUPPORTING THE FAMILY

The Khmer Rouge regime, which lasted four endless years, made Cambodia into a huge work and concentration camp, and consequently left the people totally devastated. Those who survived and were able to flee, and who are now secure in a Western country, continue to look for surviving members of their lost families. Following ten or fifteen years of silence (Cambodia remained closed until the end of the 1980s), they attempt to gather more details about their family—their lives, and also their deaths. Some have discovered family members who are alive in a new place—in Cambodia, Vietnam, Hong Kong, or elsewhere—but many others still have no information about the fate of family members.

When the borders were finally opened in the beginning of the nineties, it was possible to communicate with relatives again. Motivated by strong feelings of duty towards their family survivors, the Cambodians from outside sent letters, money, and parcels with medicine inside that could be resold for a good fee in Cambodia (when and if they reached their destination). In addition, some among the new "French Cambodians" sought to bring some surviving family member to France—or at least one member from the remnant that remained. These activities were less an attempt to remove them from Cambodia, and more a desire to reconstitute the family in a situation that promised greater security and economic well-being (both are central elements in Cambodian culture). It is difficult to know whether this sense of family duty will continue in the future. What is more clear is that this concern for family is one element that links Cambodians overseas with persons and events "back home."

COMPASSIONATE SOLIDARITY

The use of the term "solidarity" refers to the voluntary cooperative activities initiated by small groups of Cambodians living overseas. The goal of the activities is to collect funds to assist their former village to initiate new programs of health, education, and the repair of religious sites. Money is collected "in the Cambodian tradition": that is, donations are made during gatherings of persons at a Buddhist feast organized at the pagoda (or at a place considered for the occasion to be a pagoda). These gatherings are highly stylized according to "the Cambodian tradition." A person or a group of family members arrives in the morning with Cambodian food and cooked rice. Entering into the gathering-place, they bow before the Buddha and the monk or monks who are there, greet the organizer of the occasion, and then give a certain amount of money to the man considered as the treasurer. They then are congratulated and receive blessings from him. They sit on the floor together with the others and carry on conversation while waiting for the prayers to begin. Following the prayers and the lesson, given by one of the monks, everybody rises and offers their meals to the monks, who, as a sign of their status and respect, eat before the others while sitting in front of them. When they have finished, everyone shares the foods that they brought with them.

Following the meal, the money that was donated is publicly counted, and the amount given by each person or family is announced in a loud voice. The money is then sent to Cambodia with a trustworthy traveler, usually one of the monks. When he returns, he tells the families how the money was spent, and sometimes shows photos and videos of their "modernized" village.

These periodic activities are occasions when "Cambodia" is actualized and brought closer to persons' sensibilities. During these gatherings they may feel almost as if they were in Cambodia. The participants include persons of all ages—children and teenagers as well as heads of families—who are at these moments linked back to their parents' or grand-parents' homeland. Will they perpetuate this traditional aspect of Cambodian relations, that is, donations in the Buddhist format?

NATIONAL AND POLITICAL COMMITMENT

It is fair to say that most of the Cambodians who were at least teenagers when they arrived in France, and in the interim have become French citizens, feel themselves to "be Cambodian," and identify themselves with the *srok khmer* (a Cambodian expression meaning the land of the Khmer, the ethnic majority). In their private as well as community lives, they try to live as they would in Cambodia, in this way making the country that they left alive and real for them. This includes elements such as the family, village, pagoda, "the earth that had fed us." These elements can be said to constitute the basis for the national feeling; for some it is mainly sentimental, a kind of cultural humanitarian expression, while for others it also includes political and occupational involvement.

While all Cambodians know that they come from the *srok khmer*, which is revered, not everyone feels the same attachment to Kampuchea, the political designation of Cambodia, and to its government. Some argue that "compassionate solidarity," focused on health, technology, and so forth, should continue to be voluntary and not be connected with the Kampuchea government, which they consider to be corrupt. Others take the position that it would be best for the present government to fall and be replaced by a more capable leadership. Those who strongly oppose the government also tend to express a strong xenophobia vis-à-vis the Vietnamese who live in Cambodia—a minority group there—and elsewhere. Thus, while there is continued concern for "Cambodia," the politics of support introduces argument and discord and at times tends to divide the overseas community. These debates are meaningful mainly for the older generation, while for the time being the youngsters do not wish to become involved.

RETURNING TO CAMBODIA?

Generally speaking, it is possible to briefly list five different attitudes regarding returning to Cambodia. First, some voice what is undoubtedly a genuine nostalgia for *srok khmer*, and when their financial circumstances permit they travel back in order to visit their former home. The second attitude is precisely the opposite: they flatly refuse to even consider returning, primarily because of strong objections to the present government. The third attitude is located somewhere between these two, and can be termed a kind of "ambiguous nostalgia." Those in this category have contrary, opposing feelings—the land that fed and nourished them is also a land of cruel bereavement, of devastated families and long periods of horror and punishment. For them, returning would open old wounds, would revive their sorrow. The fourth group is more definitive: it is composed of the small number of Cambodians who, faithful to their land and sensing its absence from their lives, decide to return and permanently settle there. Finally, the fifth category may be the majority: when financially able to, they travel and spend their holidays "at home," "where everybody has the same skin and the same nose as ours." During their stay in Cambodia they typically engage in a kind of comparative critical review—of their own lives in France, their reinvention of a Cambodia now in transformation—and they may then realize that nostalgia has become the basis of their community organization in France.

Despite the small number of sociological and anthropological surveys concerning them, we can assert that most of the refugees' children have a good cultural and identifying balance between Cambodia and France. Among those who were born in Cambodia and came to France as infants—up to the age of five—they know that Cambodia is their country of origin. For them it is a palpable fact, and they may have memory flashes, even though they don't know whether those frequently repeated and evocated images are really theirs or are those of their parents. Cambodia may represent for them, too, the place of a certain sense of belonging and identifying, justified by the presence of a family group there. Country and family are mixed and give to their "Cambodianity" an unquestionable reality; this is not a nationalistic feeling, however, since their link to Cambodia is not of a patriotic nature.

Whether born in Cambodia or France, they all continuously measure the difference between their own "Cambodian culture" and that of their relatives in Cambodia. They are familiar with and feel close to them, and yet it is impossible to jump the gap between the two places. The fact that in Cambodia they are seen and designated as "French" seems insurmountable.

Is Buddhism a Link Between All Cambodian Communities?

The Buddhist religion does not demand or depend upon active participation, particularly on the part of children and youngsters. Children's participation may be passive, for example, as they accompany one or several members of their family to the place of worship, playing together and remaining outside for much of the time. With the exception of rules of politeness that include persons of all ages, from youngest to oldest, no one imposes any behavioral or ideological conformity upon them. Consequently they learn, as it were, in spite of themselves, and mainly by absorbing the required behavior. This essentially informal mode of activity can be observed in Cambodia as well as in France, and it may be said to produce a certain relaxed serenity vis-à-vis religion that includes both children and adults. For them, as it were, "religion never causes a problem."

In France, this serenity is reinforced by the positive image that Buddhism has succeeded in projecting in European and other Western societies. This is perhaps best symbolized by the well-known "smile of the Dalai Lama in exile." On a more practical or pragmatic level, preoccupied by religion and fidelity, the adults have in recent years begun to construct pagodas where they are able to meet, meditate, and pray. In France, a secular state in which public and private areas are kept separate, these newly built pagodas are not negatively perceived, apparently since Buddhists are not feared as potential religious competitors or as "trouble-makers." [11] Whether positive or merely patronizing, this "accepting" attitude is also expressed with regard to many other cultural features.

If we take the example of language, we can see that while many parents are pleased to see the efforts of some of their children to speak Khmer (the Cambodian national language), they do not actively fight for its reproduction. During the first years of their settlement they organized Khmer language courses, but the difficulty of the syntax as well as the writing system (the alphabet is derived from Sanskrit) discouraged many children from continuing. It may be that even though they felt that retaining their language was necessary in order to maintain their identity, this sense was not strong enough for them to continue. Interestingly, when they traveled to Cambodia as visitors, children who spoke Khmer at home with their elders discovered how far they were from the way the language is spoken in Cambodia. Thus, in effect, the parents' attitude towards learning Khmer was pragmatic and relaxed. While Buddhism is an important part of "Cambodianity," [12] and the loss of the Khmer language a sad consequence of migration, mastering the French language was more important to them in their present life.

The accepting attitude of the dominant majority influences the attitudes of the Cambodian children as they grow up, and it is undoubtedly significant in forming or constructing their own individual identities. Overall, they can be seen to express the desire to reproduce their "native culture," to belong to their own particular group, without at the same time preventing their full membership as citizens within the larger collectivity.[13]

These kinds of relations can also be seen in many other features of everyday life—for example, in relations between elders and youngsters, food preparation, and in family interactions. In brief, with regard to their sense of adopting the ways of living of urban Western society, we may conclude that Cambodians in France have become acculturated. At the same time, however, in many situations and contexts they continue to "be Cambodian."

This does not mean that they are under the influence of a permanent determinism over which they have no control—such a view would support the critics who accuse anthropologists of "making traditions," more real in the anthropologist's mind than in the facts on the ground. Nonetheless, there is no doubt that "culture" is deep-seated and unlikely to be entirely transformed or to disappear in a generation or two. Indeed, while we do not wish to essentialize them, we might conclude that in spite of the torturers, the vicissitudes of migration, and living as a minority in an urban Western milieu, "cultures" are quite healthy!

If we now attempt to answer the question, "Can one be a Cambodian in the dispersion?" we may be able to give a tentative answer for the first generation and their children in France. While they have been changed culturally in comparison with their previous ways of life in Cambodia, they also have created specific forms of cultural identity in their new places of settlement. Indeed, this diversity is based on some of the major features of "Cambodian culture" as these can be observed in Cambodia itself. They have built places of communal presence where "traditional" rites and practices continue to be very much alive, so that a newcomer from Cambodia can "feel at home" in the dispersion. This poses an additional series of questions: Do they express the same cultural and other formats wherever they have settled in the world? In other words, is it possible to find or recognize what might be termed "Cambodianity" in the diaspora?

Is "Cambodianity" a Link Between All Cambodian Communities?

At the beginning of this chapter I briefly discussed the *a priori* use of the concept of "diaspora." Among other features, it contains the idea of an original place of departure (a real place of origin, or an imagined or mythical one); many places of settlement eventually linked by commercial, religious, family, and other networks; and the idea of long-term establishment or stabilization of communities. While many authors mention and even emphasize the internal diversity of diasporas, the ways in which they are represented in effect often underscores their homogeneity. Thus they are named or called "the Cambodians," "the Chinese,"[14] "the Armenians," "the Algerians," and so on. Applying the term "diaspora" to them may therefore have the effect of reifying these groups, precisely because it implies the sense of long or unlimited time, and, by extension, of stability and the continuing reproduction of cultural elements. To be sure, the vocabulary of the social sciences has not yet found a term which would better describe the spatial dispersion of collectivities that arise from a specific ethnic group (or from a supposed or imagined ethnicity) and the process of change and diversification that occurs as the result of long-term contact with members of their host society, and that is able at the same time to deal with notions of cultural reproduction as well as cultural transformations.

In this regard, "diaspora" seems to primarily emphasize a kind of "static conception of culture"—it suggests permanence rather than movement, change, and heterogeneity. The very conceptualization that typically is phrased in category terms such as "the Cambodians" or "the Chinese" has the result of reinforcing an image of stable, on-going cultural systems, despite the new and dramatically different experiences as well as the new contexts in which the "diasporized groups" find themselves. Facts on the ground, however, give us another interpretation. As time goes on, the social actors operate selectively in a multiplicity of different cultural frames. Some features of their previous lives may no longer be relevant; they may develop other features that become much more fundamental (and may re-interpret or rephrase their previous or original *cultural focuses*). They are thereby able to both design and lend a certain novel coherence to their newly established migrant collectivities.

Returning to our analysis of "the Cambodians," the concept of diaspora might lead us to omit their own heterogeneity in Cambodia itself, as well as the intermarriages and other "mixtures" that take place following their migration. If we refer to them all as "Cambodians," we may be accused of assigning individuals to a specific group, a kind of labeling with an indelible marker. In this and other ways, their very existence in the imagination of the members of the host society is emphasized if not created. For them, "Cambodians" becomes a legitimate term and suggests that they are the same wherever they live, in Cambodia and elsewhere. In what sense can this be an adequate depiction of "the Cambodians" 's social reality and the concrete situations of their everyday lives?

In other words, are all those persons who are called "Cambodians" (and who define themselves as "Cambodians") and presently live in Cambodia, Paris, Rennes, New York, Philadelphia, Los Angeles, Sydney, Quebec, and Montreal: are they all "the same"? If we call them "Cambodians," are we not thereby justifying their naming as well as their classification as a "diaspora"? If we accept the implications of the terminology, there is the possibility (even more, the risk) of being classed together with those ideologists who "racialize differences"; on the other hand, when we criticize this position we also take the risk of being accused of opposing ethnic diversity, being anti-pluralist and pro-assimilationist, suffering from a kind of "ethnic blindness." Moreover, if the collectivities are distinctive and different from one another, can we also locate common links (or at least one link) between them irrespective of where they live so that they can be defined as a "diaspora"? If so, what are the characteristics or features of this link?

It is possible to identify and list a few clues or criteria: country of origin, dispersion from a particular place, relationship to the original territory, maintenance of national consciousness, becoming a minority in the host society, having relations with the various dispersed collectivities, and so forth. Indeed, if we focus upon the issue of how "Cambodianity" is constructed, we may be able to deal with these criticisms as well as free ourselves from ideological constraints. In this sense it will be useful to examine the ways in which "ethnicity" is expressed. No matter what the host society's policies are regarding ethnic minorities, it is likely that individuals can attain some diversity, either by themselves or as part of a more encompassing collectivity.

It is probably fair to conclude that a kind of "Cambodianity" has in fact developed. This can be seen both at the level of individual behavior as well in the ways in which the various collectivities[15] become organized. Of course, assimilation into the different "host societies" takes place, and yet there also are distinctive features that appear to be common to all of them. Putting it more generally, there are certain cultural traits that continue to structure the group, making it active and alive within the new global society while at the same time maintaining a myriad of ties and relationships with the society of origin. Paradoxically, the cultural manifestations that appear to be "common" or "defining features" also lend the scattered "Cambodian" collectivities their apparent homogeneous appearance.

Whether their host society is multiculturalist or assimilationist in ideology and practice, certain features can be said to characterize the immigrant generation of Cambodians and their children wherever they now live. Buddhism is undoubtedly one of the most important. It is one of the principal cultural traits of Cambodian culture, both with regard to everyday domestic practices as well as in more encompassing collective activities. It not only serves to build social and cultural bridges between different subgroups, it also finds expression in the performance of rituals during the "diasporic" meetings that take place in the growing number of pagodas. Modeled more or less after those that one finds in Cambodia, the pagodas themselves are designed differently depending upon the country and locale where they have been built. The important dates on the Buddhist calendar provide an opportunity for followers to gather there in communal celebrations.[16] In addition, each religious site includes a mausoleum where, to an increasing extent, funeral urns are kept. The periodic religious gatherings tend to strengthen the collectivity; indeed, if these practices had not emerged, the "Cambodians" might have withdrawn within their extended families and would have lived a kind of "passive ethnicity." Yet these and other religious activities are practiced, and they project an image of "the Cambodians" as a homogeneous group in the diaspora.

While a more-or-less common Buddhist religious pattern can be observed in the different places where they live, over time religious practices are also being re-adopted, country by country, to their host society. "Being Cambodian" therefore varies somewhat from one place to the next, even though Buddhist practices outwardly lend them a common structure. These religious frameworks serve to transcend the conflicts within the collectivity (individual, political, hierarchical), and they can be seen as principal elements in the affirmation of "Cambodianity." It is because Cambodian Buddhism presents a certain specificity in practice and belief that the "Cambodians"— including the offspring of intermarriages—maintain their identification with the collectivity.

Conclusion: Are the Cambodians a People in Diaspora?

The emergence and development of pagodas is a vital feature in the formation of a "Cambodian ethnicity" in the various overseas communities. They are important on several levels: the pagodas are a setting for interaction between members of the collectivity in each particular place of settlement, they provide links between the different settlements (this is best illustrated by the main temples situated in the Paris area), and also between some individuals and Cambodia itself.

The new pagodas are usually built in small local neighborhood houses, some without any outward sign that would suggest that they are religious places. While externally they often are different from the structures in Cambodia, the pagodas tend to have the same internal organization, including the presence of one or more monks. The monks typically have ties to other pagodas, both new and traditional—those situated in France, Cambodia, and sometimes in other places in the world.

Interestingly, the present-day revival of Buddhism in Cambodia itself is actively supported by Cambodians living overseas, especially those who were born and socialized there. As noted earlier, they have a continuing, long-term link to their *srok*—the earth where the placenta that bred them was buried—and to their village and pagoda. Buddhism was attacked during the Khmer Rouge regime, when many monks were killed and pagodas and *chaddei* (family monuments in which the urns are traditionally deposited) were often destroyed. Now, however, many of those living overseas take part in religious festivities that are organized at their own local pagodas. These events often are sponsored as a means of gathering money to rebuild or furnish a particular pagoda in their village of origin. As a result, the building trade is now flourishing in Cambodia, especially in places where the old temples were destroyed and new ones are being constructed. The industry of religious "art" is also having a revival; for example, some American-Cambodians prepare for the future by having large *chaddei* built for them in a quiet place near a newly constructed pagoda.

This is a main link between Cambodians in the dispersion and their former country and its inhabitants. Those who live abroad are thought to be very rich, and yet "back home" they also have become strangers, aliens in Cambodia. Those who live in France are called "the French." Youngsters born in France do not feel at ease when they travel to their parents' mother country, even if they had been told about or dreamt of it for years. Moreover, the Cambodians have not created supranational organizations—social, political, or economic—that might successfully range between the various communities in the dispersion, or between those communities and Cambodia itself.

Finally, should the Cambodians living overseas be classified as a diaspora? The data are not entirely clear-cut, and it is difficult to make a final judgment. Overall, however, it is probably most accurate to conclude that at present they are not a diaspora. The migration is too new to make this claim, and the other links are still too weak to confirm it. As has been emphasized, for those living overseas there are many ties of memory and activity that focus upon Cambodia, and "Cambodianity" is also emerging as a broad, somewhat vague pattern of behavior among those who have settled in Europe and North America. Yet these patterns are still being fashioned, and Cambodians living overseas seem mainly concerned with becoming established in their new lands. For the time being it appears that they are culturally distinctive communities living in a number of host societies, and their expressions of ethnicity provide the common links that together bind the immigrant-refugees and their children.

REFERENCES

Bastide, Roger. 1960. "Problemes de l'entrecroisement des civilisations et de leurs oeuvres." In *Traite de Sociologie*, ed. Georges Gurvitch, vol. 2, pp. 315–22. Paris: Presses Universitaires de France.

Bruneau, Michel. 1995. "Espaces et territoires de diasporas." In *Diasporas*, pp. 5–23. Montpellier: GIP-Reclus.

Chan, Kwok B., and Doreen Marie Indra, eds. 1987. *Uprooting, Loss and Adaptation: The Resettlement of Indochinese Refugees in Canada.* Ottawa: Canadian Public Health Association.

Chandler, David P. 1991. *The Tragedy of Cambodian History: Politics, War and Revolution Since 1945.* New Haven, Conn.: Yale University Press.

Choron-Baix, Catherine. 1986. "Mo lam du Sud Laos réfugiés en France." Thése de 3e cycle. Ecole des Hautes Etudes en Sciences Sociales, Paris.

Cuche, Denys. [1996] 2001. *La notion de culture dans les sciences sociales.* Paris: La Decouverte.

Furnivall, John S. 1939. *Netherlands Indies: A Study of Plural Economy.* Cambridge: Cambridge University Press.

Giraud, Michel. 1995. "Acculturation." *Pluriel recherches. Vocabulaire historique et critique des relations inter-ethniques* 3.

Haines, David W. 1989. *Refugees as Immigrants: Cambodians, Laotians, and Vietnamese in America.* Totowa, N.J.: Rowman & Littlefield.

Hassoun, Jean-Pierre. 1997. *Hmong du Laos en France. Changement social, initiatives et adaptations.* Paris: Presses Universitaires de France.

Ledgerwood, Judy L. 1990. "Changing Khmer Conceptions of Gender: Women, Stories, and the Social Order." Ph.D. diss. Cornell University.

Ma Mung, Emmanuel. 2000. *La diaspora chinoise. Geographie d'une migration.* Paris: Editions Geophrys.

Marienstrass, Richard. 1975. *Etre un peuple en diaspora.* Paris: Maspero.

Safran, William. 1990. "Ethnic Diasporas in Industrial Societies: A Comparative Study of the Political Implications of the 'Homeland' Myth." In *Les Etrangers dans la ville. Le regard des sciences sociales*, ed. Ida Simon-Barouh and Pierre-Jean Simon, pp. 163–77. Paris: L'Harmattan.

Scheffer, Gabriel. 1986. *Modern Diasporas in International Politics.* New York: St Martin's.

Simon, Pierre-Jean. 1997. "Classements sociaux." *Pluriel recherches. Vocabulaires historique et critique des relations inter-ethniques* 5.

Simon-Barouh, Ida. 1990. *Le Cambodge des Khmers rouges. Chronique de la vie quotidienne. Recit de Yi Tan Kim Pho.* Paris: L'Harmattan.

———. 1995. "Enfants de Cambodgiens, Chinois, Hmong, Japonais, Lao, viétnamiens et enfants au college et au lycee a Rennes." *Migrants Formation* 101.

———. 1999. "Immigration and Age at Arrival: Integration and Cultural

Transmission among Cambodian Refugees in France," in *Roots and Routes: Ethnicity and Migration in Global Perspective*, ed. Shalva Weill. Jerusalem: Magness Press, Hebrew University.

———. 2003. "Are the Cambodian Refugees in France and Their Children an Element of a Cambodian Diaspora?" In *Deux mille ans de diasporas?*, ed. Lisa Anteby and William Berthomiere. Rennes: Presses de l'Universite de Rennes.

Smith-Hefner, Nancy J. 1999. *Identity and Moral Education in a Diasporic Community: Khmer American*. Berkeley and Los Angeles: University of California Press.

Stein, Barry. 1981. "The Refugee Experience: Defining the Parameters of a Field Study." *International Migration Review* 15(1).

Welaratna, Usha. 1993. *Beyond the Killing Fields: Voices of Nine Cambodian Survivors in America*. Stanford: Stanford University Press.

Willmott, William. 1967. *The Chinese in Cambodia*. Vancouver: University of British Columbia.

NOTES

1. In reference to Marienstrass 1975.

2. I intentionally speak first of "dispersion" instead of "diaspora" because I don't know *a priori* if the people I am speaking about *are* a diaspora. This word is a concept, a tool for analysis, but it is rather polysemic, too, and I prefer to see about using it for the "Cambodians" after a description of the people. Is "diaspora," applied to them, an operational concept? What reality does it cover? Does it allow the best comprehension of Cambodian ethnicity?

3. Hundreds of thousands of Cambodians of all conditions—peasants and city dwellers, rich and, in most cases, very poor—fled the Khmer Rouge regime between 1975 and 1978, and after January 1979, when the Khmers Rouges were overthrown by other, pro-Vietnamese, communists. Alone or, more often, in family groups (parents and children, grandparents, uncles and aunts, etc.), most of them went to Thailand first and then to the West. The United States, Canada, Australia, and France were their main host countries.

About 65,000 of them went to France and scattered after their arrival to many cities. Now half of them live in the Paris area (in the 13th, 18th, and 19th *arrondissement*, or district), in its eastern district, and in the southeast of France, with the others scattered elsewhere. They created Cambodian niches where they live, structured by a few pagodas. But the most important group is centralized in the Paris area. Their children are integrated into French society, and occupationally speaking they follow the same paths as their French peers. Some (higher educated) have become doctors, others are workers, and others failed to find work (see Simon-Barouh 1995).

In regard to their occupations, all of them changed to other occupational categories once in France. Many of the women were mothers, as well as farmers, workers, seamstresses, or shopkeepers (and a very small number were in intellectual or medical occupations) and the men could be found in every occupational category (peasant, policeman, soldier, shopkeeper, school master); however, in France, neither men nor women could find equivalent jobs. The French census of 1990 counted Cambodians, Laotians (including Hmong), and Vietnamese together, as if they were an indistinguishable whole: workers, 57 percent; skilled workers, 6.3 percent; office workers, 20 percent (with a quarter of them in the trades), "cadres" (higher graduates, staff, managerial staff, senior executives), 3.1 percent; entrepreneurs, 6.9 percent; farmers, 2.7 percent.

4. Cf. Furnivall 1939.

5. I would like to mention that such a complexity is rarely shown by the researchers (sociologists as well as geographers) who seem to prefer "communities," with well-defined boundaries. They very often reduce Cambodians to "Chinese," so that, in the migration, one can perceive only Chinese people. It is as if the reference to China conferred on the individuals to whom it is applied a social value lacking to the Cambodians, who are less well known and so few, compared to China's immensity. But maybe this very point is part of another discussion, though I am not sure that this "invention" of "communities" by some scientists does not corrupt a more precise vision of ethnic groups or collectivities.

6. The numbers vary according to the authors. Some authors suggest that the total reached 1.5 or 2 million (of a total population of 7 million). Cf. Simon-Barouh 1990.

7. I developed this argument a few years ago at a conference in Jerusalem. Cf. Simon-Barouh 1999:45–64.

8. Bastide 1960:315–22.

9. Even if they have ignored the works of the Chicago School, some contemporary sociologists and anthropologists (in France, for instance) still like to criticize their ideas and ideologies. What they forget is that although the history of the disciplines necessitates cutting off what seems outdated or maybe wrong nowadays, it is not necessary to erase or deny all they gave us. The Chicago sociologists constructed explicative schemas. Today we question them and we try to go further, but they gave us descriptions that one can hardly dream of finding the equivalents of today. Their analyses, when revisited and made more flexible, are still operant for us. The schema of the "race relations cycle" seems fertile if one tries to use it as a tool. Rid of a kind of systematism, one can see situations globally, with their multiple sides, taking into account the migrants as well as their place of settlement so as to have a better understanding of hierarchized relations. Paying greater attention to the populations with whom we work, and making evident the situation of minorities, which many studies seem to have forgotten, helps us to be more circumspect and avoid hasty explanations.

10. I have developed this argument in Simon-Barouh 2003.

11. This attitude is not shared vis-à-vis the development and the recognition of Islam, the second most important religion in France, nor toward Islamic religious schools.

12. Nancy J. Smith-Hefner (1999) titled one of her chapters, "To Be Khmer Is to Be Buddhist."

13. This remark calls for another. My formulation could allow us to understand that ethnic belonging results from the choice of the individuals who would shape a culture as they wish it be. In taking into account the role of individual freedom in the way one constructs one's life, however, we must not forget that culture is the product of social transmission and contact, themselves fruits of the interweaving of the historical, political, economical, and social situations.

14. See, among many references, Ma Mung 2000.

15. Though we do not have enough time here to develop this aspect of intra-community relations, one should not fail to notice that the way the Cambodians gather together at present follows the old ethnic divisions in Cambodia. As time goes by, Cambodians move from solidarity between refugees, without any ethnic distinction, to solidarity limited to the extended family. In doing so, they will have found again one of the pillars of the Cambodian social organization. This means that the gatherings are selective. At present, only the pagoda includes everybody.

16. Such celebrations as Cambodian New Year, Buddha's Birthday, the festival of the dead, the festival of the monks, et cetera.

CHAPTER 11

Défrancophonisme in Israel: Bizertine Jews, Tunisian Jews

EFRAT ROSEN-LAPIDOT

Shortly after the May 1999 elections, an Israeli newspaper published an alphabetical lexicon reviewing some of the clichés that had been featured during the campaign (Spector and Nuriel 1999). One of the clichés mentioned was associated with a famous Israeli actress. During a political support event for Ehud Barak, she condemned the conduct of the "rabble" and its blind support for Binyamin Netanyahu. Her statement triggered a rapid mechanism of semantics reversal; one manifestation of this process was the appearance of stickers bearing the slogan, "I'm a proud rabble." Her utterance also reverberated in the article's central caricature, which shows a couple exchanging the following comments:

SHE: "My father is Tunisian and my mother's from Lithuania."
HE: "Is that considered rabble or élite?"

This exchange, which rhymes in the original Hebrew, could serve as an *avant-propos* to several discussions concerning contemporary Israeli society, such as the tendency to view ethnic categories as part of a binary formation—East versus West, Mizrahi versus Ashkenazi, right-wing versus left-wing, rabble versus élite. It might also highlight the growing prominence of hybrid identities and the implied necessity to refine research strategies, or indicate the deconstruction of old clichés, replacing them with subtler ones. It might also serve as an illustration of the tendency to define immigrant groups according to their national origin.

In contrast to this national labeling, the present research takes as a starting point one Jewish-Tunisian community—that of Bizerte, a city on the northern coast of Tunisia. It also deviates from common Zionist periodization, extending its time span to include the period before the establishment of the State of Israel and the consequent waves of immigration. In addition, following the paths taken by emigrants from Bizerte leads the present fieldwork beyond the Israeli borders, especially into France and Tunisia. Last, the diaspora research orientation is exclusively Jewish, focusing on the intrinsic perspectives of the Bizerte Jews, who formed but one part of a multi-ethnic urban fabric.

Like many other cities throughout the Maghreb, Bizerte was emptied of its local Jewish community around the middle of the twentieth century. In general, this mass departure was conceptualized as a "one-way tearing . . . a no less important or traumatic event, perhaps, than the Spanish Expulsion" (Sitbon 1994). The Jewish communities in the Maghreb were declared eliminated, uprooted, dispersed.[1]

However, while visiting Bizerte in 1995, I saw the first signs of the community's *post-mortem* revival. As a descendant of this community, I was invited by a French relative to join him on his trip to Tunisia. His son had just been married, and he decided to show the young couple his native village. This small family excursion turned into an extended family reunion comprising a group of thirteen family members, six from France and seven from Israel. Possibly as part of the trend described by Levy (1997)—of organized tour groups of Israelis of North African origin traveling back to their native land and to their "childhood districts"[2]—we made a three-day "roots pilgrimage" to Bizerte, and spent four additional days as tourists traveling around the country. The first place we visited in Bizerte was the Jewish cemetery, where we saw that all the tombstones were broken. However, renovation work was being carried out, and I was informed that it was the result of the activities of an association of Bizertine Jews (AJOB[3]), established in Paris two years previously.

As the research developed, it became obvious that the institutional revival of the Jewish community of Bizerte was not exceptional. At the time AJOB was founded, several other Jewish-Tunisian associations were already active. This proliferation is often conceptualized as an attempt to overcome uprooting, displacement, dispersal, and elimination. Courses of action revolve around anchoring, placing, centralizing, and preserving past entities, providing a sense of continuity and transmitting these themes to the younger generation.

Despite the emphasis put on continuity, it is evident that new organizational formations are being molded, led by a generation younger than that of past community leaders. Nevertheless, these organizations are a first generation phenomenon, initiated and implemented by leaders born in Tunisia, although some of them left their native country in their childhood or adolescence.[4] In the course of acting on behalf of their displaced but continuing communities, they draw heavily on past identities, while at the same time constructing new configurations of identity.

This chapter focuses upon these processes of collective identity construction. Enriched by the multiplicity of research layers, the analysis is fed by different crosscuts: past versus present, Israel versus France, and personal versus public narratives. The examination of the present identity constructions in light of parallel reconstructions of the past will clarify that the former are the outcome of reworking mechanisms. A comparison of developments in Israel and France will highlight the differential influences shaping Jewish-Tunisian organizations in these two societies. Last, examining personal reconstructions of the past against the public, collective constructions of present communities will demonstrate the place allocated to different identities that are available to Tunisian actors.[5] Francophone identity, one of the components in this repertoire, will be given special attention.[6]

Taking the Bizerte community as a starting point reveals the sense of uniqueness that this label carries. It often evokes memories of a small community, guarding its symbolic boundaries through practices of solidarity, familiarity, and mutual assistance. What the label also implies is the community's ultimate hallmark—that is, being the most European, or the most French, of all the Jewish communities in Tunisia. However, the present organized activities of the Bizerte descendants do not present Francophone identity as a definitional one; neither is this the case with the other Tunisian Jewish associations.

The following ethnography, then, will supply an additional perspective to earlier accounts concerning the decline of *francophonie* in Israeli society (Miles 1995), and the fact that "the North African community as a whole hardly retains [the French] language, one of its rare valued resources, over generations" (Ben-Rafael 1994:193).

Starting in Another Place and Time: The Bizerte Story

Bizerte was conquered in April 1881, a month before the Bardo treaty was signed, turning Tunisia into a French protectorate (Abun-Nasr 1987:291). The strategic naval base built in the city remained under French control until as late as October 15, 1963 (Renaud 1996:174), several years after Tunisia became an independent state. The final eviction of the military base was preceded by the Bizerte Crisis, armed conflict between the Tunisian and French armies, which erupted in July 1961, following Habib Bourguiba's demand that French president Charles de Gaulle evacuate the French bases at Bizerte (Laskier 1994:299). After four days' fighting, including battles in the streets of the city, the Tunisian army was roundly defeated. Official reports spoke of a thousand dead, almost all Tunisians (Bensimon 1988). This armed military conflict over one of the last vestiges of French colonial past accounted for further Jewish emigration. During the two to three months following the battles, approximately four to five thousand Jews left for Israel and France.[7] For the local Jewish community, these events brought about its dispersion. Already accused of collaboration with the French forces, several of its young members were arrested by the Tunisians and accused of espionage and subversion (Tirosh 1988:3).[8] The vast majority of the Jews of Bizerte left the city, making their way to France or Israel.

At the end of October 1961, the information service of the Bizerte navel base published a booklet summarizing the fighting. The front page of this booklet shows two photographs. The top photograph represents the old Banzart[9]: it depicts the old port of Bizerte, with its small fishing boats. In the background one may see one of the Arab quarters, with its densely constructed two-story houses. The lower photograph represents the new Bizerte—it shows a twelve-story apartment block surrounded by palm trees. The caption reads: "Today's Bizerte is essentially a French creation. Thanks to the enormous works undertaken at the beginning of the century by bold individuals, France managed in less than eighty years to change the face of Bizerte more than the preceding millennium had done" (Les Services Information de la Base Strategique de Bizerte 1961:n.p.) This perception of Bizerte as a "French creation" was internalized by the members of the Jewish community. They place their collective history on an evolutionary axis leading from the old quarter of the city, where they lived alongside the Muslims, to the new European section.[10] As an eighty-year-old man living in France describes it:

> At first, we lived in the *Ksibah*. But then the Jews began to say: "How can we live here? We need a house with electricity, water, and all that stuff. Here there is only a well." . . . Although they didn't do anything to us. The Arabs used to say "Al-Nabi—the Prophet—ordained that we should have such neighbors." So some of them took us under their protection. . . . So when the Jews had money, they wanted to go along with the French, to live in the French quarter. . . . The women used to dress *à l'arabe*, but then they took off all that stuff and began to dress *à la française*. . . . After the [Second World] War, many [women] did not want to change [their dress]. They said, "No, no—people will laugh at me." But then the children used to ask them:

"Mommy, don't wear Arab clothes." So they wore it, the Jews too. They went into the city with pants and a waistcoat and everything. You see?

In addition to the changes already noted—the transition in the place of residence as economic circumstances improved, and the replacement of traditional clothes by European dress[11]—the interviewee emphasizes two more central processes: first, the adoption of the French language, which within a single generation replaced Judeo-Arabic as the mother tongue, and second, the transformation in the attitude to education. Like his peers, this interviewee attended a French school until he obtained his *certificat d'études* at the age of thirteen or fourteen. When he spoke to his friends in Arabic during recess, the teachers and principal used to say: "*Mon dieu*, you are at a French school now! Speak French, not Arabic!"[12] He reports that few of his generation continued their education on to junior high or high school. Most found their place in the job market to help their families make a living. By comparison, he describes the younger generation (i.e., those born around the mid-1930s) as more intelligent and more aware of the importance of education. High school education expanded in this generation, although university education was still rare.

By that time, the Arab children in Bizerte typically attended separate Franco-Arab schools, while the children of the Jewish community—boys and girls alike—studied at French schools alongside the Christian children. There was no Alliance Israélite Universelle (AIU) school in Bizerte, but until their Bar Mitzvah, the boys received Jewish religious instruction at the *kuttab* that operated alongside the synagogue. Here they were taught by rabbis, not all of whom spoke fluent French.[13]

By the middle of the last century, most of the Jews lived in the European quarter. There was no separate Jewish quarter (*hara*) in the city, which had a Jewish population of approximately two thousand.[14] The community was stratified into a small number of wealthy merchants and professionals, followed by a vast middle class composed of petty merchants, craftsmen, and employees (Allali et al. 1989:99). The socioeconomic structure also included disadvantaged families,[15] as well as a newly emerging category of *fonctionnaires*—salaried workers employed in administrative positions and at the French military installations.

However, the rhetoric stressed in the interviews is often egalitarian, focusing on two arenas of *communitas*.[16] The first arena is that of the single synagogue that operated in the city, where "everybody was equal." As a symbol of tolerance, the synagogue enabled different patterns of religious observance to co-exist under a single roof. This was, however, a male arena, and it was here that decisions were made regarding community affairs. The second arena, and the ultimate expression of equality, was the Jewish cemetery. To this day, the wall surrounding the cemetery bears signs in French and Hebrew: "Rich and poor all meet for eternity."[17]

"The Evolution Started in Bizerte": The Construction of Collective Identity

Despite the variance in the level of religious observance, Jewish identity continued to form the basis of individual and collective identity. Indeed, Jewish identity provided the sense of equality and fraternity, with institutional support from the official communal bodies—*la Caisse de Secours et de Bienfaisance* and other mutual aid associations.[18] Many of the interviews include descriptions of the ways in which these voluntary societies worked to promote the welfare of the Jewish population, particularly the poorer members.

The collective identity was also defined vis-à-vis other Jewish communities. The underlying claim is that Bizerte was the most French of the Tunisian communities. For example, when I asked a sixty-year-old man who immigrated to Israel in the 1970s from France whether he and his family are identified as Tunisians, he replied:

> "They call us French, but I say, 'I'm not French, I'm Tunisian. From Bizerte.' When I say that I'm from Bizerte, it isn't like saying that I'm Tunisian. It isn't the same thing."
>
> HIS WIFE: "For you! For other people it's the same thing." [An argument ensues.]
>
> HUSBAND: "No, it's not the same thing at all! Not at all. . . . Take a Jew from Tunis and a Jew from Bizerte, for example. They're as different as day and night. It's not the same thing. There was a fierce war between us. The person from Bizerte was a human, educated and clean. Someone from Tunis—well, even their language wasn't at all the same as ours. . . . We were much more European, because Bizerte was a French base. 80 percent of the population of Bizerte was French.[19] . . . Our education was really French education. . . . Now what do they write here in your passport and all that stuff? 'Country of birth: Tunis.' That's wrong! It isn't Tunis, it's Tunisia. . . . Try to explain that to some clerk here, and he says, 'No, you were born in Tunis.' I said, 'I'm sorry, I wasn't born in Tunis. I was born

in Tunisia, in Bizerte. It's not the same thing.' They don't understand this."

EFRAT: "When you say that to Tunisians who don't come from Bizerte,
how do they react when you say that Bizerte is something
different?"

HUSBAND: "They know that this is the case."

EFRAT: "Really?"

HUSBAND: "We were . . . the snobs of Tunis."[20]

In structural terms, the distinction between Bizerte and the other Jewish communities of Tunisia is described as being *réservé* (reserved or constrained), as compared to the typical Tunisian *exubérance*. Sometimes, the distinction is broader, relating to French culture as opposed to Arab culture. It also has a broader geographical context, differentiating between the north and south of the country.

This broad distinction did not escape external observers' attention. For example, Haim Zeev Hirschberg, an Israeli historian who has researched the Maghreb countries, visited Tunisia at the end of the 1950s. In describing the north, he states that "there are clear signs of assimilation," by which he means intermarriage (1957:222). As he describes the journey south from the capital Tunis, he states that: "South of Sfax, one enters a different cultural world. In Gabès, some of the Jews still speak French, but they are mostly Arabic-speaking, and after Gabès one no longer finds any French-speakers among the Jews. In the south, all the boys attend religious school and speak Judeo-Arabic" (p. 41).[21] He later describes Jerba as one of the most important Jewish religious centers of Tunisia.[22]

The distinction between north and south is rooted in two Jewish cultural models, perceived as mutually exclusive—one that kept an open approach to French cultural influence, and the other that waged a fierce war against it. As demonstrated earlier, when the "northern, French model" is described and evaluated from within, it implies self-esteem. But when it is evaluated from without, this is not necessarily the case. When described from a Zionist perspective, for example, the basic point of reference becomes the question of loyalty: "The force of attraction of the French language and culture was at times so powerful in the eyes of the westernized Jewish stratum, so far as amongst it grew the phenomenon of preference to the ideals of France, rather than to national and Zionist Jewish identity, accompanied by a total self-effacement" (Abramski-Bligh 1997:12; see also Hirschberg 1957:45). But the affinity to French culture was not limited to the realm of collective representations and the dynamics of their mutual reflections. In the colonial situation, it was bound up with questions of personal juridical status. This is illustrated in the next section, which considers the dispersal of the Jewish community of Bizerte.

Narrating Beyond the Bizerte Crisis — Mourning and Repair

In the Bizertine narrative, two historical events are central. Each relates to the evacuation of the Jewish community. The first evacuation came during the Second World War, when the military port in Bizerte was bombed.[23] The community members found refuge in Tunis and other cities, some of them among relatives and acquaintances. This event ended with the reintegration of the community. After the war, many of the Jews returned to the city, and later a synagogue was built to replace the old one that had been destroyed. The second departure from the city began around the time of the Bizerte Crisis, in July 1961, and led to the final dispersion of the community. The Jews left the city during the fighting, and this continued for the next two months. However, their fate was determined by their civic status. Those Jews who held French nationality and valid passports were able to leave as part of the repatriation process, together with the other French residents of Bizerte. This option was not available to the Jews who held Tunisian nationality. As the *aliya* director for Tunisia described it: "The city of Bizerte is emptied of Europeans: the Italians emigrate to Italy, the French to France, while the Tunisian Jews find themselves in a catastrophic situation" (translated from Bensimon 1988:8). Some of them managed to obtain passports, but approximately 250 Jews remained, mainly people who were not granted Tunisian passports (Laskier 1994:299). Later, they were assisted by the *Misgeret* (the "Framework") a joint body formed by the Jewish Agency and the Israeli *Mossad*. With reluctant help from France, they were later able to reach Marseilles and then continue on to Israel (Laskier 1994; Bensimon 1988).

From the perspective of four decades later, it seems that the members of the community recognized the irreparable detachment between those who moved to France and Israel. Interestingly, however, they conceptualize their present collective actions as a restorative process that began to emerge some three decades after the tragic events of the early 1960s.

As mentioned earlier, an association of Bizertine Jews was established in Paris in 1993. Its main objective was defined as the renovation and preservation of the Jewish cemetery in Bizerte. These activities were carried out in cooperation with the local authorities in Tunisia. In the past few years, representatives of the board of the association and other members have visited the cemetery and undertaken further renovation work. A gate was installed in the wall surrounding the cemetery, and a marble plaque has been erected on one of the inside walls, bearing the family names of the deceased. In addition, all the fragments of tombstones bearing letters have been placed on a concrete structure with three steps, with an additional plaque that gives the full names of the deceased.

Since the association was established, it has been headed by a native of Bizerte born in the early 1930s. During the course of his medical career as a hematologist he treated cancer patients, and gradually came to be involved in psychosocial oncology, and later in aspects relating to coping with death. He states that it was at this point that he began his work on behalf of the cemetery. As he relates:

> The cemetery was for me some internal death. A feeling of obligation to repair. We had to repair something. This is what I felt. . . . I think that, of course . . . it's not at all the same dimension with what happened to the Jewish community in Eastern Europe. But in a sense it's a similar thing. I think, here, that we had a catastrophe. The catastrophe is that we had a community living there—nobody remembers from when, probably for thousands of years—but now nothing, nothing is left. And it's not a catastrophe, it's like a death. . . . After death, when people die, there is a psychological, internal necessity for a bereavement process, and I think that this bereavement process has not been done for the Jewish community. . . . And in addition, here, with the profanation of the cemetery, something has been made which is . . . absolutely terrible, because it's like a loss of human dignity. Then, this is part of the mourning process, to repair something.

Formal activities relating to the cemetery have been implemented for several years. A team of several officials has been established to take responsibility for the different aspects of renovation. Donations are collected and the work is monitored. The question arises as to why it was the descendants of the community in France who undertook the burden of this "duty-memory" (Nora 1989). And more fundamentally: what was the process that enabled collective action to become organized on behalf of the past community?

Reviving Communities: From a Statutory Kehilla *to a Voluntary Association*

In common with other basic concepts in the social sciences, the term "community" is polysemic, denoting and connoting a variety of semantics. It is applied to a wide range of social entities, differing in their scope, degree of institutionalization, and mode of functioning. Sometimes it marks primary affective social relations, and elsewhere, secondary instrumental ones. It may be used as a synonym for a social group characterized by cohesion and feelings of "we-ness," or as an inclusive term imposed upon a social category of citizens, "ethnics," professionals, or others.

Implementing reparatory actions on behalf of the past community of Bizerte necessitates more than a narrative sequencing bridging thirty years of rupture. More fundamentally, it requires the perceptual transformation of the *Kehilla*—the basic unit of Jewish diaspora existence, a statutory entity regulated externally—into a voluntary community. As an areligious community, the new structure allows its members a high degree of agency. No functional imperatives exist, nor are there Halachic obligations that dictate its existence or its modus operandi. The sole initial requirement is a desire to create the new community and to belong to it.

Such a desire seems to have been readily and abundantly present over the last two decades. As mentioned earlier, the institutional revival of the Jewish community of Bizerte forms part of a wider phenomenon of the revival of past Tunisian communities, Jewish and non-Jewish alike. The space that enables this plurality, vitality, and institutional activism may be affiliated in broader terms to the Third Sector. In the absence of a more positive definition, the Third Sector is located between the commercial sector and the public sector. Third Sector organizations do not aim to secure economic profit, and they are not statutory governmental or municipal organizations. Rather, they are termed voluntary, philanthropic, or nonprofit organizations (Gidron 1995). The growth of such organizations during the last two decades has been a prominent phenomenon not only in Israel and France (Gidron 1992; Mizrahi-Tchernonog 1992), but also in other countries, as part of the "global associational revolution" (Salamon 1994, cited in Gidron 1995).

What institutional formations did the "Tunisian associational revolution" produce? A brief comparative description is required to understand the range of associations that have been formed. In France, several associations have been constituted on the basis of past Tunisian experience. The 1994 bulletin of Arts et Traditions Populaires des Juifs de Tunisie (an association active in this field) mentions fifteen Tunisian emigrant associations. Nine of these function as *landsmanschaften*, bearing the names of the cities of origin: Ariana, Béja, Bizerte, Jerba, Gabès, Sousse, Le Kef, Nabeul, and Sfax (1994:24–25). Two additional *landsmanschaften* that are known at the present stage of the research are that of Ferryville (Berreby 1995:61) and an additional association of Bizertines active in Toulon in the south of France. Several of those associations are not exclusively Jewish; some of the exclusively Jewish associations are loosely grouped under the umbrella organization of *la Fédération Française des Associations Juives Originaires de Tunisie.*

In Israel, by contrast, at least two highly institutionalized associations represent the Tunisian community. Both attempt to recruit members of general Tunisian origin. One of them is AMIT (*Association Mondiale des Israélites de Tunisie*), and the second is La'Ghriba (*Amouta Le-moreshet Yahadut Tunisia ve-Jerba*). Other organizations are also engaged in Jewish-Tunisian heritage, but do not define themselves exclusively on this basis.[24] To the best of my knowledge, only one Israeli association is organized according to the city of origin—that of Bizerte.[25]

Organizational patterns in France and Israel are clearly different. The French Jewish-Tunisian Third Sector is more highly differentiated than Israel's, embodying and preserving past diaspora community structures to a larger extent. Differing patterns of geographical dispersion in the two countries may have contributed to this situation. The Bizertine Jews, for example, arrived in Israel in several different time periods, and they are now dispersed throughout the country. Most of them live in the large main cities, some in development towns and other small towns, and a minority in small communal settlements. Even where there are relatively large concentrations, the members of the community do not necessarily maintain close ties. The dispersion is France is different. From a list of some 150 people prepared by the Bizertine association in France after its establishment, the majority lived in Paris and its surroundings, with a minority in the south of France and outside the country.[26] In fact, the French association developed in Paris among a small group of friends who had maintained contact after the emigration.

An additional explanation for the differential preservation of past community structures relates to the pattern of organization within the Third Sector. As mentioned earlier, the Jewish emigration from Tunisia is part of a wider context of decolonization that created a broad category of repatriates from the Maghreb countries and stimulated the formation of *landsman-schaft*-type organizations (Jordi 1993). In addition, the Jewish-Tunisian associations in France do not operate in a vacuum. Prior to their proliferation, dozens of Jewish *landsmanschaften* and *Amicales* were active in Paris (Boyarin 1991). To this day, issues relating to burial and commemoration form a central part of their activities. This vitality of the institutionalized Jewish community also facilitated the reception and integration of the North African Jews into French society (Zytnicki 1999). In Israel, there was also intensive activity by *landsmanschaften* of East European Jews; after the Second World War, they devoted their efforts to commemorating their communities by establishing communal tombstones and publishing communal commemorative books (Thidor-Baumel 1995; see also Yablonka 1997). However, these communal activities were closely linked to the Holocaust, the commemoration of which was also undertaken by the state and its official institution Yad Vashem.[27] Thidor-Baumel (1995:385) notes that at least one practice of commemoration was initiated at the level of the community (in several *kibbutzim*), became institutionalized at a higher level (that of the settlement movement), and disappeared after its replacement with an equivalent pattern of commemoration in the state level.

Whether the centrality of state commemorative practices should be seen as the consequence of weak *landsmanschaften* activity in Israel, or as their cause, is an important question, but one that lies beyond the purview of this presentation. However, comparison with the French Third Sector shows that as far as collective identities are concerned, those based on past Tunisian cities of origin were blurred in Israel. To put it differently, adhesion to one's community-of-origin may be seen as excessively "exilic" or "Diaspora-like" from an Israeli point of view, while in France communal identities may form a prominent part of the search for a positive definition of Jewish identity. As will be demonstrated below, in Israel these identities were subordinated to national identity. The latter development includes two distinct processes: first, the construction of a broader "Tunisian community," or a sense of "Tunisian-ness," and second, its subordination to Zionist identity while constructing the collective Jewish-Tunisian narrative in Israel.

A third point to be inferred from the inventory of the Israeli Tunisian associations is that none of them explicitly embodies Francophone identity as a constitutive component. Moreover, examination of the activities undertaken by an Israeli association in which Francophone identity receives relative visibility highlights the fact that in the public sphere *francophonie* is instrumentally muted, and its symbolic value is confined to the private sphere. Francophone identity, as a highly exclusive identity in the past, is absent from present attempts to mark the space and the terms of collective meaningfulness. Instead, prominence is given to Zionist identity as an imperative condition for meaningful participation in Israeli society.

Défrancophonisme *and Integration*
into the Zionist Narrative

Miles (1995:1024) defines *francophonie* as varying from the aim of "creating an institutional solidarity among French speakers and French-speaking nations" to its loosest sense: "facility with or mastery of the French language." This analysis takes the loose definition as a starting point, but adds to it the affinity to French culture. Both the French language and culture are conceptualized as a cultural capital,[28] that is, symbolic capital capable of transformation to different kinds of capital, and of marking the distinction between social groups.[29] Miles (ibid.) characterizes the nature of Israeli *francophonie* as diffuse, dispersed, and discrete. Among the six "categories of *francophonie*" in Israel, he states that the numerically largest is that of Francophones of North African and Near Eastern origin. Upon arrival to Israel, their attachments both to France and to *francophonie* as a culture were profoundly weakened.[30]

Practical knowledge and later historical knowledge asserted that "the attractive force of Zionism was weakened as far as the more 'modern' elements of the Jewish society were concerned" (Abitbol 1989). By definition, then, those North Africans who immigrated to Israel were considered the less French, more traditional, and poorer section of their reference group. In the discourse that emerged from the 1950s onward, *francophonie* became but one component in an "identity kit" that the immigrants were required to demonstrate: that they were thoroughly French, "modern" enough, kosher Jews, and loyal Zionists.

The next citation will illustrate the delegitimization of Francophone identity in Israel.[31] It is taken from a book published in 1957,[32] written by a social worker and teacher of social work. The introduction to the book notes that it is intended for social workers, teachers, counselors, and nurses. Since the book was published posthumously, the Hebrew version was approved for publication by distinguished researchers (including President Itzhak Ben-Zvi, S. D. Goitein, C. Frankenstein, and H. Z. Hirschberg). The book notes that "in many cases, what the natives see as French culture is no more than a thin coat of external manners by which they disguise their North African self. Accordingly, the Jewish youth run the risk of falling into superficiality, devoting their time to cheap and even questionable amusements imported from Europe instead of to serious efforts" (Tahon 1957:57).

Left without a "thin coat to disguise their North African self," the Tunisians Jews were integrated into Israeli society and acquired Israeli identity.

As mentioned earlier, in recent years they have established several voluntary associations, including one in which Francophone identity enjoys relative visibility. Established in Netanya in 1994, this association claims to represent the entire community of Tunisian Jews in Israel.[33] It publishes a bilingual newsletter in Hebrew and French that is also distributed in France, and is promoting its plans to establish a world center for Tunisian Jewry based on the model of the synagogue in Tunis. Despite what might be inferred from its French name (*Association Mondiale des Israélites de Tunisie*), it is one of the associations grouped under the French Federation of Jewish-Tunisian Associations.

In late 1998, the association published a book entitled *How the Mighty Have Fallen* (Attal 1998), according to the Biblical verse. The book commemorates over three hundred members of the Tunisian community who died during active service in the Israeli Defense Forces or in terrorist attacks. The book begins with greetings from the president of Israel and the minister of defense. The entire text appears in Hebrew and French.

The families of the deceased and public representatives were invited to an event to mark the publication of the book. The formal part of the event included the traditional *Yizkor* memorial prayer, sung for the first time with a Tunisian melody. A resident of Netanya who won the International Bible Quiz gave a speech about the biblical Jewish heroes, who were presented as the first links in a chain continuing through to the heroes commemorated in the book. A collective memorial day for the martyrs of the Tunisian community was announced, to take place each year on November 20, the date when the "Oslo Children" perished.[34] It was also announced that Tunisian Jewry would file a collective claim for compensation for damage to property and life caused under Nazi rule. The mayor of Netanya also participated in the event, beginning her speech by noting that she had met with the prime minister that afternoon and cut short her meeting in order to attend the event. She announced that she had signed the permits for the establishment of the World Center of Tunisian Jews, and that the plans would be brought before the municipal council over the following days. The editor of the book also made a speech, in which he expressed the hope that his work would ease the pain of the bereaved families, some of whom cannot read the existing commemorative works written in Hebrew. Because of this fact, he stated that half of the Tunisian community, which "still lives in France," is unaware of the sacrifices made by the Tunisian community during Israel's wars. The editor read the second half of his speech in French, noting the difficult emotional task involved in honoring the memory of the fallen and in creating communal memory. This process, he stated, would add to their Jewish heritage, strengthening ties among Tunisian Jews in Israel and among their Francophone co-religionists.

During the same week that the event took place, the Tunisian Jews celebrated the Feast of Jethro. This event is traditionally marked in the family or the synagogue in the Hebrew month of *Shvat* (around late January or the beginning of February). The most common explanation for the event relates to a plague that affected the Jews of Tunisia during the nineteenth century, and which struck mainly the younger boys of the community. The plague ended during the week when the Torah portion entitled "Jethro" is read.[35] To commemorate this miracle, a festive meal was celebrated (on Thursday of the week prior to that of the Jethro weekly portion), served on miniature dishes. In recent years, this traditional meal has been celebrated in public, and new semantics have been given to the traditional symbol.[36] In 1999, the event was celebrated by at least nine night-time balls that took place in different areas—in Netanya (three separate dinners), Jerusalem, Beersheba, Ra'anana, Beit-Shemesh, Akko, and Nahariya.

Three days following the event marking the publication of the commemorative book, the same association celebrated its Feast of Jethro at a hotel in Netanya. Approximately four hundred people from throughout Israel attended. Apart from conversations in French among the guests, the only use of this language on the podium was to repeat in French the numbers drawn in the lottery, the first prize being a plane ticket to Paris. This time the mayor left her sick bed to attend the event, noting that she made every effort to get better, since it was unthinkable that she would not attend the association's first celebration following her election. She mentioned her visit to the Feast of Jethro celebrations the previous year, when the political atmosphere was sensitive and many candidates were competing for the position of mayor. When she felt the love in the air, she said, she knew that she was going to be the next mayor of Netanya. She mentioned the plans to build the world center and the publication of the book, and spoke of the unity of the people. Despite her illness, she took off her jacket and joined the circle of dancers, who responded with enthusiasm, closing around her in circles. A red *shashia* was placed on her head, with gold sequins spelling out the word "Tunis."

Before the mayor arrived, two of the association's leaders went up to the podium and attempted to secure the guests' attention. "Just three or four minutes," they promised, "not more. Let us talk, and then you can dance as much as you like." Holding the new commemorative book in their hands, they described the characteristics of the traditional festival, connecting the historical sons for whom the festival is celebrated with the sons of the present century commemorated in the new book. They added that a scientific study they had undertaken showed that while the Tunisian community in Israel constitutes less than 1 percent of the population, its sacrifice in the wars is almost 1.5 percent. "This is a book of pride," they said, "a book of honor for the Tunisian community." "And when it comes to pride," they added, "you can only have pride if you present invoices. This is our invoice!"[37]

In this fashion the Tunisian community proved that it does not devote its time to cheap amusements, but recognizes and obeys the rules of the game, demanding as these may be. The evidence was clear: the association's world center for Tunisian Jews is being erected in Israel; Feasts of Jethro are celebrated around the country; members of the Tunisian community are well-represented in Israeli politics, communications, and art. And, in fact, the members of the association, on behalf of the entire Tunisian community, showed themselves, the Israeli people, and their Francophone co-religionists, that with or without a thin coat of external manners, they no longer need to disguise their "North African self."

Challenging the Binary Model: Ethnics in Hebrew, Diasporics in French

In the 1970s, Edward Said's *Orientalism* (1979) analyzed the manner by which the Orient was constructed as a homogeneous and primitive category, an antithesis to the rational, enlightened West. Fifteen years later, he wrote about the disappearance of binary oppositions and the creation of new formations, which are crossing borders, nations, and substances (Said 1993). In the debate on the politics of identity, he claims that all cultures are mixed. None are any longer pure—they are all heterogeneous and non-monolithic.

A comparison of the "Tunisian" Third Sector in Israel and France shows that although they set their own agenda, in their form of organization voluntary associations in Israel do not challenge the monolithic vision of the North African past. They do not articulate the heterogeneity of the past *kehillot*, nor their sense of uniqueness and distinction.[38] Rather, they are compatible with the fixed structure of identities that has emerged in Israeli society based on geographical and national distinctions. As such, they fit into the category of "Tunisian-ness" that has developed, influenced by the prominence of other Mizrahi sub-identities. However, the associations' public social action draws from the rich repertoire of symbolic capital that is available to Tunisian actors. Paving the way for a Tunisian renaissance, shared resonating symbols are brought to the fore. In contrast, symbolic elements carrying the potential for tension, such as Francophone identity, are muted. Not only has *francophonie* failed to crystallize as an identity marker for the entire Jewish population in Tunisia[39]; it has also never gained legitimacy in Israeli society when attributed to North Africans. *Francophonie* in the public sphere is reduced to its instrumental, communicative capacity, confining its symbolic value to the private sphere and thus limiting its transformational possibilities to other discursive capitals.

In the late 1960s, with the revival of the *Mimouna* festival in Israel, Weingrod notes, it was "the first time [that] Moroccan immigrants who previously may have sought to identify themselves as 'from the South of France' were joining together under a specifically Moroccan ethnic banner. If anything, they had come in order to join in a public demonstration of their 'Moroccanness'" (1990:103). If we accept Weingrod's commentary, this demonstration could be seen as the formative reaction to the delegitimization embodied in the joke that depicts North Africans as originating in "southern France." The latter draws an analogy between, on the one hand, a historical (multi-)cultural category, capable of crossing borders and nations and combining Jewish, Moroccan, French, and Arab identities, and, on the other hand, either-or, inflexible territorial categories. In Israeli society, then, a social group can be regarded either as Moroccan or French; Mizrahi or European; rabble or élite. Only individuals are capable of being Francophone North Africans—as numerous as such individuals may be.

Thus the *Mimouna* has become not only the prototypical Israeli ethnic celebration (Weingrod 1990:104), but also a model of the mechanism of semantic reversal. It may be seen as a product of the struggle with the stigmatized connotations of the term "Moroccan," created in the new Israeli milieu; as a process in which the term "is filled with positive content relating to one's ethnic background, and relating one's own ethnic categorization to an overall Israeli identity" (Goldberg 1977:181–82). Thus Moroccan Jews may have paved the way for other "ethnic communities" to demonstrate their uniqueness and successes as full participants in Israeli society. The Tunisian community is but one example.

By drawing a thread bonding the Feast of Jethro—back then, back there—with *How the Mighty Have Fallen*, a statement is made regarding the continuity of the Jewish community in Tunisia with the Tunisian community in Israel. By commemorating death and institutionalizing it as part of the Zionist narrative, the Tunisian community demonstrates its participation in Israeli society and its claim to be recognized as such. But this claim is presented in bilingual form, and accordingly it is addressed not only internally. In its French version, it is also addressed outward, to the diaspora Francophone North African community, thereby demonstrating its successful integration into Israeli society.

Israeli society might refer to this demonstration as purely ethnic. However, a more challenging reference would be the decoding of the French version as a statement made by Tunisians in Israel about their belonging to a transnational Francophone community. This statement is pronounced in their mother tongue, although as a group they have never presented invoices to claim its symbolic value.

REFERENCES

Abitbol, Michel. 1986. "Tahalikhei Modernizatzia Vehahitpathut Baet Hachadisha." In *History of the Jews in the Islamic Countries*, vol. 2, ed. Shmuel Ettinger, pp. 363–468. Jerusalem: The Zalman Shazar Center. [Hebrew.]
———. 1989. "Leheqer Hatzionut Veha'aliya Beqerev Yehudei Hamizrah—Hebetim Metodim." *Pe'amim* 39:3–14. [Hebrew.]
Abramski-Bligh, Irit, ed. 1997. *Pinkas Hakehillot: Libya, Tunisia*. Jerusalem: Yad Vashem. [Hebrew.]
Abun-Nasr, Jamil M. 1987. *A History of the Maghrib in the Islamic Period*. Cambridge: Cambridge University Press.
Allali Jean-Pierre, Annie Goldmann, Paul Sebag, Claude Sitbon, Jacques Taïeb, Claude Tapia and Lucette Valensi, eds. 1989. "Bizerte." In *Les Juifs de Tunisie — images et textes*, pp. 98–99. Paris: Editions du Scribe.
Attal, André, ed. 1998. *Comment sont Tombés les Héros au Milieu du Combat*. Netanya: Association Mondiale des Israélites de Tunisie (AMIT). [Hebrew and French.]
Ben-Rafael, Eliezer. 1994. "A Sociological Paradigm of Bilingualism: English, French, Yiddish and Arabic in Israel." *Israel Social Science Research* 9(1–2): 181–206.
Bensimon-Donath, Doris. 1970. *Immigrants d'afrique du nord en Israël: évolution et adaption*. Paris: Éditions Anthropos.
Bensimon, Agnès. 1988. "Le Pourim des Juifs de Bizerte: Le récit des principaux témoins du sauvetage de la communauté juive de Bizerte." *Tribune Juive*, February 26, 1988, pp. 8–12.
Berreby, Haï William. 1995. "Naissance et disparition d'une communauté juive: Ferryville, Menzel Bourguiba." M.A. thesis. INALCO, Paris.
Boyarin, Jonathan. 1991. *Polish Jews in Paris: The Ethnography of Memory*. Bloomington and Indianapolis: Indiana University Press.
Brown, L. Carl. 1974. *The Tunisia of Ahmed Bey: 1837–1855*. Princeton, N.J.: Princeton University Press.

Brubaker, Rogers. 1985. "Rethinking Classical Theory: The Sociological Vision of Pierre Bourdieu." *Theory and Society* 14:745–75.

Chouraqui, N. André. 1968. *Between East and West: A History of the Jews of North Africa*. Translated from the French by Michael M. Bernet. Philadelphia: The Jewish Publication Society of America.

———. 1975. *La Saga des Juifs en Afrique du Nord*. Tel Aviv and Jerusalem: Am Oved and "Hassifria Hatzionit." [Hebrew.]

Deshen, Shlomo. 1996. "Southern Tunisian Jewry in the Early Twentieth Century." In *Jews Among Muslims: Communities in the Precolonial Middle East*, ed. Shlomo Deshen and Walter P. Zenner, pp. 133–43. Basingstoke, Hampshire: Macmillan Press Ltd.

Deshen, Shlomo, and Moshe Shokeid. 1974. *The Predicament of Homecoming*. Ithaca and London: Cornell University Press.

Deshen, Shlomo, and Walter P. Zenner, eds. 1996. *Jews Among Muslims: Communities in the Precolonial Middle East*. Basingstoke, Hampshire: Macmillan Press Ltd.

Editorial. 1963. "Sauvez J. Hakoun avant qu'il ne soit fusillé." *Le Journal d'Israël* 17, February 8–14, 1963, pp. 1–2.

Ganiage, Jean. 1994. *Histoire Contemporaine du Maghreb*. Paris: Fayard.

Gidron, Benjamin. 1995. *Mipui Hamigzar Hashlishi be-Israel*. Tel Aviv: Migzar Hahitnadvut Vehamalkarim. [Hebrew.]

———. 1992. "A Resurgent Third Sector and Its Relationship to Government in Israel." In *Government and the Third Sector: Emerging Relationships in Welfare States*, ed. Gidron Benjamin, Ralph M. Kramer, and Lester M. Salamon, pp. 176–95. San Francisco: Jossey-Bass.

Goldberg, Harvey. 1977. "Introduction: Culture and Ethnicity in the Study of Israeli Society." *Ethnic Groups* 1:163–86.

Handelman, Don, and Lea Shamgar-Handelman. 1997. "The Presence of Absence: The Memorialism of National Death in Israel." In *Grasping Land: Space and Place in Contemporary Israeli Discourse and Experience*, ed. Ben-Ari Eyal and Yoram Bilu, pp. 85–128. Albany: State University of New York Press.

Hever, Hannan, Yehouda Shenhav, and Pnina Motzafi-Haller, eds. 2002. *Mizrahim in Israel: A Critical Observation into Israel's Ethnicity*. Jerusalem and Tel Aviv: Van Leer and Hakibbutz Hameuchad.

Hirschberg, Haim Zeev. 1965. *Toldot Hayehudim Be-Africa Hatzfonit*. Vol 2. Jerusalem: Biyalik Institute. [Hebrew.]

———. 1957. *Me'eretz Mevo Hashemesh: Im Yehudei Africa Hatzfonit Be'artzoteihem*. Jerusalem: The Department of Youth and Pioneers of the Zionist Histadrut. [Hebrew.]

Jordi, Jean-Jacques. 1993. *De l'Exode à l'Exil: Rapatriés et Pieds-Noirs en France*. Paris: L'Harmattan.

Knafo, Michel-Meir. N.d. *The "Egoz" Ship, Its Period and Its Last Journey.*

Irgun Pe'ilei Hamahteret, Haha'apala Ve-asirei Tzion Bitzfon Africa. [Hebrew.]

Laskier, Michael M. 1994. *North African Jewry in the Twentieth Century: The Jews of Morocco, Tunisia and Algeria.* New York and London: New York University Press.

Les Services Information de la Base Strategique de Bizerte. 1961. *A Bizerte: De Juillet à Septembre 61.* Bizerte: Ici Bizerte.

Levy, André. 1997. "To Morocco and Back: Tourism and Pilgrimage among Moroccan-Born Israelis." In *Grasping Land: Space and Place in Contemporary Israeli Discourse and Experience,* ed. Ben-Ari Eyal and Yoram Bilu, pp. 25–46. Albany: State University of New York Press.

Lewis, Bernard. 1984. *The Jews of Islam.* Princeton, N.J.: Princeton University Press.

Memmi, Albert. 1969. *The Colonizer and the Colonized.* Boston: Beacon Press.

———. 1975 [1974]. *Juifs et Arabes.* Translated from the French by Aharon Amir. Tel Aviv: Poalim. [Hebrew.]

———. 1976 [1966]. *La Libération du Juif.* Translated from the French by Zvi Arad. Tel Aviv: Am Oved. [Hebrew.]

Miles, William F. S. 1995. "Minoritarian Francophonie—The Case of Israel, with Special Reference to the Palestinian Territories." *International Migration Review* 29, 4(112):1023–40.

Mizrahi-Tchernonog, Viviane. 1992. "Building Welfare Systems Through Local Associations in France." In *Government and the Third Sector: Emerging Relationships in Welfare States,* ed. Gidron Benjamin, Ralph M. Kramer, and Lester M. Salamon, pp. 215–37. San Francisco: Jossey-Bass.

Nora, Pierre. 1989. "Between Memory and History: Les Lieux de Mémoire." *Representations* 26:7–25.

Renaud, Patrick-Charles. 1996. *La Bataille de Bizerte (Tunisie), 19 au 23 Juillet 1961.* Paris: L'Harmattan.

Saadoun, Haïm, ed. 1989. *Les Enfants d'Oslo: Quarante Ans après la Catastrophe d'Oslo 20.11.1949.* Tel Aviv: Yad Tabenkin, Histadrut, Union des Juifs Originaires de Tunisie en Israel. [Hebrew.]

Said, Edward W. 1979. *Orientalism.* New York: Vintage Books.

———. 1993. *Culture and Imperialism.* New York: Alfred A. Knopf.

Salamon, Lester M. 1994. "The Rise of the Nonprofit Sector." *Foreign Affairs* 73(4):111–24.

Saraf, Michal. 1995. *Séoudath Itro: Le Fistin de Itro.* Lod: Haberman Institute. [Hebrew and French.]

Sitbon, Claude. 1994. "Kri'a she'ein mimena hazarah." *Sfarim Magazine, Ha'aretz,* August 3, 1994. [Hebrew.]

Spector, Dana, and Yehuda Nuriel. 1999. "Me'alef ('Ani ma'ashim') Ve'ad Tav ('Tiki Dayan')." *7 Yamim Magazine, Yedi'ot Aharonot,* May 20, 1999, pp. 16–22, 102. [Hebrew.]

Tahon, Hanna H. 1957. *Ha'edot Be-Israel: Praqim Bekorotehen Vehavlei He'ahzutan Be'Eretz-Israel.* Jerusalem: Rubin Mass. [Hebrew.]

Thidor-Baumel, Yehudit. 1995 "'Lezikhron Olam': hanztahat hashoa bidei haprat vehaqehilla bimdinat Israel." *Iyunim Bitqumat Israel* 5:364–87. [Hebrew.]

Tirosh, Abraham. 1988. "This Is How the *Mossad* Rescued the Jews of Bizerte." *Maariv.* February 19, 1988, p. B3. [Hebrew.]

Turner, Victor. 1985. *On the Edge of the Bush: Anthropology as Experience.* Tucson: University of Arizona Press.

Udovitch, Abraham L., and Lucette Valensi. 1984. *The Last Arab Jews: The Communities of Jerba, Tunisia.* London: Harwood Academic Publishers.

Weingrod, Alex. 1990. *The Saint of Beersheba.* Albany: State University of New York Press.

Yablonka Hana. 1997. *Qlitat Nitzolei Hashoa Bimdinat Israel — Hebetim Hadashim. Iyunim Bitqumat Israel* 7:285–99. [Hebrew.]

Zytnicki, Colette. 1999. "L'arrivée des juifs d'Afrique du Nord en France, 1961–1962: Role et consequence de la crise de Bizerte dans la mise en place d'une politique d'accueil communautaire." In *Histoire Communautaire, Histoire Plurielle: La communauté juive de Tunisie* (actes du colloque de Tunis organisé les 25–27 Février 1998 à la Faculté de la Manouba), pp. 267–74. Tunis: Centre de Publication Universitaire.

NOTES

This chapter is part of wider research conducted at the Hebrew University. My gratitude is due to both supervisors—Prof. Harvey Goldberg and Dr. Esther Schely-Newman—for their devoted and inspiring guidance. I would also like to thank readers of earlier drafts of this chapter, Orit Abuhav, Osnat Lapidot-Amit, Susan Weiss, Gad Yair, Eyal Ben-Ari, François and Mylène Zittoun, Robert Zittoun, and the Doctoral Forum of the Department of Sociology and Anthropology at the Hebrew University. The research was supported by the Israel Association of University Women, the Shaine Center, Yad Tabenkin, the Levi Eshkol Institute, the Ben-Zvi Institute, the Department of Sociology and Anthropology at the Hebrew University, the International Center for the Study of Moroccan Jews, Misgav Yerushalayim, and the French Embassy in Israel.

Note on translation: Several citations in this chapter were originally published in French or Hebrew.

1. Deshen and Zenner, for example, dedicated their book to "the memory of the many Jewish communities of North Africa and Southwest Asia which have been deserted, destroyed and transplanted in the course of the twentieth century" (1996:vii). Abitbol (1986:467) indicates that "North Africa . . . was almost completely emptied of its Jews." He adds that the 25,000 Jews still liv-

ing there in 1985 are the "miserable vestiges of a Jewish gathering dating from the second temple era." Lewis (1984:191) laments the "Judaeo-Islamic symbiosis . . . [a] great period of Jewish life and creativity, a long rich, and vital chapter in Jewish history . . . [which] has now come to an end." Chouraqui indicates that "Jewish life in the Maghreb was almost completely decimated" (1975:309), and that "communities that were rooted in the country for more then two thousand years were condemned to disappear within less then a decade, leaving no remainder or trace" (p. 11). Memmi speaks of North African families, which were "uprooted, destroyed, dispersed" (1975 [1974]:14).

2. Interestingly, Levy found that while his informants left to search for their Maghrebi roots, they actually found the roots of their Israeli identity.

3. *Association des Juifs Originaires de Bizerte.*

4. This is not to say that younger generations do not participate in the different organized events, but that they did not take any central leadership positions.

5. A similar approach was the basis for the work of the Forum for the Study of Society and Culture in Israel in the Van Leer Jerusalem Institute (Hever et al. 2002). Its members claim that "there is no one distinct and clear Mizrahi identity, but there are multiple identities which are being molded simultaneously out of complex relationships of inclusion and exclusion" (p. 10). They refer to Mizrahi identity as a "site of establishment, as a fluid phenomenon, which enables 'to be and not to be'" (p. 17).

6. Albert Memmi deals extensively with the Jewish-Tunisian hyphenated identity. He conceptualizes North African Jews as Arab-Jews (1975 [1974]), but describes their cultural drama (1976 [1966]) as stemming from their status as colonized, maneuvering between Jewish, Arab, and French cultures and identities. According to Memmi, the cultural drama begins with the language (1976 [1966]:151).

7. Laskier (1994:299) mentions three thousand five hundred Jews who arrived in France from the end of July 1961 until late September that year, and an additional five to six hundred Jews in transit in Marseilles on their way to Israel. Zytnicki (1999:271n10) cites a source who mentions five thousand Jews leaving Tunisia between July and October 1961.

8. One of them was accused of assassinating a commander of the Tunisian army, condemned to death penalty (Editorial 1963), and released only after putting into action a vast public campaign for his release (Bensimon 1988:10).

9. This is the old Arab name of the city.

10. "Evolution"—like closely related terms such as "the march toward the West" and "modernization"—makes an object of contemporary academic debates. Their meaning here is tied with that given to them by my interviewees. Bensimon-Donath's definition can clarify that point of view: "For the North African Jew, the concept of 'evolution' had a particular content. It signified not only change and modernization, but also acculturation, assimilation to the

West, in other words, in this case, frenchifying (*francisation*). . . . The West presented itself in his eyes not only as the ideal of technical progress, of comfort, of well-being, of richness, but also as the knowledge, as know-how and enfranchisement from an old-age physical and moral burden" (1970:39–40).

11. A change that was carrying a deep symbolic value. Adopting Western artifacts was highly connected with affinity to the West, and with a commitment to the European-oriented new order. See, for example, Brown (1974), who discusses an earlier period of Ahmad Bey's rule (especially pp. 315–21). In the Jewish-Tunisian experience it was sometimes related to unwelcome situations, like the institutional pluralism that split Twansa and Grana in Tunis.

12. At home, sometimes cross-pressures existed. For example, another interviewee spoke of his grandmother, who used to tell her grandchildren: "You are not Jews! You don't know Arabic! French is a foreign language, it isn't our language."

13. Deshen (1996:136) states that "the gap between the standard of traditional learning of the Jews of the south and of the Jews of other parts of Tunisia gradually increased. . . . The northern communities were compelled to appoint rabbis and other religious functionaries from Jerba and the south. This greatly strengthened the sense of worthiness and exclusivity among the Jews of Jerba." Several interviewees mentioned the common practice in the *kuttab* of translating Hebrew texts (that they did not understand) into Judeo-Arabic (that they did not understand either). Learning consisted of oral memorizing.

14. Abramski-Bligh (1997:289) notes that by 1946, 1,037 Jews dwelt in the city, not including Jews of French nationality. Her estimate is that by 1961, there were an additional nine hundred French Jews in the city.

15. For example, the 1951, 1953, and 1954 budgets of the American Joint Distribution Committee indicate that 125 persons in Bizerte took advantage of the canteen project. The budget estimates for 1957 mention 100 persons, and the 1961 budget, 110 persons (Givat-Ram AJDC Archives, Geneva I, box 10c, file C-56.601—"Budget-financial Tunis, 2/48–11/56"; Geneva I, box 49A, Tunis C-56.601 "A"—"Budget-financial 1957–1963–1964").

16. "A generic human relationship undivided by status-roles or structural oppositions, which is also vouched for by myths and histories stressing the unity and continuity of the widest group to which all belong by birth and tradition" (Turner 1985:233–34).

17. This is the translation for the Hebrew version. The French version is: "*Riches et pauvres ici se rencontrent.*"

18. La Caisse de Secours et de Bienfaisance was established in Bizerte in 1904, following the Bay's decree (Hirschberg 1965). Like other Jewish communities, it was responsible for conducting the internal religious life of the community as well as promoting the well-being of its members. Victor Nataf's *Annuaire Sioniste*, published in Tunis in 1931 (pp. 96–98), lists several additional bodies that comprised the institutional community of Bizerte: *Société de l'hôpi-*

tal Israélite; Société des Veuves et Orphelins Israélites de Bizerte (for orphans and widows); *Société Israélite de Secours Matrimoniaux; Qeren Qayemet Le-Israel; Eclaireurs Israélites de France; Talmud Thora; Or Haqodesh.*

19. The breakdown of the civil population of Bizerte in 1931 was 60.2 percent Muslims, 39.8 percent Europeans and Jews (Ganiage 1994:460). In 1946 it was 72.2 percent and 27.8 percent respectively (calculated on the basis of Allali et al. 1989:99). However, the pattern of dispersal of the different ethnic groups throughout the city, the occupational stratification and educational segregation, as well as the French military presence, may have contributed to the sense that the Europeans constituted the majority in the city.

20. The fact that he is referring to the common label, Tunis, in spite of his criticism, emphasizes its strength.

21. A similar description can be found in Chouraqui (1968:194), Deshen and Shokeid (1974:32–34).

22. Jerba was extensively researched by Shlomo Deshen and by Udovitch and Valensi (1984).

23. It was bombed first by the Germans and the Italians in 1939 and second by the Allies in November 1942, following the German occupation of Tunisia (Abramski-Bligh 1997).

24. For example, North African Pioneer Youth Movement Veterans (Yotz'ei Tnu'ot No'ar Halutzi'ot Mitzfon Africa), whose hard-core activists are of Tunisian origin; "EDUT"—Association for the Advancement of Education and Society in Beit Shemesh (organizers of the Feast of Jethro, and the pilgrimage to Rabbi Slama's grave); the Haberman Institute. In addition, different local groups organize the yearly feast of Jethro (to be discussed later).

25. This move was directly influenced by the French Bizertine association, and I suspect that my presence in the field also has some part in it. The association was established in 1998, and since then it held several social gatherings of Bizertine Jews.

26. Data kindly provided by AJOB.

27. Commemoration included the *Encyclopedia of Jewish Communities* (*Pinkas hakehillot*), a series of volumes dedicated to Jewish communities "that existed for generations in the Diaspora until brutally eradicated in the Holocaust and its aftermath" (Abramski-Bligh 1997:vii); the "Valley of the Destroyed Communities" within the Yad Vashem compound (comprised of tombstones for hundreds of communities annihilated in the Holocaust), and, more recently, the project "Each Person Has a Name." See also Handelman and Shamgar-Handelman 1997.

28. According to Bourdieu's terms. See, for example, Brubaker 1985.

29. The following citation from Memmi (1969:110) could demonstrate the non-instrumental approach toward the French language: "Is the French language only a precise and efficient instrument? Or is it that miraculous chest in which are heaped up discoveries and victories, writers and moralists, philoso-

phers and scholars, heroes and adventurers, in which the treasures of the intellect and of the French soul are transformed into one single legend?"

30. Leaving North Africa and arriving in Israel means, in Memmi's terms, being freed from the status of colonized. This change could explain the different attitude granted to the French language, because "in the colonial context, bilingualism is necessary. It is a condition for all culture, all communication and all progress.... [But] colonial bilingualism ... is a linguistic drama" (1969:107–8). Memmi adds that this "possession of two languages is not merely a matter of having two tools, but actually means participation in two psychical and cultural realms. Here, the two worlds symbolized and conveyed by the two tongues are in conflict; they are those of the colonizer and the colonized" (p. 107).

31. This is not, obviously, the only possible illustration of this vast phenomenon. Chouraqui, for example, states that "the Maghrebi Jew, even if he was cut off from his Jewish origins and became a total stranger to the Arab world, nevertheless did not turn into a real Frenchman. While remaining in North Africa he did not know the French civilization, but only its caricature, as it was presented before him in the colonial society that, within its margins, he was developing" (1975:307). Bensimon-Donath writes that "in the process of acculturation, the Jew was often far from crossing all stages. He adopted rapidly the ways of life, the behavior, the fashions, the language, everything that was, after all, external and easy to imitate.... Between the desire for westernization and the assimilation of the values of the Occident there is a gap, a margin" (1970:42).

32. *Ha'edot Be-Israel: Praqim beqorotehen vehavlei he'ahzutan be'Eretz-Israel* (1957), Jerusalem: Rubin Mass (Hebrew). My gratitude to Orit Abuhav, who referred me to this book.

33. Several Bizertine Jews are active in this association and participate in its activities.

34. This tragic event occurred on 20 November 1949, while twenty-eight Jewish-Tunisian children were being transferred from Tunisia to a health resort in Norway. In fact, they were making their clandestine *aliya* to Israel, organized by Aliyat Hano'ar, while the Dutch aircraft that carried them crashed about thirty kilometers from Oslo. Twenty-seven children, the three adults who accompanied them, and the four aircrew personnel were killed. Only one child survived. He made his way to Israel, where he lived until his death. This event, similarly to the sinking of the *Pisces-Egoz* on January 1961, carrying Moroccan immigrants to Israel, symbolizes the affinity to the Zionist narrative and ethos. For a detailed description of the two affairs, see Saadoun (1989) and Knafo (n.d.).

35. Two more common explanations are evoked. The first concerns the biblical meal that is mentioned in that week's portion (Exodus 18:12), and the second deals with the fact that *kuttab* children started reading the Ten Command-

ments this week (Exodus 20:1–13), and for the first time they read about the giving of the Law. The traditional festive meal included white pigeon, candies, and cakes. See Saraf 1995.

36. This issue calls for a more elaborate comparison to the earlier revival of the Moroccan *mimouna*, in the late 1960s (Weingrod 1990:101–6). Like the *mimouna*, the Feast of Jethro has been transformed in recent years into a national Tunisian-Israeli holiday, but it is held indoors.

37. This macabre metaphor can be understood figuratively as presenting proofs, usually of a successful performance; and literally, meaning receiving an invoice following a payment. In this case, of human life.

38. The Internet is an additional social space, which sets its own agenda, and where collective representations are constructed and maintained. See for example <www.harissa.com> "the site of Tunisian Jews." Another site that preserves the alleged reputation of different cities in Tunisia is <http://i-cias .com/m.s/tunisia>. Bizerte is defined there as the oldest and the most European/French city of Tunisia.

39. Bizerte is obviously a rare example in which *francophonie* served as an identity marker for the entire local Jewish community.

CHAPTER 12

Visit, Separation, and Deconstructing Nostalgia: Russian Students Travel to Their Old Home

EDNA LOMSKY-FEDER AND TAMAR RAPOPORT

The tale of visiting the native home emerged as a meaningful chapter in "immigration stories" that were narrated to us by Jewish-Russian university students in Israel. The visit-journey to the native home was depicted as a highly significant and important event which made the visitors reflect upon their past and present lives, here and there, and evaluate their immigration to Israel.

The salience of the visit-journeys, and the colorful and lively descriptions of them, attracted our attention and stimulated our curiosity. We probed the visitors' sentiments toward their old home while they were there, their conceptions and images of the old and the new place, as well as the impact of the visit-journey on their valuation of the cross-cultural transition they had experienced. In reading these visiting tales, we conceptualize the experience as a "disruptive event" in terms of temporality and space. Embarking from this conceptualization, we explored the meaning that the "little journey"—the visit—assumes in the context of the "big journey"—immigration.

Little Journey and Big Journey — Visit and Immigration

Immigrants at all times and in all places have desired, dreamed of, and planned to visit their native home—their relatives, their friends, their country. In former times, traveling to visit the native home, especially in the case of distant places across the sea, was rare and particularly exciting. For many immigrants, who were unable to ever set foot in their old homes, the visit remained an unfulfilled dream; people and places could be retained only as pictures in their minds. By cultivating memories and fantasies and fueling their longing, immigrants were engaged in reinterpreting and reconstructing a vision of the life and land they had left behind. There is little doubt that today, in the transnational era, visit-journeys that crisscross the boundaries of countries and continents are becoming a commonplace activity for many immigrants (Glick-Schiller et al. 1995; Hannerz 1996), thereby significantly influencing the way in which the old home is perceived. While these trips (and the old practice of writing letters) can now be supplemented by diverse electronic means of communication (telephone, fax, e-mail, video), the visit-journey to the native home remains a unique experience of contacting and connecting with it. The unmediated experience of actual travel—involving the conduct of face-to-face interactions and a physical contact with familiar places, people, and culture—has a significant impact, meaning, and importance, and differs from any other experience of contacting home.

The "little journey" to visit the native home is conducted within the context of the "big journey" of immigration. Both journeys entail crossing of spatial boundaries and movement in time, yet the meanings of time and space differ for each. Whereas the immigration-journey entails uprooting and displacement for an indefinite period of time, the circular movement of the visit-journey is marked from the outset by clearly defined boundaries of time and space. The immigrant crosses boundaries to visit her/his native place and returns to the new society after a fixed period of time. In the process of connecting here and there and past and present, visit and immigration become intertwined.

The visit is a terrain that reconstitutes the immigrant's relationship with both the old and the new places by elaborating and refining the images, perceptions, and attachments (negative and/or positive) that they carry from place to place. Being neither a total stranger nor entirely local, situated both here and there, the visitor, who is (in our terms) a "transient homecomer," is located in a hybrid position. From her/his hybrid vantage point, the visitor is compelled, yet relatively free to observe and interpret the new and old places and to figure out "who s/he is" and where s/he can best realize her/himself. Experiencing ambiguity and oscillation, her/his hybrid state entails a constant change and redefinition (Chambers 1994; Bhabha, interviewed by Thompson 1994).

In his seminal article "The Homecomer," Schutz (1945) argues that homecoming is a unique experience in that it shatters the "taken for granted." To a large extent the visitor—the "transient homecomer"—is in a position of "phenomenological strangeness," a position that is largely unexpected since this strangeness occurs in a place that used to be familiar. Thus the visitor moves from "natural" to "phenomenological" examination of the old and new places. Returning home disrupts the "natural" and spontaneous continuum that guided the visitor in interpreting his home reality. According to Mead's conceptualization of time and temporality (1981), returning home disrupts the spontaneous experience of time. The circular movement of the visit in time and space creates a moment that disrupts the linear and teleological nature of the immigration journey. Thus the visit raises a "problem" that seeks a "solution" in linking past, present, and future. The self-narrative is a major practice that provides such a solution by constituting a subjective sense of self-continuity (Ezzy 1998).

Immigration and Self-Narration

Any immigration story renders meaning to the immigrant's movement through time and space. The immigration experience elicits a story that encompasses both a collection of events, characters, and experiences which the individual (consciously or unconsciously) chooses to represent, and the rhetorical resources which s/he utilizes in describing and valuing them. This narrative expresses the complex interrelations between the external reality and the inner world of the narrator. Hence there is no "real" narrative of immigration, but rather different versions created by individual immigrants, reflecting the multi-faceted nature of their lives (Linde 1993).

The personal narratives related by immigrants designate the manner in which their experiences are embedded in cross-cultural transition (Benmayor and Skotnes 1994; Denzin 1989; Rosenwald and Ochberg 1992; Sarbin 1986). It is a cultural text which links and mediates between personal and cultural meanings that preoccupy the immigrants, while they reshape their old-new identity (Corradi 1991; Greenbaum 1985; Rosenwald and Ochberg 1992; Samuel and Thompson 1990).

While telling the story, immigrants examine, clarify, and define where they are coming from and where they are going to, as well as where they belong and who they are. Within the larger context of the immigration story, the visit tale is a chapter that intensifies reflexivity, because the visit is an event that disrupts the continuity of time and space. As such the tale is a vital practice of identity construction employed spontaneously by the immigrant.

The immigrant is also expected and requested to relate her/his immigration story. Different kinds of people s/he encounters in the new home and while visiting the old home, in formal (bureaucratic, professional, etc.) and informal settings (primary groups) alike, are ready to hear what s/he has to tell. In this regard, the research interview is a special setting: as a structured conversation, the interview is designed from the outset to encourage the immigrant to narrate her/his story and to be reflexive. It consequently animates and revitalizes memories and experiences.

Interviews and the Interviewees

Our research is based on the analysis of forty-three stories narrated by students (twenty-three men, twenty women) who came to Israel from various republics of the former Soviet Union in the "big wave" of the 1990s.[1] All of the interviewees arrived in Israel after 1989, studied at least three years in an institute of higher education (mostly university, but also a music academy, a technical college, and a nursing college). At the time of interview, the interviewees ages ranged from nineteen to twenty-five. Most of their parents had academic degrees (85 percent). Only two were married.

We conducted open, in-depth interviews in Hebrew with the students, all of whom had very good command of the language. The interviews were conducted by three interviewers, one of whom is an immigrant from the former Soviet Union and two of whom were born in Israel. We asked the interviewees to freely tell their immigration story, interrupting them to clarify obscure points and to elicit a wealth of description. On the average, the interviews lasted about three and a half hours, and most required more than one session. All of the interviews were recorded and transcribed.

At the time of the interview, four to five years after their arrival in Israel, 65 percent of the forty-three students had already returned to visit their native home, and 90 percent referred to the subject of visiting. Thus our analysis was based on almost all the stories—both on concrete and imagined visits to the native home.

Analysis of the visit tales was carried out in numerous group sessions. It was conducted on three levels: (1) the individual story—ascertaining the central themes in each narrative and their content, as well as rhetorical analysis in the context of the entire body of narratives; (2) the narratives as a whole—classification and interpretation of the central themes and variegated voices that appear throughout the narratives; (3) the general context—analysis of the narratives as a whole in the context of immigration processes, Jewish life in Russia, and Israeli society.

Little Journeys: Deliberation and Actualization

All of the students, both visitors and non-visitors (i.e., those who as yet had not visited their native home) alike, ascribed special meaning to traveling back home. While some of the non-visitors expressed a desire to visit Russia, others admitted that they were hesitant to do so, and a few rejected the possibility altogether. The reflections and deliberations of all the students made it clear that the visit does not begin or end with the physical action; the visit is alive in the students' minds well before they depart, and remains with them long after they return.

There are many concerns and anxieties surrounding the visits. While some of the non-visitors worry that a visit could shatter their nostalgia, others fear the opposite—that a visit might evoke or strengthen their longing for the past. Ella (all names are fictitious) articulated her fear that making contact with the familiar might awaken negative feelings towards the native home: "I have seen people going there and they didn't really like it there." Nastya's advice to Ella is to avoid a nostalgic view of the past, so that one suffers no risk of disappointment and can safely make the journey: "You should not idealize. I always remember that it was not so great there, but I went because I wanted to see my friends."

On the contrary, Sasha wasn't concerned about losing an idealized vision of her past. Her hesitation stemmed from the fear that such a journey would reinvigorate her attachment to the old place: "Before the first visit I was very much afraid to go, I thought it would be extremely difficult. Only a year and a few months have passed, and I will see everything again and I still remember everything so well, and it will be very, very hard. And this did not happen." Like Sasha, Sergey sensed danger, and he dared to take the trip only after he was sure that he was mentally strong enough to withstand its influence: "While rationally I knew I wouldn't want to stay there . . . I also knew there was an irrational possibility [of being tempted to stay] and I stopped myself [from going]. It wasn't until after a year and a half [in Israel] that I felt I'd overcome my doubts. I entered the Soviet Union very relaxed in this respect."

Daring to take the trip that some of her friends are afraid to take, Lera traveled to Leningrad to prove to herself that leaving Russia had been the right thing to do, and that she had not missed out on anything while she'd been away: "I had to explore what they [my friends] did during the year I was here [in Israel]. Maybe I missed something. . . . After all, it [migrating to Israel] was not irreversible, I can return there [if I want]." The visit di-

minished Lera's "total" experience of the big journey, making her realize
that immigration need not be feared because it is not necessarily a one-way
street.

There is no single model of visiting home, and many versions and variations exist. Some students had made a single visit home: Lyuba went with
her boyfriend to visit her family, Sveta traveled to Moscow to represent a
kibbutz firm in an industrial fair, and Dan returned to Russia as a representative at a conference on democracy. Quite a few of the immigrants have
made more then one trip back, and some visit Russia regularly. Yana visits
her father once a year, Sergey travels often to visit his girlfriend, and Daniel
goes frequently to work with his brother in Moscow. Others, including Lera,
Sasha, Lena, Jacob, and Karina, have traveled as *shlichim*[2] and visited their
native home at least once a year in the framework of summer camps, seminars, and the like. These students, hired to do educational work with groups
of Jewish students, are able to take advantage of their working trips to visit
the people they are close to and the places they have left behind. The students' travels are by no means exceptional; travels to Russia and to other
countries are commonplace among many new immigrants. Structured according to personal motivation and opportunity, the visits differ in many
respects: the timing of the first visit, the duration and frequency of visits,
the sites and the people visited, the goal of the visit, and its organizational
framework.

The Experience of Separation

Interpretation of the visit tales indicates that, in contrast with other other
journeys, visits to Russia substantiate and intensify separation from the old
home. These visits differ from the "searching for roots" trips (for the Israeli
case, see Levy 1995; Israeli 1991; Kugelmass 1995), because the students
make their visits relatively soon after leaving their native home. The Russian students are too young to be searching for roots—the roots they have
pulled up are still short. Also, in contrast with other immigrants, they are
not potential homecomers (Jones 1984). That is, while back home they do
not explore the possibility of returning there for good. Nor are they "vaca-
tioning homecomers," visitors who plan from the outset (although they do
not necessarily pursue the plan) to return home (e.g., university students,
guest workers). Furthermore, the visit does not induce them to preserve
their ties to the old home or to move constantly between homes like transmigrants (Glick-Schiller et al. 1995). In this regard, what is common to these

other various types of visits to the old home is that they do not induce separation.

While telling her visit tale, Karina articulates our "scholarly thesis" regarding separation from the old home:

> First the feeling of being pleasantly surprised, great, Moscow is mine! In her
> dirtiness and dilapidation, it is as if . . . it is mine and this is my homeland.
> . . . And I know every nick and cranny here, and I can walk by foot through
> every yard, I know how. . . . The whole city is mine and it has not changed,
> but let's say I go into a store, I see people with stacks of money and that
> is strange to me. In the streets near the entrances to the restaurants, I see
> young women all dressed up, and they step out of fancy cars, it is very
> strange for me. . . . They have not become rich because they were intellectu-
> als or because they made an effort. They became rich by stealing and by all
> kinds of businesses of the sort that are not so clean, yes. And that is strange
> to me, you understand? Afterwards . . . on the last day I said no! I cannot
> live here. . . . This is my homeland and what a beautiful memory, but it does
> not belong to me and now it is not mine, certainly not mine. What I under-
> stood was that Israel means progress and Russia means going backwards.

"Moscow is mine," exclaims Karina in presenting her strong attachment to the city, but she simultaneously deconstructs her affinity by focusing on the city's repulsiveness. She arrives at the conclusion that the future lies in her new home. Step by step, she unveils the three interlinked practices of separation from the native home: (1) linking up with the familiar, (2) distancing from the old home, and (3) appraising personal growth in the new place. Following her insights, our analysis considers how separation is effectuated through the employment of the three simultaneous and contrary practices.

ENCOUNTER WITH THE FAMILIAR

Once the students arrive at a decision to return for a visit, they are excited about making the trip home. They anticipate the welcome they'll receive and the opportunity to reunite with what they have left behind. Lera expressed a hunger to set foot in familiar territory. After a year and a half in Israel, she felt compelled to take action to ease her longing: "Suddenly I felt that I had to return, I cannot take one step in my life without going back. I must walk in the street where I lived, travel in the underground. . . . I was really depressed . . . it was a longing for the place."

Anya, who was also homesick for her native city of Leningrad, saved money for the visit. Even before the actualization of her dream, she had a very clear idea in her mind of what she would do upon arrival: "First I will go to all the museums, all the theaters, to the Philharmonic and to the conservatory, to bookstores to buy as many books as I can carry back . . . and to all the exhibitions, and I will walk around the whole city." Clearly, Anya voices the longing for Russian culture that is repeatedly expressed by Russian immigrants in Israel (Nudelman 1998; Ben-Raphael et al. 1994).

During the visit, the boundaries of time and space melt away. "Each time I come," says Yana, "I feel that nothing has changed, nothing, that I walk in the same streets, that I go into the same places . . . and when I go to visit my friends at my old university, my knees tremble with excitement." Yana relates how she ran around Moscow "like a crazy person," visiting all her old friends, cooking together and gossiping just as they used to. Being eager to reunite with her friends, Yana was not interested in, nor aware of, the changes which had taken place in her native home during her absence. Yana voices the eagerness—which she shares with other visitors—to reinstate old friendships, in the hope of an instant and complete return to associations unaffected by the physical separation or the time that has elapsed.

The familiar experience of returning to one's parents' home is undoubtedly one of the major motivations behind the students' visits: the expectation of being able to experience the unconditional love and trust of home and relive the sensual feelings of childhood, eating familiar food and smelling familiar smells (Ganguly 1992). Sasha enjoyed the experience of linking up, even temporarily, with her childhood home: "When I got home, I told my mother, 'Remember, this is my room and nobody is allowed to enter,' and I regained a little of the life I had there before."

Recollecting the positive experiences of the visit, the students emphasize the cultural aspects as well as the comforting sense of familiarity they experience as they reconnect with beloved people and places. This unmediated, bodily connectedness heals homesickness and impedes the development of nostalgia. Yet these comforting experiences do not dominate the stories of the visit-journeys, since they are inextricably linked with contrary experiences that paint the visit in darker colors.

DISTANCING FROM THE OLD HOME

The visit terrain is a site of criticism, judgment, and reinterpretation. When referring to day-to-day life in the old home, the dominant voice in the stories of the visit-journeys is highly critical, expressing observations and evaluations regarding the essence of "Russianness," the character of the Russian people, and the poor quality of day-to-day life and relationships there.[3]

The students offered two major explanations for the situation in Russia:

"national character," an expression that alludes to the "deep structure" of Soviet-Russian society across historical times, and a more history-specific explanation that attributes the deterioration of the Soviet Union to the dramatic and rapid geopolitical transformations it has undergone in the last decade. Russia is portrayed in dark colors both by students who believe that "nothing has changed there" and by those who claim that "everything has changed there." It appears that the visit may confirm and strengthen negative images and beliefs that were formed during childhood and adolescence, and/or it may evoke new criticism.

In portraying Russia's current realities, the students use dramatic imagery: "everything is entirely rotten," the country suffers from a "chronic disease," "an eternal curse," "physical and social decay." These metaphors, which are commonly used to represent states of impurity (Douglas 1966), emerged primarily when the students were relating the stories of their visit-journeys. They did not appear in the immigration stories themselves. Thus, for example, when the students were critical of Israeli society, they used such expressions of cultural inferiority as "primitive," "uncivilized," and "Levantine." However, while they depict their new home as culturally inferior, they portray the old home as morally inferior.

A Destructive Society

The students point to the ills of the Russian mentality, repudiating its extremism and its oppressive culture. Karina sounds the dominant voice:

> It is an unhealthy country, it is as if this country is cursed. There is a certain
> extremism—before one type of extremism and now another—and they
> never can be normal. Now it is money and wealth of other people and capi-
> talism and all that. Before it was the other way around, all the Russians were
> scared and miserable, and I do not want to live in such extremism. I want to
> have the ability to decide and now nobody has this [ability] and they did not
> have it [in the past].

Karina believes that Russia and the Russians are doomed to instability and to living in a state of extremism that leads to self-repression. She explains the inner- and outer-repression as a product of the constitutive codes of the Russian soul over the course of time and of different types of regime. In her words we can trace the liberal model that celebrates moderation, autonomy, and free choice—cultural codes that, according to her, the Russians have never been able to develop.

Lena is concerned as well about the nature of the "Russian soul," especially its inherent "sickness":

> . . . not liking the ugly and the stinking and not caring for the regime that suffocated everyone . . . that same utter disgust that I described to you in terms of the external is also there internally, there is something sick and oppressive in the Russian being, in the Russian soul, people eat themselves from within. . . . they are never satisfied with themselves, every one is a Dostoevsky, continuing to ask big questions but continuing to be a real pig in his private life. . . . This combination of spirituality and stench is unbearable.

According to Lena, self-destruction is inherent in the "Russian soul" (embodied in Dostoevsky's writing) that sanctifies inner torment and spiritual conflict. This exact description of the tormented soul is often used in other chapters of the immigration story to emphasize the superiority of Russian culture vis-à-vis Western culture, and, even more, to deprecate Israeli culture.

Deviant Society

Destructiveness is not the only thing that bothers Lena. She is also deeply concerned about the inherent moral ills of the Russian character:

> The Russian scum, in my hometown the people lay like drunk pigs in the mud. They are all drunk and beating up people everywhere, really that is my picture of Russia. Everything is disgusting and reeks, and all the people have droopy faces and no one smiles and everything is utterly disgusting. . . .
> and the clothes are all ugly and the people do not know how to eat well and healthily, and they don't know how to have fun and to be happy. That is to say, the classic Russian happiness is to be in a sealed room, to smoke a lot and to drink a lot and to talk and I have never liked that, ever since I was little. My hatred of Russia is aesthetic.

Lena portrays moral deterioration and obscenity in terms of ugliness and sickness; she draws a parallel between morality, aesthetics, and health. In her belief that the deep structure of Russian culture and society will dominate the country forever, Lena explains away the external changes that she has witnessed on her visits as nothing more than the carefully applied make-up, which cannot obscure an ugly face.

Dan points to another deviant aspect of his homeland related to the lack of a social contract—the social contract which he believes is the cornerstone

of every civil society. Dan describes his former life in Russia in terms of being deeply immersed in the "mud of the society." At that time, he explains,
he was aware neither of its deviant nature nor of being embedded in it himself. In such a society, he emphasizes, it is impossible to conduct a decent life.
Much of Dan's criticism is based upon negative interpersonal encounters in
the public sphere that he experienced during his visit: "I simply did not feel
good there. I felt that everybody behaved arrogantly towards me, and
screamed at me for no reason, [even though] I didn't do anything, and I was
not treated like a human being." Dan criticizes the corruption, hypocrisy,
dishonesty, and lack of personal freedom in his old home, with particular
emphasis on the Russians' "inhumane," hot-tempered, and rude behavior.

In judging his former society, Dan applies the academic knowledge concerning public management and bureaucracy that he acquired while studying political science at an Israeli university. In his studies he was taught that,
in a modern society, particularistic and universalistic orientations should not
be intermingled in public service:

> [People in public service] are supposed to do their job, exactly as I am sup-
> posed to do my work in my place, no more and no less. They should not at-
> tack me and I should not fall into their arms. I demand what they are sup-
> posed to do according to the social contract. . . . the only interaction I am
> supposed to enter into with a person who sells ice cream is to give money
> and get the ice cream, and if I feel like saying thank you this is already a per-
> sonal gesture. This is something that never works [in Russia], usually.

Dan uses recourse to mundane, somewhat minor events to convey his
general idea regarding the rudeness that is part of the Russian mentality. His
dramatic presentation is nevertheless meant to convince the interviewer of
the perniciousness of the deviant "rules of the game" that regulate the public sphere in his former country.

A Backward Society

The poor conditions they found in Russia, and the neglect of basic needs—
such as healthy and tasty food, clean water, and basic communication facilities (telephone and transportation)—were also a source of criticism. Lena,
for example, recalling her experiences in a summer camp where she worked
as a *shlicha*, describes a series of everyday hardships she had to struggle
with: horrible food, the endless waiting for equipment, recourse to bribery

and flattery in order to get minimal service, and the need to negotiate every little item with Russian bureaucrats. For Jacob, who also traveled as a *shaliach*, the visit afforded an opportunity to reflect on his former life in Russia: "Life is really sad there . . . How could I live in such conditions using rough toilet paper like a Brillo pad and without water in the summer? . . . No wonder people who live like animals are so mean, so bitter."

The students contrast the poor physical conditions and low standard of living in their former home with the better conditions in Israel. It is easy to get used to a higher standard of living, they say. In other parts of their immigration story, these same young people express anger with Israelis for looking down on Russia as an underdeveloped society. In the course of their visits, however, they adopt the same critical point of view.

A Materialistic Society

During the course of Sasha's visits (especially during the second one), she realized that the deteriorating situation in the Soviet Union, epitomized for her by growing materialism, has ruined her friendships. "It breaks my heart," she says. In her interview, she describes a joyful and fulfilling life during her childhood and youth, a life full of intimate friendships. During her first year in Israel, she experienced a great deal of nostalgia and suffered greatly due to separation from her friends. But her disappointing encounters with "old" close friends, who did not pay enough attention to her, have left her with a dismal picture of Russian society today.

Her disappointment in the old home leads her to search for an explanation for the growing gap between her old friends and her: "I did not understand what they were doing." She attributes this gap to their new pragmatic and materialistic orientations. Sasha is highly critical of their powerful "addiction" to making money:

> Their only goal in life is to live normally from an economic standpoint . . . to adapt to the conditions that they have there. They do not need any substantial change. My friends did not understand what happened in my head, inside me, why I decided to save money to travel and not to buy a car, why I am searching all the time and why I am not worried [like they are] about material things. I told my friends this [their material world] is a world I do not know, that I am afraid to enter. This is something that is not related to my life there, *something that didn't use to be there* and [the change] is difficult for me (authors' emphasis).

Deploring the dissolution of her friendships, Sasha pronounces a criticism common in the West concerning the greediness of the "New Russians." She accuses her old friends of betraying the Russian code of friendship (Markowitz 1991),[4] describing herself as much more committed to applying this code: "I have always said that relations with people are the most important things . . . and here [in Russia] it is really not like that [anymore]." According to her, only distancing from the decaying homeland has allowed her to adhere to and fully realize "genuine" close relationships in the new place, and, at the same time, avoid developing a materialistic orientation like that of her old friends.

The immigrants express a pessimistic view of their former society, judging it harshly without pity or empathy. Their representations de-idealize and de-romanticize their native home. Criticizing the old home makes it difficult to develop a yearning for it and facilitates separation from a place to which they will probably never return permanently.

When Alexander's friend suggested to him that he would get used to the things that disturbed him upon his return, Alexander's response was adamant: "I shouted at him, no, no way. I do not want to get used to it, damn it! That's it!" Using a historical analogy from the Russian past, Alexander reiterates his reluctance: "My friend said I was like a White officer [a Russian officer from the civil war between the 'Whites' and 'Reds'] who came back to Russia and saw what was going on there, but unlike [the Whites], who wanted to return to Russia, I never did."

APPRAISAL OF PERSONAL CHANGE

During the "little journey" the students re-evaluate their "big journey" in terms of personal change, measuring their new selves against the old. Expressions such as "I have changed very much," "I see things differently now," "I am not the same person anymore," and "I have become more significant" recur in the stories of the visit-journeys.

The stories illuminate transitional insights and deliberations that convey personal transformation, self-development, and maturation. Sergey's visit makes him aware that he "thinks differently now and has changed a lot." Comparing himself to those who stayed behind whom he met during his visit, Sergey explains his accelerated maturation and the opportunity he has had to expand his knowledge as a result of having experienced a different reality:

> A person who really left his country is very different from the one who always stayed there. . . . The experience of breaking ties changes a person.

Leaving Russia lets you lead an independent life in a more definitive manner, lets you see the world differently. You know of something which it is impossible to find within the boundaries of a particular state, language and culture.

Reflexivity is engendered in the new home by everyday social encounters and cultural experiences, and consequently the students' revelations about themselves and their sense of personal change often became clear only upon their return from the visit. The interview, as such, is a setting that stimulates memories and intensifies reflectivity and self-appraisal. During the four-hour recital of his migration story, Dan was preoccupied with reflecting upon and depicting his personal progress. This growth became clear to him when he visited his homeland because it forced him to confront himself: "This trip to Moscow was *proof* of how much I changed, because it was very difficult for me there, very difficult (authors' emphasis)." Life in Israel has assisted him, he says, to clarify many things for himself and about himself, to become the Dan he wished to be, the Dan he likes better.

The young immigrants attribute the personal change they experience to the processes of cross-cultural transition and/or to their coming-of-age.[5] Their use of the rhetoric of change and personal realization is ingrained in the psychological models of self and identity that are deeply rooted in Western thought (e.g., Bauman 1996).

The images the students use to represent personal change signify openness and expansion. From the vantage point of their visit, the "big journey" is seen as a prospect of new horizons and a tearing down of inner obstacles that allows for the realization of an expanded, enriched self.

Psychological Growth

Comparing himself to his compatriots, Dan utilizes the model of a "communicative self" to represent his sense of personal transformation. This model dominates the discourse in the different "encounter groups" he attends in Israel.

Attending a conference on "Civil Communication" in Moscow allowed Dan to appreciate his emotional superiority. At this conference, he said: "I understood something very significant about the Russians," especially their problems in personal communication. "They are intellectualizing life instead of saying I feel this way. . . . their speeches are in slogans, supposedly loaded with emotions, but really just explaining emotions." The Russians, Dan claims, are unable to talk directly about or share their emotions, so instead they use dramatic words. Rather than being spontaneous, they explain and rationalize what they feel, detaching themselves. They apologize for their emotions because they do not recognize or admit the legitimacy of their or other persons' feelings.

Dan uses interpretative models he acquired in the new land to explicate his newly emerging self.

> The most important change that I have gone through is communicating on an emotional level. How I feel and how you feel. And I discovered in it an awful lot of honesty and pleasure. It is simply enjoyable because I do not have to hide anything, I do not have to think about the next step, I do not regard the other person as an enemy. If I tell him that I fear him I neutralize many things at once. . . . This openness stems from communication on the emotional level that is much deeper, more pleasant, direct and honest [in Israel].

In Israel, Dan is deeply engaged in searching for and finding himself. He is looking for his authentic voice, eager to establish relationships based on trust, openness, and directness.

Professional Growth

The widening of professional horizons, especially via studies, is another dimension of personal change which the students became aware of during their visits. Lena reflected upon her professional development during the course of the interview. While sharing a story of what happened when she went to visit friends who work in advertising, she relates: "I realized suddenly that they looked at me as a professional, as if I were a colleague who came from another place and can evaluate and give advice. And suddenly I became an independent person, totally not an appendage to someone, and that was strange, that is, suddenly to wear another hat."

This newfound recognition served as evidence of her achievement and success in her new society. Lena attributes this recognition to the new knowledge and enriching experience of her professional studies and M.A. degree, and to her work in public relations in Israel. She is a very ambitious student, intent on an academic career in communications. Lena considers Israel as the place that enabled her to develop a new persona and to improve her self-image (to put on a new hat) and understanding.

Identity Expansion

The visitors' self-development is also manifested in the expansion and elaboration of their "identity cluster." During the visit they substantiate their Jewish and/or Israeli identity. For example, Lera comes in touch with her Israeliness during her many trips to the old home. On her first visit, a year and a half after her immigration, she proudly told the interviewer that everybody she met told her that she was already "very Israeli." At the time, she related: "I was very patriotic. . . . I felt I was the representative of Israel there, and I told my friends about Israel as if it was my country, and said that the [native] Israelis are not Israelis—we are the Israelis. In the world I felt Israeli and probably I wanted to feel Israeli."

By representing herself to her former friends as the genuine Israeli, Lena exercised her Israeliness and tested the limits of her newly acquired identity. Later on, when she traveled to Russia several times in the official capacity of a *shlicha*, she was prompted to reexamine these boundaries and began to express ambivalence and doubt regarding " being an Israeli."

Karina's story articulated an "a-Zionist" version of Israeli identity. During her visit as a *shlicha*, she realized that it was very hard for her to accept the ethos of a "return to Zion" and to convey the official ideology to her former compatriots:

> When I worked for the Jewish Agency, we were supposed to promote this
> thing about the Jew. I simply could not. I do not regard *Eretz Israel* [the land
> of Israel] as the country of Jews. I do not relate to Jerusalem and to Israel as a
> country for me being a Jew. That is to say, as a Jew, I want to go to the United
> States. This [being Jewish] does not hold me here [in Israel] at all.

Her experience as a *shlicha* induced Karina to deconstruct the ideological congruity between living in Israel and being a Jew: according to her, a Jew can live as a Jew wherever s/he chooses. Karina says she will stay in Israel as long as it fulfills her need for self development and career ambitions.

Edward's encounter with the "other," an Israeli-Palestinian, during his visit to Russia, extended his Israeli identity, which is committed to the national religious groups and their ideology. A national religious Jew who lives in the occupied territories, Edward went to visit his parents four and a half years after his immigration, immediately after completing what he defined as a very difficult period of military service. While traveling to Leningrad, Edward by chance met an Israeli-Palestinian student on the train. "There were many other Arabs on the train," Edward related, recalling the journey:

In the morning I came out [from my compartment] with a skullcap and *tsit-sit* [a religious garment] to put on my shoes, and suddenly someone was standing there and we looked at each other and it turned out he was an Israeli-Arab, an Israeli citizen and just like that, really in fun, we spoke for a long time. 'I also have an Israeli passport,' he said, showing me his Israeli passport and said, 'What fun! I haven't spoken Hebrew in a long time' [here Edward imitates his Arab accent]. We became friends. It is like in the story by O. Henry, like two enemies from a hole in Texas suddenly meet in New York and suddenly they hug.

Only on foreign soil does Edward have a chance to meet the "other" on pleasant, non-confrontational grounds and find a common language with him. For a moment, his identity draws upon the civil, non-ethnic definition of the Israeli collective.

The visit terrain may also elevate Jewish identity. Jacob, who went to Russia to work as a *shaliach* in summer camp, is a good example. Although he was sure that after six and a half years in Israel he was totally detached from his own people, the Russian Jews, during the visit he experienced an instant, spontaneous and almost primordial affinity with them: "They suddenly understood me, something that never happens to me in Israel. . . . in Israel we [the Israeli and I] do not talk the same language. . . . I felt there mentally like a fish in water, I blossomed. . . . there I really felt like a Jew, we [the people in the camp and I] have a common background, both in the distant and recent past."

The visit distanced Jacob further from his native home ("everything there is in black and white"), but at the same time brought him closer to his Jewish cultural roots. Following the visit, he developed a strong urge to go back to Russia as a *shaliach*, and to work there in order to foster and strengthen the Jewish community. His vision is to do this by reviving the Eastern European Judaism of the nineteenth century. Following his arrival in Israel, Jacob studied Yiddish at the university. After his visit "back home" he decided to join an institute that is involved in Jewish education in the diaspora, where he cultivates and implements his ideas about Jewish revival in Russia.

Visits, Separation, and Deconstructing Nostalgia

Immigration and nostalgia are conceived as inseparable: *nostos*, which connotes a return home, and *algos*, a painful condition, together comprise the idea of nostalgia (Kaplan 1996:34). It is assumed that the experience of nostalgia is embedded in the immigration-journey, in accordance with the primary axiom of nostalgia, "there's no place like home" (Casey 1987:201).

Hence, nostalgia is a cultural scheme that is alive in the immigrants' minds while narrating their immigration/visit-story. This ancient, powerful, and romantic idea renders meaning to their interpretations of their relationships to the old home, and enables them to develop a continuous sense of time and place.

The literature on nostalgia commonly focuses on how it emerges, develops, and is nourished. Yet little effort has been given to examine the manner in which nostalgia is or may be surmounted. We contend that the immigrant may yield to nostalgic feelings and cultivate them, or conversely, reject and eliminate them.

The stories we collected clearly suggest that in narrating their stories, the students in effect deconstruct nostalgia: "the temporary *nostos*" (the visit) does not allow nostalgia to develop, the *algos* (the pain) is relieved by connecting with the familiar. Lena's words of wisdom allude to this divergence, "It really helps to travel to the place one came from. The moment you feel nostalgic and stuff like that, you have to return, not to be ashamed, it really works like a psychological treatment."

Like some of the other immigrants, Lena was able to uproot nostalgia before it had a chance to grow deep inside. The intimate encounter and joy of reconnecting with the familiar relax and satisfy the hunger to reunite with what was lost, while revitalizing positive experiences and memories. However, this encounter is not accompanied by the preservation or revival of an attachment to the old home. Needless to say, the deterioration of Russia is a critical determinant in this respect. The students do not wish to reestablish their lives in Russia, nor are they seeking to form social and economic networks which would enable them to move between the two places. They do not, in other words, try to establish lives of transmigrants.

Expressions of satisfaction with the visit are simultaneously countered by harsh criticism of their former home. During the visit, the students uncover its ugly face, distancing themselves from it as they apply various cultural models which they have acquired in the new society, in their stern judgment of the old. They do not conceive of the native home as a stable source of values or meaning.

The young Russians refrain from using a rhetoric that conveys longing for "the golden age," homecoming, and the pastoral (Tannock 1995). On the contrary, the phenomenology of the visit removes each of the four sources of nostalgia proposed by Turner (1987): "individual freedom and autonomy," "personal wholeness and moral certainty," "homefulness," and "personal authenticity and emotional spontaneity." Each of these sources addresses a different target of longing, or (in our terminology) power of gravitation.

Criticism of Russia as a destructive and repressive society negates the nostalgic power of freedom and autonomy. The students' conceptions of the native home as a corrupt, delinquent society halt the development of longing for any personal wholeness and moral certainty which may have been lost. For those who never experienced "homefulness" in Russia, their negative feelings of alienation are reconfirmed during the visit. Finally, descriptions of the Russian national character as violent, closed, and materialistic prevent the emergence of nostalgic feelings concerning "the loss of simplicity, personal authenticity and emotional spontaneity" (Turner 1987:151).

The phenomenological removal of the major sources of nostalgia is interwoven with the evaluation of the emerging new self. The depreciation of the old home is accompanied by a new appreciation of life in the new home, a life which is seen as allowing for personal growth. The visit-journey tales do not portray the present new world as deficient or repressive, nor the immigration as a "lapse." The past is absent from the description of the current "me"—the self that is developed in the new society belongs to the present and the future, not to the past. Thus the experience of "who I was" does not serve to construct a sense of self-continuity.

According to the literature on nostalgia (Davies 1979:chap. 2; Lowenthal 1985:4–13; Tannock 1995), negative feelings in the present, such as a sense of insecurity, fear or dissatisfaction, as well as mistrust of the future, induce the immigrant to harness nostalgia in the service of self, thereby constituting a sense of self-continuity. Applying the same line of reasoning, we argue that the opposite is true with respect to the young Russians: their sense of personal gain from the cross-cultural transition hinders the development of nostalgia for an "old" self.

Contrary to the popular models about immigrants that dominate both the academic literature and fiction (King, Connel, and White 1995), the visit to Russia does not bring about a traumatic or crisis-laden experience. Quite the opposite, it engenders positive conceptions of personal change that strengthen the students' interpretation of their immigration as an enriching, beneficial move. Their experience of gain is definitely related to their positioning in the new society as young, educated adults who are in the midst of developing their personal capital. The semi-protected environment of the university enables the student to expand her/his identity while relatively freeing her/him from day-to-day struggles that older, less-educated immigrants often have to confront.

Contextualizing Nostalgia

Exploring the context of the immigration journey helps us to account for the phenomenology of deconstructing nostalgia that we have discovered. Having left Russia, where they lived as a suppressed Jewish ethnic minority, the main thing that the immigrants bring with them is their revered Russian culture, which they relocate "inside" themselves and take with them wherever they go. Culture in this sense is a transferable commodity which can be dislocated from place. Russia is the culture that they want to retain, nurture, and protect within themselves wherever they go (Horowitz and Leshem 1998).

Thus, the immigrants detach their cultural identity from the land, freeing themselves of any moral obligation towards their old home. This disconnection between Russian culture and "Mother Russia" is by no means a new practice of Russian Jews—it had already characterized their individual and collective identity even before their immigration. Russian culture serves the newcomers in cultivating their ethnic identity in the new home, paving for themselves a distinctive place in the new society.

The deterritorialization of the Russian culture is supported and reinforced by the visits to the native home, which is, as we know, a fairly common practice among the Russian-Jewish immigrants. As with other contemporary immigrants, the crisscrossing of boundaries that is entailed in the visit-journey both characterizes and is enabled by the transnational era. However, the celebration of Russian culture does not nurture nostalgia for Mother Russia.

In common with other Jewish immigrants, the students are accepted in Israel as "homecomers." Israel, the "Zionist-immigrant society" and the Israeli state that is defined as the "home of the Jews," officially welcomes Jewish immigrants and grants them citizenship under the Law of Return. Indeed, the young immigrants perceive Israel as a kind of "promised land," a home that will always be secure for them, whether they commit themselves to stay in Israel or decide to continue their immigration-journey (Lomsky-Feder and Rapoport 2001). "Israel is like a home that is waiting for me," said Karina.

Our contention is that the Russian-Jewish immigrants-homecomers we studied construct their relationship with their old and new homes within an interpretative field that contains two constitutive meta-narratives—national homecoming and transnationalism. These meta-narratives define contradictory movements and opposite orientations towards person-place relations:

homecoming entails unidirectional linear movement, which fixes the migratory journey in the new place. According to Bauman (1996), homecoming is
a pilgrimage, a journey that is a constant search for meaning, and is regulated by the meta-narrative of personal and national "salvation." Homecoming as realization of nostalgia toward an ancient fatherland negates the
diaspora and does not endorse nostalgia toward the native home.

Nevertheless, the movement of homecoming cannot be indifferent to a
parallel cultural narrative that puts constant motion between places and
homes at the center. From the outset, the transmigration narrative denies an
ideological affinity to and embeddedness within one place. In such migration,
affinity to the old home is an inseparable element of the immigrant process
of relocation in the new society (Brettell 2000; Glick-Schiller et al. 1995).
The construction of diaspora is not foreign to this kind of migration, but is
rather an integral part of it, while nostalgia to the old home is a useful tool
in this context (Brah 1996; Clifford 1994).

These counter-narratives meet during the visit to the native home,
thereby constituting an interpretative field within which the immigrants
consider and evaluate their linkage to the old and new homes. The students'
experience of Israel as homeland, and their perception of immigration as return to home, counters (but does not entirely eliminate) the development of
a transnational identity.

Indeed, the analysis of the visit tales indicates that homecoming is meaningful in the students' representations of their relation to both homes. Even
though individual immigrants may not necessarily perceive their immigration to Israel in terms of returning to the "national home of the Jews,"
they do embrace and thereby support the national ideology of homecoming
(Lomsky-Feder and Rapoport 2001). Based on the paradigm of the "ingathering the exiles," Zionism constitutes a historical-natural linkage between homeland, immigration, and identity and seeks to delegitimate the development of nostalgic discourse and feelings toward other native homes.[6]

By exploring national homecoming in a transnational world, our study
problematizes the relationship between immigration, nostalgia, and identity.
By showing that the immigrants' identity does not draw on the cultivation
of nostalgia, we suggest a model of identity construction in immigration that
contrasts with contemporary models of Diaspora and Diasporic identities.
These models are preoccupied with constructing and substantiating a direct
link between the constitution of Diaspora, nostalgia to the native home, and
the immigrants' politics of identity.

More generally, our research indicates that post-modern thought has been
too hasty in discounting national homecoming as an active meta-narrative

in constituting person-place relations. Studies dealing with homecoming mainly investigate homecomers who have permanently or temporary returned to their birthplace as part of transmigration (Brettell 2000). Yet the post-modern project, which undermines and questions the power of the nation-state, remains nearly blind to the issue of returning home as part of a national movement in which people go back to their motherland. Its preoccupation with diaspora (Brah 1996; Clifford 1994) has overshadowed the study of immigrants who leave their diaspora to become newcomers in their imagined homeland. When belonging to the new home directs and manages the newcomers national/ethnic sentiments, nostalgia for the old home does not color the immigration stories. Nostalgia is contingent and context-bound, and understanding its role requires that we deconstruct nostalgia.

REFERENCES

Anteby, Lisa. 1998. "Processes of Ethnic Revival among Ethiopian Migrants in Israel." Paper presented in the Annual Conference of the Israel Anthropological Association, Beer Sheva, March. [Hebrew.]

Bauman, Zygmunt. 1996. "From Pilgrim to Tourist: A Short History of Identity." In *Questions of Cultural Identity*, ed. S. Hall and P. DuGay, pp. 18–36. London: Sage.

Benmayor, Rina, and Andor Skotnes. 1994. "Some Reflections on Migration and Identity." In *Migration and Identity*. ed. R. Benmayor and A. Skotnes, pp. 1–18. New York: Oxford University Press.

Ben-Raphael, Eliezer, Elith Allstien, and Idith Geist. 1994. *Aspects of Identity and Language in the Absorption of Olim from the Former USSR*. Jerusalem: Hebrew University NCJW Institute for Innovation Education. [Hebrew.]

Bhabha, Homi. 1994. "Between Identities (Interviewed by P. Thompson). In *Migration and Identity* ed. Rina Benmayor and Andor Skotnes, pp. 183–99. New York: Oxford University Press.

Brah, Avtar. 1996. *Cartographies of Diaspora*. London and New York: Routledge.

Brettell, Caroline, B. 2000. "Theorizing Migration in Anthropology—The Social Construction of Networks, Identities, Communities, and Globalscapes." In *Migration Theory — Talking Across Disciplines*, ed. Caroline B. Brettell and James F. Hollifield, pp. 97–135. New York and London: Routledge.

Casey, Eduard S. 1987. *Remembering: A Phenomenological Study*. Bloomington: Indiana University Press.

Chambers, Ian. 1994. *Migrancy, Culture, Identity*. London: Routledge.

Clifford, James. 1994. "Diasporas." *Cultural Anthropology* 9(1):302–38.

Cohen, Eric. 1973. "Nomads from Affluence: Notes on the Phenomenon of

Drifter-Tourism." *International Journal of Comparative Sociology* 14(1–2):
    89–103.
Davies, Fred. 1979. *Yearning for Yesterday — A Sociology of Nostalgia*. New
    York: Free Press.
Denzin, Norman, K. 1989. *Interpretive Biography*. London: Sage.
Douglas, Mary. 1966. *Purity and Danger*. London: Routledge & Kegan Paul.
Ezzy, Douglas. 1998. "Theorizing Narrative Identity: Symbolic Interactionism
    and Hermeneutics." *Sociological Quarterly* 39:239–52.
Ganguly, K. 1992. "Migrant Identities: Personal Memory and the Construction
    of Selfhood." *Cultural Studies* 1:27–50.
Glick-Schiller, Nina, Linda Basch, and Cristina Szanton-Blanc. 1995. "From
    Immigrant to Transmigrant: Theorizing Transnational Migration." *Anthro-
    pological Quarterly* 2:48–63.
Hannerz, Ulf. 1996. *Transnational Connections*. London: Routledge.
Horowitz, Tamar, and Eliazer Leshem. 1998. "The Immigrants from the FSU
    in the Israeli Cultural Sphere." In *Profile of an Immigration Wave: The Ab-
    sorption Process of Immigrants from the Former Soviet Union, 1990–1995,*
    ed. Moshe Sicron and Eliazer Leshem, pp. 291–33. Jerusalem: Magnes
    Press. [Hebrew.]
Israeli, Raphael. 1991. "Back to Nowhere: Morocco Revisited." *Jerusalem
    Quarterly* 1:15–27.
Jones, Fred M. 1984. "The Provisional Homecomer." *Human Studies* 7:
    227–47.
Kaplan, Caren. 1996. *Questions of Travel*. Durham: Duke University Press.
King, Russell, John Connel, and Paul White. 1995. *Writing Across Worlds*.
    London: Routledge.
Kugelmass, Jack. 1995. "Bloody Memories: Encountering the Past in Contem-
    porary Poland." *Cultural Anthropology* 10(3):279–310.
Levy, André. 1995. "Ethnic Aspects of Israeli Pilgrimage and Tourism to Mo-
    rocco." *Jewish Folklore and Ethnology Review* 17(1–2):20–24.
Linde, Charlotte. 1993. *Life Stories*. New York and Oxford: Oxford University
    Press.
Lomsky-Feder, Edna, and Tamar Rapoport. 2001. "Homecoming, Immigration,
    and the National Ethos: Russian-Jewish Homecomers Reading Zionism."
    Anthropological Quarterly 74(1):1–14.
Lowenthal, David. 1985. *The Past Is a Foreign Country*. Cambridge: Cambridge
    University Press.
Markowitz, Fran. 1991. "Russkai Druzhba: Russian Friendship in American
    and Israeli Contexts." *Slavic Review* 50(3):637–45.
Mead, George Herbert. 1981. *Selected Writings*. Chicago: University of Chi-
    cago Press.
Nudelman, Rafael. 1998. "Between the Empire and the Ghetto." *Panim* 4:10–
    16. [Hebrew.]

Rosenwald, George, and Richard L. Ochberg. 1992. "Introduction: Life Stories, Cultural Politics, and Self-Understanding." In *Storied Lives*, ed. George Rosenwald and Richard L. Ochberg, pp. 1–18. New Haven and London: Yale University Press.

Samuel, Raphael, and Paul Thompson. 1990. "Introduction." In *The Myths We Live By*, ed. R. Samuel and P. Thompson, pp. 1–22. London: Routledge.

Sarbin, Theodore R. 1986. "The Narrative as a Root Metaphor for Psychology." In *Narrative Psychology: The Storied Nature of Human Conduct*, ed. T. R. Sarbin, pp. 3–22. New York: Praeger.

Schutz, Alfred. 1944. "Stranger: An Essay in Social Psychology." *American Journal of Sociology* 49(4):499–508.

———. 1945. "The Homecomer." *American Journal of Sociology* 50(5): 369–76.

Tannock, Sally. 1995. "Nostalgia Critique." *Cultural Studies* 9(3):453–64.

Turner, Bryan. 1987. "A Note on Nostalgia." *Theory, Culture and Society* 4:147–56.

Yacobson, Jacob. 1987. "Secular Pilgrimage—Travels of Young Israelis to Distant Places." M.A. thesis, Tel Aviv University. [Hebrew.]

NOTES

Previously published in *Journal of Contemporary Ethnography* (2000) 29(1):32–57.

Authors' names appear in alphabetical order. This paper is the product of a joint research project entitled "From 'Being a Stranger' to 'Being a Local': Personal Stories of Russian-Jewish Migrants to Germany and Israel."

1. The migrants from the former Soviet Union and the Israeli public use the terms "Russia" and "the USSR" interchangeably when discussing the former Soviet Union. Likewise, "Russia" and "the USSR" will be used throughout this paper to refer to the former Soviet Union.

2. *Shlichim* is the Hebrew word for emissaries who are sent to represent Israel and to work with Jewish communities abroad. *Shlichim* are sent by the Jewish Agency, the Israeli government, and other organizations to encourage immigration to Israel and to strengthen ties to Judaism and Israel through educational programming and community organization and involvement. A male delegate is called a *shaliach*, and a female, a *shlicha*.

3. Their old and new homes were represented differently by the students when they talked about them in the contexts of the little or the big journey. In their visit tales they expressed a stronger ambivalence and more negative feelings towards their old home, often portraying it in darker colors. Conversely, the visit tales communicated a more positive image of the new home; it is within the context of telling about visits to their old home that the students elaborated upon the new opportunities they have in Israel to realize themselves

and to develop individually. Generally, leaving the USSR was represented in the visit tales more positively than in the other chapters that weave together the immigration stories. For instance, at other points in their immigration stories, when the students wanted to stress the negative aspects of Israeli society, they emphasized the personal price they had to pay for leaving their native homes.

4. This code of friendship is mentioned in the immigration stories when comparing (genuine) friendships amongst Russians to interactions with Israelis.

5. Traveling, as such, induces a process of self-exploration and self-discovery for all people in all times, and particularly for young people who are eager to explore and experiment. Young travelers often represent the "trip" as a process of uncovering their authentic self (Anteby 1998; Yacobson 1987; Cohen 1973).

6. A good example can be found in the press coverage of the visit to Russia of Nathan Sharansky (the prominent "refusnik") as a Minister of Absorption (in the Israeli government). "Nathan Sharansky returned to Moscow after 20 years with the same fur hat but without nostalgia," wrote the biggest newspaper in Israel, underlining the non-nostalgic character of the visit (*Y'diot Acharonot* January 31, 1977, pp. 24–25).

CHAPTER 13

Claiming the Pain, Making a Change:
The African Hebrew Israelite Community's
Alternative to the Black Diaspora

FRAN MARKOWITZ

In place of the essentialized identities that formed the categories of understanding in the past . . . critics now look at the ways in which the pure
is always contaminated. Thus, one hears of hybrid identities, diaspora
identities, borderland identities—all terms intended to designate such
historical conditions as interaction, interdependency, cultural transformation, and movement. It follows then that every appeal to some originary, authentic, pure identity . . . can only be an appeal to a *mythical*
purity.

— KAWASH 1997 : 2

Diasporas bring the force of the imagination, as both memory and desire, into the lives of many ordinary people. . . . The key difference here
is that these new mythographies are charters for new social projects,
and not just a counterpoint to the certainties of daily life.

— APPADURAI 1996 : 6

Heralding the analytical shifts that were to occur later in the decade, David
Scott (1991) urged ethnographers studying black Americans to change the
thrust of their project. Instead of striving to authenticate Africanisms (Herskovits 1941) and slave memories (Price 1983), Scott suggested investigating
how black people have built "traditions" that link the trauma of slavery—
that inaugural event of diaspora—to *these* contemporary thoughts, memories, and enactments of it.

Writing as the racial categories of "black" and "Negro" gave way to a cul-
ture-and-place label of identity in the United States, Scott was prescient in
his call for thinking about African-Americans as a diaspora.[1] The concept of

diaspora, which "offers a critique of fixed origins while taking account of a homing desire" (Brah 1996:197), has been instrumental in looking beyond primordialist notions of any ethnic or minority group, and in the particular case of African-Americans, for busting ontological blackness (cf. Anderson 1995). Within the scope of diaspora, African-American culture reemerges as a complex, often internally contradictory bundle of overlapping, sometimes creative, sometimes coercive hybridities that remain linked to remembrances of dispersal—the inaugural horrors of kidnapping, the middle passage,[2] and chattel slavery—while also suggesting ways to overcome and go beyond them (see, for example, Dyson 1993; Gilroy 1993, 2000; Hall 1995; hooks 1990; Howe 1998; Kawash 1997; West 1990).

By contrast, although the people and subgroups who constitute the Black Diaspora have yielded an astonishingly wide array of cultural products and expressions, their hybridity, at least in America, has been all but invisible and defied narration.[3] Color, as a legal if not social fact in a racially constituted world, is always manifest. A black/white categorical dichotomy obviates overlaps, denies or denigrates mixture, and subverts alternative versions of history and identity. This dichotomy is manipulated and invoked to create morality, the identification of one color with the nation, while objectifying the "outsidership" of the other (Torres and Whitten 1998:24; Williams 1930). The dynamics of the African-American Diaspora—as both a yearning for and critique of anterior origins—have always been animated and deflated in their push against such a relentless color line.

The seemingly impossible meshing of diasporic fluidity with the fixity of race has constituted a black identity in which homeland has played a fleeting and fragile role. Like that of several other diasporas, African-American group identity has been based on "a shared, ongoing history of displacement, suffering, adaptation or resistance" (Clifford 1994:306), but homeland has minimally and ambiguously directed the attachments of that identity. It may well be that the initiatory events of captivity and deracination, followed by centuries of slavery and second-class citizenship, have overridden all else in black collective memory (Scott 1991, cf. Safran 1991; Clifford 1994; Cohen 1997).[4] Color, stigmatized, objectified, and essentialized through slavery and perpetuated ever after in a starkly racist discourse, put attachments to Africa and an African-American group identity at risk (Thomas 1993, esp. p. 190). The black/white dichotomy swallowed up Africa-as-peoples-cultures-places and obviated the variety of social forms and cultural expressions that resulted from its mergers with America (Brodkin 1997, esp. chaps. 2 and 3; Dominguez 1997; Kawash 1997; see also Lewis 2000 for a fascinating analysis of blackness in Mexico).

The power of the color line to thwart the central tension of *diaspora*—a term that evokes movement and mergers as it conjures up as well images of prior purity rooted in one specific place (Brah 1996; Young 1995)—is by now well recognized. The Black Atlantic, as Paul Gilroy (1993) has so convincingly demonstrated, has always been a site—or nexus of sites—of creolization and hybridities, yet it had rarely been theorized as such by whites or blacks. The power of diasporic critique to disarm and destabilize fixed social categories was not to be recognized in a racially bifurcated world dependent on the stability of that model to perpetuate its asymmetrical social system (Bhabha 1994:37–38). As a result, although fusions of many sorts occurred between Africa and America over the centuries, their variety was usually overlooked and unrecorded, and Africa, the earth's second largest continent, was castigated and deprecated as that dark, pagan land that yielded necessarily black slaves.

Africa as homeland, despite its entanglement in a cruelly racist discourse, never disappeared from black people's longings for anterior origins.[5] And after decades of struggle for civil rights and black pride, in the late 1980s this theoretical desire became social fact when the term "African-American" contested racial or color categories and emerged as the identity label of choice. "The African diasporas of the New World," Stuart Hall (1995:9) explains, "have been one way or another incapable of finding a place in modern history without the symbolic return to Africa." But it is an uneasy return, because Africa-as-homeland cannot be singular or pure. It has been vilified and pillaged by Europeans and white Americans for centuries, even as it took on mythical proportions for (some) New World blacks. Swathed in layers of prior text and refracted through the trials of modernity, *contemporary* Africa is being re-appropriated as homeland in African-Americans' narratives of authenticity.[6] As primordial or authentic as one may wish it to be, Africa has been cast as cartographic fact and mythographic concept as the result of centuries of hybrid fusions and ruptures, and ambivalence and messiness persist despite the promise of (symbolic) homecoming (Sivanandan 1970:11).

Just as Africa emerged from the invisibility of hybridity and the *bricolage* of Black American culture, so too did the African Hebrew Israelite Community (AHIC, or more broadly, Black Hebrews) take form through the dynamics of diaspora to become a multi-sited community centered in the dusty desert town of Dimona, Israel. In fact, according to the group's creation story, it could not have come into being any other way but as a result of exile, sojourns through Africa, and then the ultimate in deracination—the humiliations of slavery and racism in North America.[7] The Black Hebrews explain

that experience of such indignities prepared black people to ponder the significance of their plight and motivated those who would to uncover the reasons for it. To do this, they sifted through and fused together all kinds
of knowledge, from the most discredited oral traditions passed on through
the family over the generations, to those at the hegemonic center of Euro-
American culture. Their search for an anterior identity ultimately led them
in two mutually dependent directions, back to the past and into the future,
for when they looked for origins in Africa, they found their way to Israel,
and that is where they discovered the messianic message and social project
of their people (see Ben-Yehuda 1975; Gerber 1977; Markowitz 1996; Singer
1979).

The African Hebrew Israelite Community is not the only group of
African-Americans to identify with the biblical Israelites or to delineate a
special mission for black people, but it is the first, and remains the only one,
to have established a social program plotted along the circular route of diaspora and return. My goal for the remainder of this chapter, therefore, is to
demonstrate how the messy ambivalence of hybridity—that celebrates both
cultural and racial mergers while also invoking an anterior authenticity or
prior purity—works its way out in and through the efforts of the AHIC to
confront and transcend diasporic displacement.

To do this, I will first trace American blacks' uneven encounters with
Africa and show how their attempts to validate an originary homeland have
been motivated and thwarted by the Africa that they found. My concern
then becomes to follow one strand of that complicated story[8] to the transformation of several thousand black Christian Americans into Hebrew Israelites as they constructed—or, as they describe it, recovered and resur-
rected—a group narrative that links them both to Africa and to Israel. This
discovery/recovery of their "true history" impels a "return" to Israel-Africa
to carry out their special mission—to bring about salvation for everyone
everywhere, but first and foremost for black people. And, although I shall
end my telling of their tale on the brink of fulfilling millenarian promise, the
AHIC in and through its locations in Israel's Negev, American cities, and on
Africa's west coast, goes on blending with and crashing against blackness,
whiteness, Judaism, Christianity, America, Africa, and Israel, to recover and
play out, while constantly amending, their always authentic, but never static,
culture.

Dueling Discourses: Recovering Africa
Through the Lens of Modernity

Hybridity necessarily involves ruptures at the same time as it speaks to blendings, but each diaspora's memories and experiences are cast in different ways so that the sides of their hyphenated fusion/divide are differentially weighted. In the case of black Americans, the inaugural terror of kidnapping and exile followed by the ordeal of chattel slavery overpowered and enveloped homeland in defining group consciousness (Scott 1991).

The dominance of pain over place in the Black Atlantic has been exacerbated by two interconnected pieces of history. The first is that the Africans shipped to America were men and women from a variety of places who spoke mutually unintelligible languages and held to different traditions. They were not and did not consider themselves one people dispersed en masse from one place. Thus, from the very beginning, what united Africans in America was the violence done to them through slavery and the color of their skin rather than a singular place of origin.[9] Second, as they developed a collective imagination of Africa-as-homeland, they learned as well that Africa and the Africans were under European control and suffered, as did they, "brutal enslavement, institutional terrorism, and cultural degradation" (West 1990:26). Under such conditions, Africa offered little solace.

By the eighteenth century, Africa was categorically constituted in white discourse as the Dark Continent, a place of savages and heathens, the depraved homeland of necessarily black slaves. These images were not only metaphors in literature or allegories in church sermons; they were also at the heart of political programs and affirmed by science. In the "Great Chain of Being," a taxonomic table devised in the eighteenth century, Robert Young (1995:67) reveals, "the African was placed at the bottom of the human family, next to the ape, and there was some discussion as to whether the African should be categorized as belonging to the species of the ape or of the human." No matter where they turned, even to civil beliefs in the rights to "life, liberty, and the pursuit of happiness," American Negroes, slave or free, were bombarded with a total knowledge system that informed them that since they were an inferior race from a land where civilization failed to develop, they deserved to be excluded from citizenship and condemned to slavery, or at best second-class citizenship, under the domination of whites.[10]

Almost from the moment that they reached America, the slaves were introduced to Christianity. They received religious instruction and were included in prayer services mainly led by slave owners and in high church denominations.[11] But most blacks did not convert because they perceived Christianity to be the white man's religion, which justified their slavery (Raboteau 1997:89–91). Although one of Christianity's central messages is that God's blessing awaits all humankind, only with the rise of American Evangelical Christianity in the latter part of the eighteenth century did these egalitarian tendencies countermand a divinely sanctioned hierarchy in which whites had exclusive hold on citizenship and salvation, and blacks were deemed depraved and damned. In ecstatic revival meetings, charismatic but often unschooled preachers taught that every man and woman, rich and poor, black and white, could get the spirit, transcend the woes of the world, and find favor in God's eyes. Responding to this promise of equality, more African-descended Americans converted as the eighteenth century turned to the nineteenth than in the previous two hundred years. And they made evangelical Christianity their own.

If, as Charles Long (1997:27) has suggested, the slaves had to come to terms with the opaqueness of their condition and at the same time oppose it by creating another reality, then evangelical Christianity gave them the means, showed them the way, and provided the authorization for so doing. In the process, Christianity, once exclusively the religion of the white man, became a black-white hybrid, which, like all hybrids, proved to be a double-edged sword. White slaveholders used Christianity, along with "science," to justify ownership of black-African slaves, while the slaves found plenty in the religion's sacred texts to oppose the rectitude of slavery and to challenge claims that Africa was damned.

Christianity provided the slaves with at least three directions for pondering their identity, and there was often overlap among them. First, acceptance of the Gospel and receptivity to the Holy Spirit provided a path for transcending earthly woes, temporarily in this world and permanently in the hereafter. Jesus, who lent solace and furnished a role model endowed the slaves' suffering with meaning while assuring ultimate redemption. Second, complementing the message of transcendence offered by the New Testament, the Old Testament provided rich illustrations of this-worldly deliverance in the personae of Daniel, David, Joshua, Moses, and Noah, and in ways that struck the imagination of the slaves (Levine 1997:98). No single story reverberated with black Americans' embodied experience and utopic vision more than that of Exodus, for it broke the equation between the African and the slave and proved that slavery completely opposes divine will.

Many African-American historians and theologians note that the slaves viewed the deliverance of Israel from Egypt as the "archetype of promise," a universal message and the ultimate proof that God abhors slavery (e.g., Long 1997:30). Others interpret it as "the prototype of racial and nationalistic development" (e.g., Wilmore 1986:37), which made it ripe for appropriation by American blacks to articulate their own sense of peoplehood. Over the decades both approaches intertwined so that it is difficult to determine if "appropriation," which implies strategizing, or "identification," which conveys emotional internalization, is the best way to characterize the relationship between African-American slaves' yearnings and the history of the biblical Israelites. Raboteau (1995:33–34) points out that "in the ecstasy of worship, time and distance collapsed, and the slaves *became* the children of Israel." They thereby rose above their sorrows and cast off the stigma of Africa, for surely as the chosen people of the God of Israel their origins were noble. This often-forgotten and severed theme of African-American Christianity later became an important historical source for the Black Hebrews' identity assertions.[12]

The third direction came from a rather obscure Old Testament line. Whereas Exodus captured African-Americans' imagination early on, it was not until the nineteenth century that this verse, "Princes shall come out of Egypt and Ethiopia shall soon stretch forth her hands unto God" (Psalms 68:31), began to circulate with regularity. The line is ambiguous and open to multiple interpretations, but one point emerges as clear: Africa is not doomed to an eternity of depravity. African-Americans grasped this passage as a divine clue for recovering their past and reading their future.

Psalms 68:31 gave to American descendants of African slaves a sacred rejoinder to the dominant discourse of Africa's depraved status. Even white folks could not deny that Egypt, the site of the earliest world civilization, and Ethiopia, the land of King Solomon's consort, the Queen of Sheba, were located on the African continent.[13] Nineteenth-century black Americans identified Ethiopia and Egypt metonymically with their own origins and pointed to these ancient civilizations as indicators of a glorious African past (Raboteau 1995:43).[14] In the twentieth century these claims have been bolstered by the discovery of fossil evidence pointing to East Africa as the cradle of *all* human evolution. Biblical verse and science converged once again, but now to refute evidence of Africa's deficiencies.

These refutations, however, were themselves open to debate: Egypt fell centuries ago, and contemporary Ethiopia never attained the status of a world power, whites would argue.[15] While it came to be accepted that the earliest humans evolved in Africa, in the nineteenth century "Darwinism and phrenology"—and I should add, in the twentieth century IQ tests and no-

tions of "cultural deficit"—"passed on new 'scientific' theories of black inferiority and the old racial stereotypes abounded in American society" (Fulop
1997:230).

After Reconstruction, although slavery had ended, "oppression contin-
ued, even worsened, and black Americans read their future in Psalms 68:31"
(Raboteau 1995:41). Some interpreted this verse as God's commandment to
American Negro Christians, who had carried the pain of exile and slavery for
244 years without knowing why, to go back to Africa and convert its people.
In so doing, they would redeem their personal suffering and that of Africa,
thereby opening the way for princes to come out of Egypt (see Becker 1997;
Wilmore 1986, esp. chap. 5).[16] In the 1920s these themes were at the heart
of Garveyism (Burkett 1978; Jenkins 1975), and in modified form they re-
emerged in the 1960s as central to the program of the African Hebrew Israelite Community.

A different but related version of this story developed within the apoca-
lyptic-millenarian vision of evangelical Christianity. In simplified form,
Egypt and Ethiopia are destined to rise again as great civilizations. A new age
is quickly dawning, "continuous with a glorious African past accompanied
by God's judgment of white society and Western civilization" (Fulop 1997:
231). This future golden age will vindicate Africa; the racial order of things
will be reversed, and blacks will be on top because of centuries of proven
moral superiority. Millenarianism is a powerful charter in the AHIC, where
it impels its constituents to educate Africans and African-Americans about
their Hebraic origins and urges them to prepare in body and soul for God's
judgment and the dawning of a new era.

By the end of the twentieth century, Africa had been reconstituted and re-
appropriated by African-Americans as both homeland and heritage in a variety of ways, but always as refracted through the lens of modernity. In an
unceasing double bind of acceptance-contestation of white discourse about
the lowliness of their origins, blacks in the New World struggled—and still
struggle—to excavate from hegemonic political writings, scientific and sacred texts, the knowledge and counter-knowledge that refutes the "darkness" of Africa. Competing and conjoining narratives circulate here, there,
and back again to remind black Americans (as if they need reminders) that
they and Africa are always threatened by whiteness (hooks 1997), vulnerable to what Cornel West (1990:26) designates as "the problematic of invisibility and namelessness" if not theft and violence as the color line thwarts
and often blots out hybridity and creativity. Africa has at last become the de-
ciding factor in shaping black American identities, yet the link between
Africa and Israel that has been expressed over the centuries through bodily

experience as well as in religious and ethical beliefs remains open to doubt and under assault by blacks and whites alike. It is here that the African Hebrew Israelite Community ties together its bundle of discursive and programmatic strands to present as essential and enduring, while it also evaluates and emends, its visions for a recovered Africa.

Claiming the Pain, Making a Change

Black Judaic sects, which blended Christian messianic theology with claims of being the chosen descendants of biblical Israel, sprang up in urban America from at least the beginning of the twentieth century (Baer and Singer 1992; Brotz 1964; Fauset 1974), but they never challenged the prominence of Christianity or even rivaled Black Muslim groups. According to Ruth Landes (1967:176) who researched "Negro Jews in Harlem" during the 1920s and 1930s, "Judaism never became significant in the Negro life of the United States or elsewhere; and it has been hardly more than a curiosity to American (white) Jews. It has made no impact on social institutions or values, though it can matter in some personal lives." The African Hebrew Israelite Community is determined to change this order of things by spreading its message and implementing a return to Israel-as-Africa and Africa-as-Israel.

In the 1960s, at the height of the civil rights movement, when a broad array of black pride political and cultural organizations spread across America's urban landscape, the AHIC emerged from an older Hebraic group. In Chicago, Detroit, and other American cities, the brothers and sisters of the community embellished and made manifest strands of discourse that over the centuries had linked African-American slaves to Israel. They fashioned a distinctive Africana-Hebraic form of dress that blends colorful African fabrics and loose, flowing designs with the modesty laws of the Old Testament, and they assumed Hebrew names.[17] When peddling incense, oils, and jewelry on street corners—which later grew into restaurants and boutiques—they handed out leaflets and spread the message that the time had come for black people in America to return to Israel and claim their patrimony.

Although the community has changed and grown since then, it remains based on Biblical passages that support the "bits and pieces of wisdom" about their origins and destiny carried northward in proverbs by older family members (see Markowitz 1996:199–200; Singer 1985).[18] In their discussions of the Old Testament in intimate study groups, the community's founders probed for the sources of these proverbs and reached the conclusion that the Bible is not only a sacred text but also the chronicle of a people—their people (see Crumbley 2000:15–16 for a parallel example of biblical exegesis in a Black Sanctified Church). Their readings revealed that the Garden of Eden, where life first began, was physically located in Israel, which as both biblical references and geographical evidence indicate, has always extended south into Africa as one continuous landmass.[19] They thus concluded that the Hebrew patriarchs and their descendants, as well the first humans, were dark-skinned Africans.[20]

"But what is history?" they asked, as they delved further into the Bible. Noting that the text moves between chronicling events and predicting the future, the Black Hebrews determined that history encompasses prophecy and allegory as well as a linear chart of the past (see Harding 2000 for a similar description of fundamentalist white Christian understandings and manipulations of the Bible). Reading and interpreting the book of Deuteronomy from this perspective revealed proof positive of their Hebrew origins and provided an explanation for why this knowledge had been concealed. These insights made explicit the once-hidden links between the(ir) historical experience as slaves in the New World, and Old Testament predictions of what would befall the people of Israel. Such exegeses enabled AHIC leaders to understand why African-Americans had been condemned to centuries of pain and namelessness. Most important of all, the scriptures revealed to them a way to end the suffering by providing the key to a future of glory.

During 1998 and 1999 Prince Asiel devoted several Sunday classes in the AHIC's Institute of Divine Understanding in Chicago to a discussion of Deuteronomy 28. In these verses, God tells his chosen people of all the rewards they will reap by following his commandments, but then warns them that should they disobey, they will be "only oppressed and crushed always," and scattered "from the one end of the earth to the other." Once in exile, they will "serve other gods . . . of wood and stone. And among these nations shalt thou find no ease" (Deut. 28:64–65). And if that is not punishment enough, the dispossessed people of Israel will be taken away by ships and sold to their enemies to serve forever as slaves (Deut. 28:68). After reading these passages, Prince Asiel rhetorically asked, "Who *but* our people fit this description?"

The answer is clear to those who have found their way into the community. The AHIC's promotional brochure explains that in the year A.D. 70, when the Romans destroyed the second temple in Jerusalem, the majority of the people of Israel fled south into the African continent to escape from the armies that invaded from the north. Over the years these Israelites spread westward across the continent, and in accordance with the prophecies, were swallowed up by other groups and embraced their gods of wood and stone.

In the sixteenth century the Portuguese, to be followed by other Europeans, established the slave trade on Africa's west coast. And there began what is referred to in the AHIC as the painful, prophetic link between Israel-Africa and America that could not be severed unless and until the bereft Children of Israel took it upon themselves to study the Bible, rediscover their Hebrew origins, and live according to God's commandments.

In the 1960s, having put together these pieces of the puzzle to explain the futility of black people's endless struggle in America, Ben Ammi, the Black Hebrews' spiritual leader and putative messiah, decided that the time had come to begin anew and reverse his people's history of exile and suffering. Viewing America as the land of chastisement, the exilic equivalent of Egypt and Babylon, in 1967 Ben Ammi led an exodus of some three hundred men, women, and children first to Liberia and then to Israel. Although more than half of the original members returned to the United States, the tiny group that settled in Dimona continued to grow throughout the 1970s. As they established a presence through their unique self-governing residential communities in Israel's south, they also attracted attention from the international press and the government of Israel.

A key tenet of the AHIC, as with other black pride and black power groups, is that after centuries of being misplaced and misnamed in the white world, blacks hold and must assert the power to define themselves. Thus the Hebrews consider their Africana clothing, vegan-vegetarian diet, "divine families,"[21] and syncretic worship style as direct expressions of their identity and testimony to their origins and mission. Others, however, might view these same characteristics as "invented traditions," borrowings, or syncretism, not as recuperation of a once-lost past. The State of Israel, for example, has never agreed with the community's claims to be the descendants of the biblical Israelites, mainly because the AHIC's teachings and practices transgress the boundaries of Judaism.[22] Yet despite being denied the right to settle in Israel under the Law of Return, hundreds of Black Hebrews continued to come from the United States using tourist visas which they allowed to lapse.[23] Tensions mounted during the 1980s, and they culminated in some fifty deportations in 1986.[24]

The African Hebrew Israelite Community responded by mobilizing international law and rallying public opinion. Hundreds of adults gathered to renounce their "second-class" American citizenship as they returned their passports to the United States embassy in Tel Aviv. With this act they became stateless refugees, who, since Israel was a signatory to the United Nations, could not be deported. Back in the United States, having already captured media attention and interest from within the wider African-American community, the Hebrews rallied support from the Black Congressional Caucus. These lobbying efforts paid off in convincing the executive branch of the U.S. government to apply pressure on Israel to stop the deportations. In addition, by calling attention to the historical injustices of their U.S. citizenship, the community prevailed in a campaign for American monetary assistance. Throughout the 1990s the daily hot lunches served to children in the Dimona communal dining hall have been subsidized by an Israeli welfare program provided with American funds. Just as important, the U.S. government granted the community $100,000 to build a twelve-grade comprehensive school, which opened in 1993. Most significant of all is that in 1992 some fifteen thousand Black Hebrews received Israeli temporary residency status, and, despite all statutes to the contrary, this status has been renewed and extended over the years. After the disappointment of not receiving permanent residence status when the millennium turned, in 2003 these long-term "temporary residents" were at last granted permanent residence status.[25] Rather than regard such assistance as an indicator of the AHIC's political dependence and economic vulnerability, its members see it as validation of their identity claims (see Markowitz, Helman, and Shir-Vertesh 2003). Often the leadership points to these events as "victories" of the power to define while seeking wider acceptance within Israel and among the black population of the United States. Improvements to the community, no matter the source, are read as signs—or further proof—that confirm God's favor, support the rectitude of Ben Ammi's program, and validate the biblical sources that document "who we are as a people."

Several men and women, who were college students when they joined their fate with the AHIC in the 1970s and 1980s, told me that upon hearing about the chastisement of the (black) Children of Israel, they immediately understood why African-Americans had such a sad history. It provided them with an explanation for why they felt like "no grow Negroes" or "no-identity black Americans," and confirmed as well that the future would bring about no change for the better. And so they entered the community to resettle in Israel, serve the God of Israel, and contribute to the establishment of a new and better age (see Markowitz 1996; Singer 1979). But many more people, black and white, Jews and Christians, react with skepticism, even amusement or ridicule, when they encounter the Black Hebrews' interpretation of the Old Testament as a vehicle to explain contemporary history.

The AHIC—without having read Foucault—learned from experience that the "power to define" is never absolute, because acceptance or rejection of definitions depends on the weight of discourse. The community has responded to doubt in the wider world by canonizing its teachings. Ben Ammi has published a number of books in which his interpretations of biblical texts are presented as self-evident, and the community has "museumized" its knowledge by constructing the African/Edenic Heritage Museum, a photographic and textual exhibit that documents historical and geographic connections between Israel and Africa. Beyond the specific teachings and texts of the AHIC, which standing alone may constitute a vulnerable, subjugated knowledge system (Foucault 1980b:82), the community has added scientific and historical data from within the orbit of authorized academic knowledge to its biblical hermeneutics. They refer to Joseph Williams' 1931 volume, *Hebrewisms of West Africa*, which, among other examples, points to the Asantes' practice of secluding menstruating women as proof of an unbroken history of observing the *niddah* purity laws,[26] and they avidly collect newspaper and magazine articles that document scientific investigations into cultural and genetic links between African peoples and the Jews. At the end of May 1999, Moriel, who heads the community's St. Louis extension, informed me that he had just read of a new genetic study that demonstrates a remarkable similarity between the DNA patterns of South Africa's Lemba and Ashkenazi *kohanim*.[27] When I remarked that surely everyone knows that all of us derive from the same source anyway, he smiled and retorted, "You and I know that, but others take a lot more convincing."

And so too did the Black Hebrews. In the 1960s and 1970s, responding to the dictum "one people, one state" and the declared desire for their own "land, language and culture," the AHIC echoed the exclusivistic position of several other black power movements and earlier Black Jewish sects that "the only true Jews were the blacks, and that white Jews were merely European offshoots of the original black African Hebrews" (Landes 1967:180).[28] Over the years as their status in Israel changed, the Black Hebrews softened their position from racial absolutism to one of pluralism if not hybridity, and abandoned the claim that they were the only original Hebrew Israelite nation (see Gerber 1977; Singer 1979). Now they acknowledge that, in the wake of the destruction of the temple in Jerusalem, some Israelites fled northward into Europe and Asia and became the ancestors of today's Ashkenazi and Sephardic Jews. Since the 1980s, the community has come to accept the sovereignty of the State of Israel and the right of all Jewish people to return to its land.

As he discussed these changes in the community's position, Prince Asiel took pride in noting the AHIC leadership's ability to take in new knowledge, ponder it, and move forward. "In 1968," he said, "we were young, we were radical, and no white was going to tell us who we were and what we could do. As we learned more we grew and we changed. The community in 1998 is not the same as the community in 1968." In the Sunday classes he offers weekly in Chicago, Prince Asiel declares that after centuries of dispersal to the four corners of the earth, the Children of Israel are like a "speckled bird."[29] He adds, "It's not about black and white. We've gotten way beyond that. It's about what's wrong and right." The Black Hebrews, accordingly, are one branch of the Jewish family, but they are an extraordinary one, for only they have fulfilled in its entirety the prophetic wisdom of the Bible. Thus they hold a special status and bear a special message for black people, Israel, and the entire world.

The AHIC's leaders' reading of the Bible reveals that no matter how hard Africans-in-America try to succeed, they will not, because America is the land of their captivity and not the land of redemption. Salvation awaits only in Israel-as-Africa or in Africa-as-Israel. It is therefore the community's responsibility to teach New World blacks to embrace Hebraic law, reconnect with their origins, break the curse of the past, and usher in a new era. It has already been thirty years since they established a beachhead for the Kingdom of God in their Dimona residential community, but this small enclave is not nor can it be the end of the story. A huge task remains in bringing all the lost children of Israel—in the Americas and Africa—back into the fold, and the sisters and brothers of the AHIC know that this is a long and arduous process that is bound to confront setbacks along the way. As a starting point, the community has established a presence in three American inner cities where it offers healthy alternatives to their residents through "Soul Vegetarian" restaurants, health food stores and juice bars, "Afrika" boutiques, and regenerative wellness centers.[30] In Washington, D.C., Prince Immanuel stressed that even in the nation's capital, where blacks on the average are better off economically than anywhere else in America, their life expectancy rates, especially for men, are shockingly low (fifty-four, vs. the national average of seventy-six). Pointing to the community's health food grocery store, its restaurant, and its holistic health center, he noted that although most will not find their way into the community, the AHIC's duty is to provide Africans-in-America with alternatives that can alleviate the awful conditions with which they have little choice but to contend.

Along with the institutions it operates in America, the AHIC has long been active in exploring business and repatriation opportunities in Africa, thereby documenting what they believe to be their diasporic route and the path of return. They had maintained a small commune and a health food business in Liberia from the mid-sixties until the military coup of the 1990s, when they moved their African center to Ghana. Over the past decade the

AHIC has opened a vegetarian restaurant in Accra, built a mill as part of an economic self-help project outside of the city, and laid foundations for "Westward in Eden," a residential community designed to replicate the Kingdom of God in Dimona. When we discussed the Ghanaian alternative to Israel, Ammi-Kam, executive assistant to Prince Asiel and a community leader in his own right, reminded me: "Africa is the cradle of civilization, but Israel is the head of Africa. We see Israel as the home of that small chosen remnant, but not everybody wants to go there; for that they need an innate love of the land." Reflecting (consciously or not) the influence of Euro-America, he continued: "Africa is a continent that's never really been developed . . . and it's time to utilize another [divine] structure of government there. We built this society in the Holy Land and it works for anybody, anytime. Africa needs a new breed of leadership that can lead Africa in a new direction. People have energy and intellect; they just need the correct direction. We're going into the continent to start over again."[31] Now, as in the nineteenth century, descendants of New World African slaves, having learned important lessons in diaspora, see themselves as returning to Africa with a message of hope and a blueprint for redemption.

Most people in the United States, however, do not give much credence to the Black Hebrews' teachings. Members of the community are philosophical about others' inability to see the truth of their origins and of their mission—after all, it had once eluded them as well. The oft-quoted passages from Deuteronomy, bolstered by mainstream historical evidence of how Europeans deceived and plundered Africa, may serve to convince some black Americans of their Hebrew origins and the divine reasons for their plight in the New World. But if it is hard to persuade Africans and black people in America that their ancestors were Hebrews, the challenge only increases when facing a white audience, especially when that audience is Jewish.

Jewish rejection is more perplexing and painful to the Black Hebrews than the incredulity that they receive from black and white Christians. This is all the more difficult for them to accept since discovering that Deuteronomy, a Jewish sacred text, offers a prophetic response to those who would wonder how it can be that only the Black Hebrews "lost" the written word, while all other Jews, dispersed from the Atlas to the Caucasus Mountains and beyond, retained connections to Hebrew and the prayers and practices of Judaism.[32]

After attending Sunday class, or just visiting the Soul Vegetarian restaurant in Chicago, I have often been asked, "Can you tell me why the white Jews don't accept us as Jews?" When I offer the Halakhic explanation that they did not adhere to the Talmud as attested to by their upbringing as

Christians, I am frequently confronted with the anguished reply, "But we
didn't know!" Brothers and sisters of the community then point to the
middle passage and centuries of slavery.[33] African Hebrews, they stress,
were ripped from their traditions and then tossed willy-nilly among other
peoples in the New World, where they were demeaned, denied literacy, and
force-fed Christianity. Recovery of once-lost knowledge is a great source of
pride, and so it comes as a painful blow when others, particularly Jews, refuse to recognize it as such.

The members of the AHIC were at first incredulous and then hurt when
they were rejected by Israel, the people and place they have determined to
be their own. Jews stress that their doubts of the Black Hebrews-as-Jews
are supported by *halakha*—after all, some of the community's teachings
and practices are incompatible with Judaism, especially their use of New Testament scriptures and acceptance of Yeshua ben Yosef (Jesus) and Ben Ammi
as messiahs.[34] But due to a long history of being demeaned if not disregarded
in America, the Black Hebrews may believe that their attempts to make
African-Hebrew-black-Jewish hybridity visible through "return" are overshadowed and blocked by the color line (on the broader incommensurability
between Jews and African-Americans, see Azoulay 1997, esp. pp. 9, 13, 90).
Since the AHIC has brought (white) Jews into their historical narrative
and acknowledges them as legitimate partakers of Israel's legacy, they can
only wonder why—beyond the answer of racism—this acceptance is not
reciprocal.

The contrasting American experiences of asymmetrical race and egalitarian religion remain salient and immediate to the Black Hebrews no matter
where they may be located.[35] The painful history of racism persists to this
day and makes them, like most black people in America, suspicious of being
silenced and also alert to rejection. But the egalitarian tradition of evangelical Christianity, which accepts one and all and authorizes anyone to preach
the word of God, plays just as influential a role. "From its inception," notes
Michael Eric Dyson (1993:230), "the black church identified racism . . . as
a heinous sin, and resolved to make its extirpation a primary goal. . . . The
black church's message [is] that all people are children of God and that everyone deserves to be treated with decency." Similarly, the AHIC is open to all
whose "inner spirit" reveals that they are part of the Hebrew tradition.
Ammi-Kam explains: "Hebrew culture and tradition are more than a written tradition. You have to feel who you are, then you look into it, and live it.
Do, as the scriptures say, as does Abraham." The Black Hebrews, therefore,
follow the egalitarian, anti-racist, individual salvation-oriented example of
black Christian churches, while offering an alternative to them.

Religion and ethnicity, however, are different sorts of social categories, and belonging in America or in Israel and anywhere else is not based solely on self-definition or individual acts (see Borneman 1992).[36] The ethnic group, as well as the majority society, draws boundaries around itself and demands certain attitudes if not behaviors from those designated as members. Ethnicity, as Emily Miller Budick (1998:3) notes, also brings with it "certain ethical and historical responsibilities," which in multiethnic societies "makes inevitable conflict and competition for cultural materials and power" (see also Dunn 1998:19–30). Blacks and Jews both carry cruel and violent histories of pain that predate and overlap with their encounters in twentieth-century America, but their criteria for group membership differ. Jews define themselves as a biological group through the matriline and as the people chosen by God to receive and practice His law as revealed to them at Sinai. Black people have been defined as a racial group for centuries by white America's "one drop rule" that assigns any individual reputed to have any African blood to the category "black"—but they may define themselves through "soul," a certain quality of spirituality and style that while linked to color can also transcend it.[37] Once tossed together, blacks and Jews compared and contrasted, mutually constructed and changed each other, while at the same time they examined themselves and ultimately rebuilt or reconfirmed their own group narratives and imperatives.

At the end of the twentieth century, both groups agreed that the Jews, who in contemporary America have, overall, become white, mainstream, and prosperous (Brodkin 1997) and in Israel an economic and military power, bear little resemblance to the biblical Hebrews enslaved in Egypt or the ghettoized Jewish outcasts of Europe.[38] Nonetheless, Jews in America and Israel hold onto and invoke their centuries-long history of persecution and stay alert to anti-Semitism in the wake of the Holocaust. African-Americans, conversely, are racially marked, remain dispossessed, and are still struggling to have their accomplishments, contributions, and their pain recognized as part of America's heritage and recorded in world history. They, therefore, express frustration with and can oppose "Jewish history as monopolizing certain tropes of enslavement and genocide, and perhaps privileging them" (Budick 1998:207; also Lerner and West 1995; Salzman and West 1997). Indeed, metaphorically if not actually, African-Americans may feel that they are the "real Jews" after all, for in the late twentieth century surely the Jews' lachrymosity (Zenner 1977) has been rendered obsolete.[39]

The Black Hebrews entered Israel from within this (American) context. Refusal of the Israeli state to grant them the biblically mandated courtesy to love "the stranger who sojourneth with you," to say nothing of their dashed

expectations of a welcome back into the Jewish family, confirmed at least
some AHIC brothers' and sisters' fears of racism.[40] In turn, this reinforced
assertions of an essentialistic, autochthonous black identity that declared
them to be the only "real Jews." However, after—and even during—the
initial years in which they attempted (unsuccessfully) to seize Israel's legacy,
they have been struggling to dismantle the boundaries dividing Jewish identity claims and diasporic yearnings from their own. As the twentieth century
came to a close, the Black Hebrews were emphasizing to the Israelis as well
as to themselves that (their) race is an American construct of little rele-
vance—except as a reminder of the harshness of the past and their mandate
to build a better future. They direct attention instead to their role in comprising the Jewish "speckled bird" by including themselves among those
who retraced their routes from Poland, Yemen, Libya, Russia, and Morocco,
replanted their roots in Israel, ditched diaspora, and made a return (see
Michaeli 2000:86). In so doing, they find that black essentialism, which just
thirty years ago was so important for recovering and forging their identity,
is now proving onerous and false. Diasporic subjectivity and self-awareness
(Said 1990), necessarily coupled with the cultural production of fluid constructed styles and identities (Vertovec 1997:289), demand recognition of
their own contingency even as the AHIC strives to construct a perfect, un-
corrupted Hebrew culture. In making their return to Israel—whether located in Africa's northeast, on Ghana's coast, or in the Soul Vegetarian restaurants of urban America—they defy the power of the white world to
define the limitations of race, write African history and determine Africa's
geography, name or un-name African-Americans, and steer the course of
their future. Likewise, in laying claim to the pain of the violence done them
in and by diaspora, they piece together a contemporary culture that makes
clear links to noble origins, while also highlighting in its multi-stranded
hybridity overlappings and blendings with other Africans, Jews, blacks, and
Americans that are the necessary results of the dynamics of diaspora and
return.

Conclusions: Ditching Diaspora?

> Today's self-proclaimed mobile and multiple identities may be a marker
> not of contemporary social fluidity and dispossession, but of a new sta-
> bility, self-assurance, and quietism. Fixity of identity is only sought in
> situations of instability and disruption, of conflict and change.
>
> —YOUNG 1995:4

In order to recover a valorized sense of identity that is recognized and accorded a place in the history of the world, black people in America, the descendants of involuntary migrants coerced into slave labor, were faced with the awesome task of first decoding and deconstructing, and then ultimately ditching—or at least redefining—their out-of-place placement as America's rightfully dispossessed underclass. As originally American as the Jamestown planters or the Massachusetts Pilgrims from England, Negro slaves from Africa were objectified and dehumanized as they cultivated America's crops and served as the in-the-midst Other against which white America could constitute itself as culture, society, and polity. Ontological blackness, forged into law and reinforced by science and religion, the twin peaks of discursive power, was America's racial reality in the eighteenth, nineteenth, and a good part of the twentieth centuries. Whereas there is no doubt that a variety of mixed biological and cultural productions occurred, these were overlooked because they had been rendered categorically impossible. The binary of race overpowered the multiplicity of hybridity, and it took a twentieth-century recasting of blackness as African diaspora to disrupt this fixed order.

In working to recover their origins and culture, the brothers and sisters of the AHIC, like the first slaves who recorded their memoirs, have been restoring subjectivity to peoples of color by highlighting history's hybridities and the multiplicity of black thought and experience. Over the past several decades, they first pieced together and then solidified—while always emending—a master narrative to make their case, and a culture and lifestyle to support it. The AHIC thereby offers a solution to the displacements of diaspora and a promise to revoke the pain that these have caused.

In the thirty years of their existence, the Black Hebrews have claimed the pain as their own. Working through the concept of Christian redemptive suffering on their bodies and in their souls, they converted it from a silent motif of endurance to the impetus for cultural regeneration and self-growth. It is at the heart of their social program and served as the impetus to impel once apathetic or politically radical black brothers and sisters to (re)turn to the Old Testament, and find their origins and the key to a future better than the past. Imbuing slavery, that most demeaning of human experience—the robber of culture, of subjectivity, of soul—with positive meaning, and linking that experience to a people whose history is told in the most sacred of texts, enables once "no-grow Negroes" to move what had been their shadowy existence into the center of world history. The AHIC's return to Israel, their mission in Ghana, and their extensions in major U.S. cities are designed to awaken African Hebrews who through no fault of their own "don't know" their heritage, and push them to move "beyond"—to what might be when hybridity becomes visible, disrupts, and even overpowers race and the lines that divide nation-states (*pace* Bhabha 1994; Gilroy 2000).

It is here that I shall falsely end this story, poised on the verge of utopic realization,[41] where "the 'return'," as Radhakrishnan (1996:166) reminds us, "takes the form of a cure, or remedy for the present ills of postcoloniality." But for those whose task it is to ponder how constructing cultures is an ever-changing constant, the return—even if physically performed—can never be total and has no end. It is always interrupted by fusions and ruptures even as it strives for completion (Kermode 1967). Thus, I will leave the African Hebrew Israelite Community in the present continuous as a transnational, diasporic, and returning society-in-the-making, always struggling to make its claims for hybridity visible while pushing against either/or ethno-racial categories, trying to perfect, while constantly amending, its always authentic but never absolute or static culture.

REFERENCES

Anderson, Victor. 1995. *Beyond Ontological Blackness*. New York: Continuum.
Appadurai, Arjun. 1996. *Modernity at Large: Cultural Dimensions of Globalization*. Minneapolis: University of Minnesota Press.
Azoulay, Katya Gibel. 1997. *Black, Jewish, and Interracial*. Durham: Duke University Press.
Baer, Hans, and Merrill Singer. 1992. *African-American Religion in the Twentieth Century: Varieties of Protest and Accommodation*. Knoxville: University of Tennessee Press.
Becker, William H. 1997. "The Black Church: Manhood and Mission." In *African-American Religion*, ed. Timothy E. Fulop and Albert J. Raboteau, pp. 177–99. New York: Routledge.
Ben Ammi. 1990. *God, the Black Man, and Truth*, 2d rev. ed. Washington, D.C.: Communicators Press.
———. 1994. *Yeshua the Hebrew Messiah, or Jesus the Christian Christ?* Washington, D.C.: Communicators Press.
Ben-Yehuda, Shaleak. 1975. *Black Hebrew Israelites: From America to the Promised Land*. New York: Vantage Press.
Bhabha, Homi. 1994. *The Location of Culture*. London: Routledge.
Borneman, John. 1992. *Belonging in the Two Berlins*. Cambridge: Cambridge University Press.
Brah, Avtar. 1996. *Cartographies of Diaspora: Contesting Identities*. London: Routledge.
Brodkin, Karen. 1997. *How Jews Became White Folks and What That Says About Race in America*. New Brunswick, N.J.: Rutgers University Press.
Brotz, Howard. 1964. *The Black Jews of Harlem*. Free Press.

Budick, Emily Miller. 1998. *Blacks and Jews in Literary Conversation.* Cambridge: Cambridge University Press.

Burkett, Randall K. 1978. *Garveyism as a Religious Movement.* Metuchen, N.J.: Scarecrow Press.

Chireau, Yvonne. 2000. "Black Culture and Black Zion: African-American Religious Encounters With Judaism, 1790–1930, an Overview." In *Black Zion: African American Religious Encounters with Judaism,* ed. Yvonne Chireau and Nathaniel Deutsch, pp. 15–32. New York: Oxford University Press.

Clifford, James. 1994. "Diasporas." *Cultural Anthropology* 9(3):302–38.

Cohen, Robin. 1997. *Global Diasporas: An Introduction.* Seattle: University of Washington Press.

Crumbley, Deidre Helen. 2000. "Also Chosen: Jews in the Imagination and Life of a Black Sanctified Church." *Anthropology and Humanism* 25(1):6–23.

Davidson, Basil. 1961. *The African Slave Trade: Precolonial History 1450–1850.* Boston: Little, Brown & Company.

Dominguez, Virginia R. 1997. *White By Definition,* 2nd ed. New Brunswick: Rutgers University Press.

DuBois, W.E.B. 1939. *The Souls of Black Folk.* New York: Henry Holt.

Dunn, Robert G. 1998. *Identity Crises: A Social Critique of Postmodernity.* Minneapolis: University of Minnesota Press.

Dyson, Michael Eric. 1993. *Reflecting Black: African-American Cultural Criticism.* Minneapolis: University of Minnesota Press.

Fauset, Arthur Huff. [1944] 1974. *Black Gods of the Metropolis.* Philadelphia: University of Pennsylvania Press; New York: Octagon Books.

Foucault, Michel. 1980a. *The History of Sexuality,* vol. 1. New York: Pantheon.

———. 1980b. *Power/Knowledge: Selected Interviews and Other Writings, 1972–77.* Edited by Colin Gordon. New York: Pantheon.

Fulop, Timothy E. 1997. "'The Future Golden Day of the Race': Millennialism and Black Americans in the Nadir, 1877–1901." In *African-American Religion,* ed. Timothy E. Fulop and Albert J. Raboteau, pp. 227–54. New York: Routledge.

Gerber, Israel. 1977. *The Heritage Seekers: American Blacks in Search of Jewish Identity.* Middle Village, N.Y.: Jonathan David.

Gilroy, Paul. 1993. *The Black Atlantic: Modernity and Double Consciousness.* Cambridge, Mass.: Harvard University Press.

———. 2000 *Against Race: Imagining Political Culture Beyond the Color Line.* Cambridge, Mass.: Harvard University Press.

Glass, David. 1980. *Ha-Cushim ha-Ivrim: Din vHashbon vHamlatzot shel havadah l'vdikat bayot ha-Cushim ha-Ivrim* [The Black Hebrews: Report and recommendations of the committee to investigate the problems of the Black Hebrews]. Jerusalem: American Jewish Committee in Jerusalem.

Goldberg, David Theo. 1997. *Racial Subjects: Writing on Race in America.* New York: Routledge.

Hall, Stuart. 1995. "Negotiating Caribbean Identities." *New Left Review* 209.

Handelman, Don. 1994. "Contradictions Between Citizenship and Nationality: Their Consequences for Ethnicity and Inequality in Israel." *International Journal of Politics, Culture and Society* 7(3):441–59.

Haraymiel Ben Shaleak. N.d. *The Holy Art of Divine Marriage.* Global Images International Press.

Herskovits, Melville J. 1941. *The Myth of the Negro Past.* New York: Beacon.

hooks, bell. 1997. "Representing Whiteness in the Black Imagination." In *Displacing Whiteness,* ed. Ruth Frankenberg, pp. 165–79. Durham: Duke University Press.

———. 1990. *Yearning: Race, Gender, and Cultural Politics.* Boston: South End.

Howe, Stephen. 1998. *Afrocentrism: Mythical Pasts and Imagined Homes.* London: Verso.

Jenkins, David. 1975. *Black Zion: The Return of Afro-Americans and West Indians to Africa.* London: Wildwood House.

Kawash, Samira. 1997. *Dislocating the Color-Line: Identity, Hybridity, and Singularity in African-American Literature.* Stanford: Stanford University Press.

Kermode, Frank. 1967. *The Sense of an Ending: Studies in the Theory of Fiction.* London: Oxford University Press.

Landes, Ruth. 1967. "Negro Jews in Harlem." *Jewish Journal of Sociology* 9(2):175–89.

Lemelle, Sidney J. 1994. "The Politics of Cultural Existence: Pan-Africanism, Historical Materialism and Afrocentricity." In *Imagining Home: Class, Culture and Nationalism in the African Diaspora,* ed. Sidney Lemelle and Robin D. G. Kelley, pp. 331–50. London: Verso.

Lerner, Michael, and Cornel West. 1995. *Jews and Blacks: Let the Healing Begin.* New York: G. P. Putnam's Sons.

Levine, Lawrence W. 1997. "Slave Songs and Slave Consciousness: An Exploration in Neglected Sources." In *African-American Religion,* ed. Timothy E. Fulop and Albert J. Raboteau, pp. 58–87. New York: Routledge.

Lewis, Laura A. 2000. "Blacks, Black Indians, Afromexicans." *American Ethnologist* 27(4):898–926.

Lincoln, C. Eric. 1997. "The Muslim Mission in the Context of American Social History." In *African-American Religion,* ed. Timothy E. Fulop and Albert J. Raboteau, pp. 277–94. New York: Routledge.

Long, Charles H. 1997. "Perspectives for a Study of African-American Religion in the United States." In *African-American Religion,* ed. Timothy E. Fulop and Albert J. Raboteau, pp. 22–35. New York: Routledge.

Markowitz, Fran. 1996. "Israel as Africa, Africa as Israel: 'Divine Geography' in the Personal Narratives and Community Identity of the Black Hebrew Israelites." *Anthropological Quarterly* 69(4):193–205.

————. 1999. "Not Nationalists: Russian Teenagers' Soulful A-Politics." *Europe-Asia Studies* 51(7):1183–98.

Markowitz, Fran, Sara Helman, and Dafna Shir-Vertesh. 2003. "Soul Citizenship: The Black Hebrews and the State of Israel." *American Anthropologist* 105 (2):302–12.

Mazrui, Ali A. 1986. *The Africans: A Triple Heritage.* Boston: Little, Brown & Co.

Mercer, Kobena. 1990. "Black Hair/Style Politics." In *Out There: Marginalization and Contemporary Cultures,* ed. Russell Ferguson, Martha Gever, Trinh T. Minh-ha, and Cornel West, pp. 247–64. Cambridge, Mass.: The New Museum of Contemporary Art and MIT Press.

Michaeli, Ethan. 2000. "Another Exodus: The Hebrew Israelites from Chicago to Dimona." In *Black Zion: African American Religious Encounters with Judaism,* ed. Yvonne Chireau and Nathaniel Deutsch, pp. 73–87. New York: Oxford University Press.

Nelson, Gersham A. 1994. "Rastafarians and Ethiopianism." In *Imagining Home: Class, Culture and Nationalism in the African Diaspora,* ed. Sidney J. Lemelle and Robin D. G. Kelley, pp. 66–84. London: Verso.

Price, Richard. 1983. *First Time.* Baltimore: Johns Hopkins University Press.

Prince Gavriel ha-Gadol and Odehyah B. Israel. 1993. *The Impregnable People: An Exodus of African Americans Back to Africa.* Washington, D.C.: Communicators Press.

Raboteau, Albert J. 1995. *A Fire in the Bones: Reflections on African-American Religious History.* Boston: Beacon Press.

————. 1997. "The Black Experience in American Evangelism: The Meaning of Slavery." In *African-American Religion,* ed. Timothy E. Fulop and Albert J. Raboteau, pp. 89–106. New York: Routledge.

Radhakrishnan, R. 1996. *Diasporic Mediations: Between Home and Location.* Minneapolis: University of Minnesota Press.

Safran, William. 1991. "Diasporas in Modern Societies: Myths of Homeland and Return." *Diaspora* 1(1):83–99.

Said, Edward. 1990. "Reflections on Exile." In *Out There: Marginalization and Contemporary Cultures,* ed. Russell Ferguson, Martha Gever, Trinh T. Minh-ha, and Cornel West, pp. 357–66. Cambridge, Mass.: The New Museum of Contemporary Art and MIT Press.

Salzman, Jack, and Cornel West, eds. 1997. *Struggles in the Promised Land: Toward a History of Black-Jewish Relations in the United States.* New York: Oxford University Press.

Scott, David. 1991. "That Event, This Memory: Notes on the Anthropology of African Diasporas in the New World." *Diaspora* 1(3):261–84.

Singer, Merrill. 1979. "Saints of the Kingdom: Group Emergence, Individual Affiliation, and Social Change Among the Black Hebrews of Israel." Ph.D. dissertation, University of Utah.

————. 1985. "'Now I Know What the Songs Mean': Traditional Black Music in a Contemporary Black Sect." *Southern Quarterly* 23 (3):125–40.

Sivanandan, A. 1970. "Culture and Identity." *The Liberator* 10(6).

Smith, Theophus H. 1994. *Conjuring Culture: Biblical Formations of Black America*. New York: Oxford University Press.

Stratton, Jon. 1997. "(Dis)placing the Jews: Historicizing the Idea of Diaspora." *Diaspora* 6(3):301–29.

Sunderland, P. L. 1997. "'You May Not Know It, But I'm Black': White Women's Self-Identification as Black." *Ethnos* 62(1–2):32–58.

Thomas, Laurence Mordekhai. 1993. *Vessels of Evil: American Slavery and the Holocaust*. Philadelphia: Temple University Press.

Torres, Arlene, and Norman Whitten. 1998. "General Introduction: To Forge the Future in the Fires of the Past: An Interpretive Essay on Racism, Domination, Resistance and Liberation." In *Blackness in Latin America and the Caribbean*, ed. Arlene Torres and Norman Whitten, Jr., pp. 3–33. 2 vols. Bloomington: Indiana University Press.

Vertovec, Steven. 1997. "Three Meanings of 'Diaspora,' Exemplified Among South Asian Religions." *Diaspora* 6(3):277–99.

West, Cornel. 1990. "The New Cultural Politics of Difference." In *Out There: Marginalization and Contemporary Cultures*, ed. Russell Ferguson, Martha Gever, Trinh T. Minh-ha, and Cornel West, pp. 19–36. Cambridge, Mass.: The New Museum of Contemporary Art and MIT Press.

Williams, Joseph J. 1930. *Hebrewisms of West Africa*. New York: Dial Press.

Wilmore, Gayrand S. 1986. *Black Religion and Black Radicalism*, 2d ed. Maryknoll, Md.: Orbis Books.

Young, Robert J. C. 1995. *Colonial Desire: Hybridity in Theory, Culture and Race*. New York: Routledge.

Zenner, Walter. 1977. "Lachrymosity: A Cultural Reinforcement of Minority Status." *Ethnicity* 4:156–66.

NOTES

1. Of course, "African-American" never completely replaced "Black." Sometimes these terms are used interchangeably; sometimes the former is invoked to delineate the particular population of descendants of Africans in the United States, whereas the latter is a more inclusive term that works better to discuss diaspora.

2. This is the euphemism for the transport of millions of men and women chained one behind the other in the dank hulls of slave ships, from the west coast of Africa to America's shores. Estimates of the deaths incurred at sea range from a conservative 10 million to upward of 50–100 million. Basil Davidson (1961:80–81) reported that "it appears reasonable to suggest that in one way or another before and after embarkation, it cost Africa at least fifty

million souls. This estimate may be about one fourth of Black Africa's approximate population today, and is certainly on the low side." The first slave ship reached Jamestown harbor in 1619 (a year before the Pilgrims landed at Plymouth), and the slave trade was not abolished in the United States until the first decade of the nineteenth century.

3. Earlier voices, most notably W. E. B. DuBois, Ralph Ellison, and Harold Cruse, called for recognition of the multiplicity of experience, identity, and culture among African-Americans but were met by doubtful, even hostile, audiences.

4. Whereas virtually all attempts to define diaspora include the idea of return—symbolically if not actually—to a historical homeland, Brah (1996: 197) asserts that "contrary to general belief, not all diasporas sustain an ideology of return."

5. There is a tone of disgust, if not horror, when Gilroy (1993) notes this throughout his book. His concluding words offer a prescription to cultural analysts, political leaders, and diasporic peoples everywhere: "Recovery of history . . . ought to be done not in order to recover hermetically sealed and cultural absolute racial traditions that would be content forever to invoke the premodern as the anti-modern [but] . . . as a means to figure the inescapability and legitimate value of mutation, hybridity, and intermixture en route to better theories of racism and black political culture than those so far offered by cultural absolutists of various phenotypical hues" (p. 223).

6. In the same spirit with which they embraced the revelation that diasporic identities are multiple, fractured, fluid, and flexible, some cultural analysts are now arguing that "authenticity" deserves more sympathetic attention that it has received of late (Dunn 1998:14; Kawash 1997:216; Radhakrishnan 1996: 166). Such authenticity, however, can be neither reductionistic nor simple-minded, because the dynamics of diaspora have made it necessarily hybrid or at least double.

7. This story is told weekly in Sunday classes offered by the AHIC in several American cities, and in written form in the books of the community's leaders. See especially Ben Ammi 1990; Prince Gavriel Ha-Gadol 1993; and the third section of this chapter.

8. Other better-known directions that this story has taken have been the formation of black churches in the nineteenth century that launched missionizing activities in Africa; the twentieth-century developments of pan-Africanism, black nationalism, and scholarly Afrocentrism; Ethiopianism and Rastafarianism; reassertions of African-Americans' Christian character through their social organizations and churches; and the rise and increasing popularity of the Nation of Islam. It should be remembered that Marcus Garvey's Universal Negro Improvement Association and African Communities League (UNIA) remains the largest black nationalist-religious movement in the history of the United States, although its apex was in the 1920s. Garveyism—which blended

themes from "the Old and New Testaments, as well as from the (white) civil
religion . . . but with a new twist; Negroes are the chosen people; Africa is the
promised land" (Burkett 1978:8)—is often pointed to as the model for other
back-to-Africa movements, including that of the African Hebrew Israelite
Community.

9. "Explicit connections between slavery and race took time to emerge;
from the date of the arrival of the first Africans in Virginia in 1619 until 1660,
when slavery first began to be fully institutionalized and regulated by statute
in the colonies, the various conceptions of difference between Africans and
others were slowly transformed into an implicit assumption that the African
was, by nature and by definition, a slave" (Kawash 1997:42).

10. Robert Young (1995:95) notes that "civilization was the defining feature of racial capacity," and to this day that formula implicitly bolsters a color
line that reserves the top of the pecking order for those deemed to have the
most civilization and the bottom for "primitives" who are considered to have
none. Since "civilization" is white and European, culture, race, and social status
are uncompromisingly imbricated in each other.

11. It is no longer a question of historical accuracy to mull over the debate
among slaveholders whether or not to convert their slaves to Christianity.
Some declared that using heathens as slaves was justified but feared that possession of Christian slaves was immoral. Others were afraid that Old Testament messages against slavery would inspire revolutionary potential and upset
St. Paul's New Testament teachings that slaves should accept their lot.

12. Crumbley (2000:15) asserts that in some independent Black Sanctified
Churches, although the parishioners do not identify as Black Jews, they consider themselves "participants in the covenant made between God and the Jewish people of the Old Testament." Like the men and women in the AHIC, the
"saints" of these churches founded their beliefs in interpretations and practices
of Old and New Testament verses.

13. This was an argument that whites had to take seriously. Young (1995:
126–29) notes that the fact that Egypt developed the world's earliest civilization in Africa presented a serious stumbling block to whites' claims for the
permanent inferiority of blacks. It then became crucial to prove Egyptians
"Caucasian"—at least those of the highest social castes and classes—to set
a historical precedent for a white society with black slaves.

14. Twentieth-century elaborations of this line would develop into Garveyism and then Rastafarianism, and Afrocentrism—all "isms" with definite social programs that emerged from the dynamics of diaspora (Burkett 1978;
Howe 1998; Nelson 1994; Smith 1994:65–66).

15. If Abyssinia maintained its independence into the twentieth century,
then its subsequent conquest by Italy in 1935 was all the more humiliating.
So too was the Ethiopian civil war of the 1970s that turned black against black
and betrayed the godlike powers of Emperor Haile Selassie (see Nelson 1994).

16. Beginning early in the eighteenth century, trickles of slaves who secured their freedom returned to Africa, but the first black missionary institution was not established until 1759. Founded by the Rev. S. Hopkins, a former slaveowner of Newport, Rhode Island, the American Colonization Society "helped to forge a connecting link between emigration, Christianity, and black nationalism" (Wilmore 1986:101) and played a central role in the founding of Liberia in 1822. Controversial among blacks and whites alike, Wilmore (ibid.) writes that "it cannot be doubted that the society gave impetus to the idea that black Americans had a contribution to make to the awakening of Africa." The African Methodist Episcopal Church, a black Protestant denomination founded in 1816, was heavily involved in missionizing in Africa. William Becker (1997: 188) observes that "the African mission provided a dramatic symbol of the Afro-American as man, as leader, as authoritative carrier of God's word to those racial brothers who do not possess it. . . . It was a symbol which sought to make some sense of the suffering of the slave past . . . and which held out high hopes for the future."

17. Following Kobena Mercer's (1990:256) insight that the Afro and dreadlocks are specifically diasporean styles that signify black people's desire to "return to the roots," I prefer to describe AHIC practices as Africana and Hebraic (rather than African and Jewish) to make their hybridity visible. Moreover, although some of the names that the Black Hebrews assume are selected from the Bible, many more are created specifically for them by the priesthood. While there is some overlap between their names and those of contemporary Israelis (like Yafa, Uri, Lilach, and Adiv) more often than not the Hebrew Israelites' names are longer (e.g., biblical names like Yehoyakim) or idiosyncratic (like Yadiel, "the hand of God," or Meimaya, "the many waters of God").

18. These, like "A small black nation is rising in the east," and "Black people in America are the Children of Israel," are in all probability folk renditions of Psalms 68:31 and the story of Exodus.

19. The promised land of Israel was to have extended from the Tigris and Euphrates rivers in the north to the source of the Nile in the south and was one land bridge linking Africa to Asia until white Europeans built the Suez Canal in the nineteenth century. See also Mazrui's (1986:29–38) critical analysis of the geography of Africa.

20. Yvonne Chireau (2000:21) offers the insight that "name transformation, or the rejection of the terms 'Negro' and 'black' in favor of 'Hebrew' was one strategy by which some blacks signified Jewish as a racial classification. African Americans who identified as Jews defined themselves not only in opposition to whites, but against other blacks, and especially black Christians." What emerged among early twentieth-century Black Jewish groups were alternative ways of naming themselves and being in the world that disrupted the inevitability of America's racial hierarchy.

21. Pointing to the marriage arrangements of the patriarchs as well as those

in most African societies, the AHIC condones polygynous marriages, but rejects that term. Instead, they speak of divine marriage as that which is pleasing to God and follows a particular order. See Haraymiel Ben Shaleak (n.d.).

22. All of Ben Ammi's books, as well as the contents of Sunday classes and worship services, liberally mix quotations from the New Testament with those of the Old. Prince Asiel explained to me that the Hebrews view the Old Testament as the direct word of God and the New Testament as a holy book written by men. Judaism does not accept the New Testament at all. Further, the rabbinate rejects the claim of the AHIC that Ben Ammi is the(ir) messiah—the latest in the chain of personages from Moses to David to Jesus, who arose to lead the Hebrews from troubles to glory (see Ben Ammi 1994).

23. David Glass (1980), a Jerusalem attorney, was appointed to head a commission that reported to the Israeli Knesset on the Black Hebrews' status. He notes that the first group of four men who arrived from Liberia began studying for conversion with a sympathetic Sephardic rabbi, but they ended the process when Ben Ammi told them that the community must assert its power to define. Virtually all the adult members of the AHIC were raised as Christians, never studied with rabbis, and did not undergo Jewish conversion.

24. In 1986, forty-six community members were arrested while working on a *moshav* (farming cooperative) near Rehovot. They and several other men were picked up for having expired tourist visas, jailed, and then deported.

25. The community had been eagerly looking forward to getting permanent residency status, which could lead to Israeli citizenship, since the end of 1995. Rumors were rife in December 1998 that this change of status was imminent.

However, it took until the summer of 2003 for those AHIC members registered with the State of Israel to be granted permanent residence status.

26. *Niddah* is the Jewish purity law that restricts women's sexual and social behaviors during and immediately after menstruation and giving birth. Williams's book was written at the height of diffusionism in cultural anthropology, and Landes (1967:176) characterizes Black Hebrewisms as having been "a scholarly vogue then."

27. The *kohanim* in biblical days were the priests of the temple. Considered the descendants of Aaron, Moses' brother and the first priest of the tabernacle, they received this status hereditarily through the male line. Today, though still a descent group among the Jews, their ritual functions have been in large part superceded by ordained rabbis. In the Black Hebrew community, spiritual guidance is meted out by men who are called *kohanim*.

28. In fact they called them "ofays" (enemies), deceivers, and usurpers.

29. Although this is the message promulgated by Prince Asiel, who is the AHIC's international ambassador and thus its key spokesman, at a Sunday class held in Atlanta in October 1998, one of the Crown Brothers (the highest rank a

man can attain short of being named a minister or prince) declared in his discussion of current events that "the Jews are New World transplants, Israel is not their land." There is still ambiguity over white/black claims of priority. These will be discussed in greater detail throughout the section.

30. The AHIC is institutionally complete in Chicago, Atlanta, and Washington, D.C. It has or had smaller outreach missions in Detroit, Memphis, Newark, New York, and St. Louis and strives to broaden its range of influence.

31. Moreover, Israel certainly does not want hundreds of Black Hebrews to come and settle in Dimona. The Ghana alternative was developed as the AHIC agreed with the State of Israel to limit, if not end completely, its *aliya* (immigration to Israel).

32. The Jewishness of Ethiopia's "Falashas" was suspect for decades because—among other reasons—although they subscribed to the laws and practices of the Torah (the Five Books of Moses), their holy language was Gez, not Hebrew.

33. "Why is it," I have been asked, "that Israelis know so little about the African-American experience of slavery, while we all know about the Holocaust?" It is beyond the scope of this chapter to consider the "battle of pain" between African-Americans and (American) Jews. Although the ancestors of today's black Americans were the only people brought to the New World to toil as slaves, this trauma has not won them a central place in world history, nor have they been the recipients of any kind of praise. Why is it, they wonder, that the Jews memorialize their Holocaust and are recognized worldwide for their sufferings? Laurence Mordekhai Thomas (1993), himself both African-American and Jewish, calls for an end to invidious comparisons: "The painful truth that the Holocaust posed a threat to the very existence of the Jewish people does not, thereby make it worse than American slavery. Nor, as we have just seen, does the greater number of deaths among blacks under American slavery than among Jews in the Holocaust of itself warrant the conclusion that the former was worse than the latter."

34. See note 22 and Ben Ammi 1994.

35. African-Americans have over the centuries forged singular, yet necessarily hybrid, connections with God through an array of churches and denominations, and these have always been tolerated, even accepted, by mainstream white America (see Lincoln 1997:289).

36. Whereas the crucial binary in the United States is that of black and white, in Israel it is that of Jews and non-Jews (read: Arabs). The Jewish category is further subdivided into *edot*, or what Handelman (1994:453) calls "equivalent categories of Jews, characterized by the same and essential qualities that allow for subcultural divisions." Thus, although both American and Israeli discourses conceive of otherness along the axes of hierarchy and equality, the axes are differently constituted. If in the United States race is ranked

and all religions are considered equal, then in Israel, religion is ranked, but an equality of skin colors and cultural heritages (theoretically) transects the religion line.

37. In another context entirely, I note the difference between the "blood regime" of belonging that typifies Jews and many other ethnic groups and nations, and what I call the "soul regime" of Russians and African-Americans. The former (after Foucault 1980a) expresses a constant concern with boundaries, for blood can be polluted and spilt, whereas soul is an expansive, all-embracing spiritual quality that thrives without limits (Markowitz 1999).

38. Of course, because of German racial categorization in the twentieth century, as well as the *longue durée* of Jewish history (among other reasons), not all Jews accept this felicitous redefinition (see, for example, Azoulay 1997: 57–60; Brodkin 1997:182–87; Sunderland 1997).

39. Budick (1998) contends that there is a supercessionist tendency in Black American literature for African-Americans to replace Jews altogether as *the* symbol of exile and homelessness. She links this tendency to Christianity, which teaches that the New Testament supercedes the Old, and that Christian redemptive suffering cancels out the Jewish pain of survival.

40. After all, the prodigal son was accepted back into his.

41. As does the Chumash, or Pentateuch, of the Old Testament.

The authorized representative in the EU for product safety and compliance is:
Mare Nostrum Group
B.V Doelen 72
4831 GR Breda
The Netherlands

www.ingramcontent.com/pod-product-compliance
Lightning Source LLC
Chambersburg PA
CBHW030636270326
41929CB00007B/94

* 9 7 8 0 8 0 4 7 5 0 7 9 0 *